A CULTURAL HISTORY OF THEATRE

VOLUME 1

A Cultural History of Theatre
General Editors: Christopher B. Balme and Tracy C. Davis

Volume 1
A Cultural History of Theatre in Antiquity
Edited by Martin Revermann

Volume 2
A Cultural History of Theatre in the Middle Ages
Edited by Jody Enders

Volume 3
A Cultural History of Theatre in the Early Modern Age
Edited by Robert Henke

Volume 4
A Cultural History of Theatre in the Age of Enlightenment
Edited by Mechele Leon

Volume 5
A Cultural History of Theatre in the Age of Empire
Edited by Peter W. Marx

Volume 6
A Cultural History of Theatre in the Modern Age
Edited by Kim Solga

A CULTURAL HISTORY OF THEATRE

IN ANTIQUITY

VOLUME 1

Edited by Martin Revermann

BLOOMSBURY ACADEMIC
LONDON • NEW YORK • OXFORD • NEW DELHI • SYDNEY

BLOOMSBURY ACADEMIC
Bloomsbury Publishing Plc
50 Bedford Square, London, WC1B 3DP, UK
1385 Broadway, New York, NY 10018, USA
29 Earlsfort Terrace, Dublin 2, Ireland

BLOOMSBURY, BLOOMSBURY ACADEMIC and the Diana logo are trademarks
of Bloomsbury Publishing Plc

First published in hardback in 2017
Reprinted 2019, 2020
This paperback edition published 2022
Reprinted 2022

Copyright © Martin Revermann and contributors, 2017, 2022

Martin Revermann has asserted his right under the Copyright, Designs and Patents Act, 1988,
to be identified as Editor of this work.

Cover image: An actor looks on as a woman dedicates a tragic
mask to the gods © Art Resource

All rights reserved. No part of this publication may be reproduced or transmitted in
any form or by any means, electronic or mechanical, including photocopying,
recording, or any information storage or retrieval system, without prior
permission in writing from the publishers.

Bloomsbury Publishing Plc does not have any control over, or responsibility for, any
third-party websites referred to or in this book. All internet addresses given in this
book were correct at the time of going to press. The author and publisher regret any
inconvenience caused if addresses have changed or sites have ceased to exist,
but can accept no responsibility for any such changes.

A catalogue record for this book is available from the British Library.

Library of Congress Cataloging-in-Publication Data
Names: Revermann, Martin editor.
Title: A cultural history of theatre in antiquity / edited by Martin Revermann.
Description: London ; New York : Bloomsbury Academic, 2017. | Series: Cultural History of
Theatre | Includes bibliographical references and index.
Identifiers: LCCN 2016048847 | ISBN 9781472585691 (hardback)
Subjects: LCSH: Theater–Greece–History–To 500. | Theater–Rome–History–To 500. |
Theater and society–Greece. | Theater and society–Rome.
Classification: LCC PA3201 .C78 2017 | DDC 792.0938—dc23
LC record available at https://lccn.loc.gov/2016048847

ISBN: HB: 978-1-4725-8569-1
HB Set: 978-1-4725-8584-4
PB: 978-1-3502-7757-1
PB Set: 978-1-3502-7782-3
ePDF: 978-1-3501-3530-7
eBook: 978-1-3501-3529-1

Series: Cultural Histories

Typeset by RefineCatch Limited, Bungay, Suffolk
Printed and bound in Great Britain

To find out more about our authors and books visit www.bloomsbury.com
and sign up for our newsletters.

CONTENTS

LIST OF ILLUSTRATIONS — vii
NOTES ON CONTRIBUTORS — ix
SERIES PREFACE — xi

Introduction: Cultural History and the Theatres of Antiquity — 1
Martin Revermann

1 Institutional Frameworks: Enabling the Theatrical Event — 17
 Martin Revermann

2 Social Function? Making the Case for a Functionless Theatre — 35
 Sean Gurd

3 Sexuality and Gender: Off-stage and Centre-stage — 47
 Ian Ruffell

4 The Environment of Theatre: Experiencing Place in the Ancient World — 63
 David Wiles

5 Circulation: Theatre as Mobile Political, Economic and Cultural Capital — 83
 Patrick Hadley

6 Interpretations: The Stage and its Interpretive Communities — 103
 Martin Revermann

7 Communities of Production: Pied Pipers and How to Pay Them;
   or, the Variegated Finance of Ancient Theatre   121
   Jane Lightfoot

8 Genres: Drama and its Many Unhappy Returns   143
   Donald Sells

9 Technologies of Performance: Machines, Props, Dramaturgy   163
   *Peter von Möllendorff (translated from German by
   Martin Revermann)*

10 Knowledge Transmission: Ancient Archives and Repertoires   181
   Johanna Hanink

NOTES   197
BIBLIOGRAPHY   229
INDEX   251

LIST OF ILLUSTRATIONS

CHAPTER THREE

3.1	Costume conventions in Old Comedy.	48

CHAPTER FOUR

4.1	The Theatre of Dionysus at the end of the nineteenth century.	65
4.2	Ground plan of the fifth-century theatre at Thorikos.	68
4.3	Remains of the theatre at Thorikos.	69
4.4	The theatre-complex built by Pompey.	77

CHAPTER FIVE

5.1	The so-called 'Würzburg Telephus'.	90
5.2	Campanian oeinochoe, later than 350 BCE.	92

CHAPTER SEVEN

7.1	Late antique ivory plaque (late fifth century CE) depicting a pantomime dancer.	129
7.2	Four crowns and two money bags for the contest between Pan and Eros.	132
7.3	Two crowns and two money bags for the musical and theatrical competitions.	133

CHAPTER NINE

9.1	Schematic rendering of the stage with crane.	166
9.2	Schematic rendering of the stage with *ekkyklêma*.	168
9.3	Clytemnestra on the *ekkyklêma*. Scene from Aeschylus' *Agamemnon* in the *mise-en-scène* by Peter Stein (Berliner Schaubühne 1981).	170

CHAPTER TEN

10.1	An actor looks on as a woman dedicates a tragic mask to the gods.	184

NOTES ON CONTRIBUTORS

Sean Gurd is Professor of Classical Studies at the University of Missouri. He works at the intersection of aesthetics, media studies and classical philology. He is the author of *Iphigenias at Aulis: Textual Multiplicity, Radical Philology* (2006), *Work in Progress: Literary Revision as Social Performance* (2011) and *Dissonance: Auditory Aesthetics in Ancient Greece* (2016). He also has edited *Philology and its Histories* (2010).

Patrick Hadley is Managing Editor at the University of Utah Press and a scholar of ancient drama and its reception. He completed his PhD in Classics at the University of Toronto in 2014, and is the author of *Athens in Rome, Rome in Germany: Nicodemus Frischlin and the Rehabilitation of Aristophanes in the 16th Century* (2015).

Johanna Hanink is Associate Professor of Classics at Brown University. She has published on many aspects of the ancient Greek theatre industry and is the author of *Lycurgan Athens and the Making of Classical Tragedy* (2014).

Jane Lightfoot is Professor of Greek Literature and Charlton Fellow and Tutor in Classical Languages and Literature in New College, Oxford. She has published editions and commentaries on Parthenius of Nicaea (1999), Lucian's *On the Syrian Goddess* (2003), the Sibylline Oracles (2007) and a Loeb edition of selections of Hellenistic poets (2008). Her articles, reviews and chapters follow her wide interests across the prose and poetry of the Hellenistic period and later antiquity. Her latest project is an edition and commentary on the corpus of astrological poetry attributed to Manetho.

Peter von Möllendorff is Professor of Classical Philology at Justus-Liebig University Giessen. He has published widely on Attic drama and imperial literature.

Martin Revermann is Professor in Classics and Theatre Studies at the University of Toronto. His research interests lie in the area of ancient Greek drama (production, reception, iconography, sociology), Brecht, theatre theory and the history of playgoing. He is the author of *Comic Business. Theatricality, Dramatic Technique and Performance Contexts of Aristophanic Comedy* (2006). In addition, he has edited (with P. Wilson) *Performance, Iconography, Reception. Studies in Honour of Oliver Taplin* (2008), (with I. Gildenhard) *Beyond the Fifth Century: Interactions with Greek Tragedy from the Fourth Century BCE to the Middle Ages* (2010) and *The Cambridge Companion to Greek Comedy* (2014).

Ian Ruffell is Senior Lecturer in Classics at the University of Glasgow. His publications include *Politics and Anti-Realism in Athenian Old Comedy: The Art of the Impossible* (2011) and *Aeschylus: Prometheus Bound* (2012).

Donald Sells is Assistant Professor of Classical Studies at the University of Michigan and researches primarily Greek drama. He is currently writing a monograph on Greek comedy.

David Wiles is Professor of Drama at the University of Exeter. He has published extensively on classical and Elizabethan theatre, with a special interest in questions of festival, citizenship, mask and space. His publications include *Tragedy in Athens: Performance Space and Theatrical Meaning* (1997) and *A Short History of Western Performance Space* (2003). He was the lead editor of *The Cambridge Companion to Theatre History* (2013). He is currently working on the history of 'classical' acting from the Renaissance to the Enlightenment.

SERIES PREFACE

A Cultural History of Theatre is a six-volume series examining a cultural practice that emerged in antiquity and today encompasses practically the whole globe. Theatre is generally acknowledged to be the most social of artistic practices, requiring collectives to both produce and consume it. Theatrical performance's ability to organize and cohere markers of cultural belonging, difference, and dissonance are the hallmarks of social life. Its production and reception have, however, altered significantly over the past two and half thousand years. Despite these changes the same chapter headings structure all six volumes: institutional frameworks, social functions, sexuality and gender, environment, circulation, interpretations, communities of production, repertoire and genres, technologies of performance and knowledge transmission. These headings represent significant cultural approaches as opposed to purely regional, national, aesthetic, or generic categories. This allows for comparative readings of key *cultural* questions affecting theatre both diachronically and synchronically. The six volumes divide the history of theatre as follows:

Volume 1: A Cultural History of Theatre in Antiquity (500 BC–1000 AD)
Volume 2: A Cultural History of Theatre in the Middle Ages (1000–1400)
Volume 3: A Cultural History of Theatre in the Early Modern Age
    (1400–1650)
Volume 4: A Cultural History of Theatre in the Age of Enlightenment
    (1650–1800)
Volume 5: A Cultural History of Theatre in the Age of Empire (1800–1920)
Volume 6: A Cultural History of Theatre in the Modern Age (1920–2000+)

Christopher B. Balme and Tracy C. Davis, General Editors

Introduction

Cultural History and the Theatres of Antiquity

MARTIN REVERMANN

THE APPROACH

Cultural history attempts to situate artistic expressions within the aesthetic, socio-economic and ideological contexts in which they were first created and subsequently received and re-iterated. Underlying this ambitious project is the conviction that these artistic expressions do not, and in fact cannot, exist as self-contained entities 'in a vacuum', and that only a contextualizing approach is capable of bringing out the complexity of what it means for art to be 'at work'. For the cultural historian of any period theatre is a promising field of study. But in the case of Graeco-Roman antiquity it is particularly rich and complex, for at least two principal reasons. One is the fact that we can justifiably speak of not one homogeneous theatre of antiquity but of an unusual and fascinating variety of theatre types which are held together by what one might call family resemblance. Different genres (tragedy, comedy, satyr play, mime and pantomime) were consumed in different languages (Greek, Latin), different media (performance, book roll) and different linguistic registers (high and low; poetry and, at least in mime, prose), at different sites (open-air, indoor, private study sites) of different nature (temporary, permanent) and in different settings (public, private). Secondly, these theatres of Graeco-Roman antiquity cumulatively had a degree of cultural presence and penetration, for the millennium from about 500 BCE to at least 500 CE, which is arguably unmatched in the history of world theatre. One of the few mass media of antiquity – only para-theatrical spectacles (gladiatorial games, animal hunts, athletic events) and coins are comparable in terms of reach, access and circulation – theatre in its various manifestations pervaded the Graeco-Roman cultural sphere, a domain which, by the standard of its time, is near-global.

The rationale for adopting a cultural history approach to Graeco-Roman theatre is therefore uniquely compelling. This has long been recognized in practice by those studying it, even if this recognition may not always have been adequately expressed, let alone fully theorized. The prevalent methodology of the nineteenth century, historicism, did a great deal to elucidate not only the dramatic texts and their transmission but also the cultural frames (institutional, architectural, religious) which surrounded and enabled them.[1] In addition, the cultural turn towards the social sciences, including anthropology, that set on in the 1960s profoundly affected the discipline of Classics in general and the study of ancient theatre, especially Greek, in particular.[2] Contextualization issues to do with gender, class, ethnicity and the social practices regularly subsumed under the umbrella term 'ideology' were increasingly prominent on research agendas, and had become standard fare by the beginning of the twenty-first century. The cultural study of Graeco-Roman theatre(s) therefore must be considered a mature field, and this volume, as a result, is not exactly starting from scratch or re-inventing the wheel.

What *is* genuinely new and excitingly different about the approach taken in this volume is the fact that in each chapter the Greek and the Roman cultural sphere are discussed *in conjunction* whereas in the field of Classics, perhaps surprisingly, they are usually studied in isolation, by scholars who, some exceptions notwithstanding, tend to specialize either on the Greek or the Roman side. While the task of bridging this dichotomy posits a genuine challenge to the contributors (all of whom have weighted the Greek and the Roman slightly differently to suit their overall purpose and argument), this inclusive and holistic approach sheds new light on the field by the sheer virtue of its comparative scope and potential for situating phenomena previously treated discreetly within a significantly larger, more complex whole. In addition, while most of the key concepts uniformly applied and investigated across all six volumes of this big and ambitious project are very much 'bread-and-butter' terms by now, some are far less common among classicists ('circulation', 'communities of production', 'knowledge transmission', even 'media' or 'technologies'). All of this provides opportunities for innovative insights and fresh angles which, it is hoped, will enable novel subsequent research: the field needs more holistic discussions of this kind.

One concern throughout this project has been to avoid the pitfall of talking exclusively about socio-cultural frames and contexts without taking into account what could actually be seen and experienced on the stage(s), public and private, of Graeco-Roman theatre(s) (that they supposedly produce 'flat literary readings' – readings, that is, which are so focused on contexts that they allegedly confront texts only superficially and without sophistication – is a criticism frequently launched at cultural history approaches). It is true that because of its very nature the study of cultural history will always to some extent prioritize context over text by default. Yet it is equally true that text and context, drama and theatre, performance and socio-cultural frame are dialectical binaries: no one component even makes sense without the other. This simple but important fact is something that the contributors to this volume have always been mindful of in their discussions, even if some chapters lean more heavily to one side of the binary than the other. Taken as a whole, the vista of the volume is integrative and driven by equal interest in what happened on and off the stage(s).

THEATRE OF GRAECO-ROMAN ANTIQUITY: PHENOMENOLOGY

The theatres of Graeco-Roman antiquity can perhaps best be described using genre as a metric, which yields a classification of tragedy, comedy, satyr play, mime and pantomime. Each of these genres is characterized by a set of distinct features (for a fuller discussion see chapter 8 in this volume by Sells). In *tragedy*, the mask and costume for both actors and the chorus in conjunction with mythical plot material, solemn diction and highly regulated rhythm of alternating speech and song gave this theatre form a distinct feel both on the stage and the page. *Comedy*, at least in the fifth century BCE, is set in stark opposition to these aesthetics. Its grotesque masks, malproportioned and obscene bodies and unlimited registers for plot selection (contemporary or mythical), diction, intertextuality and metatheatricality make for a pronounced contrast which, while it diminishes in the fourth century BCE, is never lost. The Roman playwright Plautus in particular has a bawdiness worthy of his Greek counterparts from the fifth century (even if much of Roman comedy's visual dimension remains elusive).[3] All of this said, by the second half of the fourth century BCE, Greek comedy has become widely domesticated, both in its theatricality and in its plot patterns (which are now increasingly under the strong influence of tragedy, especially Euripides). So stark is the contrast between late fourth-century comedy, which for us is synonymous with the comedy of Menander (its only reasonably well-preserved representative) and that of the fifth century (for us, mainly the eleven comedies by Aristophanes and a fair amount of fragmentary evidence from his rivals Cratinus and Eupolis) that since antiquity there has been a strong sense of caesura. Modern scholarship therefore distinguishes between 'Old Comedy' from the fifth century and Menander's 'New Comedy' from the late fourth century.[4] *Satyr play*, which at least at the Great Dionysia in Athens until about the middle of the fourth century BCE would conventionally follow the performance of a tragic trilogy, is distinguished by its chorus of satyrs as a signature feature. These satyrs, who may assume additional identities, engage in daring and often erotic adventures involving heroes from the mythical past (hence from tragedy, too). Situated somewhere in between tragedy and comedy, satyr play combines comic antics with tragedy's decorum.[5] The ancient critic Demetrius (*On Style* 169) therefore refers to it as 'tragedy at play'. *Mime*, the fourth art form in this classification, was widely considered to be the lowest of theatre arts. Only in this genre there were actresses, often in central and dominant roles (to many critics' chagrin). Performers were usually unmasked and may have been barefoot. Of all dramatic genres, mime most stubbornly resists rigid classification.[6] It could be performed in poetry or prose or a mixture of both, by a single performer or pairs or a troupe, and with a variety of linguistic registers reminiscent of comedy. Mimes existed in both sub-literary and literary formats (examples of the latter are the mimes of two Greeks, Sophron and Herodas, as well as those of the Roman Laberius). Slapstick, stage violence and physical acting in general seem to have been typical. Of its many stock characters, the Fool (*môros, stupidus*) was its most emblematic one, and mime plots were known for their realism (the mime actor was regularly referred to as *biologos*: 'speaker of life'). Plots could revolve around erotic adventures, love and adultery as much as mythological subjects or thinly disguised contemporary political and social issues (hence its proximity to satire). Parody of religious rituals, including those practised by Christians, was evidently within the domain of the mime, even if it may not have been as prominent as suggested by the Christian writers dealing with this art form (usually, but not always, polemically). Last but certainly not least, mime was a keeper: it is the only dramatic genre which appears to have been continuously popular and regularly performed throughout the whole millennium of theatre history in Graeco-Roman antiquity covered in this volume. *Pantomime*, finally, is at its core a mimetic solo dance performed by a silent masked male dancer who through his movements tells a mythical narrative and who would adopt the various roles of the narrative himself, regularly changing his pantomime mask (which, by contrast with the tragic mask, had a closed mouth).[7] The solo dancer could perform his mimetic choreography with a narrator or solo singer or choir (pantomime libretti were probably always in verse). He could be accompanied by a solo instrument (including the very loud water organ) or a whole orchestra. Pantomime performance was extraordinarily flexible and adaptable, which was a key reason for its enormous success: amphitheatres, open-air theatres, roofed theatres (the so-called *odeum*) and private dining halls of various sizes could function as performance sites. Street and market-place performances too were common. Pantomime had a distinct sound to it, as its performance was punctuated by the metronome-like rhythm of the *scabellum*, a small percussion instrument attached to the sandal of a musical accompanist. Despite predecessors, the genre only seems to have come into its own in the first century BCE and was a huge success across the whole social spectrum, in the Latin West of the Roman Empire as well as in its Greek East. Its cultural and educational role in the dissemination of myth (often as shaped by tragic playwrights) cannot be overestimated.

While such generic distinctions are helpful, they should not obscure the fact that there were constant overlaps, interactions and instances of cross-fertilization. This is abundantly clear for the relationship between fifth- and fourth-century tragedy and comedy, while the interaction between tragedy and satyr play could even be institutionally fixed (at the Great Dionysia in fifth-century Athens one satyr play would follow after a tragic trilogy). But comedy and satyr play surely fed off each other too, as did comedy and mime. Pantomime has plausibly been seen as a continuation of tragedy by means of dance and, in turn, as an important influence on (Senecan) tragedy. Cross-fertilization between mime and pantomime would also seem natural and intrinsically likely. Similar dynamics were operative between these five forms of theatre and the many para-theatrical entertainment genres of antiquity such as gladiatorial shows, animal hunts, chariot races, acrobatics, staged sea battles and choreographed public executions. The latter, for instance, could become 'fabulous' (to use Katherine Welch's memorable phrasing) if staged according to a mythical plot that had been theatricalized by pantomime and/or tragedy.[8] Thus the opening festivities at the Colosseum in 80 CE featured at least two such 'fabulous' executions, along the Pasiphae and the Prometheus plot respectively, which Martial celebrated in two epigrams of his collection *On Spectacles* (nos. 6 and 9). We happen to know that both stories had been performed as pantomime in the theatre under Nero (and that both had also been treated in tragedy, by Euripides in his *Cretan Women* and Aeschylus (?) in the *Prometheus Bound*). These para-theatrical events staged in the huge Colosseum therefore gave the story a gruesome 'reality show' character which was beyond the reach of any theatre.

THEATRES OF GRAECO-ROMAN ANTIQUITY: EVIDENCE

The body of evidence for theatre in Graeco-Roman antiquity is diverse, complex and often challenging. It can, most broadly, be classified into textual and visual evidence. Both types of evidence are often fragmentary and may be difficult to contextualize, Roman tragedy of the Republican era being a notorious example. In addition, there is the issue of mediation, especially in the form of diachronic transmission which was sure to affect the quality of the playscripts which were circulated and, finally, in one way or another made it into the mediaeval manuscript tradition which has reached us.[9] Also, there may be strong imbalances between the two types of evidence respectively, with quantity of textual evidence far surpassing that of visual evidence, and vice versa, in any given period.

A good example is Greek theatre of the fifth century BCE, the age of the most important and best-known Greek playwrights. Here the (large) body of preserved evidence (forty-four plays in total) is primarily textual. There are thirty-two tragedies (seven by Aeschylus [525/4–456/5 BCE], although *Prometheus Bound* may not be by him; seven by Sophocles [497/6–406/405 BCE]; seventeen or eighteen by Euripides[10] [c. 480–406 BCE]), one satyr play (the *Cyclops* by Euripides) and eleven comedies (all by Aristophanes [shortly after 450–after 388 BCE]). In addition, there is a wealth of fragments from plays by these playwrights and some important others, especially the comic playwrights Cratinus and Eupolis. For the subsequent fourth century BCE, however, much of the evidence is visual (there is extremely little textual evidence for fourth-century tragedy, although the situation is better for fourth-century comedy, especially Menander [342/1–c. 292/1 BCE]). In particular, there are far more theatre-related vase-paintings from the fourth than from the fifth century, although most of it was produced not in Attica but in Southern Italy. This evidence, though difficult to handle, is gold-dust, as it provides us, among other things, with a great deal of information about the visual and performative dimension of Greek theatre.[11] There are also very important inscriptions from Athens and its surroundings (Attica) which, despite their often fragmentary nature, provide crucial insights into the organizational structure of the Athenian dramatic festivals, the playwrights competing at them and the financial model sustaining them.[12] Last but not least, there are still-extant theatre sites: Epidaurus, the best-preserved and best-known (built in the fourth century BCE); Athens, with its long history and messy excavation record, and the equally impressive theatre of Syracuse which goes back to at least the early fifth century BCE; or the Hellenistic theatres of Priene or Pergamon in Asia minor (the west coast of modern-day Turkey).

Roman theatre, for us, starts with the large corpus of completely preserved comedies by Plautus (c. 250–184 BCE, twenty comedies) and Terence (c. 195/4–159 BCE, six comedies).[13] Later Roman comedy is lost, as are the predecessors of Plautus and Terence. Of Roman tragedy there are only fragments from the Republican and early imperial era.[14] But we have complete texts of eight tragedies preserved under the name of Seneca, who is probably identical with Seneca the Younger, the well-known philosopher (c. 4 BCE–65 CE). Two further tragedies (*Hercules Oetaeus* and *Octavia*) whose authors are not securely attested are part of the same manuscript tradition. *Octavia* is the only preserved sample of a unique sub-set of Roman tragedy, the *fabula praetexta* which dealt with historical (including near-contemporary) Roman figures (in the *Octavia* both Nero and Seneca are dramatic characters). By significant contrast with

Greek drama, at no point did theatre-inspired scenes adorn Roman pottery, and our knowledge of the visual and performative dimension of Roman tragedy and comedy rests entirely on written sources.

Mime existed in both the Greek and the Roman theatre tradition. Of the latter only fragments survive (especially by the first-century BCE playwright Laberius).[15] But for Greek mime there is one important papyrus (*P. Oxy.* 413, published in 1903) in particular which contains substantial portions of two mime scripts (one on adultery and a jealous mistress, the other on Charition, a woman rescued by Greeks from captivity in India).[16] New, albeit less spectacular, mime papyri have been published more recently.[17] For pantomime, finally, the discrepancy between popularity and level of preserved documentation is extreme. There is a fair amount of (not rarely polemical) discussion of the pantomime and its practitioners, including an intriguing treatise by Lucian on pantomime dancing, as well as solid iconographic and epigraphic evidence. But despite the fact that famous and high-calibre poets like Lucan or Statius are known to have composed pantomime libretti, no single such libretto has come down to us. The best candidate is a papyrus (now kept in Barcelona) which contains a Latin hexameter poem with a gripping narrative (in the first-person present tense and third-person past tense) of the death of Alcestis. That the 'Barcelona Alcestis' is part of a pantomime libretto has been argued very plausibly by Edith Hall, but at least for now the case must ultimately remain inconclusive.[18]

NATURE OF ANCIENT PERFORMANCE CULTURE

Greek theatre starts to materialize in the late sixth century, in two different places. There is Athens, where tragedy and comedy, both written in the local Attic dialect, became institutionalized, as part of a general self-promoting expansion of the city and its ruling class, in an urban festival dedicated to Dionysus (the 'Great Dionysia') as a major platform for competitive dramatic performances.[19] And there is Sicily (especially Syracuse) where the playwright Epicharmus wrote comedies in the local Doric dialect (there is no evidence for Sicilian tragedy). Of these two the Athenian situation is, in every respect, incomparably better documented than that in Sicily.[20] What emerges with reasonable clarity is that within the existing landscape of Greek poetry, tragedy, comedy and satyr play are innovative hybrids which combine in novel ways long-existing traditions of choral song, poetic solo narrative and personal invective. They also all develop out of ritual practices which, certainly in Athens, had strong connections with Dionysus, who becomes the deity most strongly associated with the theatre.[21] Finally, Greek drama is embedded within a larger and very diverse performance culture which included recitations of epic or elegiac poetry, solo and choral performances at large public festivals as well as private performances of whole pieces or extracts at the drinking parties (symposia) of the elite. Other areas of public and political life (assemblies, funerals, law-courts) were also heavily performative in nature, which meant that competences acquired through theatrical spectatorship could be re-applied in other areas of social life, and vice versa.[22] Given the low overall literacy levels in Graeco-Roman antiquity,[23] communicative exchanges in these societies were predominantly oral, aural and visual. This meant that, although a sizeable book market existed by the fourth century BCE, performance rather than reading remained a main, and for many the only possible, mode of consumption of theatre.

None of the above appears to be fundamentally different in Roman culture – with one important exception. This is the level and nature of the anxiety, at least on part of the ruling elite, surrounding theatre as a cultural (and therefore also political) activity, at least until the end of the first century BCE. The production of a play (or plays) in Latin at Rome in 240 BCE by Livius Andronicus, a Greek apparently from Tarentum who had been owned and subsequently enfranchised by an elite Roman family, has since antiquity been regarded as the beginning of Roman drama, even if it is certain that well-established traditions of indigenous (i.e. Italiote and Etruscan) as well as Greek theatre had long been thriving on the Italian peninsula.[24] This is a watershed for Roman cultural life in general, not least because Livius Andronicus is also said to be the first to have written Roman comedy and epic (which turns him into something like the prime mover of Roman literary culture). Comedy, tragedy and mime quickly established themselves as fixtures in the festival and entertainment culture of Rome. But despite several documented efforts in the second century BCE Rome lacked any permanent and purpose-built performance venue (plays were staged in front of temples or in multi-purpose venues) until Pompey erected a permanent theatre, which bore his name, in 55 BCE, followed in around 13 BCE by the 'Theatre of Balbus' and, around the same time, by the 'Theatre of Marcellus' which was sponsored by Augustus.[25] Cultural anxiety about theatre as a (mainly) Greek intrusion and somewhat 'un-Roman' activity seems to be part of the reason for this delay. Another vital element is politics, since non-permanent performance venues added power and leverage to the officials in charge in running festivals and sponsoring other performance occasions.

A defining feature of Graeco-Roman theatre culture is its intense competitiveness, of both social and artistic nature. At least since Jacob Burckhardt's *The Greeks and Greek Civilization* (1872), ancient Greek culture has correctly be labelled 'agonal' (derived from the Greek word *agôn* = 'competition').[26] If a competitive element did not already exist intrinsically in a social practice (as in athletics, for instance), Greeks were eager to introduce it, and the dramatic festivals were no exception.²⁷ This agonal spirit is not only inscribed into the technical lingo in which, by the late fourth century BCE if not earlier, the actor is called a 'competitor (*agônistês*) and where 'to compete' (*agônizesthai*) becomes the predominant expression for 'to act'. It also pervades the organizational structure of both Athenian festivals for drama, the Great Dionysia and the Lenaea, where judges would adjudicate first, second and third prizes for playwrights and actors. Victorious *chorêgoi*, wealthy aristocrats, that is, who would fund individual dramatic (and dithyrambic) performances as part of their obligation to finance public endeavours (the so-called *leitourgia*), would proudly erect large and prominently positioned monuments to display their prize for dithyrambic victory, a tripod, and the achievement it represented to the city at large.²⁸ There is evidence for judges at dramatic festivals in Sicily (Epicharmus fr. 237 Kassel-Austin), and it seems safe to say that competitive performances of tragedy, comedy and satyr play are the norm throughout the Greek world in the fifth and fourth centuries and beyond. Comedy, especially that of the fifth century BCE, responds to this ubiquitous competitiveness in the most overt manner by openly, and often aggressively, addressing both its intra- and inter-generic dimension (i.e. competition between rival comic playwrights on the one hand, and competition between comedy and others genres, especially tragedy, on the other).²⁹ But there can be no doubt that this kind of responsiveness also informed tragic playwriting, acting and production techniques in a similarly fundamental way, even if generic convention pre-empted overt acknowledgement of these dynamics in the scripts (and, presumably, in performance). An exception, at least a partial one, to this ubiquitous hands-on artistic competitiveness seem to have been mime and pantomime. In the dialogue *On Dancing* by Lucian (second century CE), at any rate, a fierce critic of pantomime is made to contrast mime and pantomime as art forms not deemed worthy of institutionalized competitions with four others that are, namely tragedy, comedy, citharody and dithyramb.³⁰ But things were changing around the time of the composition of Lucian's dialogue in the 160s, and there is sound inscriptional evidence that by the end of the second century CE pantomime competitions were a regular part of Greek festivals, including the most prestigious ones (mime would be following suit shortly thereafter, albeit on a more humble scale).³¹ In addition, it seems safe to assume that the occasions for performing mime and pantomime were regularly and from early on socially competitive to a high degree, with one sponsor (or sponsoring body) trying to outdo the other in the lavishness of the support provided.

This would seem to apply in particular to the Roman cultural sphere, where theatre too is steeped in the pressures of both social and artistic competition, and again it is comedy where these pressures find some articulation.³² It is not known from the evidence currently available whether in Rome, where by the second century BCE there were six regular festivals of ever-increasing length featuring drama as well numerous one-off performance occasions (funeral games for leading politicians and generals, for instance), the competitive nature of dramatic performances was as institutionalized and openly acknowledged as in Greece, although remarks in the prologue to Plautus' *Amphitruo* (64–85, date and festival unknown) clearly presuppose the existence of a competitive element of some sort. But even so it is clear that in Rome social competition using theatre as its outlet was even fiercer than in Greece, and theatrical events were consequently more closely connected to the complex and harsh dynamics of high-powered politics. This is because in the Roman world, theatre and the various types of entertainment provided by it – drama, mime and pantomime, not to mention para-theatrical genres like gladiatorial games, animal hunts and public executions – are closely tied to the interests of the moneyed elite, either in power or aspiring to it, and the competing interests among the individual members of these power circles. Thus theatre is a crucial communication channel between the ruling class and the masses, and between competing individuals within that class. While members of the elite could demonstrate their status and prowess to the masses, and to rival aristocrats, by their largesse in the form of running established festivals or sponsoring, often as part of electoral campaigns, one-off events as 'gifts' (*munera*), those masses in turn would signal their loyalty and support during large gatherings in public space (bearing in mind that the Roman political system since the Republic had a strong plebiscitary element). As a result, Roman theatre and theatre in Rome became a catalyst, and focal point for this multi-dimensional and bi-lateral 'give and take' between elite and non-elite: it became some kind of a pulse or even litmus test indicative of the current political climate. It is important to note that because the social dynamics in these large venues could be unpredictable and, to a certain extent, uncontrollable, the Roman theatre, together with the amphitheatre and the circus, was one of the very few sites where relative freedom of expression for the masses can be said to have existed. This remained so even as the political system became ever more oppressive under the emperors (who had reason to make sure that soldiers were on stand-by).[33]

For the mid first century BCE, for example (a particularly tense, even explosive period in Roman history), Cicero provides a number of instances where sometimes minute interventions to established scripts made by actors in performance – a particular emphasis, a certain gesture, an inserted line – had an immediate and profound impact on alert and politically sensitized mass audiences, and this remarkable phenomenon continued into the imperial period.[34] In the same vein, a contemporary and social peer of Cicero's, the knight-turned-mime playwright (and at least one-time mime actor) Laberius, was infamous to contemporaries and later generations for his outspokenness and witticisms on and off the stage.[35] In the Roman world, therefore, theatre was arguably *even more political* than it was in the classical Greece of the fifth and fourth century, with the Hellenistic courts of the third and second centuries functioning as models and pre-cursors to the overt and self-interested exploitation of theatre art for personal political ambitions.[36]

This pervasive politicization of theatre affected the whole range of the real or aspiring political class, from the offices of aedile and (later) praetor (who were in charge of regular festivals) as mandatory steps in a political career up to the emperor himself (who might impose caps on how much others were allowed to spend on theatre entertainment, evidently with a view to securing his own position as the supreme benefactor). When, for instance, Augustus publicly recapitulates his life-time achievements in a major inscription to be set up prominently in Rome and replicated throughout the empire, he points out that he renovated the 'Theatre of Pompey' (*Pompeium theatrum*), an entertainment complex centred around Rome's first permanent stone theatre built by his adoptive father's arch rival, at his own expense ('without any inscription in my name', as he emphasizes in false humility). In addition, he mentions that he erected what was known as the 'Theatre of Marcellus' and made 'innumerable expenses' to fund theatrical and other spectacles.[37] The top pantomime artist of the day, Pylades, probably belonged to Augustus whereas his equally famous rival Bathyllus belonged to Augustus' close associate Maecenas (in the western part of the empire at least, most performers – be they actors, mimes or pantomimes – seem to have been freedmen or slaves owned by the elite).[38]

But this kind of public display of 'theatrical prowess' by the elite is only part of the picture. In the private residences (or, more precisely, 'show-homes') of the elite across the empire there is also a thriving home entertainment culture which included pantomime, mime and, among the top-tier sponsors, drama.[39] At this level too, socio-political competition, display of wealth and bonding among peers are key driving forces, to such an extent that the distinction between 'public'/'open' and 'private'/'hidden' display of social status and cultural prowess effectively collapses. In fact, the smaller and more personalized ambiance of the 'show-homes' provided even better opportunities for tailored and targeted self-promotion to select target groups than could be offered by any public venue.

AUDIENCES

Theatre is a mass medium throughout antiquity. From its beginnings in the sixth century BCE to the end of antiquity, theatre found large audiences, even if there were shifts in what kind of theatre found wide-spread favour. If tragedy, comedy and satyr play held the day initially, mime and especially pantomime are the predominant and most visible performance genres of later antiquity. In addition, there are para-theatrical events, most notably gladiatorial games, animal hunts and public executions, which could be elaborately staged following their own, often myth-inspired, dramaturgy. These, too, attracted very large audiences in Roman amphitheatres which were architecturally distinct venues built specifically for some of these para-theatrical purposes.[40]

Venues are indeed crucial evidence for audience-related cultural history, and the implications of their size, architecture, location and geographical dissipation lie at the heart of the claim that theatre was a mass medium in the Graeco-Roman cultural sphere. The well-known fourth-century theatre of Epidaurus, the best-preserved and most often illustrated theatre venue of antiquity which was situated in the sanctuary of the healing god Asclepius, eventually seated well over 10,000 people and was state-of-the-art, especially as far as its (still) impressive acoustics are concerned.[41] The most important theatre in the Greek world, that of Athens in the sanctuary of Dionysus on the southern slope of the Acropolis which hosted the initial key performances of the fifth-century classic playwrights, had a similar seating capacity by the second half of the fourth century when it underwent major changes and updates.[42] Sicily, the other long-time 'hotspot' for drama, had several old and large theatres (Syracuse, Segesta, probably Gela), and, by the fourth century, theatres can be found (or are attested) all over the Greek cultural continuum, including its very edges where theatre was an even more important vehicle for expressing Greek cultural identity.[43] Thus the Black Sea region has an impressive density of Greek theatre sites (even if what exactly went on at them is not at all clear).[44] Another telling example is the Graeco-Bactrian settlement at Ai Khanoum in present-day Afghanistan which had a theatre with a seating capacity of at least 5,000 people.[45]

The Roman conquest and expansion picks up and amplifies this cultural trend. Initially, before the construction of Rome's permanent theatres in the late Republican and early imperial period, the (non-permanent) performance sites, often so-called 'temple theatres' with the temple stairs functioning as auditoria, were relatively small compared to their Greek counterparts, allowing for no more than about 1,500–2,000 spectators.[46] This changed for good with the construction of the Theatre of Pompey (55 BCE, seating at least 11,000 and perhaps up to 40,000), the Theatre of Balbus (13 BCE, seating c. 8,000) and the Theatre of Marcellus (13 or 11 BCE, seating c. 15,000).[47] As a result, permanent Roman theatres, architecturally distinct both from their Greek counterparts and the Roman amphitheatre (where the audience was completely surrounding the performance space), became standard accessories in cities across the whole empire. Impressive remains can still be seen in a number of places in addition to Pompeii, including Taormina (Sicily), Lebda (Libya), Bostra (Syria), Orange (France), Belkiz (ancient Aspendus) and Pamukkale (both in Turkey). In addition, there were of course always less permanent venues and *ad hoc* performance sites as well (these were the norm for the lowly genre of the mime). It is also important to point out in this context that there is compelling epigraphic evidence for regarding actors as perhaps the most mobile of all itinerant professionals in antiquity. Actors would, of course, travel to wherever they would find audiences – which seems to have been just about anywhere.

While this big picture is surely established by the monumental evidence, it is much harder to describe, let alone understand in full, what exactly being an audience member in the ancient theatre was like on the basis of the existing sources.[48] No eyewitness accounts are preserved (unless they are part of a fictional narrative like the description of a pantomime performance at Apuleius *Metamorphoses* 10.30–4), and there is little theatre-related legal documentation which can be mined for information.[49] Moreover, audiences were not a major object of interest to theorists (like Aristotle) or vase-painters. Much of the evidence that does exist consists of anecdotes preserved in a variety of text types, explanatory commentary from ancient scholars, insights by implication or collateral information as part of narratives with a non-theatre focus (in a historiographical text or a court speech, for instance). Very important too are texts which belong to what Jonas Barish has influentially termed 'the antitheatrical prejudice', like parts of Plato's *Republic* or Tertullian's treatise *On Spectacles*, because when highlighting what for them constitute the depraved and despicable features of theatre these polemicists regularly concentrate on its performative aspects.[50]

Most important of all, finally, are the preserved playscripts themselves, especially those of comedy (both Greek and Roman) which is the most openly metatheatrical of all dramatic genres, regularly addressing its audiences and seeking to interact with them. Some portions of comedies like prologues or, in fifth-century Greek comedy, a major section of speech and song reserved for the chorus (the so-called *parabasis*) are particularly prone to metatheatrical play and contain a wealth of information.[51] But here too we encounter limits. A notorious example is the question of whether or not women were allowed to attend the theatre in classical Athens, since the evidence provided by the playtexts currently known is inconclusive. All preserved audience addresses are to male spectators only. But this need not imply that no women were present. What this evidence does provide is the important insight that in classical Athens male spectators constitute the notional audience, i.e. the audience that matters as a communicative partner and target, while the actual audience may still have been of mixed gender.[52]

Despite the gaps and shortcomings of the evidence, some important characteristics of ancient theatre-going nonetheless emerge with reasonable clarity. Thus the seating of the audience was commonly regulated in such a way as to mirror sociological distinctions that structured the world outside of the theatre, turning the performance venue into a material manifestation of the body politic and society at large. In classical Athens already, 'zoning by tribe' (with additional zones reserved for council members, young military recruits, non-citizens and perhaps women) may well have been the ideal, if perhaps not meticulously enforced, ordering principle of the Theatre of Dionysus,[53] while the preferred seating for magistrates, priest, foreign dignitaries and the like (*prohedria*) added an element of privilege to an otherwise quite egalitarian social space which juxtaposed differences more than it prioritized them. Roman theatrical space, on the other hand, is blatantly and visibly hierarchical. From the early second century BCE senators, conspicuously dressed in their long white gowns with a broad purple band (*toga laticlavia*), would be separated from the rest of audience, occupying the front seats in the *orchestra* (which used to be the performance space for the chorus), while behind them in the next fourteen rows were the knights, the next social class in the pecking order. Under Augustus the compartmentalization of audiences, which apparently had not been fully enforced everywhere, was regulated more strictly, with separations along the lines of not only class but also gender and age (Suetonius *Augustus* 44). Violations of these ordering principles were certain to generate social tensions, as Caligula reckoned when, according to Suetonius (*Caligula* 26.4), he deliberately gave tickets (or ticket subsidies?) for the riff-raff earlier than usual so that they would also fill the knights' seats.

In terms of comportment, ancient open-air theatre audiences were a far cry from the passive, domesticated and often sanctimonious onlookers in darkened auditoria that have been the norm in Western theatre history since the late nineteenth century. The loud, energized, demanding, interventionist and at times even unruly nature of theatre audiences in both Greek and Roman theatres is well-attested, not least by playwrights themselves (Plautus *Poenulus* 1–45 and Terence *Hecyra* 29–57 are the most explicit instances). The sheer existence in Athens of security personnel, so-called 'rod-holders' (*rhabdouchoi*), to control and potentially discipline the audience is telling enough. Towering above the stage in relative comfort (wine and snacks were readily available), playgoers exerted a considerable amount of power over the performance and would always made their presence felt. It therefore stands to reason that while in Greece, where formal head-on dramatic competitions were the norm, the vote on which production would be victorious was formally lying 'in the laps of the judges' (to draw on a, perhaps proverbial, phrase used by Epicharmus), in reality no judge could or would have ignored the acclamations of the audience at large.[54] Disruptive audience interventions during performance appear to have been common. The actors Hegelochus (Athens, fifth century BCE) and Eros (Rome, first century BCE) were (in)famously hissed off stage, the former after having mispronounced a single word.[55] And in the *Poetics*, Aristotle repeatedly uses the expression that a play 'fell out' (*ekpiptein*) in a way which suggests that it was a technical term to denote something which occurred quite regularly and may, at least sometimes, have meant that an ongoing performance actually had to be aborted.[56] Given the above-mentioned degree of politicization in the Roman theatre, it is hardly surprising that here the evidence for theatre claques, surely often planted and paid, is strong (starting as early as Plautus), and there could be serious riots as a result.[57] Graeco-Roman audiences, in other words, had a real presence and vitality to them. Their significance and level of engagement are perhaps the most powerful indicators of just how much theatre, in its varied manifestations, actually mattered in antiquity – as art and as a socio-cultural fixture of life.

CHAPTER ONE

Institutional Frameworks

Enabling the Theatrical Event

MARTIN REVERMANN

HERO(ES), FESTIVAL, TRAGEDY: AN INTRODUCTORY CASE STUDY

In book 5 of his *Histories* Herodotus (5.67) tells an intriguing story involving Cleisthenes, tyrant of Sicyon from c. 595 to 575 BCE, hero cult and the reorganization of a festival:

> Cleisthenes had been at war with Argos, and for one thing he put an end to rhapsodic contests in Sicyon because of the Homeric epics, which are all the time singing of Argos and the Argives. In addition, he wanted to expel from the country Adrastus son of Talaus [a former King of Sicyon and leader of the first Argive expedition against Thebes], who had and in fact still has a hero shrine in the agora of Sicyon. So he went to Delphi and asked the oracle whether he could remove Adrastus. But the Pythia replied in her oracular response that Adrastus was King of Sicyon and Cleisthenes a mere thrower of stones.[1] Since the god would not give permission, he went back home and tried to devise a way of making sure that Adrastus would leave on his own. [. . .] [Cleisthenes then decides to introduce to Sicyon a hero cult of Melanippus from Thebes, a mortal enemy of Adrastus whose brother and son-in-law had been killed by Melanippus.] When Cleisthenes had assigned him [i.e. Melanippus] the precinct, he took away from Adrastus his sacrifices and festivals and gave them to Melanippus. [. . .] In many ways they [i.e. the

> people of Argos] gave honour to Adrastus, but in particular they celebrated him with tragic choruses for his sufferings. These were not in honour of Dionysus, but of Adrastus. Cleisthenes gave the choruses to Dionysus instead, and the rest of the cult to Melanippus.

This very important passage, about a period which precedes all preserved dramatic texts we have by a century or so, illustrates a number of features which are to be characteristic of the institutional frameworks within which ancient theatre will operate for the next millennium. First, there is the simple yet crucial fact that there *is* an institutional frame to begin with. Sicyon, like most cities in classical antiquity, surely had a host of festivals which showcased various art forms. Herodotus explicitly mentions contests of epic poetry as delivered by travelling bards (the so-called 'rhapsodes') and 'tragic choruses' as part of Adrastus' hero cult. What exactly these 'tragic choruses' in Sicyon of the early sixth century would perform, and especially how much resemblance this had with what would be 'tragedy' (*tragôidia*) in Athens by the second quarter of the fifth century (when our textual evidence starts with the early plays by Aeschylus), is impossible to say with the evidence currently available. But Herodotus clearly assumes a generic similarity between those 'tragic choruses' at Sicyon and what he, writing in the second half of the fifth century BCE, conceptualized as 'tragedy'.[2] From the viewpoint of institutional organization, it is important to note that these are not *ad hoc* performances but dedicated performance slots which were integrated into an organizational framework (in this case hero cult) which secured (re)performance in stable conditions and within predictable intervals. The existence of such stable frameworks enabling performance is a defining characteristic of much of Graeco-Roman theatre, especially its canonical genres (tragedy, comedy and, in Greece, satyr play), even if less rigid, more improvisational frameworks must have existed and were in fact the norm for mime (possibly also for pantomime, especially in its early history). None of this is surprising given the nature, extent and prominence of ancient festival culture in the lives of individuals and communities (of whatever size). Theatre is an integral though not exclusive part of this festival culture.[3]

The second important general feature well illustrated by Herodotus' account is the complex socio-political nature of this framework. Overtly, it is entirely religious, since the tragic choruses are part of the hero cult for Adrastus, celebrating his sufferings (presumably, for instance, the loss of his brother and his son-in-law). Secular concerns, however, are the overwhelming driving forces: Herodotus' narrative makes it abundantly clear that under the veneer of cult and religion, the performance of tragic choruses is, or at least can very easily become, an extremely political and socially competitive business, a state affair even. By replacing Adrastus, the leader of the (first) Argive expedition against Thebes, with his Theban death enemy Melanippus,

Cleisthenes' tactical shifting of heroes and their cults is designed to make an all-too-blunt point about his relationship with hostile Argos, and the tragic choruses of the hero cult are nothing but pawns in this chess game of inter-state war politics. So are, incidentally, the gods: at the order of Cleisthenes attempting to outmanoeuvre the Delphic oracle, the tragic choruses of Sicyon are re-allocated from the hero Adrastus (who, *qua* hero cult, functions as a minor deity in his own right)[4] to the god Dionysus, while the rest of the cult is re-assigned to the newly created local hero cult of Melanippus. The concept of Greece as a 'militant festival culture', endorsed by Slater,[5] seems particularly apposite in this instance. The potential for self-interested manipulation seems limitless indeed, and institutional frameworks for theatre are to remain deeply politicized throughout antiquity, no matter whether these are city-run drama competitions in fifth-century Athens, theatrical performances under the tutelage of Macedonian kings and their successors, Plautine comedies staged at a Roman festival sponsored by a high-ranking Roman official, or pantomimes performing at the villa of a wealthy Roman while also competing at a prestigious festival in honour of the Roman emperor. The strength of the nexus between theatre, power and the moneyed elite that characterizes Graeco-Roman culture is arguably second to none in Western and non-Western cultural history, and the institutional frameworks for theatre are the nodal points where these inter-connections become most clearly and visibly articulated, hence particularly interesting not just for the cultural but also the political and the economic historian.

Lastly, the Herodotus passages also at least hints at the fact that the question 'Who enables the theatrical framework?' often has a less straightforward answer than one might initially think. The sole ruler Cleisthenes, of course, pulls the strings here. But Herodotus also says that 'the people of Argos' celebrate the hero cult of Adrastus, including the tragic choruses in his honour. Theatre is a highly collaborative art form both in terms of its production and its reception, and looking more closely at the workings of any institutional framework for theatre in antiquity usually reveals complex dynamics and ongoing negotiations between individual and collective, private and public, sponsors of theatrical events and those who make them materialize, be it as actors and choruses or as spectators. This is the key reason why in the current volume this (first) chapter on institutional frameworks has as its natural complement the (seventh) chapter on 'Communities of production' (by Jane Lightfoot), which should be read alongside.

THEORIZING THE ANCIENT THEATRICAL FRAME

The notion of the 'frame' is a sociological one. It was popularized by the influential micro-sociologist Erving Goffman (1922–82), notably in his book entitled *Frame Analysis: An Essay on the Organization of Experience*.[6] As indicated by the book's sub-title, frames are a means of social organization and one of the prime elements which make social order possible in the first place. They therefore have, by default, a stabilizing and affirmative function which enables social cohesion.[7] While Goffman was particularly interested in the discursive frames of everyday talk, he was keenly aware of the special connection shared by social frames and the theatre (exploring the theatricality of human social life is a key theme in all of Goffman's work). He also realized that frames usually manifest themselves as frame*works*, i.e. as complex clusters of organizational patterns which interact with each other as well as with the individuals or groups using them. While 'frame' and 'framework' have, for some time now, been common lingo in Theatre Studies and Cultural Studies more broadly, it is very important to bear in mind the sociological pedigree of these concepts.

Frames can be physical (a theatre building, for instance) or conceptual (that is, the frame of mind adopted when viewing theatre). The institutional frameworks which are the subject of this chapter are both. There is a physical demarcation – often the sacred space of a sanctuary, a 'theatre temple' or a tomb but also the profane space of a market-place or the villa of a wealthy patron – which provides the site and location of the theatrical event. And there is the conceptual frame, or 'frame of mind', of the performer(s) and the playgoer(s). This conceptual frame has cognitive but also socio-historical and emotional aspects to it. In the case of Graeco-Roman theatre, the very strong link between theatre and festival meant that notions of feasting, licence, worship, relaxation and socializing were powerful ingredients of any institutional framework for the theatre arts. A festival also constitutes what may be branded a 'strong' institutional frame: it is highly visible and socially sanctioned by perhaps the strongest of all collective bonding mechanisms, religion; its continuity and iteration are usually guaranteed, with financial resources being quite readily available; and it affords numerous opportunities for pronounced and visible social differentiation: note, for instance, the social capital gained and displayed by the sponsors (*chorêgoi*) of classical Greek drama, or the hierarchical seating order of theatres in Rome which put the senatorial class, with its conspicuous dress, centre-stage (literally).[8] 'Weaker' institutional frames for theatre did exist, in the form of street or market-place performances, theatre acts done for the Roman military, or private performances in the luxury show-homes of the moneyed elite. But overall, ancient theatre stands out for the ubiquity of 'strong' institutional frames. These functioned as extraordinarily robust, predictable, reliable, structured and effective communicative networks of power and politics. As regulated contact zones, they helped channel, express and negotiate relations between the elite and the masses, the few and the many, the human and the divine, the past and the present, the real and the imagined, the indigenous and the foreign, the Greek and the Roman.

SOME DISTINCT FEATURES

Much of what follows in this chapter will have to be concerned with details of the taxonomy of Greek and Roman festival culture. It is therefore important to step back at this point and outline some distinct features that characterize ancient theatrical frameworks. *Competitiveness*, as mentioned in the Introduction, is a key defining feature of ancient theatre. It is inscribed differently into the frameworks that are attested: competitions between productions with prizes being awarded to rival playwrights and rich individual sponsors (classical Athens); actors' prizes (Greece); peer-driven competition between sponsoring magistrates who aspire to climb the political career ladder and in effect use theatre as part of their electoral campaign (Rome); competition of theatre with rival leisure-time attractions (gladiatorial combat, horse racing etc.) which are being offered at the same occasion (Rome); and theatre art forms (mime and pantomime) that successfully exist for a long time outside of these competitive institutional frameworks before, eventually (in the late second century CE), being at least partially integrated into them. One remarkable difference between Greek and Roman theatrical frameworks is a relative shift of competitiveness, from competition between producers of parts of the theatrical event (actors, playwrights, sponsors of individual productions) to competition between the enablers of wholesale theatre festivals (the presiding magistrate, including the Emperor, trying to outspend and outdo his elite peers). This is in part to be explained by the different social standing of theatre practitioners in Rome, who were hirelings and often socially stigmatized.[9] For the Roman situation, this also means that while the content of the frame (i.e. the actual plays) are often politically neutral (usually dealing with things Greek, often Greek myth), the context (i.e. the frame itself) remains politically charged: it is here, in the sphere of the frame, that competition, conflict and ambition 'play out'.

Graeco-Roman antiquity also saw an increasing *privatization* of theatrical frameworks, alongside the continued existence of public frames in the form of large-scale festivals. This phenomenon, articulated and explored in a pioneering study by Eric Csapo,[10] brings actors and their art into secluded performance contexts outside of the public festival calendar and with more filtered access, although audiences of private performances were not necessarily small but could number hundreds or thousands: the court theatres and banquet performances sponsored by the Macedonian kings or the Roman emperors are, from the perspective of institutional frameworks, as private as the dinner theatre given in the courtyard of a senator's villa for the entertainment of a handful of close friends and useful associates. Here the political element of theatre functioning as a display of munificence and an occasion for bonding was not smaller than in public frameworks but, if anything, much amplified: privatized frames enabled significantly more targeted, hence more efficient, use of theatre as socio-political capital. Privatization also privileged theatre art that was highly mobile logistically and adaptable thematically. Thus full-scale tragic productions (with a chorus and all) increasingly gave way to virtuoso performances of highlights by star actors. Mime continued to be very popular in both private and public contexts. And the rise of pantomime, a hugely adaptable theatre form, which began in the early imperial period, seems intricately connected with privatization.

A related, and from the modern perspective striking, general feature of ancient theatrical frameworks is that they are *not purely economic*. The notion of theatrical entertainment for nothing but profit is, in fact, alien to Graeco-Roman culture which instead conceptualized theatre as an exchange not primarily of money but along other axes, especially that of *religion* (worship of the god(s) is exchanged for divine protection) and publicly displayed *largesse* (the sponsor funds the theatre festival in exchange for political support, loyalty and enhanced or at least maintained social status). Actors and others of course did make money with theatre, and we know that some of them became very wealthy indeed. But the façade of theatre as a different, less ordinary kind of exchange was meticulously maintained.

HISTORY AND TAXONOMY

In the city which provided the opening case study of this chapter, Cleisthenes' Sicyon in the early sixth century BCE, hero cult had functioned as the framework for the performances of tragic choruses (however much or little those may have resembled tragedy of the classical period). Despite lack of concrete evidence this practice may well have been more widespread, especially when considering how popular hero cult was in the sixth and notably the fifth century BCE.[11] The intriguing remark by the anonymous author of the *Life of Aeschylus* that after Aeschylus' death in Sicily around 456 BCE theatre artists would flock to his tomb at Gela and 'conduct sacrifices and perform his plays' points in the same direction and is consistent with the otherwise attested heroization of poets.[12] The standard institutional frame for theatre in antiquity, however, is not hero cult but the festival in honour of an Olympian deity (often, but not always, to the widely popular god Dionysus), either featuring only drama (and possibly a related art form like dithyramb) or combining musical competitions (*mousikoi agônes*), which could include theatre, with athletic ones. There is uncertainty as to the organizational structure of theatre productions in sixth- and early fifth-century Southern Italy and Sicily where Epicharmus' comedies were performed. Some structure was clearly in place: there is sound evidence for the existence of some kind of choregic system in the Sicilian city of Gela in the early fifth century as well as for a competitive adjudication procedure of drama in performance which involved judges.[13]

But a more fleshed-out history and taxonomy of institutional frameworks for ancient theatre cannot start in Western Greece: one has to turn to the Greek mainland instead. It is classical Athens of the fifth and fourth century BCE where we are in the best position of all to (re)construct the institutional framework for theatre and its complex interfaces with what was seen by audiences on stage. This is not so much because we have particularly good evidence about the framework itself (although this is indeed the case). Rather, the case of classical Athens stands out for its unique combination of good epigraphic, at least decent archaeological and exceptionally rich textual evidence (notably in the form of playscripts by Aeschylus, Sophocles, Euripides, Aristophanes and Menander). Here, if anywhere in Graeco-Roman antiquity, it is possible to catch some sense of a 'framework in action' and at least make an attempt to reconstruct what a 'festival experience' may possibly have looked and felt like.

It is for this reason, and the overall constraints of space, that the taxonomy presented here will focus on Athens in the classical period (and, for comparable reasons, on Rome of the middle and late Republican period). This comes at the expense of the Hellenistic period (where epigraphy provides quite rich and fascinating information) and of later antiquity. For these the reader is referred, again, to Lightfoot's chapter in this volume which discusses these periods quite extensively from the different but related vantage point of production. In addition, there is a growing number of excellent publications that can be consulted.[14]

CLASSICAL ATHENS

The city of Athens had two major theatre festivals, the Great Dionysia (or City Dionysia) and the Lenaea festival, in addition to local ones in the demes (smaller administrative sub-units of the city-state) of surrounding Attica.[15] The creation of the Great Dionysia, which were held in the month *Elaphêboliôn* (late March), is associated with the tyrant Peisistratus, who ruled Athens from around the mid-sixth century to 527 BCE. Peisistratus' new urban festival, created around 560 BCE to solidify and endorse the socio-cultural and political cohesion of his new and centralized rule of the city-state, built on long-existing festivals of Dionysus in Attica and beyond. What subsequently made the Great Dionysia unique was the gradual introduction of chorus-based art forms. Thus the first performance of tragedy, by Thespis according to an invaluable inscription now commonly referred to as 'The Marble from Paros' (*Marmor Parium*) dating from about the middle of the third century BCE, took place around 534 BCE (whatever *tragôidia* in Athens may have looked and sounded like at that point in time). Or perhaps, as has more recently been suggested, the introduction of tragedy occurred as late as c. 500 BCE when the political system of Athens had just morphed into a democracy.[16] This is about the time when dithyramb, a cult song delivered by large choruses of fifty men or fifty boys recruited from each of the ten tribes of Athens, was probably introduced into the festival. Performances of comedy became part of the Great Dionysia in 486 BCE or thereabouts.

As a result of its Dionysiac nature and origin, the ritual frame of the Great Dionysia was pronounced. During the 'introduction' (*eisagôgê*) the centre of attention was the cult image of *Dionysos Eleuthereus* ('Dionysus from Eleutherae', a small village on the border between Attica and Boeotia, from where Dionysus was said to have come to Athens; note that this cult name of Dionysus also invokes connotations with *eleutheros*, the Greek word for 'free': 'Dionysus the Liberator', then). The cult image, a wood shaft with a mask, was dressed, garlanded with ivy and taken in a procession from the temple of Dionysus on the southern slope of the Acropolis to a grove outside of the city and then, after some fairly short interval, returned to the Athenian theatre (which was situated in that very Dionysus sanctuary). The festival proper commenced on the tenth day of *Elaphêboliôn* with a 'procession' (*pompê*). While its precise route is unknown, the sociological order of the procession is revealing: a virgin from aristocratic background at the head of the procession, followed by male citizens, foreign residents ('metics') and their daughters, the sponsors of the dramatic and dithyrambic competitions (*chorêgoi*) in lavish dress, and young men of military age (*ephêboi*). Each of these groups was, according to their rank, carrying items of real or symbolic value to the ritual proceedings (fruits, wine, bread, water and a bull as the main sacrificial victim). The end of the procession was formed by men carrying large phalloi (even phallic 'floats', known from vase-paintings, were being conspicuously paraded), and the songs performed by these phallic choruses included not just hymns but also aggressive and derogatory pieces. Therefore, while the phallos, like the mask, is a key symbol of Dionysiac worship, the phallic choruses were, beyond their ritual role, a paratheatrical event in its own right. As a result, the boundary between the end of the ritual procession and the beginning of the proper dramatic contests was emphatically fuzzy and fluid, and the phallic choruses stood in an intriguing cross-fertilizing relationship with drama proper, especially comedy.[17]

The timing of the Great Dionysia in late March meant that the sailing season had resumed and full connectivity within the Greek cultural continuum had been re-established. This mobility attracted an audience that was drawn from beyond Athens and Attica, and helped to turn the festival into a showcase of

Athenian cultural and political prowess to the whole of Greece. The dramatic competition proper began with a ritual purification of the theatre, a wine offering to the gods not by the priest of Dionysus but by the ten generals of the Athenian city-state (in effect the most important Athenian officials). Subsequently, the festival took on ever more overtly a civic character: the names of distinguished citizens and of benefactors to the city of Athens were announced by a herald;[18] the tribute from the allies of Athens that now, with the sailing being resumed, had become due was brought from the treasury on the acropolis down to the theatre for ostentatious display; and Athenian war orphans, who had reached adulthood, were invited to sit in the front-row seats wearing suits of armour.

At this point of the proceedings the selection of the ten judges appears to have taken place, with the state official in charge of the festival (the so-called 'Name-giving archon', or *archôn epônymos*, whose name was used to identify years in Athens) drawing one name from each of the ten sealed jars which contained the names of possible judges submitted by each tribe respectively. The judges thus selected then came forward, took an oath of impartiality and were seated in a separate section of the theatre. As far as the dramatic competition was concerned, these judges would cast their votes not on individual plays or poets but on whole productions (i.e. not as scripts but as embodied performances, and in the case of tragedy not a single play in performance but a proper tetralogy of three tragedies followed by a satyr play). What the actual voting procedure looked like is not entirely clear (especially in the case of dithyramb, where the choruses were tribally recruited – like the judges who were supposed to adjudicate them).[19] The most reasonable (if not entirely fail-proof) procedure, at least for drama, is that not all of the ten votes cast actually counted, but that initially only five were drawn. If no winner emerged at this point, the draw would continue one vote at a time until a winner had been established. This procedure would leave a fair amount to chance or, conceptualized differently, to the inscrutable power of the divinity Dionysus who was presiding over the festival as a whole. But in view of the clear and persistent systemic efforts at guaranteeing fairness in these much-coveted competitions such a partial deferral to chance and divine supervision would in fact make good sense, also bearing in mind that comparable procedures were followed in the political practice of the Athenian democracy (like allotment from an elected shortlist to determine ten 'statute setters', or *thesmothetai*).

If the precise voting procedure remains ultimately unclear, further uncertainty surrounds the details of the 'order of play' during the Great Dionysia (on *Elaphêboliôn* 11 to 14). All five comedies on the first day and one tragic tetralogy on each of the subsequent three days? Or were individual comedies somehow combined with a tragic tetralogy? Was there a reduction in the number of comedies (from five to three) during the Peloponnesian War, a once fashionable view which has been rendered somewhat unlikely by a papyrus (*P. Oxy.* 2737) published by Edgar Lobel in 1968?[20] And how were the two dithyrambic contests placed, one for men's and boys' choruses respectively? This is not a minor, entirely technical question but something which quite fundamentally shapes the festival experience and the ways in which the theatre art on competitive display at this festival would be perceived. Tragic playwrights – this much is certain – competed not with a single play but with tetralogies, i.e. three tragedies which, at least in the fifth century and for part of the fourth, were followed by a satyr play.[21] Comic playwrights competed with one play each, which left them with significantly less time to make an impression. Actors' competitions were added to the Great Dionysia in 449 BCE, a clear indication of their growing importance (which was to culminate in the pan-Hellenic stardom of some of them in the fourth century and beyond).

Those who competed had been pre-selected at an early stage. It was one of the first annual duties of each incoming *archôn epônymos* to select, in mid-summer about eight months before the Great Dionysia, the eight *chorêgoi* needed to finance the three tragic and (presumably) five comic productions, and to match each of them both with an *aulos*-player and one of the poets to whom he had decided to 'grant a chorus' (*choron didonai*, cf. Cratinus fr. 17 Kassel-Austin).[22] The sheer existence of such pre-selection and subsequent matching is, of course, remarkable, and invites suspicions of censorship and other repressive acts (especially for comic poets, who could be very outspoken about contemporary events). This, however, is not suggested by the extant evidence. Euripides, a notoriously controversial poet, was regularly being granted choruses, as was Aristophanes who launched vitriolic criticism against the general Cleon (especially in his *Knights* from 424 BCE) at a time when Cleon was at the height of his political influence. Part of the explanation for this may be public awareness and scrutiny, as is suggested by two, only fragmentarily preserved, passages from comedy which question chorus-allocations that had been made, including the denial of a chorus to Sophocles.[23] The only known case of what may be considered actual censorship was not the result of control mechanisms within the institutional frame of a festival but a retroactive ban by the Athenian people. According to Herodotus (6.21), Phrynichus' *Capture of Miletus*, staged shortly after 494 BCE, outraged the Athenians so much 'for reminding them of their own troubles' that they fined the poet 1,000 drachmas and prohibited reperformances.

We know that a few days before the beginning of the festival (by the eighth of *Elaphêboliôn* at the latest) some advance information of all competing plays had been given to at least part of the prospective audience as part of the so-called 'Pre-contest' (*proagôn*). On this occasion, which after c. 440 BCE took place in the Odeum right next to the Theatre of Dionysus, the playwrights would appear together with their actors and chorus members, mount a platform and, as our sources put it, 'announce their poetry (*ta poiêmata epangellein*) before the announcement in the theatre' or 'point out the content (*epideixesthai logous*)'.[24] The actors were neither in costume nor wearing masks, a rare instance of full disclosure of the performer as performer in the Greek theatre. They were, however, wearing garlands: in response to the news of Euripides' death in 406 BCE Sophocles, we are told, asked his chorus and actors to appear without garlands at the *proagôn*, while he himself put on a dark cloak.[25] The performative implications of this pre-festival 'oral playbill' event are hard to assess: what kind of advance information would this sub-section of the actual audience be given, and what difference would it make to how, for instance, surprise effect or dramatic irony worked in performance? Especially for comedy, which at least in the fifth century capitalizes a great deal on the comic potential of surprise and unpredictability, the implications are potentially far-reaching: *if* comic playwrights were in fact part of the *proagôn*, which is not entirely certain, they may have been very keen to provide only partial, somewhat enigmatic or perhaps even deliberately misleading information at this event. All of this said, providing detailed advance information cannot have been the main point of the *proagôn* which was primarily designed to create visibility and promote the event itself, quite conceivably also generating what modern advertising professionals call 'hype'. And, very much in keeping with the competitive (or 'agonal') character of Greek society more generally (especially among its elite), it celebrated the spirit of competition itself.

This spirit, of course, thoroughly pervaded the institutional frame of the Great Dionysia as a whole, and it is only fitting that the festival ended with a celebratory procession (*kômos*) of the victorious playwright and his sponsoring *chorêgos*.[26] The competitive pressure operative within this institutional framework was intense and must have been one main reason for the high degree of professional specialization of those who were active in it: playwrights, actors and whole troupes stuck to either tragedy (including satyr play) or comedy only. There also seems to have been a concomitant sense that 'fair play' and a 'level playing field' had to be ensured, which manifests itself in a number of features: the probable element of sortition, chance and divine will in the judges' voting procedure has already been mentioned; there also was a limit of speaking parts, at least in tragedy though probably not comedy, to three ('three-actor rule'); last but certainly not least, performance time, one of the most basic and crucial theatrical resources of them all, was probably regulated to slots of about 90 to 120 minutes (which helps to account for the remarkable uniformity of the length of preserved Greek playscripts, none of which exceeds 2,000 lines).[27] Another aspect of the regulatory framework is the fact that at the Great Dionysia only Athenian citizens were allowed to perform in choruses or to become *chorêgoi*.

Based on all this evidence about the festival framework of the Great Dionysia in Athens, what would the 'festival experience' of a playgoer have been like in, say, 458 or 423 BCE when Aeschylus' *Oresteia* (placing first) and Aristophanes' *Clouds* (placing 'only' third) were performed respectively? It was certainly a very intense, engaging, diverse, multi-sensory and 'multi-generic' experience, combining phallic processions, sacrifices, plenty of food and drink, prayers, announcements, state propaganda, large-scale dithyrambic choruses, comic licence and aggressiveness, tragic abyss followed by satyric abandon. Anticipation, suspense, partisanship and fandom must have surrounded the various competitions for 'best tragic actor', 'best adult dithyrambic chorus performance', 'best tragic production' and so forth. Tensions within the festival framework also certainly existed. Thus Aeschylus' *Oresteia* is clearly (also) a political intervention engaging with the recent reform of the Areopagus by Ephialtes and apparently trying to mediate between opposing views. And if, as Aelian reports (*VH* 2.13), the real Socrates did indeed stand up in silence among thousands of seated spectators while the Aristophanic caricature 'Socrates' of *Clouds* was performing his antics in the huge theatre, this incident was likely to be 'the talk of town' that day. Whether, as present-day critics continue to debate, fifth-century playgoers and playwrights perceived an intrinsic tension between Athenian democratic ideology as promoted by some aspects of the festival framework and the brilliant dynasts from the great mythical past who they saw experiencing both downfall and greatness on the tragic stage must perhaps remain open.[28] If such perception existed, it is not articulated in the sources currently available to us.

The second major dramatic festival in the city of Athens, the Lenaea, was celebrated in late January (in a month called *Gamêliôn*). It was considered to be the lesser of the two big drama festivals[29] and, because foreigners were not yet able to come at this time of year, had a more 'all-Athenian' vibe to it, as is acknowledged by the comic protagonist Dicaeopolis in Aristophanes' *Acharnians* of 425 BCE (501–8). This, however, did not prevent the elite of playwrights from competing there. Aristophanes' *Frogs*, for instance, one of the best comedies and most important plays we have, was performed at the Lenaea in 405 BCE. The Lenaea too were a Dionysiac festival but much older than the Great Dionysia, and overseen not by the *archôn epônymos* but the *archôn basileus* ('King archon'). Fewer details about its structure are recoverable. Initially performances probably took place on the Athenian market-place before being moved, by around the mid-fifth century at the latest, to the Theatre of Dionysus; by contrast with the Great Dionysia, tragic poets competed with only two tragedies each (there was apparently no satyr play); two or three tragic and three or five comic poets may have competed against each other.

In addition to these two grand occasions, many frameworks for drama, yet again all in honour of Dionysus, existed at the level of the so-called demes of

Attica, the smallest territorial sub-division of the city-state of Athens. Evidence (often epigraphic) for dramatic performances at these rural Dionysia, which took place over the winter months, comes from thirteen of the 139 demes that existed in total, but the practice will have been more wide-spread. In the big demes, such as Piraeus (where the harbour was located) and Eleusis (the site of the most famous mystery cult of antiquity), the rural Dionysia appear to be local versions of the Great Dionysia at Athens, with all the usual bells and whistles (Dionysiac procession, tragic and comic competitions, even dithyramb). Some of the deme theatres are still visible in some shape or form, the one at Thorikos, discussed by Wiles in chapter 4 of this volume, being a particularly well-preserved and interesting one.[30] Inscriptions from Thorikos show tragic and comic competitions, with otherwise known playwrights and actors as contestants.[31] No lesser a playwright than Euripides competed at the Dionysia in Piraeus, as did Sophocles and Aristophanes at Eleusis.[32]

REPUBLICAN ROME

By sheer geographical location, Rome was, throughout the centuries of its meteoric rise from small town via local champion to global super-power, in a position of easy access and exposure to two thriving theatre and entertainment traditions. There is the Greek one as practised in Sicily and Southern Italy (especially Campania and Apulia), which was extraordinarily vibrant in the fifth and fourth century BCE and even appears to have been trend-setting before that. And there is the Etruscan tradition (itself very heavily influenced by the Greeks) which, however, is much harder to pin-point, as the evidence here is mainly iconographic, etymological and based on much later Roman literary accounts such as Livy's important excursus on the origins of the 'scenic games' (*ludi scaenici*) in Rome (Livy 7.2.4–13).[33] Fundamental performance-related terms in Latin like *histrio* ('actor') and *persona* ('mask') are Etruscan in origin, and while the Etruscans may possibly have lacked a fully-scripted plot-based drama they were highly-skilled (mimetic) dancers and accomplished musicians (especially pipers): when in 364 BCE Roman officials thought of ways to combat the plague and appease the gods, it was to the services of professional Etruscan dancers and musicians that they turned (Livy 7.2.4). The great prominence of music on the Roman stage, palpable for us in the works of Plautus, seems to be a result of this influence. In addition, the Etruscans had to offer something that Rome too was lacking: a fully-developed festival and entertainment culture, with sport contests, gladiatorial combats, cult songs with musical accompaniment, mimetic dance and so forth.

That year, 364 BCE, is the first watershed in the institutional development of theatre in Rome, since it marks the addition of 'scenic games' (*Ludi Scaenici*) to the 'Roman games' (*Ludi Romani*), until the end of the third century the only regular festival in Rome. This change to the institutional framework had a major impact. With the introduction of 'scenic games' the festival acquired not only a more secular character but significantly broadened its horizon beyond the local and the parochial. The novel forms of entertainment not only invited but required exchange and internationalization, and Rome now entered the nexus of festivals which covered all of the Mediterranean. It joined a trans-regional communicative framework, thereby transforming the notion of what 'Rome' was and how it presented itself to its neighbours and the rest of the Mediterranean.

While it remains unclear what precisely was put on stage at the time,[34] it is uncontroversial that the formal introduction of theatre entertainment to this pre-eminent festival of Jupiter is intimately connected with, and clearly the result of, a major re-organization of the Roman political system a couple of years prior which, in essence, now granted 'plebeians' (i.e. non-aristocrats) access to the highest levers of political power that had until now been the sole preserve of the 'patricians' (i.e. the aristocracy). The offices of the praetor and the curule aedile were created (the latter being in charge of the *Ludi Romani*) and two consuls, one from the plebeians and one from the patricians, were to share the highest command each year. This extraordinarily strong connection between the institutional frameworks available for theatre and the political system as embodied by high-level magistrates was to remain a crucial defining feature of Roman theatrical culture, which in turn was always dependent on a 'top-down' hierarchical power structure that enabled the theatrical event in the first place while aggressively attempting to capitalize on it in political terms.

The third century BCE saw the gradual defeat by Rome of Carthage, its biggest and most powerful adversary, and the establishment of Rome as a Mediterranean super-power. These changes are reflected in Roman festival culture which was now even more designed to impress, assert and command attention. Qualitatively, the landscape changed in that festivals and the stage were now co-opted for the creation of a Roman *literary* culture which, via translation, adaptation and other forms of cultural transfer, built on, appropriated and re-shaped its formative model, Greek literary culture. Thus the *Ludi Romani* in 240 BCE, the year after Rome's victory in what turned out to be the first of three Carthaginian Wars, saw a major innovation which reflected, by way of cultural politics, Rome's new role and self-positioning: for this occasion Livius Andronicus, a Greek from Tarentum (and probably a former slave who had by enfranchised by his elite Roman owner), was commissioned to stage, for the first time, a play (*fabula*) in Latin.[35] What precisely is meant here by *fabula* is, contrary to what is sometimes asserted by modern scholars, not entirely clear from the extant sources: a tragedy or a comedy (Livius was active in both genres)? A translation, in the strict sense, of a Greek play, or an adaptation, or a new play following the standard conventions (metrical, lexical, dramaturgical) of the Greek model genre?[36] What mattered, in the perception of Livius' contemporaries, was that a Greek artefact had now, for the first time, been fully, officially and publicly Romanized: performed in Latin, on a stage in Rome and as part of the *Ludi Romani*, Rome's premier showcase event. The institutional framework of the festival, in other words, functioned as an indispensable component in this highly symbolic act of appropriation, self-validation, propaganda and cultural conquest.

In quantitative terms, too, the landscape changed in the second half of the third century BCE, because now five new major festivals, all featuring theatrical entertainment, started to complement the venerable *Ludi Romani* as the previously sole regular festival (held in September, eventually over ten days, in the *Circus Maximus*, first under the curule aedile then, after Augustus, the praetor).[37] The 'Plebeian Games' (*Ludi Plebeii*), like the *Ludi Romani* dedicated to Jupiter and clearly designed to rival them, were established in 220 BCE. They took place in the *Circus Flaminius* in November, under the supervision of the plebeian aedile (Plautus' *Stichus* is known to have been performed at this festival in 200 BCE). Also under supervision of the plebeian aedile were the *Ludi Ceriales*, held at the temple of the deities Ceres, Liber and Libera in April (Ceres, the goddess of agricultural growth, was particularly popular among the plebeian part of the population). Two of the new festivals were dedicated to Greek gods: the *Ludi Apollinares*, run by the urban praetor, in honour of the god of the lyre, and the *Ludi Megalenses* in honour of *Magna Mater* ('Great Mother', i.e. Cybele). The latter took place at the Temple of *Magna Mater* on the Palatine, which was dedicated in 191 BCE. We know that Plautus' *Pseudolus* was performed there in that year, a piece of information which provides a rare opportunity to estimate the size of the audience on that occasion (c. 1,500, i.e. only 10–20 per cent of what its size would have been in classical Athens) and to reflect on performance dynamics.[38] Finally, there were the *Floralia* or *Ludi Florales*, which were annual by 173 BCE but had been celebrated since at least 241 BCE. They stand out for being the only regular second-century festival for which performances of the lowly mime with its female performers and farcical, often obscene plots are attested.[39]

Ennius, Plautus and their fellow second-century playwrights were therefore producing for and within a wide, visible and well-established regular institutional framework funded by individuals who occupied high magistracies that came with an explicit 'entertainment mandate' (especially the aedileship, but also the praetorship). A matching of plays and festive occasion, however, is unfortunately possible only in a very small numbers of cases,[40] and the existing evidence does not seem to permit generalizations. Since none of the institutional frameworks was exclusively theatrical but always also incorporated other attractions like horse racing, gladiators, boxing and the like, playwrights and troupes constantly had to fight for attention – not always successfully, as Terence facetiously reminds his audience in the second prologue to his *Hecyra* (29–48).

This regular, magistrate-sponsored framework was increasingly being supplemented by a host of occasional festivals (commonly referred to as *munera*, 'gifts') which celebrated particular politicians and their exploits. As a 'life-time achievement' occasion of sorts, funeral games with theatre performances are one variety of such occasional festivals. Both the *Adelphoe* and the second *Hecyra* by Terence, for instance, were performed in 160 BCE at the funeral games for the former consul Aemilius Paulus, who was both an ardent admirer of Greek culture and a fierce military adversary who ended the Macedonian monarchy, and with it the notion of any kind of Greek political autonomy, with his victory over King Perseus at Pydna in 168 BCE. On such an occasion, the staging of not one by two Terentian comedies based on Greek models therefore was not only fitting but also made a point about cultural appropriation itself. Military victories and a subsequent triumph in Rome similarly provided *ad hoc* performance frameworks, even with the possibility of permanent extension: both the regular *Ludi Victoriae Sullanae* (where mime too was being performed) and the regular *Ludi Victoriae Caesaris* originated as one-off victory celebrations of Sulla (in 82 BCE) and Caesar (in 45 BCE) respectively. In addition, there could be repetitions of regular festival days (a practice known as *instauratio*), courtesy of a magistrate who used his private money to garner more support from the masses.

The fierce competition among the Roman elite for status, power and money via bought elections to magistracies led to spending sprees of enormous dimensions. Anti-sumptuary legislation was regularly being passed,[41] but its sheer existence and frequency only serve to indicate that these laws must have been largely ineffectual in practice. In view of the fact that the sponsoring magistrates in fact purchased the scripts from playwrights or from impresarios there would seem to be little room for subversive tendencies within the socially affirmative frame of the festival – or, put more precisely, at least not subversion directed at the magistrate or other ambitious individuals who were sponsoring the (partisan) theatrical event. One exception appears to be mime which, at least in the politically charged and turbulent atmosphere of the late Republic, apparently could pick up and capitalize on politically hot and controversial topics.[42] In general, the current overall-mood and potential dissatisfactions of the urban masses could, and were, being expressed in any large venue where crowds assembled, including theatres (Tacitus *Annals* 6.13). Thus the frenetic applause for Accius' tragedy *Tereus* which was performed at the *Ludi Apollinares* in July 44 BCE was, at least in Cicero's partisan judgement, in truth nothing but a thinly disguised endorsement by the masses of Caesar's assassin Brutus who had been forced to leave Rome shortly after the assassination in March but nonetheless sponsored the *Ludi Apollinares* of July 44 *in absentia*.[43] Full-scale breakdowns of institutional frameworks in the form of riots are attested for pantomime.[44] In 115 BCE, two Roman aristocrats who in that year occupied the magistracy appropriate called *censor* even banned 'the performing arts' (*ars ludicra*) from the city of Rome, probably because they saw them as a potential threat to social and political stability.[45] But the drama business appears to have gone on as usual nonetheless. Theatre was socially too compelling and politically too useful to suffer exile from the Eternal City.

CHAPTER TWO

Social Function?

Making the Case for a Functionless Theatre

SEAN GURD

AFFECT AND SOCIAL FUNCTION

In the Homeric hymn to Hermes, Apollo hears a lyre for the first time (it has just been invented by the infant Hermes), and thrills with a surprising and erotic desire to hear and know more of this remarkable instrument.[1] This episode contains an intuition about the function of art which was widespread among ancient theorists: that it had its first and perhaps most powerful effect on the psychic experience of those who see, hear, touch, taste, or otherwise sense it. Interest in affect was associated with Athenian musical drama from at least the middle of the fifth century, when the Athenian theorist Damon proposed that there was a relationship between the tonal structures of specific musical modes and the structures of the soul which listened to it.[2] Though his ideas were appropriated by Plato as an argument against musical innovation,[3] Damon may simply have been exploiting widespread assumptions about the material nature of the soul to account for the way music seemed to communicate affective atmospheres: in Empedocles, for example, sensation and cognition occur because material structures are communicated through the senses to the blood: the resonant reproduction of these structures in the blood was experienced as thinking.[4] Gorgias of Leontini was building directly on theories like this when he voiced the first explicit surviving discussion of the effects of drama: because logos is a powerful master which enters through our ears and takes control of our soul, it causes us to rejoice when we behold the suffering of others in a play.[5]

In one of the most important intellectual developments of the fifth century BCE, medical theorists – whose materialist commitments were strong and who show a broad and sophisticated awareness of many strains of natural philosophy, from the Heraclitean to the Pythagorean – recognized the effects art could have on the soul. This recognition was so strong that in the Hippocratic Regimen it is advised that we should listen and sing because doing so alters our psychic constitution and makes us smarter and healthier.[6] Such theoretical insights found institutional expression in the growing affiliation of tragedy and the medical god Asclepius: by the second half of the fifth century the art form of Dionysus was being performed within view of Asclepius as well, and in the Hellenistic period major sanctuaries of Asclepius included theatres as part of their health-oriented complexes.[7]

In theories that attributed a social function to drama, accounts such as these played a crucial role because art was thought to affect society through the mediation of individual experience. The idea that musical performances had a direct, quasi-physical effect on souls was the underlying assumption of both Plato and Aristotle; both modulated this into a theory of the way drama affected supra-individual organizations, via the assumption that the constitution of a polis expresses the character of the souls that comprise it. For Plato, a democracy will be one in which the majority of souls has a democratic character, while in a tyranny the plurality of souls is tyrannical, and so forth.[8] (This theory could well be seen as an extension of the physical model that saw souls as expressions of musical structures because both of these were ultimately constellations of matter; the configuration of units is simply projected up a level, such that poleis appear to be constellations of souls.) Drama affects souls, which constitute cities, and so drama has a social function, though this function is mediated by the individual.

Plato's take on drama's influence on the structure of the polis is notoriously pessimistic. The *Republic*'s first swipe at it comes in the context of a general assessment of musical culture, in which Damon's theory that musical modes can produce certain psychological dispositions is invoked by name; given that the city Socrates and Glaucon are fantasizing about must be made of souls that are martial and energetic, Socrates assumes that only music in the Dorian (martial) and Phrygian (energetic) modes should be performed there.[9] This follows a general discussion of musical genres in which tragedy is at the centre of attention. Tragedy is to be treated with mistrust, says Socrates, because its representation of gods and heroes is both untrue and not exemplary. It lies to treat gods as vengeful, angry or lustful, and it sends the wrong message to show heroes lamenting and mourning their misfortunes. Indeed, the representation of lamentation will incline audiences to be ready to weep at the drop of a hat.[10] In book 10, Socrates claims that drama can only appeal to the part of the soul that delights in imitation: that part of the soul is sensual and appetitive, and a lower psychological capacity. Because it flatters this inferior part of the psyche, drama is a danger to the city.[11]

Plato's student Aristotle accepted that musical structures had direct effects on souls. But he seems not to have thought that drama was a danger to the state. Indeed, in the *Politics* he generally condones the seeing and hearing of dramatic performance as beneficial to the soul and hence the city.[12] Tragedy specifically, he claimed in the *Poetics*, caused audiences to feel pity and fear, and through this brought about a catharsis or purification; his position has close ties with medical theories of purification.[13] More than one modern scholar has surmised that drama had a positive function for Aristotle in that the purification of pity and fear left the citizen more rational and better equipped for the performance of civic duty.[14] The same fundamental assumption – that drama affects souls, and that this can have a decisive effect on the condition of the city – informs Cicero's view, expressed in the *De re publica* ('On the State'), that it was the responsibility of the governing classes to provide games and entertainments to the city: doing so made the plebs happy, and consequently preserved social order.[15]

Though Plato also objected to the content of dramatic mimesis, his main emphasis was on affect as it was associated with drama. This was entirely in keeping with pre-Socratic ideas about the functioning of sensation and the aesthetic nature of art. But there was another approach that paid more attention to drama's representational content, asking what effects certain kinds of stories or speeches could have on a city and its citizens. The earliest extant expression of this concern comes in Aristophanes' *Frogs*, produced in 405 BCE. In a netherworld contest between Aeschylus and Euripides, the two dramatists' works are compared on a series of criteria, including the 'weight' of their words and the variety of their metrics; but the arguments that ultimately sway the presiding judge, Dionysus, concern the civic status of the playwrights' works as examples. Euripides, who (we are told) had a penchant for using rhetorical devices in his plays, has 'taught the populace to quibble', and imitating his argumentative characters has made Athenians more litigious and less likely to obey their leaders. In contrast, Aeschylus' characters, who breathe the martial valour of the generation of Marathon and Salamis, make the citizenry stronger and tougher by providing them with compelling models of civic virtue. Ultimately, the issue boils down to which playwright shows things that are better for the city.[16]

A similar approach is taken by Aristophanes' slightly younger contemporary Alcidamas, a rhetorical theorist and teacher who studied with Gorgias and is today best known for his attack on the pedagogical value of writing. It is probably from his work *Mouseion* that the text describing a fictional contest between Homer and Hesiod descends: in this tale, the two bards compete for supremacy before a king. As in the *Frogs*, the contest covers a series of skills, including the ability to solve riddles and to complete previously composed lines of verse, but the laurels are ultimately awarded to Hesiod because his talk of peace and farming was more edifying, morally speaking, than Homer's tales of war.[17] Why Alcidamas, who as a student of Gorgias might have been expected to emphasize materialistic affect-based theories, turned to the question of representation in the *Contest between Homer and Hesiod* may be an unsolvable mystery. What cannot be doubted is that we are dealing with a quite different model of how art affects souls: here it is the communication of meanings, of what Aristotle would call the mental images (*phantasiai*) prompted by words, that is ultimately at stake, not how words might make one feel.

Though Aristotle's main defence of the functional role of tragedy has to do with its capacity to communicate and thereby bring about the purgation of pity and fear, it is clear that he also took representation seriously. For Aristotle, tragedy's affect is ultimately caused by its representation strategies, since only a certain kind of character undergoing a certain kind of story can cause tragic emotions. His definition of tragedy as the imitation of an action, the important related idea that drama is more philosophical than history because it deals with what is likely to happen, and his willingness to treat drama as a purely written form independent of any performance are all derived from his innovative and influential theory of language, in which words are imitations of images in the soul.[18]

Both the emphasis on the role of affect in conditioning the citizen-soul and an interest in the role of mimetic 'content' can be found in authors of the Hellenistic period. On the one hand, inheritors of the Platonic/Aristotelian doctrines made a case for the positive influence of well-formed plots and decorous character representations (this strain of interpretation is most evident in the tradition of rhetorical education and was presumably central to the teachings of Neoptolemus, a major source of Horace's *Ars Poetica*). On the other hand, materialist theories underwrote a concern with the sound of poetry, driving some critics to the point of claiming that it was exclusively the sensuous presence of poetry that distinguished it from other arts.[19] Such a strong denial of the role of meaning could be seen as the result of a radicalization of the difference between affect and representation, but by the second century BCE compromises had begun to emerge, with Crates of Mallos and then Philodemus of Gadara attempting to claim that poems were distinguished 'not by the meaning, but not without the meaning.' The idea that poetry was at once meaningless sensual pleasure and yet also meaningful got a social-functionalist spin from the speaker of Horace's *Ars Poetica*, where we find the claim that art must both 'please' and 'instruct'.[20] Whether it was Horace who first articulated this agenda or someone before him, it has since become a cliché that to be both socially useful and sensuously delightful is to be artistically and commercially successful.

Widely acceptable as it may have been, however, the ideal is incoherent so long as the basic psychological division between sensuality and reason promulgated by Plato prevailed – and prevail it did, for most of antiquity. Plutarch's advice in *On How a Young Man Should Read Poetry* tries to reconcile the benefits and the harms of art by suggesting that adequate positive gains can be realized from a programme of reading, so long as we approach it in a paranoid frame of mind that keeps us constantly alert to the many dangers poetry presents.

Proclus Diadochus (fifth century CE) may have been thinking of Horace when he insisted that what pleases harms, and that whatever benefits might come from an attractive sensual form are counterbalanced by the inherent dangers of sensual attractiveness.[21] By Proclus' time it seems to have been accepted by the philosophically minded that both affect and representation were potentially harmful. Augustine described his own youthful addiction to the theatre as a wrong-headed kind of ocular and emotional lust, a desire to feel emotions that he would avoid in other contexts;[22] in the City of God he complained that the Romans' theatrical depictions of pagan gods were either blasphemous or proof that those gods were not worthy of worship.[23] Here, drama is attributed not with a function, but with dysfunction, and, in a fashion recalling Plato, the result is an iconoclastic scopophobia.

SIGNS OF THE NON-FUNCTIONALITY OF THEATRE

The existence of a long-term ancient discussion about the social function of drama is, in one sense, a surprise: that institutions had social functions was so widely taken for granted and so fundamental to most thinking and acting among the ancient elite that it is barely afforded much in the way of remark. Indeed, as classical scholars have demonstrated over and over again for the past quarter-century or more, discovering the social referent of an ancient practice is surprisingly easy.[24] Finding explicit theoretical statements concerning these social functions is, on the other hand, quite difficult: you have to read critically and pay attention to basic assumptions, unspoken prejudices and unacknowledged tendencies. And yet in the case of drama functionalist analyses were a continuous and explicit concern, as we have seen.

One reason for the constant theoretical protestation of what was taken for granted almost everywhere else could be the fact that, despite its clear grounding in civic practices and its persistent association with practices of elite self-advertisement, drama seemed frustratingly dis-integrated from its social context. It was not by any means the only theatrical form in antiquity, if by that we mean an institutionalized practice in which a small group of agents performed in front of a larger group of onlookers.[25] At both Athens and Rome, political decision-making involved a dynamic in which orators made extended arguments before larger groups – in the democratic assembly or the senate, for example. The rule of law, too, implied similar agonistic-spectatorial engagements, as advocates argued out cases before juries that could number in the hundreds. Religion also involved forms of mass spectacle; sacrifices, processions, mystery cults all entailed a kind of actor-audience relation. But these other spheres of civic life involved the audience in the performance much more directly than did drama. Audiences of rhetorical performance in deliberative fora and the law courts not only interacted vocally with the speakers, but also concretized the proceedings by voting for or against an agenda or a prosecutor. We have little evidence that this took place at dramatic performances. To be sure, the performances at the festival of Dionysus were judged as part of a competition. But the judging did not directly involve the assembled audience. Ten judges, one representative of each tribe, were selected before the festival began: *they* voted. How the voting worked is unclear, but there is no reason to suppose that the judges were substantially swayed by the rest of the audience.[26] Indeed, one piece of evidence suggests a desire to preserve their independence: in 468 BCE, audience passions in support of rival productions were so enflamed that the usual judges were replaced by elected generals.[27] The implied motivation is that the generals, who in the fifth-century democracy were the only directly elected public figures, had the security of stature to be able to make judgments independent of the public pressure in the rest of the theatre. In Rome, dramas were not directly judged, as far as we know – though there is one case in which the heckling of a performance was so great that the show was stopped. It is typical that this interruption is presented in our source as an aberration and that the play was reperformed, albeit revised, at a later date.[28] Spectatorial involvement in ritual practice was at times much less direct than it was in the assembly and the law-courts, and the affinities between drama and ritual were much closer, in this regard at least. But participation in a ritual was broadly understood to have a transformative effect on the participants, and in the case of mystery cults like that at Eleusis the ritual was actively continued by the initiated in the form of the observance of secrecy. Drama never lost its association with cult (Christians in the fourth century CE criticized it as idolatrous partly for this reason), but at the same time its relation to cult consistently seemed like a problem – the idea that tragedy had nothing to do with Dionysus voiced a widespread confusion as to how exactly drama was integrated into the transformative practices of ritual.[29]

Another indication of the 'non-functionality' of drama on the social scene may be gathered from the fact that, in remarkable distinction from dithyramb (which used fifty chorus members in each performance), tragedy and comedy involved a very small number of performers – eighteen in tragedy (fifteen chorus members and three actors; initially there were twelve chorus members and one actor) and twenty-seven or twenty-eight in comedy (twenty-four chorus members and three or four actors). So while a single festival of Dionysus would involve 1,000 dithyrambic chorus members, there would only be fifty-four tragic performers and up to 140 comic performers (my count excludes musicians, mute actors and children). To someone expecting a civic institution to maximize citizen involvement, 'nothing to do with Dionysus' might also have meant 'nothing to do with us'.

Perhaps the resistance of drama to easy integration within well-known patterns of social causality was a provocative anomaly, one that theorists tried to obviate by demonstrating how it was, in fact, socially productive or, failing that, at least socially deleterious. An early sign of the need to explicitly theorize function may have been the association between drama and Asclepius. It is tempting to read this association as the result of an attempt to assert a function for a form that seemed to exceed or at least to resist integration into its other cultic context. Aristotle's theory of catharsis could also be taken as the attempt on the part of a talented theorist to offer a rational account of a mysteriously intransigent phenomenon. In the end, however, the theory of drama as socially *dys*functional seems to have won out, with Plato's iconoclastic impulses appearing barely transformed in the works of Augustine and others in late antiquity.

A major element in the unsettling apparent non-functionality of drama was the fact that, with very few exceptions, the performances at the core of the dramatic event depicted fictional action. The exceptions – Phrynichus' *Capture of Miletus*, the same playwright's *Persians* and Aeschylus' *Persians*, all plays with historical subjects from the early fifth century – were controversial and may have ended up reinforcing the tendency for tragic playwrights to fashion entertainments whose stories were drawn from a mythical world widely separated from the here-and-now (on comedy, see below).[30] Freedom to innovate in the handling of mythical detail, such as we find in Euripides, also speaks to the centrality of narrative plasticity – simply put, new stories could be made to replace old ones, new points of view developed, and all of this for no explicitly stated purpose. Liberty with the facts could never be admitted to in court or the assembly (though it surely happened) and can hardly be contemplated in ritual. But it may be said of self-conscious, unapologetic fiction that its most basic ontological principle is independence from the realia of its historical manifestation: the actor is not an actor, the chorus is not a chorus, the *skênê* is not a *skênê*. One attempt to deal with the fictionality of drama can be found in the Socratico-Platonic theory of mimesis: because it is a degraded copy of realer-than-real ideas, dramatic fictionality can be treated as the kind of falsehood that emerges when the truth is corroded beyond recognition. Aroistotle's explanation is more conciliatory: here fictionality explores what is probable and is therefore a sign that drama is 'more philosophical' than history (*Poetics* 9, 1451b5f.). Each of these approaches could be taken as an attempt to 'functionalize' the fiction at the heart of dramatic performance.

In the case of old comedy, 'real' historical personages were singled out as targets of satire and represented on stage – and the author himself seemed to speak in the convention of the parabasis. But it is hardly worth pointing out that the appearance of historical characters in a play does not make their story any less fictional – otherwise we would have to assume (for example) that the story of the *Women at the Thesmophoria Festival*, in which Euripides and Agathon appear, actually transpired. In fact, *Women at the Thesmophoria Festival* is clearly and self-consciously meta-theatrical: its material is copied from the plays of Euripides and it ostentatiously points to its own status as drama, so even here we are dealing with a play that self-identifies as fictional. Hubbard and others have demonstrated, similarly, that the parabasis cannot be taken as autobiography. Its concerns are usually motivated by the theme and structures of the play in which it appears;[31] the 'author' is a creation of the comic text. What is remarkable, however, is how rarely ancient theorists acknowledge this. From Cicero to Evanthius it is said that the distinctive characteristics of old comedy are (1) for historical figures to be singled out for public shaming and (2) for the author to speak in his own voice in the parabasis. The best explanation for this curious blindness is that a social function has been invented for plays that are often self-consciously fictional and actually very hard to pin down as political or social statements. This is a move analogous to Aristotle's denial that the fictionality of drama is different from the truth-telling of philosophy. In both cases, fiction posed the question of usefulness in a critical fashion and demanded a response.

THE FUNCTION OF DRAMATIC NON-FUNCTIONALITY

It is possible, however, that drama's apparent non-functionality actually had a function, though this was a function theorists may have been unwilling or unable to aver. Certainly a clear motive for drama's canonical form is legible in the story of its institution at Athens. Enough evidence survives about this to make it likely that the dramatic forms that became normal in the Graeco-Roman world were not the result of a slow or 'natural' evolution: drama was a designed art form, one whose components, financing, and institutional context were intensely political at the beginning and may well have reflected a lucid agenda.[32] Whatever its predecessor forms happened to be, the decisive moment for drama was its association with the Athenian festival of Dionysus known as the City Dionysia. Tragedy's affiliation with this festival, as well as the contriving of its basic formal elements, took place under the tyrants of the family of Pisistratus.

Changes to the festival brought about after the institution of a democratic form of government are unlikely to have significantly altered tragic form, although they were decisive for the other musical competitions (especially the dithyramb).[33]

We know little of the earliest productions, but again what has survived suggests a conscious attempt to develop artistic forms that would be specific to the festival and distinct from what was performed elsewhere. Economic self-interest alone could have provoked the Pisistratids, the family of tyrants who ruled Athens for most of the second half of the sixth century BCE, to develop a festival and art form of international remark: Athenian businesses can hardly have suffered from the influx of an international clientele wanting to witness the musical *agônes* and needing – at minimum – something to eat and drink and somewhere to sleep. There were probably also geo-political ambitions at play. Delphi developed extraordinary influence thanks in part to its oracle and the quadrennial games, and any city wanting to increase its profile on the international scene could well have considered the festival format an important tool. That the Athenian tyrants were aware of the diplomatic significance of festivals is suggested by their role in the revivification and control of the pan-Hellenic festival site of Delos.[34] The most important considerations, however, may have been local and civic. Older, family-and-wealth-based forms of influence had become problematic as early as Solon, and attempts were made in numerous parts of the Greek world to control them. One method was to weaken families' ties to cult by shifting religious practice away from family-based organizations to the city and making it a civic responsibility. 'Civic cult' caused symbolic capital to migrate from families to the polis, and offered the opportunity for the creation of a new ideological focus: that of the collectivity or the commonwealth. Emphasis on pan-Hellenic gods rather than local heroes seems to have been a significant part of this shift in emphasis. At Sicyon, Herodotus reports that the tyrant Cleisthenes transferred 'tragic choruses' from a local hero cult to a cult of Dionysus: he did this, we are told, as part of what amounted to a large-scale re-engineering of Sicyonian social relations.[35] Sixth-century Athenian statecraft engaged in exactly the same practices, with the design of large-scale festivals such as the Panathenaia and the City Dionysia, whose organization and funding were controlled by the polis.

A conflict between the wealthy individual and the civic collective seems to inform the structure of dramatic productions at another level as well: in the relationship between *choreîa* ('dance') and the *chorêgia*. *Choreîa* was more than merely an element in the structure of drama: it was close to the heart of the festival's operations. Choruses played a fundamentally pedagogical role – indeed, choral participation was a basic element in pedagogy in the archaic period.[36] It was through dance that young men and women learned how to move in sync with each other – a crucial kinetic metaphor for social coherence. And through the singing that coincided with dance, they learned a heritage of story and song.[37] The young men selected to be part of a tragic chorus were subjected to an intense and probably extended period of instruction which must have forged lifelong social ties and left an indelible mark on attitudes and personalities. *Choreia*, in other words, was a collective, participatory form of civic education. By contrast, the *chorêgia*, as it was called, emphasized individual display and wealth. Tragedies were financed in nearly all respects by a single, wealthy individual: the financial contribution of the *chorêgos* was considered a *leitourgia*, a word which originally meant 'work for the people'.[38] The fact that every festival involved three tetralogies, and therefore three *chorêgoi*, meant that the display of wealth was transformed into an *agôn* just as in the fictions of the plays the display of aristocratic greatness was tested by the agony of unanticipated misfortune. Indeed, that tragic stories emphasized problematic aspects of kingship and aristocratic standing either through the representation of misfortune or ill-character, and juxtaposed these with the figure of collectivity embodied by the chorus, allowed dramatic storytellers the opportunity to explore the same tension between individualized 'excellence' and collective well-being.

It is tempting to see drama's resistance to easy integration within the normal functioning of the polis as another example of this dramatization of the conflict between the agonies of the few and the solidarity of the larger collectivity. Jacques Rancière has suggested that art becomes political not when it begins to speak directly about social reality (in a Shavian or Ibsenite fashion, perhaps), or even when it offers itself as a utopian alternative to politics (as is suggested by Adorno or Bloch), but rather 'because of the very distance it takes' from such political functions and 'because of the type and space and time that it institutes, and the manner in which it frames this time and peoples this space'.[39] This suggests that drama's projection of an autonomous imaginary world contains the most vital social function of all. For Rancière, politics is a movement in which groups who have been excluded from the normal operation of power occupy common spaces and insist on their prerogative to speak, to be heard, and to participate in governance.[40] Citing Aristotle, he observes that the links between humanity's status as a political animal and its possession of logos implies that 'the whole question is to know who possesses speech and who merely possesses voice' (24). Social regimes are founded on the establishment of a line that excludes certain groups as, in effect, not possessing logos; politics consists in the insistence on the part of these excluded groups that they have speech as well as merely voice. Rancière's focus is on the positive, expansive aspect of politics, in which space is reconfigured to be more inclusive; but it may be that in ancient drama we witness the inverse of this movement, in the form of the expulsion of certain groups from the sphere of power.[41] It seems hardly accidental that tragedy depicts exactly that class of citizens whose influence was watered down under the tyrants and in the nascent democracy. Just as the *chorêgia* tamed and deployed the competitive impulses of the rich in a civic practice, so does the fictional representation of kings and demigods transform aristocracy into a function of artistic representation. In effect, nobility is being afforded a presence in the public sphere on the condition of its being imaginary. The fictional representation of aristocrats would, then, be a kind of democratic delegitimation of a real historical class with a tendency to enjoy disproportionate amounts of power and influence. Indeed, we note that the element of lamentation in tragedy does nothing other than replace speech with voice in this newly disempowered group – a noble who makes a persuasive political speech is very different from one who cries out *otototoi popoi da*. Tragedy from this perspective looks (or rather sounds) like politics in reverse, like an act of exclusion through representation. This casts the trajectory of comedy in a new light, too: it is telling that the comedic styles of Menander, Plautus and Terence, all of whom were working in a far from democratic age dominated by great men, does not play with the rich or with public figures as old comedy and tragedy did: instead, it places at the centre of attention the agency of slaves, who, though they often outmatch both their owners and their owners' adversaries in wit, act only on stage: here too, in other words, agency is awarded to a dis-enfranchised group only on the condition of its being unreal.

We could imagine, in other words, that drama's social afunctionality was in fact its function – that, as a reconfiguration of civic space such that certain groups were afforded visibility at the expense of historical agency, drama fulfilled a social function by having none, by, as it were, isolating the disenfranchised behind the hermetic boundary of ontological difference (i.e., of fiction). The idea that art can have a 'functional afunctionality' is best known from Adorno. For Adorno, modern art was a radical negation of history and social context – and yet this very negativity became the means by which capitalist modes of production are reasserted within the work, since in both an unmitigated productive sovereignty over 'passive' materials is asserted.[42] Thus for Adorno the modern artwork repeated the dialectics of domination prevalent in its society through its own autonomy. Ancient drama's afunctionality operated differently: it was predicated on a tactical attempt to secure certain forms of agency within the closed aesthetic monad. That is, its autonomy was determined by immediate practical concerns within its historical context. The result was an artwork that did not repeat social structures internally (as Adorno's modern artwork does) but rather presented itself to its contemporaries as an enigma ('What does this have to do with Dionysus?'). Again, this enigma, this functionlessness, in fact has a function. That, however, leaves us to contemplate an unsettling consequence; in asserting that drama had a civic role, functionalist theory such as we see emerging as early as the mid fifth century BCE in fact denied the role it actually had.

CHAPTER THREE

Sexuality and Gender

Off-stage and Centre-stage

IAN RUFFELL

The drama of Greece and Rome reflects societies which by law or convention tightly policed hierarchies of gender and sexuality. Locating women in the Greek theatre is problematic, slightly less so at Rome, but the content of plays demonstrates a great interest in gender and sexuality, almost in inverse proportion to women's involvement as producers or consumers. Often the focus is on the social norms themselves, for reinforcement or scrutiny, but within civic orders which depended upon subordination of women and regulation of sexuality, representations of women on-stage also became particularly useful to think with, as both implicated in and apart from their political systems.

PRODUCTION

The gendered nature of ancient theatre is conspicuous on the production side. There is little or no evidence of female playwrights or, in most genres, performers or women in other production capacities. Conventions that developed at Athens facilitated male-only performance, both mask and costume – stately (if exotic) dress in tragedy, grotesque padding in comedy. Both, however, seem to have originated in or been adopted for their ritual associations.[1] It was only in the less formal genres of mime and pantomime that came to displace comedy and tragedy as performance genres that it is possible to see greater involvement of women on the production side.[2]

The restricted number of speaking actors (rising from one to three for tragedy; occasionally more in comedy[3]) and the civic nature of performance perhaps also inhibited any pushing at production boundaries. The provision of choruses and, in some sources, actors was closely regulated. The contests of both actors and poets were public affairs. The *chorêgoi* sponsored choruses as a form of taxation, and were necessarily male given the law on property.[4] Although the financial framework changed in the fourth century, the civic dimension remained. The performance conventions were exported along with the drama.

The only area where female participation has been suggested was in mute roles.[5] An important closural element of many fifth-century comedies was the use of women stolen or won as sexual trophies. The most conspicuous example is Reconciliation in Aristophanes' *Lysistrata* (411 BCE), introduced as a tantalizing object of desire, on whose body a punning diplomatic settlement is traced (1114–88) by sexually starved Athenian and Spartan representatives. Given the costume conventions, however, male actors could easily have played such sexualized roles, and almost certainly did. Vase-painting and terracotta figurines show that comic costume was based on a body-stocking that went over substantial padding – arguably more grotesque for male characters, who also had a large (usually dangling) phallus (Figure 3.1). Both desire and the desired are essentially grotesque.[6]

FIGURE 3.1: Costume conventions in Old Comedy. Red-figured wine bowl (bell-krater), attributed to the McDaniel Painter. London, British Museum F151. © The Trustees of the British Museum.

The grotesquerie of Old Comedy was increasingly toned down in the fourth century until the New Comedy of Menander and his contemporaries, but did not entirely disappear. Its conventions then transferred to the Roman stage, which was heavily indebted to Greek models.[7] Roman adaptations of Greek comedy (known as *fabula palliata* or 'drama in Greek dress') adopted costume conventions from the later Greek incarnation; in most other genres too, Roman drama in the Republic was masked,[8] except for the mime, the least respectable form, where female performers were allowed. Later, there is even evidence for a female leader of a mime company (*archimima*).[9] Ancient pantomime, which became increasingly important in the imperial period, also admitted female participation.[10]

CONSUMPTION

There is more evidence for women as consumers of theatre in classical antiquity, and there may be a distinction to be drawn between Athens and Rome. There has been a long dispute over whether women attended the theatre in classical Athens, centred on problematic literary evidence. Aristophanes is ambiguous. In *Peace* (422/1 BCE), as part of a sacrificial ritual, the central character Trygaeus and his slave start throwing goodies to the audience (a practice elsewhere both condemned and used in Aristophanes):

Trygaeus	Throw some barley to the spectators.	
Slave		There.
Trygaeus	Have you given any yet?	
Slave		Yes by Hermes, so that
	out of all these spectators,	
	there's not one that doesn't have any barley.	965
Trygaeus	But the *women* didn't get any.	
Slave		Yes, but tonight
	their husbands will give it to them.	
	(Aristophanes *Peace* 962–7)	

Superficially, this would seem to imply that women were in the audience, perhaps too far away to receive the barley-grains (also slang for the penis).[11] The joke could, however, be that women were not in the audience at all, as might seem to be implied in *Birds* 793–6, where the chorus of birds suggest that wings would allow (male) spectators, if they observe their lover's husband in the council seating (*to bouleutikon*), to fly off at lunchtime for an adulterous liaison. Some women, at least, were not at the theatre, but that is not decisive evidence for all. However large the theatre was at that time, by no means everyone could attend.

The fourth-century evidence is less equivocal. Plato clearly suggests that women attended the theatre (*Gorgias* 502d, *Laws* 658c–d, 817c) and some evidence locates women in the outer wedges,[12] which would be consistent with the joke in *Peace*. Some have suggested that Plato is not referring to the main Theatre of Dionysus or the principal festivals (Dionysia and Lenaea), but to local (deme) theatres and festivals or even non-Athenian theatres. It takes special pleading, however, to detach Plato's dialogues from the Athenian public sphere and most likely women of some status did attend, conceivably those around whom there were fewer social anxieties or inhibitions: older women, resident foreigners (metics) or *hetairai* ('courtesans').[13] In the post-classical context and beyond Athens, women clearly did attend. Hence such colourful and unreliable anecdotes as that the chorus of Aeschylus' *Eumenides* scared pregnant women into miscarrying.[14] In the Roman period, seats in the Theatre of Dionysus were reserved for female dignitaries.[15]

The intended audience, however, was unquestionably male.[16] Down to the third century, comedies refer to their audiences as *andres*, 'men' (in a gendered sense). In the fifth and early fourth centuries, citizen males are the notional audience. Only infrequently are other types of spectators directly acknowledged, notably boys and metics (resident foreigners). Non-resident foreigners (representatives of allies and others) certainly attended the Dionysia, but are rarely acknowledged.[17] Even in the era of New Comedy, there was a reticence about female spectators: thus the finale of Menander's *Dyscolus* (965–7) invites many categories of spectators to applaud, but all male. Thus women were onlookers not only on the events on stage but on a communication process between two groups of men.

Roman theatrical practice drew heavily on Hellenistic Greek antecedents, but in much more informal spaces (until the Theatre of Pompey was built in 55 BCE) and there seems to have been no restriction on who could attend.[18] In the early second century BCE, the prologue of Plautus' *Poenulus* ('Little Carthaginian') refers to women of various social statuses, notably *matronae* (wives) and nurses (probably slaves):

> Let no clapped-out tart sit on the stage,
> and let no lictor or his rods make a sound,
> nor an usher walk in front of anyone's face
> or lead anyone to a seat while there's an actor on the stage.   20
> As for those lazy-bones who have slept too long at home, it is fitting
> that they stand now without complaint, or else sort their sleep out.
> Slaves should not sit in the way, so that there is a place for free men,
> or else they should pay head-money; if they can't do it,
> let them go home, let them avoid double trouble,   25
> in case they are beaten with rods here and whips at home,
> if they have not attended to their tasks, when their masters come back
>   home.

> Nurses should look after their tiny wee boys
> at home and let none bring them to watch,
> in case they go thirsty themselves and their boys die of starvation   30
> or they bleat hungrily here like young goats.
> Let wives watch quietly, laugh silently,
> avoid ringing out with their sing-song voices,
> let them take their chattering conversation home
> and not be trouble to men both here and at home.
>   (Plautus *Poenulus* 17–35)[19]

Women's attendance continued in the imperial Roman period (Tacitus *Annals* 3.23). Nonetheless, the struggle to build a permanent theatre indicates Roman ambivalence towards this Greek import. Anxiety over gender roles, specifically, can often be seen in Roman responses to Greek cultural imports, as in sanctions carried out against worship of Dionysus (*Senatus consultum de Bacchanalibus*, 186 BCE). Anxieties about women attending the theatre persisted into late antiquity. Christian writers complain about the theatricality of pagan culture. Specific regulations targeted mime actresses. The Theodosian Code regulated female mime artists' dress (15.7.12, 394 CE), displays of wealth, and their status (15.7.8, 381 CE). It is the pagan emperor Julian who recommends that women be banned from the theatre (*Letters* 304c). Theatre thus continued to be available to women as producers and consumers was also thereby a source of cultural anxiety.

SOCIETY

The differences in consumption and production of theatre between Greece and Rome reflect broader gender roles within these societies. In classical Athens under its democracy, regulation of women appears as the corollary of political powers being extended to all male citizens. The transfer of political deliberation away from family relationships towards public debate undermined one vector of informal involvement women had in the Archaic period. Unlike other Greek states (notably Sparta), Athenian women were not allowed to own property, and invasive legal mechanisms maintained property within the male family. Thus orphan 'heiresses' (*epiklêroi*) were attached to the household's property and married off to the nearest willing male relative.

Socially, our texts suggest a high degree of social segregation. Women were excluded from the drinking party (*symposion*) except as entertainment, the gymnasium and warfare, and all aspects of direct political involvement. Some texts suggest separate male and female domestic spaces, notably Lysias 1 'On the Killing of Eratosthenes', but this is not supported by archaeological evidence.[20] Texts also often suggest texts that women should not be let out of the house, or at least not unchaperoned. There was, however, no general proscription: such ideas were strongly linked with class and social status.

The only formal public role for women was in religion. A number of high-profile priesthoods were held by women, notably the priestess of Athena Polias, the chief civic cult, and Athene Nike (goddess of victory), whose temple was built conspicuously on a bastion abutting the entrance to the Acropolis. Most Athenian festivals were open (on some level) to both sexes (the Mysteries of Eleusis, exceptionally, open to all Greeks), but some cults were segregated by gender, such as the female-only Thesmophoria festival in honour of Demeter and Kore.

The clearest regulation came in Pericles' citizenship law of 451/0 ([Arist.] *Ath. Pol.* 26.4), that citizens must have both an Athenian father and Athenian mother. Thus the Athenians established a category of 'citizen wife' distinct from other women (girls, metics, slaves). Segregation (actual or claimed) particularly applied to this category, with more freedom attached to older women beyond child-bearing age or to poorer, working women. These ideas are fundamental to Aristophanes' plays, especially *Women at the Thesmophoria Festival* (probably Dionysia 411 BCE), where separate ritual space functions as women's political space, and *Lysistrata* (probably Lenaea 411 BCE) and *Assemblywomen* (392/1 BCE?), where citizen wives involve themselves in (male) politics. *Lysistrata* is the first surviving comedy where respectable citizen women speak. Lysistrata herself is an exception to the rule that respectable women without a clearly defined public role are not named by men in Greek comedy; this reticence seems to reflect a general Athenian taboo.[21] Earlier plays featured *hetairai* within the plot, but not respectable citizen women.[22] In *Lysistrata*, the 'citizen wives' gather surreptitiously to plan a sex strike, whereas the older women have openly gone up to the Acropolis on religious business and seize it (for symbolic, defensive and economic reasons: it holds the Athenian treasury). The shock troops are the old women and the poorer market-traders who square up to their male counterparts. In one confrontation, the female semi-chorus construct a ritual progression for becoming a female citizen-equivalent, analogous to male rites of passage (638–47). Lysistrata fences with the *proboulos* over the competence of citizen wives to engage in politics (mainly war and economic management). To break the comic mould, Lysistrata is suggestive of the most prominent public woman in Athens, the priestess of Athena Polias, Lysimache (the names mean much the same thing). Two other important characters, Myrrhine and Lampito also have significant names, the former being the name of the priestess of Athena Nike, the latter that of the Spartan queen mother.[23] Aristophanes is not *identifying* these fictional characters with real-world counterparts, but is using public women to increase the plausibility (and, no doubt, acceptability for the male audience) of women taking an active political role.

As theatre expanded beyond Athens, comic drama retained much of its Athenocentricity. While many social restrictions were common across different Greek cities, distinctive Athenian elements such as civic legitimacy and economic regulation of the household (*oikos*) continued. Even under oligarchic rule, which covered much of Menander's career, the old citizenship principles (strengthened in the fourth century) continued in New Comedy, whether the play is set in Athens or (like *Perikeiromenê*) elsewhere. Similarly, the heiress (*epiklêros*) was a plot point in more than one play.[24]

Both Greek and Roman cultures gave great power to the male head of household, the *kyrios* and *paterfamilias* respectively, over both sons and daughters. This relationship underpins many fractious interactions between fathers and sons in New Comedy and its Roman adaptations. Both cultures saw marriage as a transfer of the woman from one household to another, but at Rome marriage was a complex and evolving institution. By the time of Plautus, many women were not marrying into the authority (*manus*) of their husbands' families. Such women (not *in manu*) remained under the authority of their original *paterfamilias*, but could become independent (by his death or by his emancipating her) and then own property (under the broad eye of a guardian, *tutor*) and enter marriage while remaining under their own authority (*sui iuris*). Roman society clearly changed rapidly: by 169, Cato the Elder complains about the numbers of wives owning property (Gell. 17.6.1); in the first century, *manus* marriages were uncommon.[25] Certainly by the late Republic, Roman wives could be identified as having more freedom than their Greek counterparts. Although *fabula palliata* is set in a stylized, even hyperbolic, Greek world (Plautus in particular ramps up the Grecizing language and locations), Roman ideas colour its presentation of marriage (e.g. Plautus *Stich.* 98, *Merc.* 405; Terence *Andria* 747). As I discuss below, they may also be responsible for some of the larger ways that Plautus, particularly, shapes his plots.

CONTENT

In both societies, drama not only reflected its cultural context, but also explored possibilities of social and political change. Sometimes the debate was concerned to police boundaries and close down questions, but often plays probe the limits of contemporary ideas.[26] Pericles' citizenship law tightened the criteria for democratic participation, but achieved this by paradoxically establishing non-citizens (Athenian women) as guarantors of male rights as citizens and implicitly acknowledging (however grudgingly) that women had a formal stake in the city. The introduction of the law followed extensive discussion around gender, democracy and citizenship on stage in preceding decades, particularly in Aeschylus' surviving plays. These bracket a turbulent period of Athenian politics, the reforms of Ephialtes (462/1 BCE), which attacked legacy pre-democratic power structures, particularly the aristocratic council, the Areopagus. Later writers saw Pericles' subsequent constitutional innovations, including the citizenship law, as concluding that process ([Arist.], *Ath. Pol.* 26). It is no coincidence that both the Danaid trilogy (probably 463 BCE) and *Oresteia* (458 BCE) interwove ground-breaking reflections on both democracy and gender.

Questions of ethnicity, gender and citizenship dominate in the earlier trilogy. Following the Ephialtic revolution, while political nerve-ends were clearly still very exposed, Aeschylus returned to marriage, gender and law as the foundation of a democratic politics in the *Oresteia*. The *Agamemnon* presents a story of power and revenge within the house of Atreus, as Agamemnon and his wife, Clytemnestra struggle for control of the household (*oikos*), and she seeks vengeance for his sacrifice of their daughter Iphigeneia to secure passage to Troy. The politics of vendetta expand in *Libation Bearers*, as Orestes avenges his father's death by killing his mother and her lover, Aegisthus. As Orestes descends into madness inflicted by the Furies, guarantors of blood-vengeance, there are competing blood-claims and a potentially open-ended cycle of violence. In *Eumenides*, Orestes has taken refuge at Delphi to be purified by Apollo, who had commanded him to kill his mother. Apollo fails to assuage the Furies (Erinyes) and they pursue Orestes to Athens. To resolve their competing claims – Apollo upholds masculine authority in the *oikos* and the Furies demand equal vengeance for female blood – Athena institutes a new murder court: the Areopagus in its post-Ephialtic guise, shorn of its political powers. Aeschylus provides a mythological aetiology for the democratic settlement and its foundational decision is between male and female. The human court is tied; Athena, a masculine goddess, born from her father's head, decides in favour of the male. Yet, along with the democratic (male) murder court, Athena still incorporates revenge and fear, as the Furies are beguiled and browbeaten into settling at Athens: integrated but subordinate. *Eumenides* founds democratic justice on this divinely sanctioned subordination.[27] Pericles' citizenship law follows the same principle.

Legal frameworks were only one way of consolidating norms of gender and sexuality. Greek drama worked with, and Roman drama inherited, many humorous and non-humorous stereotypes around gender. Tragedy inherits from myth the idea of women as irrational and reflecting untamed nature,[28] but also uses the stereotype as a wedge to open up ideological questions; in Seneca, such irrationality, coded as Stoic *furor*, becomes a clearer object of psychological investigation (so *Medea* and *Phaedra*). Often, women and children are passive victims, used as an index of suffering, even where a play seems critical of violence (so Euripides' *Trojan Women*). In Aristophanic comedy, women are typically obsessed with sex and alcohol – again drawing on an inherited male anxiety.

The most aggressive policing of norms comes in humorous drama. Dicaeopolis' wife in *Acharnians* (426/5 BCE), who watches from the roof as her husband (and young daughter) hold a festival celebrating his personal peace, is an eloquently silent testimony to the role of comic wives before *Lysistrata*. In the thoroughly domestic New Comedy, their silence is even more marked. Pollux's list of masks revealingly comprises six courtesans, two slaves, three old women (at least one also a slave), and six young women. The mature wife is conspicuously absent.[29] The wife of Callipides (mother of Sostratus) in *Dyscolus* is typical, in that she instigates an important scene, a sheep taken to Pan for sacrifice, but is entirely offstage herself. Women's main role in New Comedy is as courtesans and young women (sometimes overlapping), and the principal plot line revolves around the marriage of a young man and young woman. This preference for the young is reflected in costume conventions: the central, normative characters become increasingly naturalistic and far less grotesque. Residual grotesquerie survives in the old and the non-free. Yet aspects of Athenian marriages are downplayed, such as substantial age-gaps or compulsory marriage within the family. Roman comedy (*fabula palliata*) took over both the plotlines and ideological orientation.

Humorous drama extended beyond comedy. Tragic tetralogies normally ended with a satyr drama: a burlesque take on ancient myth, with most humour focused through the satyr chorus and Silenus, usually both oppressed and out of context. In 438, Euripides produced the odd tragedy *Alcestis*, apparently in place of a satyr drama, with many elements of humorous drama,[30] including its highly normative gender roles. Here the model wife, Alcestis, speaks and has agency, but only to volunteer to die for her husband. None of the males resemble model citizens – Apollo reneging on a deal with Death, Admetus trying to persuade someone, anyone, to die for him, his father Pheres angrily repudiating any such suggestion, Admetus (again) entertaining Heracles instead of mourning his wife, and Heracles himself getting riotous in a house of mourning. The contrast between the virtuous, self-sacrificial Alcestis and the men behaving extremely badly might allow an instructive deconstruction of ancient gender norms. Yet the play remains far more interested in masculinity than femininity. Alcestis' virtue is rewarded, once Heracles has learned the truth, sobered up and departed to wrestle Death and return her to her husband. The final scene, where Heracles teases Admetus over who he has brought with him, is uncomfortable viewing, and suggests that Heracles believes that Admetus had managed to skew his priorities. Alcestis' actions are heroized and validated; alternatives are not explored.

In terms of sexuality as well as gender, ancient comic discourse is frequently normative, not least through its characteristic humour of aggression or dominance. Superficially, this is encoded in the (usually) visible male phallus in Old Comedy and for satyrs. The acquisition of women (and occasionally boys) by comic characters as sexual markers of triumph fits the pattern. Yet the phallus often indicates vulnerability or lack rather than potency.[31] The use of sexual aggression to enforce norms of behaviour is particularly evident in our one complete satyr play, Euripides' *Cyclops*. The satyrs and their father Silenus are in servitude to the Cyclops; Silenus' shameless venality, cowardice and flattery are rewarded by being carried off by the drunk Cyclops to be raped (582–9), a fate conspicuously not mourned by his children.

Humiliation of male characters through enforced crossdressing occurs repeatedly in both Greek and Roman comedy. Examples include the Probulus in *Lysistrata*, losing both the argument and his authority, Praxagora's husband Blepyrus, forced to put on his wife's clothes to go outside to defecate (she has gone to the assembly in his). In Plautus' *Casina* (from a Greek original by Diphilus), the crossdressing is used to create embarrassment for others. Two slaves, Chalinus and Olympio, have been promised Casina by their mistress and master respectively. They draw lots, but the contest is rigged, as the lecherous master, Lysidamus, wants access to her for himself at his country estate, which Olympio runs. In revenge, Chalinus and Lysidamus' wife Cleostrata devise a scheme where Chalinus impersonates Casina at the supposed wedding, realized on stage, and the wedding night indoors with its double encounters. First Olympio emerges in a distressed state after finding something – unusual in the encounter: he is interrogated by a highly entertained Cleostrata. Lysidamus exits the house pursued by Chalinus *déshabillé*, and forced to confront his lechery in front of his wife.

The intersection of gender, sexuality and class or social status is significant here. Both male and female adulterers faced severe penalties, including (in Athens) the possibility of killing any male adulterer caught *in flagrante* and adequately witnessed (thus Lysias I 'On the Killing of Eratosthenes') and punishment by anal rape with a large radish (akin to a mooli) could result from more formal proceedings – a punishment shrugged off by the Weaker Argument in Aristophanes' *Clouds* (1083–5), a mark of his dissolution. There was clearly, however, a distinction to be drawn between the social status of the targets: sex with a citizen's wife or daughter outside marriage was clearly a different matter from sex with a slave (of either sex) or non-citizens (metics in Athens, freedwomen in Rome), including prostitutes (or more upmarket *hetairai*). The same licence did not extend to respectable women, who were closely hedged around with male anxieties over adultery and the production of (illegitimate) offspring. It is this (rather than incest) which is the sexual offence that drives Euripides' *Hippolytus* (less so Seneca's *Phaedra*). Much of the sexual activity in New Comedy and *fabula palliata* has to be understood in terms of this cultural double standard; and the resolution of rape plots by marriage is one of the many fantasies by which that genre tends to resolve conflict, violence and social anxieties.

Yet both tragedy and comedy were concerned to test norms as much as to consolidate them. The double nature of male fidelity within marriage is scrutinized in both *Agamemnon* and Sophocles' *Trachiniae*, with very different wives but equally fatal results. Sophocles' Deianeira is from the beginning both dependent and lonely; her husband Heracles likened early on to a farmer who only rarely visits a distant field (32). On his latest sojourn he acquires a captive, Iole. Deianeira's fear of being supplanted (a theme also explored through the less sympathetic Hermione in Euripides' *Andromache*) prompts her to send her husband a robe impregnated with the blood of the centaur Nessus. As he died, Nessus had extolled its ability to prevent Heracles loving another like her (555–81). Rather than a love potion (as she believes), it is deadly poison (Nessus had been shot with Heracles venomed arrows) and Heracles dies in agony. The play turns, then, on Deianeira's precarious dependency, framed by this cultural double standard.

Deianeira never actually meets her husband again, and indeed (mis-)communication is one key problem in the play. By contrast, the compelling figure of Clytemnestra meets and dominates Agamemnon in similar circumstances, as he returns chariot-borne with his captive Trojan princess, Cassandra. In his absence, Clytemnestra has taken control of the household – amply demonstrated in the watchman's eloquent silences (36–8) and her commanding interaction with the chorus, and further confirmed by the stage-management of her husband's entrance into the house.[32] Agamemnon's possession of Cassandra is, however, only the last of his many hybristic actions, particularly with women and children as victims, from his sacrifice of Iphigeneia to the wider population of Troy, sacked by his army. Although Clytemnestra does not claim the murders of her husband and Cassandra as retribution for all these (and indeed she adds her own female victim), both the thematization of male violence against women and Clytemnestra's easy control of both her husband and her lover Aegisthus (whose belated claims of agency are none too convincing) challenge easy notions of masculine authority. Certainly, masculinity reasserts itself subsequently, as Orestes avenged the dead Agamemnon in *Libation Bearers*, and the social and political settlement in *Eumenides* is founded on the subordination of women. Yet, all the interesting questions are posed by Clytemnestra: the gendered nature of political power in *Agamemnon* or the relationship of mothers to sons in *Libation Bearers*, memorably embodied by Clytemnestra indicating her breast as Orestes is poised to strike (896–8), or (through her proxies, the Furies) forcing the foundational judgement to be based on nothing beyond Athena's extraordinary personal circumstances and affiliations. A Greek male audience would no doubt find Clytemnestra and her man-scheming heart (*androboulon kear*, 11) monstrous, but the trilogy hardly imposes complete ideological closure.

Social norms are tested elsewhere in Greek tragedy, if perhaps less dramatically. Ideals of seclusion and subordination are often played with.

Sophocles' *Antigone* begins with a dispute between the model daughter Ismene, who only exits the house because summoned (18f.) and urges obedience to Creon the *kyrios*, and the convention-breaking daughter Antigone, who puts loyalty to her brother, a rebel and a traitor, ahead of such obedience. Antigone claims to follow the laws of the gods in burying her brother as opposed to the city's laws (a more innovative opposition than it might now appear[33]). Antigone is sentenced to death for her rebellion, but Creon's household is ruined, and it emerges that the gods do regard non-burial as an act of pollution. Not all of Antigone's actions or claims are thereby endorsed, but the rebellious daughter does here display a fundamentally better understanding of the world than her *kyrios*.

Equally resistant to closure are the female revolutionaries Lysistrata and Praxagora in Aristophanes' *Lysistrata* and *Assemblywomen*. Their interventions, respectively to end war and to replace democracy with a female-run communist utopia, are absurd (for Athens), but are also well motivated, whether by association with conspicuous public women (as above), by the suffering inflicted on women by war, or by the incompetence of male politicians. The latter gave Praxagora the opportunity to acquire her unusual facility with public speech (*Assemblywomen* 240–5). Both women are politically effective within their fictional worlds, and much more comprehensively than any male counterparts in other plays. Certainly, Lysistrata and Praxagora are somewhat exceptional, and have difficulties training or restraining the younger wives. More significantly, perhaps, their brave new worlds are designed to benefit men, and both protagonists retreat into the background towards the end of each play. Yet, like their tragic counterparts, these comic women open up possibilities that cannot entirely be controlled, as the reception history of *Lysistrata*, in particular, shows, where it has been co-opted as much for feminist as for anti-war interpretations.[34]

While Lysistrata and Praxagora have no direct descendants in New Comedy, that genre does test some boundaries, not least by exploiting typical characters. In Menander, courtesans are afforded much more agency, spontaneity and generosity than their (grasping) stereotype might demand (reflected in mask types such as the 'golden' *hetaira*). Thus in *Men at Arbitration*, Habrotonon is responsible for clearing up the truth about Pamphile's baby (product of a rape by her future husband Charisius) and for engineering a happy ending (winning her freedom only as a secondary motivation). Nor is New Comedy entirely about citizen boy meets (quasi-citizen) girl. In *Samia*, the restoration of a long-term relationship between Demeas and his *pallakê* (contracted mistress) Chrysis is one key outcome of the play (she was suspected of an affair with his son, Moschio, because she was generously nursing his baby by Plangon, the girl next door). Plautus, by contrast, prefers to play the stereotype of the *meretrix* in a very broad fashion: the two *meretrices* of *The Bacchis Girls* are instructive examples of the grasping type of *hetaira*,[35] although he also has a line of younger and (perhaps) more naive *meretrices* who live with similarly young love-interests, albeit with correspondingly less agency within the play.[36] Terence uses the grasping older *meretrix* in the Bacchis of *Heauton*, but also has examples closer to the Menandrian heterodox version (Thais in *Eunuchus* and Bacchis in *Hecyra*); in these cases, even the *bonae meretrices* themselves are very conscious of playing against expectation (*Eun.* 197f. and *Hecyra* 756f.).[37]

Whereas in Menander the citizen wife was largely not represented, she figures greatly in Roman comedy. Plautus, especially, specializes in nagging wives doing battle with hen-pecked husbands (often, indeed, up to no good, as in *Casina*). In one of the two instances where we can see Roman comedy adapting a Greek comedy in detail, a key element is amplification of just such a marriage: thus Caecilius Statius' *Plocium* (*Necklace*), extracts of which are discussed by Aulus Gellius along with their Menandrian models.[38] The relatively greater social and economic freedom afforded Roman women (above) may explain such amplification by Roman comedians. The economics of marriage, too, are similarly treated quite cynically, with some of Plautus' younger male heroes pursuing love affairs that lead to marriage regardless of dowry. It is reasonable to see *fabula palliata* exploring the steadily evolving nature of Roman marriage through its alternative world that is self-consciously not Roman.

In terms of sexuality, Euripides' *Hippolytus* and *Bacchae* investigate superficially convincing moralists, whose extreme stances rebound upon them. Hippolytus' rejection of Aphrodite leads that goddess to gain revenge by instilling in his stepmother Phaedra sexual desire for him. She resolves to starve herself to death to maintain her honour. Coaxed by her nurse, who has a more pragmatic attitude towards desire, she reveals the nature of her passion and allows the nurse to find a solution. Hippolytus' devotion to Artemis, hunting and to sexual abstinence may look like the acts of a laudable ascetic, and his horrified reaction to the nurse's revelation of Phaedra's desire seems entirely consonant with Greek social norms. Yet he winds up into a spectacular misogynist rant that leads Phaedra not only to commit suicide out of shame at her secret being revealed but also to accuse him of rape. Theseus, who returns to find his household in uproar, escalates his own hastiness in response to Hippolytus' high-handedness, and calls down his father Poseidon's curse on his son. When Artemis arrives to set matters straight and console the dying Hippolytus, she repeatedly emphasizes his virtue, but he has arrogated a virtue appropriate only for those like Artemis herself. Her promise of future cult for Hippolytus at Troezen confirms his exceptionalism: young women will dedicate their girdles to him before marriage. In death, as in life, Hippolytus' abstinence represents a stage which humans pass through; Hippolytus will never leave.

Bacchae sets similar human rigidity against a similarly implacable divine foe. Dionysus exacts vengeance on Thebes because his mother's family deny his divinity. Her sisters and the other Theban women have been driven mad onto the hillsides, and the play focuses on male responses to Dionysus, who is posing as the long-haired leader of (voluntary, female) devotees from the East. Cadmus (his grandfather) and the old prophet Teiresias opt to dress as Dionysus' followers and go to the hills themselves (although for self-serving and fanciful reasons respectively). Left holding the fort is the young king Pentheus. He responds to the old men with mocking incredulity, and to Dionysus with insecure hostility, tinged with increasing fascination. Pentheus' fails to control the situation, the stranger and eventually himself, as Dionysus asks whether he wishes to see the women on the hillsides and proposes that to infiltrate their rites, he should dress and act accordingly. Dionysus supervises Pentheus' dressing as a maenad, and he is delivered up to the Theban women by Dionysus to be torn apart in their delusion that he is a lion. As in other crossdressing scenes, one point is to humiliate the king, but both in well-observed presentation (such as Pentheus' concern with hemlines) and in the overall context of the play, the effect is rather more sophisticated. The play distinguishes between those who voluntarily embrace Dionysus (the chorus, Teiresias and in a more limited way Cadmus) and those who do not. As with Aphrodite, there is a need to embrace what the god stands for: that includes a more relaxed (but controlled) stance towards gender and identity, an element that was recognized in cult and elsewhere within Greek life.[39]

In focusing on crossdressing, and in other respects, *Bacchae* draws on elements familiar from comedy, especially *Women at the Thesmophoria Festival*, which deploys two contested modes of crossdressing, intertwined with different approaches to theatricality. Here, the Athenian women intend to vote on condemning Euripides to death for depicting a series of bad women: Medea, Stheneboea and Phaedra (particularly the Phaedra of the first *Hippolytus*, far less innocent than in the surviving second *Hippolytus*[40]). Euripides looks for someone to infiltrate this women's assembly to speak on his behalf. First he tries the tragedian Agathon, represented as habitually dressing as characters, both women and men, in order to write them. A poetics of realism and of emotional sympathy between poet, character and audience is suggested, also with sexual overtones (130–3). Agathon has more sense than to accept this assignment, so Euripides turns to his coarse, hairy relative instead (another forced crossdressing scene ensues). Euripides' relative is both figuratively and literally exposed, and tied up under the guard of a Scythian archer (who acted as a police force). A series of parodic escape attempts follow, orchestrated by Euripides, including *Andromeda* and *Helen*, with the relative as the damsel in distress. Neither the women nor the Scythian archer are prepared to entertain this role-playing: they have seen his phallus and for them biology is destiny. Euripides thus adopts a more physical, less conceptual approach, and introduces a dancing girl to distract the Scythian archer. The audience, by contrast, have to process parodic tragic storylines alongside the comic events on stage with a flexibility that their fictional counterparts lack. Certainly, this is exposing the limits of tragic fictionality and its pretensions towards realism and naturalism, while celebrating the flexibility of the comic imagination, where the fictional contract is foregrounded. Yet in so doing, two different modes of crossdressing are explored (broadly 'passing' and 'drag' modes respectively). Whether the comic mode, whereby everyone knows who everyone 'really' is, ultimately presents a conservative position or demonstrates the performativity and constructed nature of gender roles, or represents a culturally-situated exploration of the broad spectrum of transgender identity or practice[41] is largely a matter of audience stance.

Dramatic treatment of same-sex sexual relations is rare outside of Greek Old Comedy, although that picture would change if more of Aeschylus' *Myrmidons* survived.[42] Greek tragedy deals principally with male homosocial relations, best seen in Sophocles' *Philoctetes* where the choices of the young Neoptolemus centre on his relationship with two older men, the pragmatic Odysseus and the marooned, crippled but principled Philoctetes. The pedagogic/social relationship between an older man and a youth on the cusp of citizenship echoes that seen in the canonical, stylized form of Greek homosexuality. Aristophanes prefers to reduce sexuality to bodily essentials, and eschews elaborate courtships and non-penetrative (inter-crural) sex as seen on vase-painting (particularly of the early fifth century) in favour of oral and mainly anal penetration – of both citizens and youths. Often penetration is linked to the poetics of invective, mainly targeted against the penetratee and works broadly with the social and sexual norms of the period.[43] Yet these too can be set aside or scrutinized. Thus Dicaeopolis shamelessly invites the general Lamakhos to penetrate him with his powerful weapon, in order to ridicule the pompous military man. In *Clouds*, there is a more sustained examination of traditional and modern ('sophistic') education. The representative of the latter, the Weaker Argument, creates citizens who are pale, weak, opportunistic logic-choppers and shamelessly promiscuous, advocates adultery (citing the gods) and fears no punishment. The Stronger Argument represents traditional education and morality, but belies his name: his interest in boys is rather obsessive and tinged with both anachronism and social exclusivity. More significantly, he cannot counter the Weaker Argument and loses the debate. Given the disastrous aftermath, the Weaker Argument is not being endorsed: both takes on sexuality are found wanting.

Some plays pushed at boundaries, others trampled all over them, notably Euripides' *Medea*. Almost in passing, Medea addresses women's public silence and domestic seclusion while tackling head-on more fundamental norms of social gender and biological sex. As comfortable as Clytemnestra is in publicly engaging with men, not only her erstwhile husband Jason, but kings Creon of

Corinth and Aegeus of Athens, Medea pointedly co-opts masculine language and ideology, especially that of elite men. Medea's confrontation with Jason is couched in the language of traditional (male) heroism: *kleos*, *aidôs*, *aretê* and *kakotês* (excellence and its reverse). Jason has failed to fulfil his social or personal obligations – after she helped him to seize the golden fleece, dealt with Pelias and bore Jason two children. Her own status has been undermined as Jason cast her aside to marry Creon's daughter after their arrival in Corinth. Contrast Seneca's *Medea*, which is much more a study of emotion: uncontrollable anger, without such appropriation of masculine language and ideology, or the direct assault on contemporary gendered norms. Medea's opening speech in Euripides condemns the social position of women in Greece and famously concludes by comparing bravery needed in battle unfavourably with that required for childbirth (248–51). Medea's initial concern for her children's welfare might suggest a parallel to Clytemnestra, but Medea's revenge on Jason is altogether more radical (and probably surprising to its original audience). After dispatching Jason's new bride (Creon's daughter) she also murders her own two children – thereby depriving Jason of any means of continuing his household (*oikos*) and severing all connection with him. She dispenses with family and blood (unlike both Antigone and Clytemnestra). While clearly no easy decision, and in many respects a self-sacrificial strategy, Medea's infanticide poses troubling questions, particularly for essentialist notions of gender. That would be true even in a society where near-natal infanticide (exposure) was widely practised and there was high infant mortality. Medea is certainly no ordinary woman – grand-daughter of the sun and a practiced witch – but this only helps motivate, but not limit her transgressive actions or their ideological force. Unlike Clytemnestra and Antigone, Medea even avoids any kind of punishment. Indeed, her grandstanding escape in a snake-drawn chariot is to Athens of all places, to continue her violent career. If one may doubt ideological closure in those cases, here there is no ideological closure at all.

Classical drama reflects the social contexts in which it was operating. The more tightly regulated norms of sexuality and gender in Athens resulted in them being more extensively foregrounded, sometimes for reiteration and reinforcement, sometimes for questioning and transgression and sometimes for exploration of wider social and political issues. In Rome, it is possible to see played out on stage the social change resulting from an expanding city state and not least its contact with Greek culture. The paradoxical position of women within the Athenian democracy led to particularly creative exploitation of gender and sexuality. In neither society, however, were the fundamental inequalities ever fully resolved.

CHAPTER FOUR

The Environment of Theatre

Experiencing Place in the Ancient World

DAVID WILES

Fifth-century Greek theatre was performed in a place, not a space.[1] We experience *places* through the way they smell, the way they crunch beneath our feet, the sounds we hear, the views we glimpse of sky and surrounding landscape, the people in or around those places, and above all the memories they hold for us and for others. We can never see a place without these additional non-optical forms of bodily encounter. Conversely, we tend to use the word *space* when abstracting places, using techniques of geometry to eliminate all their felt particularity. It is easy for the theatre historian to reproduce diagrams of *spaces* generated by precise archaeological investigations, much harder to imagine and convey what it once felt like to inhabit a *place*. A diagram satisfies the demands of scientific accuracy, but fails to catch the qualities that once made a performance work its effect on an audience. In the twenty-first century we live highly mobile lives, inhabiting buildings and cities designed through methods of abstraction, and forgetting our physical selves as we gaze at photos and graphics on computer screens that are devoid of scale and texture. It is an important task for the historical imagination to engage with the way other cultures have inhabited place and interpreted space, and in today's world of environmental degradation this is perforce a task with political implications. I shall undertake in this chapter what I see as the job of all historians: to capture other possible ways of living, and by this means offer some direct or indirect explanation of why we live today in the peculiar way we do.

Avoiding the loaded term 'development', I shall describe in this chapter a crucial shift that took place in both Greece and Rome. A transition from irregular and temporary performance places to prestigious urban monuments consolidated the actor-audience relationship in ways that were less open to artistic innovation, but more conducive to political control. We today have inherited these monuments, and the traditions they embody, and it is all too easy to superimpose the dramatic scripts that we have likewise inherited upon these magnificent monuments and suppose we are in touch with an authentic point of theatrical origin. In this chapter I shall also compare how the two cultures of Greece and Rome were characterized by distinctively different relationships to the environment. Greek inhabitants of small city-states were in close touch with the surrounding landscape, which they imbued with spiritual values, and in the theatre as in other architectural projects they sought to create a balance between human reason and the unpredictability of the natural environment. The inhabitants of the sprawling Roman metropolis, on the other hand, worked tirelessly to impose human order upon nature. Their theatres were not accommodations to the hillside, but rose from the ground, and shut the natural world from view.

In his tragedy *The Persians*, Aeschylus, the first great writer of Athenian tragedy, represents the father of the defeated Persian king in the person of a ghost, and this ghost, aware of what lies beyond the visible world, blames the failure of the Persian army in 480 BCE on its hubris. 'When they reached the soil of Greece, they had no respect, stripping the altars of the gods, and burning temples. Altars obliterated, sanctuaries of the immortals completely uprooted, their foundations overturned!' (809–12). In modern warfare, emotions are more likely to be whipped up by the murder of innocent civilians or the looting of people's homes, than by such religious sites – but we should not forget the huge passions stirred in recent times by the Temple Mount in Jerusalem or the Babri Mosque in Ayodhya. We should be wary of painting the culture of classical Athens, and antiquity in general, in our own image and regarding it as humanistic. Aeschylus helps us picture the way his countrymen felt about the sacredness of space when he evokes the collective cry uttered by Athenian oarsmen at the naval battle of Salamis, where he himself may well have been part of the onshore army, a refugee from his home across the bay. 'Sons of the Greeks, forward! Liberate the fatherland! Freedom for our children, wives, and the shrines of our patronal gods, and the tombs of our forebears! Now the fight is for everything!' (402–5). The soil of Athens was understood as a kind of parent, and there was a continuity between the living family, the gods associated with the land, and great-grandparents whose bodily remains were housed by the land. Human beings were conceived not as isolated individuals but as part of the cycle of reproduction. This way of thinking created a bond and overlap between self and place that is alien to modern Western culture.

Of course there was no single Athenian mode of seeing the world, and humanist principles were part of the mix. A famous chorus in Sophocles' *Antigone* describes how humankind has managed to master the environment, both land and sea. It has not only learned to sail the seas in winter, but also 'wears away that most august of goddesses, Earth, tireless and imperishable, with ploughs that circle round, year upon year, drawn by animals, turning her over' (337–41). To control nature by means of agriculture is one thing, but what Creon attempts to do in Sophocles' play is another – to refuse the claim of Mother Earth upon the body of a dead human being. It was an important belief in Athens, talked up for political reasons, that the Athenians were an indigenous race, born from the land, and had never been migrants. Euripides' play *Ion* helped publicize the relevant mythology. Sophocles' *Oedipus at Colonus* in a related vein promulgated the story that Oedipus King of Thebes was buried in Athenian soil, a prophylactic against the invading Theban army in 406 BCE. Half a century earlier, Aeschylus ended his Oresteian trilogy with the image of Earth goddesses taking up residence in a cave under a crag facing the Acropolis, portrayed as forces capable of bestowing not only fertility upon the land but also plague, sterility and drought. The cave of the 'Furies' had great emotional significance in the classical period, but today it no longer features in the tourist itinerary and is conveniently used as a toilet by persons caught short. The modern tourist is interested in products of humankind like the Parthenon, not in the countervailing forces of the earth.

To sit today amid the rubble of the Theatre of Dionysus on the slope below the Parthenon is not for most people a rewarding experience (Figure 4.1). One

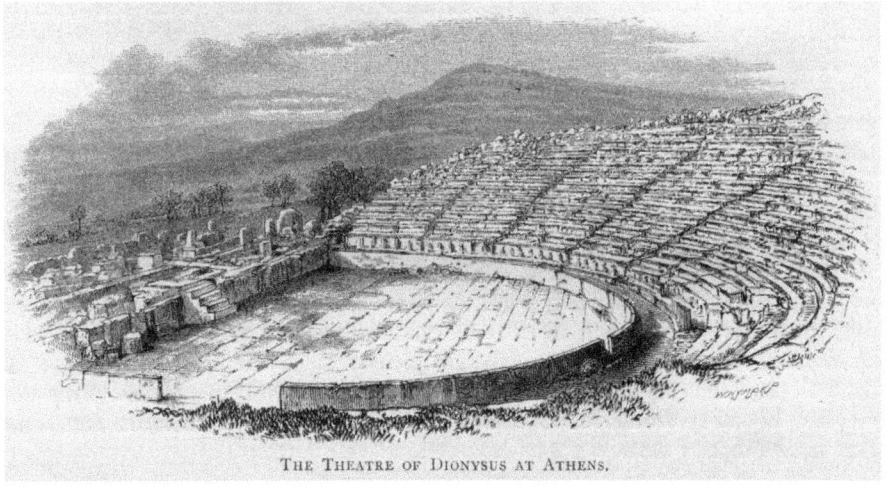

FIGURE 4.1: The Theatre of Dionysus at the end of the nineteenth century. Drawing by J.P. Mahaffy (1890).

gets little imaginative feel for how the place used to be. In today's urban environment there is no silence that lets us imagine the power of language, the air is polluted so we cannot readily picture the sharp patterning and colour of the costumes, and there is no darkness in the modern city so we cannot intuit the connection between night and the idea of the enfolding earth, nor begin to think why it was so important that the Festival of Dionysus took place at full moon.[2] We can no longer access the archaeological site via the old processional route. Though the foundations of the old sixth-century Doric temple still stand, the classical audience in the fifth century sat on wooden rostra erected for the duration of the festival. The stage area is predominantly Roman, while the stone auditorium is fourth-century, built a couple of generations after the death of Sophocles and Euripides. It is frustrating, therefore, that we do not know what the fifth-century acting area was like, and are forced to build our conclusions upon the ambiguous evidence of dramatic scripts, supported by knowledge that the space also served for circular dithyrambs performed by groups of fifty. The auditorium was erected by freelance entrepreneurs, and its configuration has likewise been the subject of controversy.[3] It was probably not symmetrical since it must have wrapped around the large square roofed building alongside known as the Odeon. The seats cannot have been set in a perfect circle since planks are straight, and some straight stone seats for dignitaries have been found embedded in the later stone auditorium.[4] Foundations of houses and wells halfway up the height of the later auditorium suggest that the earlier audience was smaller than the fourth-century audience, even though the population was probably larger. We must remain cautious in jumping to conclusions. In theatre festivals of the Middle Ages, wooden seating could be erected over the top of mere private housing, in a world that privileged the collective over the individual.

Increasingly, historians are turning their attention to the one stone theatre on Athenian soil that does survive from the age of Euripides and Sophocles, sited in the coastal mining town of Thorikos, over thirty miles by road from the city. I have chosen to focus my discussion in this chapter upon that fascinating theatre rather than wrestle with the complexities and imponderables of Athens itself, where so many layers of history are superimposed. I shall also not dwell upon the well-known theatre of Epidaurus, built in a pilgrimage site for purposes to which tragedy and comedy were incidental.[5] The quirky particularity of Thorikos helps us understand better what it actually felt like to be an Athenian theatregoer.

The lower part of the Thorikos auditorium was built along with Dionysus' Temple in about 450 BCE, and the upper section of seating was added in the fourth century.[6] Much of Athens' wealth and power derived from silver mined in the region, so the town was affluent enough to build a theatre, and when the veins of silver were exhausted the place was abandoned, allowing the theatre to survive for posterity. The wooden Theatre of Dionysus in Athens was used for only one or two weeks in the year, but the theatre of Thorikos was built in stone because it was in permanent use as a place for assemblies and sacrifices, as well as for tragedy and comedy. It was central to the working of Athenian democracy that the inhabitants of places like Thorikos should play a part in self-government just like men who lived in the city, and Thorikos functioned as a miniature democracy, with traditions that recalled the days before it was swallowed up in the Athenian federation. The size of the theatre is disproportionate to the size of the local community with some 2,000 seats available for a population of some 500 adult male citizens, and the units of seating are tightly packed by later standards, so it has been suggested that the theatre was also a gathering place for the 'tribe' – the population of Attica being divided cross-regionally into ten tribes for military and festive purposes, including the performance of dithyrambs at the City Dionysia. According to another theory, it may have been used to reunite this coastal deme with its two associated demes in the city and in farming country.[7] There would have been many leaseholders who lived temporarily in the town to work their mines and supervise their slaves. And one function of the theatre was undoubtedly prestige, drawing in visitors from surrounding villages and from Athens to enhance the reputation of an unattractive industrial location.

The ground plan does not conform to modern expectations based largely upon the iconic status of the Theatre of Epidaurus. The space is not rectilinear, not circular, not symmetrical, and thinking through its rationale will help us understand better how the Greeks of the classical period related to their environment. The acting area was a terrace on the sheltered south slope of Mount Velatouri, abutting houses and mines to the west, while on the east side a path led to the sea, which came in closer then than it does today. The theatre is laid out in relationship to a temple and an altar. Geometrically, it was planned on the basis of three imaginary circles, one of which is small, resulting in a tight curve on the west side corresponding with the sweep of the hill.[8] Nothing here is random, but the precise logic eludes us (Figure 4.2).

The statue of Dionysus housed in the temple looked not towards a central position in the acting area but towards the doorway of a large closed chamber with seats carved into the rock, probably associated with some form of religious initiation. Perhaps the statue was moved from the temple to a plinth at the focal point of the small circle in order to view tragedies and comedies, just as the wooden statue of Dionysus in Athens was carried from its temple to view performances alongside the audience in the city. The geometry of Thorikos results in a feeling of harmony, but also of instability, for there is no single centre point. The theatre is not a place to *be* at, but a place to *arrive* at, the culmination of a processional route up from the bay. The tight asymmetrical curve of the western seating allowed an arriving procession, in a dithyrambic

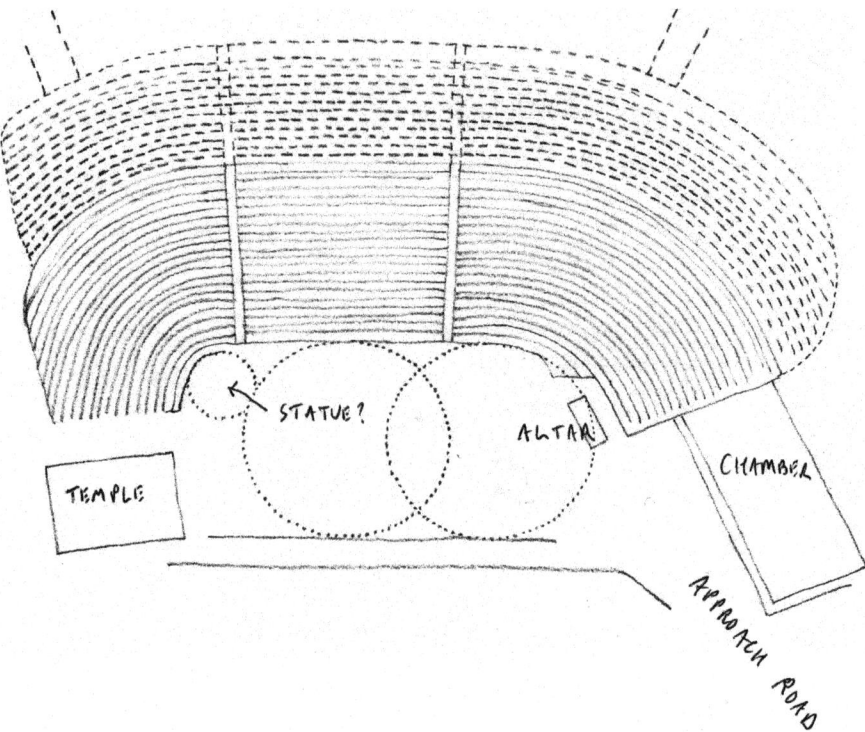

FIGURE 4.2: Ground plan of the fifth-century theatre at Thorikos. The upper section of the auditorium was added in the fourth century. The dotted circles indicate the basis on which the theatre was laid out. Drawing by Gayna Wiles.

dance for example, to feel that it was being greeted by a sea of faces beside the temple, and had reached its destination.

The central rows of seats appear to be arranged in one straight line, but in fact each comprises two straight lines which meet at a slight angle at the centre. The straightness is an illusion, designed to prevent a feeling of rigidity, which was an important goal also for the architect of the Parthenon who famously eschewed perfect straight horizontal and vertical lines. The slight angle meant that people sitting in these seats could be aware of the reactions of others further along in the same row. Since the excavators have not identified any technical reason why the auditorium was not rounded to a greater depth, we must look to function: the optimal relationship, not to an actor orating from a static command position, but to an advancing procession.

The eastern seats are wrapped around the sacrificial altar. We possess part of the calendar of annual sacrifices carried out in Thorikos, many of which would have taken place here in this central gathering place. Sacrifices embedded the people of Thorikos in their environment. There was a deified 'hero' who bore the name of Thorikos; there were deities whose names and cults helped to define the perimeter of the community: Over-the-plain, Gate-keeper, Save-boat; and finally there were mythological figures whose stories were associated with the immediate landscape: Helen who consummated her love with Paris on an island visible offshore, the nymph Philonis seduced by two gods, and finally Cephalus and his beloved Procris whom he accidentally killed.[9] The seduction of Cephalus by the goddess of the Dawn makes sense when we reflect on how the coast faces east, with the temple aligned to catch the first rays of the rising sun. The most important local figure was Demeter, who landed at Thorikos and began here a journey across Attica looking for her daughter Persephone. Her sanctuary lay below the theatre close to where she landed, not on the rocky hillside but in the fertile floodplain befitting her status as goddess of crops. Her story reminds us of the cultural importance of journeys as we seek to understand the placeness of Thorikos (Figure 4.3).

The spectators sat on the hillside, on marble carved out of the hill, and this connection to the land necessarily affected their response to performances. The hillside beneath them was honeycombed with mineshafts, the source of their wealth but also of human suffering, with far more lead extracted than silver, and amid the nearby workings archaeologists have uncovered a shrine to the goddess of health. Though it is unlikely that the slaves who worked inside the mines would have been allowed to sit in the theatre, many citizens would have been involved in working underground. Higher up the slope, Mount Velatouri contains impressive tombs dating to the Mycenaean period. The world which we abstract as the world of myth was experienced in Thorikos as

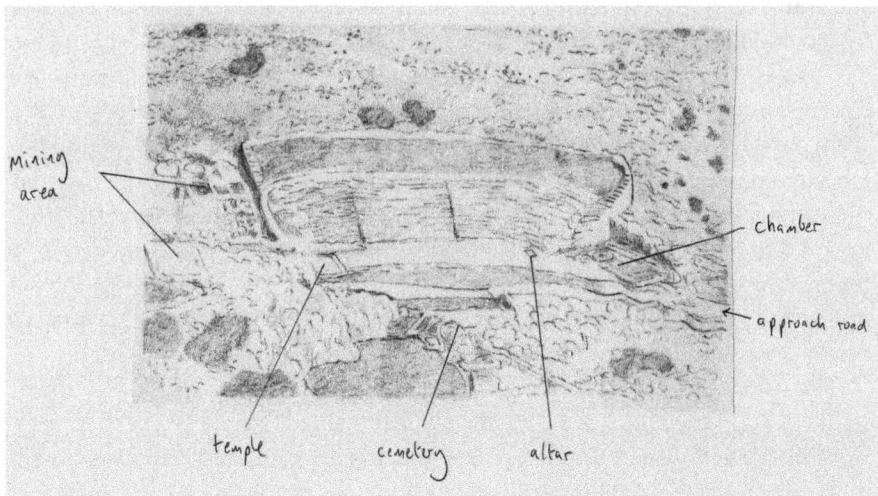

FIGURE 4.3: Remains of the theatre at Thorikos. Drawing by Gayna Wiles.

the world of heroic ancestors, still connected corporeally to the present. In the gully immediately beneath the theatre, a burial site was still in use during the classical period, reinforcing the idea of connection between the worlds of the living and the dead.

Although we only have a shadowy picture of the relationship between performances at the Great Dionysia in Athens and performances in the townships or 'demes', the idea that plays were written to be performed just once in the huge theatre of Athens has become increasingly hard to sustain as more deme theatres come to be excavated.[10] Plays reached the mass of the citizen community not because the population of places like Thorikos were all willing to make the long hike to Athens, where seats were in short supply, but because there was scope to reperform plays with professional actors and local choruses in the major deme theatres. A series of fourth-century inscriptions confirms that comedies and tragedies were played in Thorikos, and at least three choruses competed against each other. It looks as though two of the most famous actors of the day, Theodoros and Pindaros, came there to compete in theatre contests.[11] On the assumption that such performances were already taking place in the fifth century, let us try to imagine how the environment of Thorikos would have conditioned the meaning of a play like Sophocles' *Antigone*. In the modern world, with its taste for humanism and abstraction, *Antigone* has morphed into a play about human rights, about the claims of an individual citizen against an oppressive State, and about the power of women in a society governed by men. If we focus our minds on the spatial context of Thorikos, we shall start to foreground different aspects of the Sophoclean text.

Antigone becomes primarily a play about burial, when performed in front of a cemetery, at the foot of an acropolis sacralized by its ancient burial places. The horror of a body lying unburied, and the importance of burial in bestowing on a community a sense of its own history and identity, would have informed the way spectators responded to the play. The cemetery at Thorikos was screened off by the painted wooden *skênê*, and some stones have been found with post-holes that once held the *skênê* upright. The *skênê* was probably erected along the original line of the terrace before it was widened at the time the seating was put in place, for this ancient inner line was used by the builders in working out the geometry of the auditorium. When the *skênê* opened up to reveal the hanged body of Eurydice at the end of the play (1294–9), the real backdrop for many spectators would have been the site where their own parent or child was buried.

The most prominent feature of the complex was the temple, home to the statue of Dionysus, though as in Athens the statue may have been carried to the front of the auditorium to give the god a better view of the performance. This physical presence of Dionysus' image would have shaped the audience's response to the celebratory hymn sung by the chorus in praise of the healing powers of Dionysus, evoking the Theban landscapes which he frequented, green and lush in contrast with the dry slopes facing the theatre of Thorikos (1116ff.). In the previous hymn, the chorus focus on Dionysus' power to induce madness (944ff.). The daemonic power of the god is associated with a chamber locked fast by bronze, a rocky prison, dark rocks and the remote cave of the north wind, and these ideas had a physical correlative at Thorikos, where the temple is aligned upon just such a mysterious chamber. The hymn accompanies Antigone's exit to the cave which is to be her tomb, the symbolic bower where she will be united with the god of death. We do not know exactly what mysteries were performed in this chamber at Thorikos. Thorikos had strong connections to the cult of Demeter, mother of Persephone, and performed in Thorikos, Antigone's exit to a living death would have had religious resonances inconceivable for modern audience. The mineshafts on the other side of the auditorium would have enhanced the feeling of just what it meant in simple practical terms to be buried alive.

The procession was the fundamental component of the Dionysia, and the theatre of Thorikos was designed as a place to view processions.[12] When Sophocles' chorus first enter (100ff.), they associate their arrival with the eye of the rising sun, and conclude by evoking nocturnal Dionysiac dances in front of temples. Arriving from the direction of the sunrise, following the main processional route up from the sea to end in front of the temple, the dramatic chorus at Thorikos would have followed in the footsteps of the communal festive chorus. Sitting in the open air, Greek audiences were attuned to the circuit of the sun – and references to the sunrise evoked not just an idea but a physical reality. In another hymn, the chorus liken Antigone's fate to the power of the north wind sweeping over the sea from Thrace (586ff.). The audience at Thorikos could look sideways at sea, but sat on the south-facing slope sheltered from the north wind, a practical necessity since the festival of Dionysus took place in midwinter in the demes.

The eastern side of the Thorikos auditorium wraps around a sacrificial altar. The smell of blood, guts and roasted meat, mingled with the smell of the surrounding furnaces, will have formed part of the audience's sensory encounter with tragedy. When Tiresias speaks about a failed sacrifice where nothing burns (1006f.), the significance of this portent will have been more dismaying to an audience at Thorikos than it can be today. By the same token, when Tiresias speaks of ominous birds, the audience would have been alert to chance interventions by birds in the landscape and soundscape about them. References to storms and weather resonated for an outdoor audience in winter, because the forces of nature are beyond human control. A certain order and harmony results from the geometry of the theatre of Thorikos, yet the basis of that order is not obvious to the human eye. There was no perfect symmetrical circle, as in fourth-century Athens, to imply a perfect balance between the rights of the individual and the rights of the collective, allowing tragedy to celebrate the triumph of reason. Rather, this was a space that invited movement, suggesting that life is flux. A stable point of equipoise, both experiential and symbolic, was fundamental to later forms of classicism, but was unavailable in fifth-century Thorikos.

The religious and political dimensions of life are not easily separated in Thorikos. Individuals were honoured by the community through a grant of *prohedria*, the right to sit in one of the front seats, which were wider than the rest, and identified by a numbering system. The occupants of these seats were conspicuous to people behind them because they wore honorific crowns of olive or sometimes gold. *Prohedria* was allocated to priests, holders of political office and honoured visitors on the basis of custom and collective approval, and the *chorêgoi* who funded and trained the choruses were prime candidates for this honour. Sophocles is vague about the legal basis of Creon's 'kingship' because power in Greek communities did not rest upon technicalities of birth and title, but upon public esteem. Victories in theatrical competitions were commemorated by inscriptions for the benefit of posterity. The theatre of Thorikos was a memorialized environment with inscriptions carved in stone everywhere, and the pursuit of victory in the competition for best chorus or best actor was a pursuit of immortality.

The theatre of Thorikos was unusual in the fifth century in being built of stone, for most theatre auditoria were temporary structures made of planks. We get a glimpse of this procedure from a contract for erecting the seating at Piraeus, the port of Athens, a theatre which we are told was frequented by Socrates when a play by Euripides was on offer (Aelian *VH* 2.13).[13] A consortium of four individuals put up a total of 3,000 drachmas – plus a 10 per cent voluntary bonus, which secured them the reward of being crowned, and would have entailed *prohedria* alongside the *chorêgoi* who supported the production costs. In return for their fee, the contractors collected the entrance money, and it has been calculated that a full house of 5,000 people over two days would mean the investment could be recouped in two days of performance. However, we do not know how much it cost them to redecorate the stage building, which must have involved hiring a painter to create an impressive stage façade. If we factor in the risk of rain, not unlikely in December, it is a reasonable calculation that the festival was scheduled to run for three days. The mathematics of the allocation (3 x 1,100 drachmas) suggests that the structure might have been erected in three independent parts, but we have no clue as to its shape. The binding nature of the contract was confirmed on a stone in the public space of the agora, so failure to create good seating and a handsome *skênê* would have been a public humiliation.

We have to turn to evidence from Athens itself to get a sense of the social or human aspect of the performance environment. *Prohedria* was particularly important because of the scrum involved in getting a seat. Taking up the reserved thrones in front commanded the attention of an audience that arrived early, and men with rods supervised the occupation of seats to prevent fights. The scraps of evidence suggest a festive atmosphere, with spectators wearing garlands and bringing picnics of nuts, dried figs, olives and of course wine, not to mention cushions to help them sit through a long day.[14] The tight packing of the crowd, the context in a wider festival involving processions and feasting around open fires, and the passions aroused by competition meant that the audience was expressive and volatile. We hear of clapping, but also a whole vocabulary of disapproval that included hissing, clucking or tutting, stamping of heels on the wooden planks, and throwing food.[15] Though public outrage is most likely to appear on the historical record, attention was the norm. Plutarch tells us of uproar when Euripides began a play with the apparently irreligious line: 'Zeus, whoever Zeus may be, for the story is all I know!'[16] A condition of such collective expressivity was silent anticipation. We have fifth-century evidence of how a subtly mispronounced tragic line went into folklore because everyone heeded the language so carefully and picked up on a double entendre.[17]

The Athenians had various reasons for building a circular stone auditorium in the fourth century, a massive enterprise that took decades to complete.[18] More people could be accommodated, in a carefully designed acoustical bowl that helped everyone to hear the words. The auditorium was available all through the year for political assemblies, when numbers were greater than the regular location on the Pnyx could accommodate. The complex system of leasing out contracts for the provision of wooden scaffolding to seat the audience could be avoided. But most important was probably prestige: tragedy and comedy were now seen as the glory of Athens, and the city needed a monument to mark its achievement. Lycurgus, who oversaw the project, fixed the plays of Aeschylus, Sophocles and Euripides as classics by maintaining definitive copies of their texts and putting statues of the trio in the theatre, and he fostered civic rituals like the Dionysia for the sake of social cohesion.[19] Tragedy came to mean something rather different when performed in this environment of stone: the texts were, metaphorically speaking, also now set in stone. Rather like Creon in Sophocles' *Antigone*, Lycurgus as long-term steward of the public finances held sway in Athens on the basis of influence rather than formal election. The building of the stone theatre can be seen as the triumph of the Creon principle, while the principle of Antigone, bonded to the earth gods, was eroded. In a surviving speech, Lycurgus quotes as an exemplary lesson in citizenship, that supposedly inspired earlier generations of Athenians, a long passage from Euripides' *Erechtheus*. The text tells how, in obedience to the gods, an Athenian father sacrifices his daughter to save the city. Moral complexities are obliterated by the simple message, articulated also by Lycurgus' monumental auditorium, that the good of the city out-values the good of the individual household (*Against Leocrates* 99–101).

The perfect circular auditorium has haunted modern imaginings of Greek theatre, thanks in large measure to the writings of the Roman architect Vitruvius, who transmitted this conception to the Renaissance. This now familiar organization of space had a meaning and social function quite unlike those of Thorikos. The Athenian decision to build such an auditorium drew inspiration from the huge theatre recently built at Megalopolis in Arcadia in the heart of the Peloponnese, seating some 20,000 people.[20] The 'Great City' of 'Megalopolis' was an experiment in large-scale federal democracy, and involved small cities transplanting themselves and their cults to a new and impressive fortified site, sufficient to offer collective protection against the Spartans. According to Pausanias (viii.32), no subsequent theatre was ever built on the same scale. The auditorium looked down onto the columned porch of a Council Hall, an indoor performance space with columns carefully arranged to allow thousands of people to have a sight line on the speaker. Weather conditions are fiercer in the mountains of the Peloponnese than in Athens, so this covered space was a necessary addition. When the theatre was used for drama rather than for political assemblies, a wooden stage building was moved into place from an adjacent storage point to create a setting visually and acoustically appropriate to theatre. The theatre was physically attached to the cult of Dionysus by means of the stadium, which ran from a sacred spring beside the theatre to the temple of the god (Pausanias viii.32). The importance of competition in binding communities together helps to explain why the traditional processional route was now transposed into a competitive running route. The theatre itself is a perfect semicircle, and reflects the Platonic ideal of a convergence between geometric, political and cosmic ordering.

To understand the principles behind this revolutionary structure in the Peloponnese, we must consider its function. Polybius, a native of Megalopolis, explains how the founders of the city required children to sing hymns to the gods and heroes of the locality. Adolescents and young men would then perform competitive dances at the Dionysia in front of their fellow citizens, which broke down the dour individualism characteristic of a mountain people.[21] According to this interpretation, the theatre of Megalopolis was built less for its prestige than for its function as a piece of social engineering. The architectural space embodied order and harmony, with different wedges of the auditorium allocated to different tribes to reflect the grouping of the population for choral dancing. Tragedies performed in this environment would not have meant what they did in the old wooden theatres of the fifth century. The theatre environment supported Lycurgus' view that the noble playwright is one who provides citizens with fine examples 'which they look upon and contemplate in order to accustom their souls to love the fatherland' (*Against Leocrates* 100).

In Rome we can trace the same move from temporary festival auditoria to stone monuments, and the playwrights whose work was most admired in antiquity likewise wrote for temporary spaces where the relationship to the audience was fluid and immediate. Since plays were performed as part of religious festivals, temple steps were a natural site for *ad hoc* auditoria. The prologues of Plautus and Terence give us a glimpse of the chaotic atmosphere when Roman plays were performed at festival time in the sprawling city of Rome. Plautus' prologue to *Uncle Gruelguzzler* is a good example.[22] The speaker silences a noisy crowd by adopting the persona of Agamemnon and the concomitant bellow of a Greek tragedian. He is concerned with people finding their seats, and sympathetic to those who have arrived too late. Officials armed with whips supervise the seating, but risk diverting attention from the stage. The audience must have intruded onto the stage itself, because ageing male whores are told to avoid such a prominent location. The speaker suggests that the play will serve as surrogate food for the hungry poor. The Parasite is a recurrent figure in Plautus' theatre, a man who has nothing to eat and tries to sponge off others, and the context of Plautus' dramas was a life of hardship, hunger and oppression. His plays construct Athens as an affluent pleasure-loving utopia, while never denying the harsh realities of Roman life.

The speaker of the prologue concludes by turning to the Magistrates who funded the performance, and asks them to be fair in judging the competition, for pressure exerted by paid claques of spectators was often used to sway judgements. There is no further mention of the senatorial class, the Roman nobility who would soon impose their claim to dedicated seats at the front of the auditorium in an undemocratic Roman version of *prohedria*.[23] Tensions between the nobility and the people were too sensitive to mention directly. Most plays at this time were part of the 'Roman Games', and would thus have been performed in the Roman Forum, the traditional centre of the community where crowds could gather to make their dissatisfactions known to the nobility. Here selling and manufacturing rubbed shoulders with buildings of religious and political significance, in a space of encounter that was perfectly suited to Plautine drama.[24] However, the sole auditorium surviving from the days of Plautus is constituted by the steps of the Temple of Cybele on the Palatine Hill, commanding an asymmetric terrace.[25] Cybele was the recipient of a new festival featuring wild Greek eunuchs round about the time when the nobility imposed their new seating arrangements in 194 BCE, and at least one play by Plautus was performed on this occasion. Ascending the Palatine Hill, the audience climbed up to a world that was higher in both a religious and political sense. The performance was in some sense a means of taking possession.

The man who introduces the comedy *Uncle Gruelguzzler* claims that he does not want any babies in the audience because their mothers' milk might dry or they might grow randy like goats and start bleating, while older women are forbidden to gossip. This was a mixed family audience, in contrast to Greece, where the audience was conceived as a male democratic citizen body, and it was not acceptable for public theatre to be merely a vehicle for sensory pleasure. We should not, however, consider a comedy by Plautus to be any less 'political' than a Greek tragedy. A comic performance was an event where for the duration of the festival social hierarchy was symbolically overthrown. Magistrates negotiated their exercise of power by allowing ordinary Romans to have what they wanted, within the framework of the festival, and in a society characterized by rigid social divides, the rupturing of the actor-audience divide had particular force as one of the means by which power was negotiated.

Republican Rome was not an orderly place, in either political or spatial terms. The Roman Forum was surrounded by a medley of buildings, which were not connected architecturally, but were invested with communal memories.[26] The Forum contained, for example, a symbolic entrance to the underworld, and a black stone associated with the death of Romulus, founder of the city. Livy records an important tussle for the soul of the city, some two centuries before the time of Plautus. The city had been destroyed by the Gauls, apart from the Temple of Jupiter on the Capitoline Hill. The starving poor wanted to migrate to a captured city nearby, where convenient abandoned homes awaited them, but the patricians, who could better afford to rebuild, wanted to stay put because of all the religious associations of the site. The leader of the patricians, Camillus, argued that his sense of homeland entailed more than just buildings. He reflected upon the landscape, and the homesickness he always felt for the hills and plains around the Tiber, and then upon the practical advantages of the site, a strategic location close to the river and sea but protected from attack. Finally, and most persuasively, he reflected on the religious associations of the setting: the Capitol founded on the basis of an omen, the ancient hearth-fire of the Vestal Virgins, the sacred shield kept in the Temple of Mars. The special 'fortune' of this place was not transferable he argued, and the poor were persuaded, so they hastily rebuilt on whatever land each could grab, leaving the streets higgledy-piggledy, with an old sewage system that bore no relation to the streets above (Livy V.49–55). The Roman sense of a *genius loci* was a crucial factor in sustaining the courage, resilience and feeling of community that made Rome so powerful.

With the disappearance of external threats, like the Gauls, or like Hannibal back in the time of Plautus, the Roman Republic became less cohesive, and warlords turned emperors imposed a new political order on the city that was also a spatial order. Stone theatres were part of a new and coherent urban landscape that was a symbolic expression of absolute imperial power. The first and mightiest stone theatre was built by Pompey 'the Great', destined to become 'dictator' but never 'emperor'.[27] It was the ethos of the Republic that theatres should be temporary structures, a gift to the people by a member of the elite who courted their approval of his transient authority, and there was no stone theatre in Rome long after these had appeared elsewhere in Italy.²⁸ Pompey's theatre was funded by the wealth he brought back from the Greek East as a gift not to the Senate but to the common people of Rome, and with it he staked his claim to immortality.

In many ways, the Theatre of Pompey rather than the Athenian Theatre of Dionysus marks the beginning of theatre as the cultural institution we know today (Figure 4.4). This building was not an adaptation of the landscape but an imposed urban monument making a statement to men and women in the street below.²⁹ Within the cityscape of Rome, this was the first realisation in stone of the three Greek classical orders: solid slender Doric columns at ground level supporting slender elegant Ionic columns on the second tier, topped in turn by ornate leafy Corinthian columns, the whole arrangement creating a feel of harmony, lightness and additional height. The columns and arches behind them were of many shades of stone, imported from across the empire to signify and embody power. The colours grew lighter as they ascended to complete the illusion of height, and the arches framed gigantic statues. It had long been assumed in the Greek world that any self-respecting city needed a theatre, and the conqueror of the Greek East brought that urban ideal with him. This theatre was to be a public amenity, not an indulgence in Greek-style holiday decadence but an inherent part of civilized life.

The sole performance space in this theatre is the stage. From at least the time of Lycurgus, the Greek performance space had been split in two: a high shallow

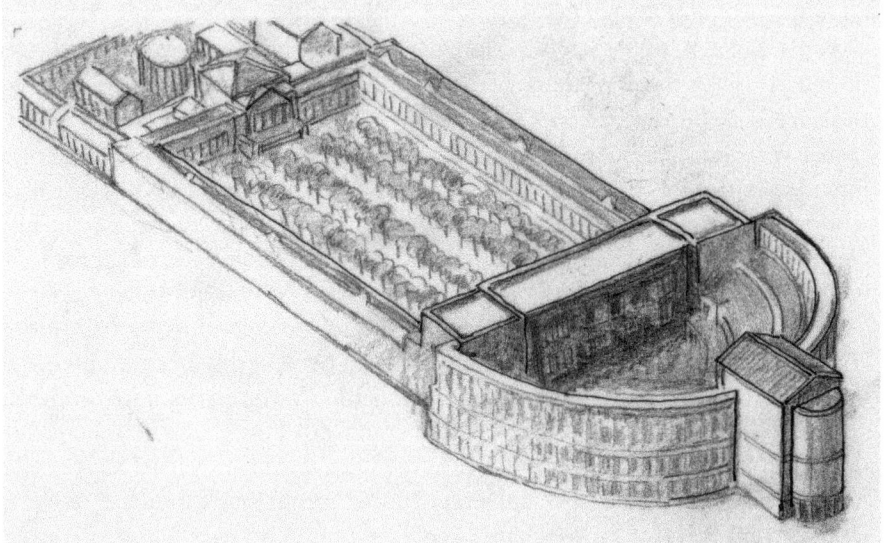

FIGURE 4.4: The theatre-complex built by Pompey. Drawing by Gayna Wiles.

stage for the three actors, and a dancing space or 'orchestra' for the chorus in the form of a part-circle. From a structuralist perspective, one might argue that this spatial divide reflects culturally significant binaries that divided speech from dance, thought from feeling, history from myth, man from god, the individual from the collective. Roman theatre preferred a single large stage, suitable for grand heroic statements rather than choral expressions of equality, and the orchestral space allocated to the Greek chorus was now given over to Roman senators, content to position themselves as the people's representatives. Greek choral dancing was seen as the expression of democratic collectivity, and deeply un-Roman.

Unlike Greek theatres, the Roman theatre was an enclosed space, sealed off from the surrounding city by high walls on all sides, allowing no sense of interconnection with the sordid and unruly world of the street, nor in Greek fashion with the natural world of sea and mountains. There was not even much contact with the sky in the Theatre of Pompey, since a huge awning was put in place to create shade for the audience, who lacked the benefit of any breeze from the side. The Emperor Nero replaced the plain awning with one made of purple, and had himself depicted in the centre, riding across the sky in a solar chariot, in an imperial fantasy which symbolized the ultimate conquest of the natural world by human technology (Cassius Dio 63.6.2). The difference between Greek and Roman theatres was a fundamental one. The Greek theatre created a bond between human society and a natural world which was also the world of the gods; Roman theatre sought to create an artificial paradise. The Romans drove straight roads through the landscape, while Athens was a maritime power – and to sail one has to reach an accommodation with the natural world, not simply master it.

Nero claimed to be a god, but Pompey did not. Pompey's theatre was dominated by a towering temple to the goddess Venus Victorious, whom he considered to be the patron of his military victories. Since in Homer's *Iliad* Venus was the champion of Troy, this new temple to Venus in Rome was intended to signify that Pompey was descended from the Trojan hero Aeneas, whom Virgil would later celebrate as a founder of Rome. The auditorium could be experienced as an extension of the temple steps, echoing the relationship of goddess and theatre on the Palatine Hill. Like Dionysus in Athens and in Thorikos, the goddess Venus was the most important spectator, and she alone could gaze from her lofty position at the world beyond the theatre, looking at eye level towards the Temple of Jupiter on the Capitol. It is hard from the perspective of the twenty-first century to gauge just how strongly Romans felt theatre to be a rite performed to please the gods, just as it is hard to conceive how the killing of gladiators once constituted a religious offering.[30] What is clear is that later theatres abandoned the notion of the Theatre-Temple, preferring the Platonic idea that the perfect circle of the auditorium echoes the circle of the cosmos. In a Greek tradition which we can trace back to Pythagoras, it was assumed that the different spheres of the cosmos generated a perfect music inaudible to the human ear. Vitruvius developed the principle that the theatre should be in essence a machine engineered to create a perfect acoustic, and in this philosophical conception of performance space, it is hard to tease human and divine worlds apart.

In recent years, as more theatres have been excavated in the Athenian demes, archaeologists have begun to question whether the fifth-century Greek playwrights could really have written such subtle and sophisticated texts for a mass audience of some 15,000, with the actors' words lacking the support of an acoustic bowl such as the Lycurgan auditorium provided. Masks helped to amplify sound and made the face seem closer and clearer, and actors devoted many hours to training their voices, but was this sufficient?[31] The shape and dimensions of Pompey's theatre present no such uncertainties about scale, though we cannot tell quite how tight the crowd was packed. His theatre probably held some 25,000 spectators, wrapping more people around the side of the stage than Lycurgus was able to do on the slope of the Acropolis, and he built a much bigger stage, 95 metres in width. Since actors on this stage could not benefit from the reflected sound bounced up by the empty Greek orchestra, and were dwarfed by a gigantic stage façade, the place was better suited to operatic singing, to dance dramas known as 'pantomime' and to other forms of spectacle, than to the spoken word. The great tragic actor Aesopus was brought out of retirement for the opening ceremonies in 55 BCE, but Cicero, who was fortunate enough as a Senator to be seated in the orchestra, complained that his voice had deteriorated (*Letters to Friends* 7.1). Cicero was dismayed by the vulgarity of the miscellaneous performances on offer – but then, the theatre was not built to satisfy the taste of men with a literary education. Although we know little about the repertoire, it is clear that in Rome as in Athens the building of stone theatres marked the end rather than the beginning of a great age of dramatic writing. This observation should not cause us to underestimate the cultural importance these theatres had in the life of the city.

What Pompey provided for the people of Rome was not just a theatre but a substitute for the Roman Forum, the traditional home of plays and entertainments. This was a new visionary city centre, sealed off from the decay, squalor and chaos beyond its walls. Behind the stage façade were arcades surrounding a park laid out with sculptures, trees and fountains. At the opposite end of the complex was a 600-seat Senate House, and as in the Forum there were shops along the south side. On the central axis, a statue of Pompey holding a globe in his hand signified that Pompey's conquest of the world had given Rome this urban paradise. It is likely that the original stage façade was a temporary wooden structure, allowing the whole complex to function as a single integrated space when plays were not being performed – and when they were, the arcades remained a convenient place to shelter from the rain, take refreshment, and inspect Greek paintings that represented the heroic world of tragedy. Unlike the Roman Forum, Pompey's architectural complex was symmetrical, cool and orderly. As a new construction it inevitably lacked the genius loci of the ancient Forum, though Pompey took care to preserve a heritage space on the east of the complex, where four ancient temples were framed by a dedicated courtyard. Pompey's rival Julius Caesar responded by creating his own Forum, complete with a Temple of Venus, and in addition planned a new theatre of his own. It was probably the Emperor Augustus who made Pompey's stage wall permanent, so the theatre was closed off, no longer to be encountered as but one part of a multifunctional urban space. Pompey's statue was at this point moved into the theatre, so posterity would remember him merely as the builder of a place for entertainment.

Ovid's guide to the art of love, written in the reign of Augustus, suggests what it felt like to be a spectator in Pompey's theatre. The poet (or rather, his fictional persona) ponders where a young man may pick up a woman, and Pompey's arcades on a hot summer's day seem an obvious choice, though in the last resort even the Roman Forum might provide opportunities. A theatre performance strikes Ovid as the ideal place to identify the choice on offer. Women arrive in groups, he says, either in an orderly line like ants or buzzing about like bees, all dressed up: 'They come to spectate, and to be themselves the spectacle. This place is the ruination of chaste propriety' (*Art of Loving* 1.99–100). Sitting so far away in this huge auditorium, Ovid has to use sign language to communicate with the women he has been ogling. He goes on to evoke the sumptuous atmosphere created by the marble stage wall, the awnings overhead and the scent from pools of saffron on the stage. To support his view that theatres are natural places of seduction, Ovid tells the old tale of how Romulus, on the grassy slopes of the Palatine Hill where theatre first began, rewarded his fellow Roman males by allowing them to abduct future brides from the audience. Ovid's behaviour in the theatre contrasts with his behaviour at chariot races in the Circus Maximus, where he is free to sit next to his beloved and make increasingly intimate physical contact, and the same freedom prevails at gladiator fights in the Forum or mock sea-battles beside the Tiber. Unlike these more dispersed viewing places given over to pure excitement, the theatre auditorium was a space for regulated public display. The principle that the most important performers in the theatrical environment were the spectators would continue to hold good in theatres from the Renaissance until the advent of modernism. Before the era of stage lighting classical-style theatres conferred exceptional permission to stare at members of the opposite sex.

Ovid's libidinous fictional persona was unable to cuddle up next to a woman at the theatre because of recent regulations which included placing women around the lip of the auditorium, protected from the sun by the shade of a portico, and safe from rich predators like himself, even if dangerously close to plebeians who could not afford the uniform of a white toga. This young man would have had to sit with other unmarried men, and indeed under Augustan legislation would have been forbidden to enter the theatre at all if he had failed to do the duty of a good Roman citizen and marry by his mid-twenties.[32] Roman Republicans had long been wary of permanent theatres as potential sites of sedition, and the reservation of orchestral seats for Senators was followed equally contentiously by the reservation of the first fourteen rows for the Equestrian order, the next tier down in the social hierarchy. Spectators dispersed along the sides of a racing track could not threaten political authority in the same way as an audience in the theatre, who might feel supported by mutual eye contact and a shared acoustic to respond with a single voice. Augustus followed Pompey in making this potentially dangerous theatre an instrument to control the forces of anarchy. The colour coding of costume, with thick bands of purple fringing the white fabric of the senator's toga, thin bands for the equestrians, and crowns of green oak for honoured soldiers, turned the auditorium into a visual map, and the dull colours of the poor contrasted with the bright unregulated colours of women on the periphery. This encircling theatre was conceived as a microcosm of the god-given cosmos, and Augustus was determined that Roman society after decades of turmoil should replicate the same perfect order. A stratified audience was an audience that could be controlled.

In both Greece and Rome, I have traced the history of a transformation, as the idea of theatre came to be associated with a particular place, built in stone to form an essential part of the fabric of a regulated and apparently indestructible urban environment. Beyond this parallel, the difference between Greece and Rome is a profound one. Pompey's theatre complex was a man-made rival to the adjacent Capitoline Hill, the home of Jupiter the sky god, patron of performances in the Roman Forum. His fountains and the neatly ranked plane trees in his gardens testify to a Roman will to subdue nature through the power of technology, treating the natural world like yet another conquered nation. We should be careful, when weighing up the Greek and Roman achievement, not to idealise democratic Greek city-states with their propensity for endless warfare. The value of the *Pax Romana* ('Roman Peace') should not be underestimated. Nevertheless, in the twenty-first century when human beings seem to have reached the limit of their ability to control the forces of nature, it is worth reflecting upon the extent to which the modern world, thanks to the Renaissance, has inherited the ambitions of Rome, while the Greek project of accommodating human beings to the natural world has become an alien one.

CHAPTER FIVE

Circulation

Theatre as Mobile Political, Economic and Cultural Capital

PATRICK HADLEY

Drama, a quintessentially Athenian creation, spread quickly beyond Athens' borders and into every corner of the ancient world, passing through a variety of media, languages and meanings with each new audience. The term 'circulation', used here as a deceptively simple catch-all to describe this process, needs some initial qualification. A concept inspired by reception studies, circulation is interested primarily in the agents who actively take it upon themselves to make a work of art mobile, and in the audiences who make that mobility possible, profitable and even necessary. These agents include actors, stagehands, painters, potters, poets, civil authorities, conquerors and their soldiers, colonizers and traders – a list only slightly narrower than the list of potential audiences for ancient drama, which would eventually include nearly everyone in the ancient world. Where traditional studies of textual 'transmission' have sought only to trace grammatical and orthographical changes in a classical text from one anonymous scribe to the next, studies in circulation cannot afford to be so narrow: while texts themselves, in the form of playscripts carried by actors and readers, did indeed move around the ancient world, so did performances, pictures of plays, schoolteachers with demanding expectations of their students' abilities to recite drama, and orators thoroughly skilled in the ability to quote from tragedy and comedy. Study of circulation thus necessitates an understanding of remediatization, of the effects that a change in medium will have on the reception of a work of art, and, more than anything, a serious and sustained inquiry into why, exactly, such widespread circulation and remediatization would take place in the first place. These are the questions that this chapter will attempt to answer.

Stephen Greenblatt has broadly suggested that all drama will be mobile, so long as a skilled writer has imbued it with 'ease or at least the illusion of ease', which would mean, inter alia, a relative lack of topical and chronologically – or culturally-specific customs, settings, or ideas driving the plot.[1] Following a similar line of thinking as new scholarship began to suggest the exportability of Athenian drama some thirty years ago, many classicists sought to explain the apparent international nature of ancient plays by both writing off their Athenian localizations and other topical elements, and by finding foreign localizations within them that would appeal to non-Athenian audiences.[2] This research has been very successful at adumbrating certain features of Athenian drama that may have aided its exportability, but the quest to excise and insert localizations and topical allusions in ancient drama can become quixotic: as some chief examples of ancient dramatic circulation will demonstrate, drama did not require 'ease' to be mobile in the ancient world. The wonder of a newborn artistic medium and the depth of its interaction with issues of importance to all of humanity,[3] combined with the cultural and (at least for a time) political hegemony of the city that created it, was enough to make Athenian drama instantly appealing to political and intellectual elites across the Mediterranean, which guaranteed its mobility.

This can be seen already in our first extant ancient drama, Aeschylus' *Persians*. Scholars have long been fascinated by a note in the ancient bibliographical tradition of Aeschylus which claims that the *Persians* received a performance in Syracuse during the reign of the culturally ambitious tyrant Hieron I. The fundamental consistence of all the ancient (albeit relatively late) sources which report on Aeschylus' sojourns in Sicily have left no doubt that the poet did, indeed, spend part of his career on the island, visiting at least twice.[4] While this is now uncontroversial, the precise timeline of the visit which saw the performance of the *Persians* has given rise to a dispute that only a philologist could love: the *Persians* was performed in Athens in 472 BCE, followed by the Theban tetralogy in 468 BCE, followed by the death of Hieron I in 467, leaving a window of only four years during which Aeschylus would supposedly have been able to reperform the play in Syracuse. Making rough estimates about the time needed to travel and prepare, many scholars have assumed that the performance of the *Persians* in Syracuse must have been in 470. This, however, would make for a very tight schedule devoted almost entirely to travel, a schedule which could only be deemed necessary, or even likely, if we assume that the first performance of *Persians* must necessarily have taken place in Athens. As Katherine Bosher demonstrated, doing away with this unnecessary assumption allows us to posit a much more realistic timeline for

Aeschylus' travels to Sicily by placing him in Syracuse at some point before 472. This could potentially explain not only the peculiar emphasis on the (otherwise unremarkable) Sicilian performance transmitted in the *Vita*, but also some troubling peculiarities of staging in the play itself. For example, while scholars have long debated how and when the ghost of Darius would have entered the action in the Theatre of Dionysus in Athens, Bosher demonstrated that the theatre at Syracuse, unlike the Athenian Theatre of Dionysus, would likely have been able to accommodate this entrance through an underground passage.[5] With the balance of probability, then, we must conclude that the very first extant play of Western Drama was first performed not in Athens, but in Syracuse, where, in the absence of a native tradition of Sicilian tragedy, it seems to have filled a distinct cultural gap.

The impetus for this performance, and for the sense of a cultural gap existing in the first place, was not a narrowly Athenian civic pride, but a broadly Greek pan-Hellenism, blossoming into temples, athletic contests, and epinician poetry all across the Mediterranean in the period after the Persian Wars.[6] Some 250 years previously, Homer's *Odyssey* had already expressed the idea that Greeks, and especially early Greek colonists, were a civilizing force in a wild and threatening world populated by frightening, cannibalistic and irreligious savages.[7] The successes of the Greek (and especially Athenian) military forces at Marathon, Plataea and Salamis solidified this self-conception and provided plenty of raw material to the Athenian propaganda machine, which set about conflating pan-Hellenic ideals with the ideals of the new (and fantastically wealthy)[8] Athenian Empire, and ensured that any Greek ruler worth his salt would seek to imbue himself in the culture of those who had driven back the tide of oriental barbarism and continued to publicly bear the mantle of the 'bastion of Greece' (*Hellados ereisma*) (Pindar fr. 76 Snell-Maehler).[9] Thus the broad praise of 'Hellas' and 'Hellenes' in the *Persians*, which only briefly lapses into specific praise of Athens and Athenians (e.g. 230–45, 347–9, 353–60), could apply equally well to the Syracusans in their continuing fight against the Carthaginians and Etruscans, as to the Athenians in their continuing fight against the Persians.[10] At the same time, the play's constant emphasis on the importance of strong, enlightened leadership, whether democratic (Athens) or autocratic (Darius), would have ensured that the play reflected well on Hieron and his regime.[11]

Drama's exalted status as *the* fundamental expression of Greekness in a colonial Mediterranean context became ever stronger in the years after Hieron's death,[12] and so did the connections between the performance cultures of Athens and Magna Graecia. These connections are borne out by records both literary and material. We will begin with the former, and in particular, with a passage from Plato, the implications of which had been very badly misunderstood until recently:

> Therefore, he who thinks he makes tragedy well, doesn't run around showing it in the other cities outside Attica, but brings himself straight here and, as is only fitting, shows it to these people.
>
> (*Laches* 183a–b)

Plato is obsessed with the theatre: he knows and uses it to the same degree that he despises and distrusts it (see also chapter 6 in this volume by Revermann).[13] His interlocutors' many statements on its ill effects upon the Athenian citizenry, its ability to beguile and mislead with nothing more than a simulacrum of a shadow, have therefore been mined time and again to ascertain the place of theatre within Athenian civic and intellectual life in the century leading up to the conquests of Alexander. Knowing this, and being broadly aware of the Athenocentric scholarship on Greek drama which dominated the field up until recently, translators of the *Laches* in years past seriously misrepresented the meaning of these lines, manipulating (or genuinely misunderstanding) them to imply that the only options for a writer of tragedy in the fifth century would be to bring his plays directly to Athens, or to take them to some of the smaller towns in Attica. Thus W.R.M. Lamb's still-current Loeb edition (1924) renders this sentence: '[a]nd for this reason he who thinks himself a good writer of tragedy does not tour round with his show in a circuit of the outlying Attic towns, but makes a straight line for this place and exhibits to our people, as one might expect'. Even Chris Dearden, in an excellent and truly foundational study of the means by which Attic drama was exported outside Athens, makes this same misreading.[14] As Chris Emlyn-Jones has recognized,[15] however, Plato's Greek clearly means that the other option for a would-be successful tragedian is to perform in cities 'around' (περὶ) and 'outside' (ἔξωθεν) Attica, with the Attic peninsula itself being the point of reference, and not its capital city. The important implication, left unstated and unexplored by scholars until recently, is that this is not the *only* other option: Laches' would-be poet would indeed be foolish to take his plays elsewhere if he were already near Attica, but the proud Athenian general cannot make the same claim for a tragedian in a region far from Attica. As he surely would have known, and as Aristophanes was already noting some forty years earlier,[16] it was entirely possible for a playwright to find success far from Attica, not only by bringing Athenian plays to other Greek audiences, but even by writing plays especially for non-Athenian audiences, just as Aeschylus did.

Plato's other interlocutors seem to think that the best place to do this was Sicily and Southern Italy, where the manner of awarding prizes was deemed more democratic and easier to work to the playwright's advantage than the Athenian system, which gave voting power only to a small number of judges (*Laws* 659c). The lure was enough, anyway, that half a century after Aeschylus was said to have died in Sicily, the comic playwright Phrynicus followed in his footsteps to seek his own fortune in the West.[17] Aristophanes, too, seems to have had no trouble having his densely topical and 'Athenian' plays reperformed in Southern Italy, as our current extant text of the *Lysistrata* of 411, with its Spartan closing song and final call for a hymn to the Doric and South Italian goddess *Athena Chalkioikos*, most likely indicates.[18] Though a late witness, Plutarch is not alone in transmitting a story which maintained that Athenian prisoners of war, held after their disastrous defeat in the Sicilian campaign of 415–413 BCE, were finally freed by their captors when they were able to teach (or perhaps simply recite) songs from Euripides' plays.[19] This would not be the only time that tragedy would help smooth relationships between Athenians and Syracusans: the first-century compiler Diodorus Siculus tells us that the Syracusan tyrant Dionysios I finally realized a long-cherished ambition when, in 368/7 BCE, a date precisely coincident with a new treaty of friendship between Syracuse and Athens, the Athenians awarded him the first prize at the Lenaea for his tragedy, *The Ransom of Hector*.[20] This fortuitous victory may be attributed to nothing more than political expediency, but the same expediency can hardly have been the reason that major Greek intellectuals continued to read and know his tragedies well into the Byzantine period.[21] Likewise, no political motives can be used to explain why Aristophanes, as early as the *Wasps* of 422 BCE, was inserting jokes from Epicharmus' Sicilian comedies into his own works (*Wasps* 1253ff.), nor why Xenophon, some fifty years later, would have Socrates himself quoting the Sicilian comedian as a moral authority (*Mem.* 2.1.20).[22] Nor were Epicharmus and Dionysius the only non-Athenian playwrights to achieve fame in Athens: precise numbers are difficult to come by, but ultimately, of the nearly 100 ancient tragedians whose names are known to us from the fifth and fourth centuries BCE, Oliver Taplin has found that 'well over 10 per cent are "foreign"',[23] meaning 'not Athenian'. Eric Csapo has even argued that many of those who are counted as Athenian citizens may only have been given that honour later in life as part of an official programme to attract and retain the best tragedians for Athens, since competition from other cities holding dramatic festivals in the fourth century had seriously threatened to dethrone Athens as the dramatic centre of the Greek world.[24] Indeed, a careful prosopography of the Hellenistic actors' guilds has demonstrated that the actors themselves, the party most responsible for the circulation of drama in performance, hailed from every corner of the Greek world, with Athens only being one of the top five sources of stage talent.[25] Though Athens always retained a certain pre-eminence as a centre of dramatic production, all the literary sources attest to 'circulation' in the truest sense of the word by the fourth century, at the very latest, with playwrights, actors and playscripts moving readily back and forth between Athens and the cities that had initially emulated her in the production of drama. Only the choruses tended more frequently to stay in place, as is most likely indicated by the mark *chorou*, or '[song] of the chorus', preserved in some later dramatic manuscripts as a remnant of a practice whereby, following the gradual decrease in the importance of the chorus as a mover of dramatic action, locally-provided choruses would be used to provide choral interludes better suited to local tastes and experiences than those written for a first performance in another city.[26]

While these literary sources are scattered chronologically and occasionally dubious, they all agree on the fundamental narrative that drama had exploded out of Athens by the end of the fifth century BCE, and become an essential part of Hellenic culture and identity across the Mediterranean by the fourth, by which point 'Athenian drama' begins to yield to 'Greek drama'. Material remains from these periods corroborate this narrative so thoroughly in terms both quantitative and qualitative that this chapter can only hope to give a brief overview of their importance, while guiding readers to the more comprehensive studies upon which the modern field is based. Though Syracuse remained an important bastion of dramatic production, the rapid expansion of drama outside of Athens proper does begin in Attica, where smaller (but still substantial) theatres are already being built in the rural demes perhaps as early as the late sixth century, and are certainly proliferating by the mid-fifth century, when inscriptional evidence attests unequivocally that they were drawing top dramatic talent.[27] This is in keeping with Laches' later insistence that talented poets come first to Attica, though not necessarily Athens itself. With all of Attica regularly producing excellent plays throughout the year, a reliable market was created for experienced and talented actors and playwrights, who were ready and able to take their act on the road.[28] They received the opportunity to do so when audiences came en masse from all over to attend these Rural Dionysia,[29] then returned to their home cities eager to reap for themselves the cultural and financial benefits that the festivals had brought to every corner of Attica.[30] Actors and audiences thus both become mobile in the fifth century, and the sphere of their circulation – especially that of the actors, whose remuneration afforded tremendous freedom of movement – only continued to expand as time went on.

Thus theatres sprout up quickly outside of Attica, numbering at least ninety-five permanent theatres by the end of the fourth century.[31] Although every truly Greek city worth mentioning was eventually required to have a theatre, the presence of a theatre at any given archaeological stratum cannot necessarily be taken as evidence of dramatic performance, as the same spaces could be used for political gatherings or for staging dithyrambic or athletic contests, for example. Some communities, however, also produced artistic evidence that attests to a rich and lively theatrical performance tradition outside of Athens. The most important of this evidence comes from the Greek colonies and their neighbouring Italic towns situated along the Gulf of Taranto in Southern Italy. Here the Athenians founded a (theoretically pan-Hellenic) colony, Thourioi, in 444/3

BCE, from which Attic vase-painters had brought their craft to the wealthy, powerful and populous Doric colony of Taras (modern Taranto) in Apulia, just across the gulf, by 400 BCE. At Taras these craftsmen soon become pre-eminent in their field, eclipsing, both qualitatively and quantitatively, the workshops of the Athenians by catering to a market the size of Athens, with two theatres and a notoriously (exaggerated) single-minded devotion to drama that would make even the medium's mother city blush.[32] At the same time, trade connections with Athens and the local colonies began to bring dramatic performances and new ceramic arts to nearby native Italic settlements, turning Southern Italy into a veritable factory of theatre-related vase-paintings, catering to an audience growing ever more familiar with ever more sophisticated performances.[33]

Not all of the vases produced for the markets in Southern Italy are equally valuable as evidence for dramatic circulation, though they do cumulatively, together with anthropological and historical research, amount to a clear picture of the spread of drama. In particular, the less explicitly dramatic iconography of vase-paintings with scenes familiar from tragedy has engendered some debate in scholars of ancient dramatic circulation, who cannot entirely reach a consensus on whether these were simply broadly mythic and inspired by a received story, or specifically tragic, and inspired by a viewed performance. Oliver Taplin, however, has convincingly argued that tragedy itself quickly became the most powerful vehicle for the spread of mythic tales, and has also catalogued several 'signs' in mythico-tragic vase-painting, which, when added together, often demonstrate with a high (though always indefinite) degree of certainty that Attic tragedy was played in Southern Italy and Sicily, and did inspire many who went on to depict its stories on vases for a public familiar with the stories primarily through performances.[34]

Comic vase-paintings are generally much more explicit than tragic vase-paintings in depicting performances of plays. Part of the reason for this is the simple fact that comic plots, unlike tragic plots, do not, as a general rule, exist outside of the play itself.[35] We can, therefore, point to numerous comic vase-paintings inspired by performances, which shed an invaluable light on the nature of the circulation of both tragedy and comedy in the ancient world. At the same time, the patent popularity of Attic comedy in the West belies any efforts to claim 'ease' as the chief motivating factor in dramatic circulation. For example, the lasting popularity of densely topical and Athenian comedies in the Greek West can be seen in a famous Apulian, most likely Tarentine, bell crater, now called the 'Würzburg Telephus' (Figure 5.1), and inspired by a scene from Aristophanes' *Women at the Thesmophoria Festival* (performed in Athens in 411 BCE).

In this scene, a playful parody of Euripides' *Telephus* (performed in 438 BCE, also in Athens), a man disguised as a woman threatens to sacrifice a 'child', actually a wineskin, if the women in attendance do not give him a fair

FIGURE 5.1: The so-called 'Würzburg Telephus'. Apulian bell crater, 375–350 BCE. Martin von Wagner Museum der Universität Würzburg (H 5697). Photo: P. Neckermann.

hearing.[36] Certain elements present on the vase, but lacking in the script for this particular play, give indications that the vase-painter was at pains to demonstrate the elements which helped make this scene funny as a comedy in performance, but not necessarily as a script for reading. The two most important such elements are the presence of a woman rushing to catch the 'blood' of the sacrificial victim with a large wine goblet, instead of the sacrificial basin called for by the text (line 754), and the old age (signalled by the mask) of the woman (called 'Mika' in Aristophanes' script) who comes to the rescue of the 'baby' wineskin (there is no indication in the script itself as to Mika's age).[37] Where the reader of the playscript can detect and appreciate the tragic parody in the text, the presence of the drinking goblet in performance would elicit from the audience a raucous laughter that simple reading could never provide, since spectators would enjoy the clash between the formal and sacrificial register of language used by the woman fetching the 'sacrificial basin', and the low-brow comic stereotype of the bibulous woman actually stumbling forward with a drinking goblet.[38] Similarly, Mika's old age adds an additional humorous dimension in performance to her claim of having given birth to the 'baby' wineskin (line 741f.). We can thus be reasonably certain that Southern Italy contained a community familiar enough with Aristophanes' *Women at the Thesmophoria Festival* to appreciate a pot inspired by a performance of it. By extension, this same audience would have to be familiar enough with Euripides' *Telephus* to appreciate the depicted scene's parody.[39] We can, therefore, be relatively certain that, when we see the numerous non-parodic depictions of the same story on Southern Italian pottery,[40] they are, at least in part, inspired by – and appealing to an audience familiar with – a performance of Euripides' tragedy, even in the absence of anything explicitly theatrical or performative on the vases themselves.

Though *Women at the Thesmophoria Festival* is the most interesting and least ambiguous case of a performance fragment of an Attic Old Comedy playing in the West, it was certainly in good company: the ceramics of the Greek West give ample evidence of comic performance, and among the handful of instances where external evidence allows us reasonably to suggest which play is being depicted, we can potentially number comedies from every member of the canonical triad of Athenian Old Comedians, including Eupolis' *Demes*, Cratinus' *Wine Flask*, *Dionysalexandros*, and *Nemesis*, and, adding to the list of Old Comedies that would necessitate some knowledge of tragedy for fullest appreciation, Aristophanes' *Frogs* and *Acharnians*.[41] Alongside these Athenian standards, native West Greek comedy from the tradition begun by Epicharmus is assuredly very well represented, even if we often lack the plot summaries and titles for these plays that would allow us to match a ceramic performance fragment to a particular Western play or author.[42]

In addition to Attic Old Comedy, we have also found fascinating evidence of the performance of Attic New Comedy in the West – evidence that provides the missing link between Greek theatre and Roman theatre, and that demonstrates how and roughly when the Greek medium began to transcend boundaries of language and ethnicity to become truly international. From roughly 330 BCE comes a Sicilian krater with a depiction of a scene, possibly from Diphilus' *Allotment*, in which a young woman is brought forward to marry a young man after a slave disguised as a woman duped the young man's lecherous father into believing that he was the object of his affection, causing him embarrassment and thereby exposing his faults and winning the young man's right to marry the real young woman.[43] This complex plot of confused identity and stock characters acting in a domestic setting – clever slave, enamoured young man, lecherous older man, and young woman of servile status who is eventually revealed to be a rightful citizen and thereby entitled to citizen marriage – is the stuff of New Comedy, which flourished in the latter half of the fourth century BCE. Though we do not have the text of Diphilus' play, we know it from its adaptation as the *Casina* of the Roman playwright Plautus.⁴⁴ Perhaps unfortunately, though, by the time the Romans were producing their own dramas in Latin, red-figure theatrical vase-painting had all but died out as an art form, with the consequence that we have no ceramic illustration of Plautus' *Casina*, as opposed to Diphilus' *Allotments*.⁴⁵

FIGURE 5.2: Campanian oeinochoe, later than 350 BCE. London, British Museum F 233.

We do, however, have at least one very late intermediary, which gives evidence of the translation of Greek drama to the Italic-speaking peoples, in the form of an oinochoe, a vase for pouring wine, from Campania, roughly 300 kilometres northwest of Apulia (Figure 5.2). Dated from some point after 350, the oinochoe features a comic character typical in most ways, but lacking the dangling phallus normal for every other depiction of a Greek (Old) comic character. Most important, however, is the presence of the name 'Santia', inscribed in retrograde letters above the character, most likely representing the Oscan version of the Greek name Xanthias, a common name for the stock slave character of New Comedy. What this vessel most likely indicates, then, is that Oscan-speaking peoples were familiar with Oscan-language versions of Greek plays by the late fourth century, and liked them well enough to want to commemorate them. Or, as Oliver Taplin neatly summarizes it, 'the Italianizing of Greek comedy well-known to us through Plautus and Terence, has begun around the Bay of Naples by soon after 350'.[46]

At the same time that the more demotic genre of comedy is making its first attested inroads into other languages, elites ruling the top-down societies of the late classical and early Hellenistic Mediterranean were ensuring the spread of tragedy as a marker of cultural, and hence political, value to non-Hellenic audiences. Not only is it likely that tragic vases, such as the famous Pronomos Vase, were produced for and by native Italic consumers familiar with tragic theatre,[47] these same vases also provide more indirect evidence explaining why, exactly, Greek drama would have appealed to non-Greek audiences in the first place. The most famous vases from Magna Graeca with mythico-tragic scenes on them likely were used at symposia and in other domestic contexts at one point or another,[48] but they were ultimately destined for use as (and preserved for us because of their use as) grave or funereal goods, whose serious themes of life, death and the will of the gods, together with their depictions of Dionysus, god of both theatre and the sacred mysteries, made them appropriate to accompany an accomplished person into the afterlife, and leant themselves to eulogistic speeches on the occasion of burial.[49] Indeed, many of the tragic vases found in Apulia could never have had any practical use, as the techniques used to fire them (and, indeed, their unfinished and occasionally even porous state) would have precluded them ever even holding liquid.[50] These goods completely bypassed the popular market and went straight to the tombs of wealthy men, and it is to these men that we must look to learn more about the spread of theatre beyond Greek-speaking communities.

Anthropological research and archaeological evidence demonstrate clearly the close relationships that existed between Italic natives and Greek colonists in Southern Italy. Grave goods and even literary evidence discussing the popularity of Hellenic Pythagoreanism among the Oscans, give clear evidence of the philhellenism of the upper echelons of native Italic societies.[51] We can see early instances of this in Italic Ruvo, whose vase-paintings certainly demonstrate a real familiarity with sophisticated travelling performances of comedy, and may even, when weighed together with the city's longstanding trade connections with Athens, have led to some of the first and most successful performances of tragedy for Italic audiences in Italy.[52] Once bonds of *xenia*, a divinely protected institution of guest-friendship, had been established between colonizers and natives, as we know they were in Southern Italy, it quickly became inevitable that the Greeks would share with their new neighbours the single most exalted and elite expression of their culture, drama.[53]

This process was given impetus by its longstanding and very successful use in the courts of the Macedonian rulers and the heirs of Alexander the Great: just as Aeschylus had written plays to flatter his Sicilian host, Hieron, Euripides joined the tragic poet Agathon and a number of other accomplished Athenian artists in Macedonia, where they turned their efforts to glorifying the kingdom's Argead dynasty. For Euripides, this meant penning such plays as the *Archelaus* in celebration of a mythical ancestor of the ascendant Macedonian king of the same name, who was on a path to hegemony in the whole of Greece, and needed badly to counter frequent Athenian accusations of barbarism and cultural poverty, while shoring up his own position amid rival claimants to the throne at home.[54] In fact, the close connections between Euripides and Archelaus have very plausibly been suggested as the primary reasons why Euripides went from being viewed as a divisive innovator within a year of his death,[55] to being considered a solid classic a generation later.[56] Philip of Macedon, Alexander's father, inherited his forebears' longstanding obsession with using theatre, and especially the speaking and performing powers of a cadre of professional actors, to present an air of culture to his new subjects in Greece, and his ancient biographers thought it all too appropriate that he was assassinated in a small theatre in 336 while presenting a spectacle of Macedonian theatrical and cultural accomplishments to an audience of international elites.[57] We certainly know that wherever his son, Alexander the Great, went, he brought dramatic performances with him, and he and his successors founded a string of theatres stretching from Egypt and Asia Minor to Afghanistan, where the theatrical remnants at Ai Khanoum, together with archaeological finds containing imprints of Greek verse which may possibly amount to a fragmentary playscript, provide our most tantalizing and exciting proof of the far-flung appeal of Greek drama.[58]

Eric Csapo and others have called the 'privatization' of theatre the single greatest innovation in Philip's and Alexander's appropriation of Greek theatre. Relocating theatre from large, public festivals to smaller, more selective performance environments, Philip and his son used highly paid professional actors to perform only select tragic odes for small groups of men who were then marked as culturally, and hence politically, elite.[59] When Alexander and his successors paid for their own performances at large banquets, military camps and ceremonies, such as the mass wedding ceremonies held between Greek soldiers and Persian women at Susa in 324 BCE, locals inevitably witnessed them, and came to associate drama, and the lavish command[60] performances thereof, with the high culture of their new ruling class.[61] When Roman mercenaries inevitably enrolled in the armies of Alexander's successors, their commanders returned home with a taste for the hierarchy-affirming power of the same type of ostentatious performances,[62] and re-integrated themselves into a society whose southern edges, areas such as Apulia, Sicily and Campania, were populated by Italic-speaking elites who had long since developed a taste for Greek theatre, and had even begun to translate it. The Roman elites created from this fertile cultural exchange a theatrical tradition that both preserved and fetishized older Greek drama as a cultural commodity, while simultaneously encouraging new generations of Roman playwrights to create and disseminate a new national drama based on earlier Greek models.

Although ritualistic mimetic performances lacking any real plot – likely an adaptation of Etruscan apotropaic ritual – may have begun at Rome as early as 364 BCE,[63] it is no surprise that the earliest playwrights working in Latin are reported to have had very close links with the Greek and Oscan-speaking south of Italy. Thus Livius Andronicus, who produced the first dramatic performances with plots at Rome in 240 BCE, came, perhaps as a prisoner of war, from Taranto, where he was assumed to have had ample contact with the Greek and Oscan theatrical traditions.[64] Andronicus' contemporary and Rome's next great dramatist, Gnaeus Naevius, most likely came from the Osco-Samnite area of Campania, near where the 'Santia' vase was produced.[65] Likewise the leading light of the next generation of Latin writers, Quintus Ennius, is said to have boasted that he 'possessed three hearts, since he knew how to speak Oscan, Greek, and Latin', having come, perhaps also as a prisoner of war, from Apulian Rudiae, near Taranto.[66]

What Andronicus introduced in 240 BCE quickly became immensely popular, so that by the end of the Second Punic War in 201 BCE the Roman calendar contained six festivals at which dramas, or *ludi scaenici*, were regularly performed. Individual votive games put on by victorious military commanders or mourning noble families could increase the number of occasions for dramatic performance significantly; while the Roman religious custom of *instauratio*, whereby a ritual would have to be repeated if any fault was found in its performance, could extend the occasions for performances almost indefinitely.[67] The communities of production that came to service this demand in Rome did, in part, overlap with those that had helped spread dramatic performance in the Greek world. Impresarios brought the troupes and props to the stage; magistrates purchased the scripts from poets, who had formed a professional/sacred guild by 207 BCE; and eventually an empire-wide umbrella organization for the various groups calling themselves the 'Artists of Dionysus', the guilds of professional actors and stagehands who had helped enable and professionalize the international theatrical business in the Hellenistic period, took over a large part of the business of dramatic production in the Roman Empire.[68]

All of these performances were hotly contested, however, for at no time did drama circulate in the Latin-speaking world without the express support of the powers that be, or of powerful men with potentially dangerous ambitions to supplant them. Thus the senate was compelled to pass laws limiting the amount spent on festivals, and particularly on the 'occasional' spectacles sponsored by powerful individuals or those seeking office, while also making a concerted effort to prevent the construction of (or simply to tear down) any permanent theatre spaces that might be used for the same end.[69] This did little to stop the truly ambitious, and it is telling that the ever more elaborate occasional festivals and attempts at permanent theatres finally culminated in the spectacular stone theatre built and dedicated as a temple by the victorious general and future triumvir Pompey in 55 BCE, which was inaugurated with an outlandishly lavish spectacle hitherto unseen at Rome.[70] Six years later Julius Caesar would cross the Rubicon, eventually defeat Pompey, and announce plans for a theatre to rival that of Pompey,[71] which would not be completed until the reign of his nephew had guaranteed the permanent annihilation of the Roman Republic, and with it the construction of 'innumerable new theatres' throughout the Roman Empire.[72]

Under the empire, access to theatrical spectacles became one of the most important public services offered by the government, and the construction of theatres remained a priority for Roman elites in need of popular support until well into the sixth century.[73] During this same period, however, we also begin to see authors focus more on a real shift in the nature of Roman dramatic performance – a shift that highlights the alternative paths by which drama had already been circulating for some time. One good example of this focus can be found in Suetonius' description of the emperor Nero's efforts at performance: where most potentates and emperors advanced their standing with the people by merely providing dramatic performances and building theatres, Nero seems to have misunderstood the lessons of Pompey and Augustus, and opted to win his people's hearts (and horrify the senatorial class) by performing in an amphitheatre carefully packed with imported Alexandrian claques (Suet. *Nero* 20–21; cf. Tac. *Ann.* 14–16; Dio Cass. 63.9–10). Of greater interest to us than the sordid details of Nero's shameless self-promotion at the theatre, however, are the details about what and how he performed: rather than acting a part in a play alongside other actors, Suetonius says that Nero donned masks to sing the parts of individual characters, including 'Raging Hercules, Blinded Oedipus, Canace in Labor, and Orestes the Matricide' (Suet. *Nero* 21.3). The same emphasis on arias is seen in a contemporary story (though of an earlier generation) that has the Parthian king's hired actor singing the part of Pentheus from Euripides' *Bacchae* for the entertainment of the gathered Parthian and Armenian courts, spontaneously seize the newly delivered head of the defeated Roman consul, Crassus, and use it as a prop to quickly switch to singing the suddenly apt part of Agave deliriously celebrating a successful 'hunt' by gloating over her son's severed head (Plut. *Crassus* 33).

This emphasis on solo arias is in keeping with a broad change in theatrical tastes that began in the imperial period. In particular, tragedies and comedies began to lose ground throughout the Roman Empire to pantomimes, balletic dances by virtuoso performers set to choral singing. Initially scorned at the higher orders of ancient performance competitions, by the early third century CE pantomime had become the most popular type of performance in the world, whereas there is almost no evidence of traditional drama being performed in large settings in the Roman Empire in this same period.[74] As tastes gradually changed, traditional drama did its best to keep pace: those who kept writing it, such as Seneca, may have been already incorporating the popular balletic and operatic elements of pantomime into their playscripts by the first century CE;[75] those who kept performing it, such as Nero (and his more-talented and professional contemporaries), abandoned the elaborate plots familiar to Plautus, Naevius and Sophocles, and focused instead on showcasing the virtuoso singing abilities that were making pantomimes so popular.

These varied means of circulation, decontextualized and detached from the traditional festival and performance contexts to become a badge of culture for the upper classes, may come to the fore in later sources, but they are not unique to the later, Roman performance traditions. In fact, Athenian Old Comedy of the fifth century BCE already shows an awareness of the various media and means by which drama was then circulating. In Aristophanes' *Frogs* of 405 BCE, Dionysus himself, as a character, discusses his favourite aspects of some famous contemporary tragedies from two very different standpoints: that of a spectator sitting and watching a performance in a theatre, and that of a person of leisure reading plays in his idle time. Dionysus appreciates the *Persians*, the play with which we began our study, from the former standpoint, excitedly proclaiming, 'I was especially happy when I heard that part about Darius being dead, when the chorus put their hands together like this and shouted, "iauoi!"' (1028f.). Dionysus' praise here is strange and, for him, somewhat embarrassing, since the death of Darius is not discussed in the *Persians* such that Dionysus could hear about it, nor does the chorus ever shout 'iauoi!' in lament.[76] It seems that Dionysus is merely excited to learn something that everyone else in the audience already knew – that Darius is dead. Dionysus' inept criticism is only appropriate to his buffoonish character in the play, however, as his inability to understand and appreciate good tragedy, simple historical facts, or even the most basic Aeschylean language[77] is played for laughs right up until the end of the play. When Dionysus excitedly proclaims his love of a play that he clearly cannot remember or properly appreciate, he is playing the part of a comically (and perhaps atypically) misinformed theatregoer to great comic effect. When he reacts to drama as a private citizen reading playscripts in his leisure time, however, he largely reflects the interests of the moneyed classes whose tastes and habits will recur time and again in the history of dramatic circulation: he loves Euripides, and he loves reading plays to himself.

This 'literary' form of appreciating the classics of fifth-century Athens far outlasted the strictly 'performative'. While its advent is ironically hailed by the chorus of *Frogs* in 405,[78] some seventy or so years later Aristotle's *Poetics* gave it real permanence by relegating spectacle (*opsis*) to a position of minor importance, as compared to those aspects of a dramatic plot which lend themselves to the minute analysis of literary details that only the wealthy have time and money to appreciate.[79] Dionysus' own description of his reading habits reflects this same class, since he is presented as a man who, though shipboard and supposedly serving in the navy like the rest of the Athenian workers (*thêtes*), has the inexperience at rowing typical of the Athenian moneyed classes,[80] and so takes to reading Euripides instead:

> And there I was onboard, reciting the *Andromeda* out to myself, when suddenly a great longing struck me right in the heart, so hard you can't imagine.
>
> (Aristophanes *Frogs* 51–4)

Dionysus must specify here that he was 'reciting *Andromeda* to [him]self' (*anagignôskonti moi pros emauton*) because the act of reading in the ancient world was often a performance in itself, intended for an audience of one's peers.[81] Reading or reciting dramatic passages aloud in front of others, and especially passages from Euripides, was such a ubiquitous type of performance by the Hellenistic period, that it became the subject of a humorous epigram by Callimachus (48 Pfeiffer), wherein a dramatic mask on the wall of a schoolroom yawns with boredom as yet another student rises to recite the *Bacchae* for his class. When the Romans learned to appreciate and exploit drama from the Hellenistic kings, they also adopted the Hellenistic elite culture of reading and recitation, which would have a lasting impact on the ways that drama circulated. This impact can be seen in the attitudes of later, more literary Roman elites, whose approaches to drama reflect the earliest Roman appropriations of Greek drama.

Cicero, for example, was perhaps the most prominent Roman of the classical era to promote familiarity with drama as a necessary weapon in the arsenal of the *orator*. This is perhaps most prominent in the *De Oratore*, where he stresses the importance of well-trained, well-read and naturally talented orators to act as statesmen and leaders for the Roman people. A central pillar of the Roman orator's education, according to Cicero's interlocutors, is the reading and rehearsing of works by early Roman tragedians. Thus Antonius gives prominent place to 'the speech of the tragedians, and the gestures of the veritably best actors' among the attributes that a successful orator must possess (*De Orat.* 1.128), and the dialogue's other participants go on to portray the comic actor Roscius, whose pupil Cicero himself may have been, as an embodiment of the grace and physical performance capabilities required of an orator.[82] Particular mention is also made in the *De Oratore* of passages from plays by Accius, Ennius, Pacuvius, and an unknown Roman comedian, to which the good orator can turn for guidance in expressing a range of different emotions (3.217–19).[83] The experience of Crassus, in the same work, is perhaps the most illustrative of the Roman nobility's approach to drama: Crassus states that he had been in the custom of memorizing and then declaiming upon works by Ennius in order to improve his ability to extemporize in a controlled manner, but that he found himself unable to improve upon Ennius' words in his own Latin declamation, so he instead decided to memorize great Greek dramatic works and declaim upon them in Latin (*De Orat.* 1.154–155).[84] In so doing, he essentially recreated the creative process of Ennius and the other early Roman dramatists, who adapted, via translation, the Greek dramatic canon into Latin.

This wholesale acquisition, via translation, of another culture's literary works is part and parcel of Roman imperialism from the earliest days of the Republic to the revival of *Romanitas* as a cultural aspiration in the Renaissance of the fourteenth century CE. While early attempts at Roman translation, such as Livius Andronicus' groundbreaking translation of Homer's *Odyssey*, may be more truly 'philhellenic' rather than 'philattic' (to coin an ugly phrase) in their goals, this process largely displays the already ancient obsession with claiming the cultural capital of Athens, even when Roman scepticism about the virtues of Greek culture may tinge this obsession with irony. Such is the case in Plautus' *Asinaria*, where the play's *adulescens*, a generically foolish and pretentious (if lovable) comic character, needlessly insists that his concubine 'know how to speak no language but Attic' (793), immediately after insisting that she use no confusing (*perplexabile*) language. Part of the humour in this passage arises from the tension between the Athenian setting of the play's Greek model(s), and the Latin language and Roman culture that inform the play's coherence in Plautus' version: a Roman audience can laugh at the *adulescens*, because the very success of Plautus' translation belies his insistence on the unique primacy of the Attic language and Attic culture.

The same pride in Roman translation and adaptation, tinged with the same tension, receives its strongest and most earnest endorsement in Cicero's *Tusculan Disputations*, where the elder statesman finally does away with his interlocutors to explain what motivated Plautus, Terence, and Ennius, and to urge his countrymen to continue their work of translating Greek works into

Latin. In so doing, Cicero explicitly invokes the cultural capital, *laus*, that he, like Hieron many centuries earlier, wishes his country to gain from such works:

> I urge all who can to steal away praise (*laus*) of this sort from Greece, which entered decline some time ago, and bring it into this, our city, just as our ancestors, by their efforts and zeal, brought thence all those relics which were worth seeking out. . . . If these studies are brought in among us, truly we will not even need Greek libraries, which today contain the vast majority of books, simply because the majority of writers have written in Greek.
> (Cicero *Tusc.* II.5f.)

Although in this context Cicero is speaking of philosophical works, in particular, he elsewhere praises the early Roman dramatists for being the first to undertake this monumental project of snatching away (*eripiant*) praise from Greece, as he does when using the 'literally translated' (*ad verbum expressae*) dramas of Ennius, Pacuvius, Caecilius, Atilius, and Terence to justify by *exemplum* his own translations of Greek philosophy (*Fin.* 1.4f.).

Theatrical performances of dramas, pantomimes and the more nebulous mimes, eventually died out entirely in the face of disapproval from the authorities of the rising Christian church, who were as horrified at the licentiousness of the sub-literary mimes as they were deeply concerned, much like Plato, with the dangerous freedom of theatrical *mimesis*; perhaps more than anything, however, the newly minted bishops and priests harboured serious anxieties about the competition that a theatrical community, complete with popular approval and the financial support of the upper classes, could present to the alternative community of the Church.[85] While dramatic performance of classical theatre withered and died, however, Cicero's endorsement of literary familiarity and oratorical utilization of drama remained salient. The *laus* that Attica and its drama could bring to the Roman West remained a necessity for Roman noblemen, even as Germans, Turks and Arabs rapidly whittled away at the very state that stood to benefit from familiarity with the brightest lights of the Theatre of Dionysus. Thus fifth-century Gaul, during the rapid collapse of Roman power, can present us with the spectacular paradox of the Church Father Salvian vehemently disapproving of theatrical performances that are not actually taking place,[86] while the Church Father Apollinaris carefully self-presents as dedicated to the regular reading of playscripts by Menander, which he could compare learnedly to the Roman adaptations of Terence.[87]

As Europe entered the mediaeval period, knowledge of Greek gradually disappeared from the Latin West. Dramatic authors such as Terence, who had earned the approval of the earliest Romans for their ability successfully to capture for Rome the *laus* of Attica, were assured of their places in mediaeval curricula, and continued to receive the literary study and schoolhouse recitations that had been such a central part of earlier circulation;[88] but the demand for all the glory and praise that original works from fifth-century Attica could bring would not be satisfied until the mechanisms of ancient circulation from Greece to Italy were re-activated in the fifteenth century CE. As Byzantine diplomats and refugees fled to Italy in search of respite and protection from the rapidly advancing Turks, they brought with them an invaluable treasure. The Latinate public of the Italian Renaissance, figuring themselves as the direct heirs of Rome and her culture, were happy to overlook any and all religious objections to Aristophanes' obscenity, when they could read on the cover of the first ever printed edition of his plays, from 1498, that Theodore Gaza, a leading Greek scholar in Italy, recommended 'just Aristophanes, because he is very acute, fluent, learned, and pure Attic',[89] while Lilius Giraldus (1479–1552) would be even more explicit, recommending Aristophanes to his contemporaries on the grounds that he contained 'all the ornaments of the Attic language'.[90] Finally, in 1585 we see the Roman ideology of translation and adaptation reaching out to again claim the *laus* of Attica for a new generation of Italic peoples in need of the lessons of Athens' greatest artistic accomplishments. That year saw the staging of a lavish Italian version of Sophocles' *Oedipus Rex* at the Teatro Olimpico in Vicenza, the first vernacular version of an ancient Greek tragedy to reach the Italian stage in some 1,500 years.[91] That the audience was largely wealthy, powerful, and concerned with being seen as culturally ascendant and sophisticated, was in keeping with the most important forces driving dramatic circulation for the previous 2,000 years.

CHAPTER SIX

Interpretations

The Stage and its Interpretive Communities

MARTIN REVERMANN

INTERPRETIVE COMMUNITIES

Ancient theatre reached many interpretive communities: the broadly stratified audiences of up to 15,000 or even more who crowded large outdoor venues, or those members of the elite who would finance performances in the more exclusive setting of their homes (bearing in mind that watching theatre is, among other things, always an act of interpretation); poets, historiographers, speechwriters and other literary artists who drew on theatrical texts for motifs, characters or quotes that might suit their argumentative goals while at the same time embellishing their products (there is no description, let alone prescription, of theatre without interpretation); visual artists working in genres as diverse as vase-painting, mosaics and the ornamentation of walls; scholars who were interested in the stories or language(s) of the scripts and the biographies of those who created them; philosophers who would argue not only about aesthetics but, more fundamentally, about theatre's position in social and moral life; and in a cognate category, religious polemicists, invariably of Christian faith, who viewed ancient theatre, its stories as well as its practitioners, as a threat to the one-and-only way of representing and talking about the divine and, even more threateningly, an obstacle to redemption, regardless of whether they encountered the theatre in ancient poetry or in its various performative manifestations (especially, in late antiquity, as pantomime or mime).

The very range and diversity of these interpretive communities and their critical responses is itself eloquent testimony to the depth and breadth of the cultural impact which the mass-medium theatre was to exercise throughout Graeco-Roman antiquity. It is also indicative of a profound lack of indifference: the medium theatre mattered, throughout antiquity, albeit in different ways to different people at different times. A reader from the incipient twenty-first century may be struck, perhaps even alienated, by the staunch anti-theatricalism of a Plato or Tertullian. But the intensity of the negatives might also be viewed by the contemporary theatre-lover with a sense of yearning and nostalgia: as eloquently hostile as they were, surely the likes of Plato and Tertullian deeply *cared* about the theatre and the central role it was evidently occupying in their respective societies. Who in our media-saturated and globalized present world, one might legitimately ask, still cares so vehemently about *theatre* as they did?

But what exactly does 'interpretation' mean? I am using it in this chapter as an umbrella term to describe the processes (intellectual, emotional, evaluative) with which ancient audiences, of whatever description, made sense of theatre. The act of interpretation(s) therefore is a necessity, not an option, to anyone exposed to the theatrical artefact (in whatever format). We should, of course, be aware not only that the interpretive outcomes may vary significantly for ancient and twenty-first-century recipients respectively, but that the very processes, negotiations and mediations involved may be very different. The question 'what does Oedipus mean for me/us?' made sense to Freud and Vidal-Naquet, and it probably made sense to ancient recipients as well. But if the somewhat garbled words by the chorus at the end of our text of Sophocles' *Oedipus the King* (lines 1524–30) are any indication, the question was framed quite differently from how psychoanalysts or structuralists would pose, let alone answer, it many centuries later: Sophocles has the chorus emphasize Oedipus' exemplary fall from greatness as an illustration of the general unpredictability of the human condition, rather than viewing him as an extreme test case for the uncanny machinations of the human soul and its meticulous dynamics of repression, or as a mythical symbol for the cognitive ordering of a messy reality by means of binary oppositions.

The notion of the interpretive community, whose members are then historically contextualized, is the conceptual and organizational centre of this chapter. Such communities can be formed by a range of common denominators, especially physical co-presence (audiences at a live performative event, for instance) or shared professional, social or ideological background. They can be real or imagined, stretching across times, geographies and other, non-physical, divides. What sets them apart from other forms of social organization is that they coalesce and become *interpretive* communities, around certain issues of cultural validation which function as 'crystallization points' and turn them into agents of cultural debate and cultural politics. Interpretive communities may be short-lived and not outlast the duration of a live performance and its immediate aftermath. At the other extreme, they may solidify as century-long traditions of cultural interpretation.

This choice of interpretive communities as the organizing principle comes, to some extent, at the expense of chronological order and the neatness of strictly sub-dividing the topic into a Greek and a Roman component. Nor are interpretive communities sealed-off monads, as one might initially take them to be: the potential overlap between the philosophical and the religious interpretive community has already been hinted at (Plato and Tertullian), and most members of the various interpretive communities discussed here will have shared the experience of being part of a live theatre audience at some point and with some frequency (even if the kind of theatre they saw differed over time). But the decisive heuristic advantage of choosing interpretive communities as the organizational principle is that this concept comes with the significant benefit of highlighting common types of responses to ancient theatre and modalities of thinking that were shared across time and societies, while also allowing for nuances and differences in historical context. If cultural history is by its very nature a messy enterprise, the notion of interpretive communities superimposes onto the mess that is culture a kind of order that is meaningfully broad yet manageable in scope.

SHOULD THERE BE A PERMANENT THEATRE IN ROME?

An example suitable to illustrate the dynamics of interpretive communities in action, as well as the difficulties of describing those dynamics, is the controversy within the Roman elite surrounding the construction of a permanent performance venue in the city of Rome for theatre productions. By the early second century BCE, Rome had a vibrant and successful theatre scene which attracted top-notch artistic talent, including the comic playwrights Plautus and Terence, neither of whom was born in Rome but who gravitated there and soon became classics. Yet, unlike other cities in Italy (especially in Southern Italy and Campania) of incomparably less political and cultural importance in the second century BCE, Rome did not have a permanent theatre venue until the mid-first century BCE.[1] Attempts were certainly made: up to four building projects, all initiated by Roman aristocrats in high-ranking administrative positions, are attested over the course of the second century BCE. But all of these projects were ultimately cancelled, at least one of them when the actual building was already quite advanced.[2] What cultural and political motivations triggered this kind of emphatic resistance is disputed and not entirely clear. It was evidently neither the theatrical performances themselves nor the prospect of a large public venue which were the bone of contention: the Roman stage was thriving throughout the second century, and with the *circus maximus* Rome of the second century BCE did have a huge sports venue, larger than any of the future permanent theatres or even the Colosseum (inaugurated in 80 CE). Instead, what appears to be at stake is the very permanence of a stone auditorium: its visibility and monumentality; the opportunities it provided for the ambitious sponsor(s) to highlight their munificence and financial prowess to the common people and rival aristocrats alike; and a concern that pervades theatre history throughout the centuries, namely the fact that the dynamics generated by a public gathering of a mass audience were even more unpredictable, and potentially uncontrollable, in a permanent structure than in a temporary one. The issue was probably aggravated by the link between theatrical performance and religious practice, with the former being perceived as potentially detracting from the validity and respectability of the latter.[3]

What masks itself as an architectural controversy is at its core politics manifesting itself as a battle between conflicting modes of cultural interpretation: Where and in what form does theatre have its place in Rome? Who is in control of that place and, consequently, the people who come there? Is being a Roman compatible with enjoying theatre entertainment, and how should this compatibility, if such exists, be expressed? By contrast, in no Greek city state did such a public controversy ever arise. In this cultural environment theatre occupied an uncontested and conspicuous place, in both physical and ideological terms. The preserved evidence gives some indication of this level of commonly shared acceptance, for instance the ways in which theatre is being used in Greek public oratory of the fourth century BCE or, at a later stage in the early centuries CE, in some of the preserved Greek novels. Thus, in a court speech given to male jurors chosen from across all strata of Athenian citizens, the fourth-century BCE politician Lycurgus quotes (and probably to some extent enacts) an extensive patriotic passage from a (now lost) play by Euripides, the *Erechtheus*, in order to bolster his case against an Athenian whom he was attempting to portray as a deserter of his own country. Possibly up to 800 or so years later, in Heliodorus' novel *Theagenes and Charikleia* which is probably the latest of the preserved Greek novels and may date from as late as the fourth century CE, theatre (especially tragedy) is regularly being invoked for the reader as a point of reference and comparison at a higher level, to make sense of the complex action as it unfolds and add grandeur as well as pathos.[4] In these communicative contexts – the Athenian public courtroom or the Greek literary space created by Heliodorus' novel and its anticipated readers – everyone involved in the process of interpretation implicitly recognizes that theatre is a socially constructive, culturally potent and hermeneutically useful tool of expression and reference. This contrast of radically different macro-level interpretations and disputes over what ought to be theatre's place, both physical and ideological, in Greek and Roman society respectively marks the enormous and often extreme range of cultural responses to the theatre that were voiced in antiquity, creating a polyphony of interpretations and interpretive communities that attests to the great vitality and ongoing relevance of theatre in the cultural history of Graeco-Roman antiquity.

PHILOSOPHERS

Poetry was a concern for the philosophical interpretive community from very early on: Plato in fact refers to 'an old quarrel between philosophy and poetry' (*Republic* 10, 607b6f.). Traces of this pre-Platonic critical and polemical discussion are preserved in fragments from Xenophanes, Heraclitus and Democritus, even though it is surely significant that the Athenian Plato (c. 427 to 347 BCE) is the first philosopher known to us who polemicized against the *theatre* in particular rather than poetry and poets (especially Homer and Hesiod) more generally (itself a further clear indicator of the standing and cultural impact which theatre had acquired by the fourth century BCE). The 'crystallization point' for this interpretive community, until (and emphatically including) Plato at least, was the question of poetry's truth value and its contribution to the quest for wisdom (*sophia*), both of which were, of course, areas to which philosophy itself laid fundamental claims. This territorial contest over claims to wisdom and moral authority resulting from them lies at the heart of the early philosophy *vs.* poetry debate which is often characterized by conflict and opposition.

Plato and Aristotle are the most prominent, best preserved and most influential members of the philosophical interpretive community engaging with the theatre, which is why these two are bound to receive the lion's share of any discussion on this topic. Post-Platonic and post-Aristotelian philosophical discourse on theatre is very hard to outline, even in the most general terms, as a result of meagre evidence (the same applies to ancient scholars of the period working on theatre, see Hanink in this volume on 'theatrical scholarship'). The work *On Poems*, preserved in fragments on papyri from Herculaneum, by the Epicurean poet/philosopher Philodemus (c. 110 to c. 40 BCE) sheds some light on issues and themes of literary theory of his time, perhaps most notably the continuing relevance to the debate of Aristotle's concept of *katharsis*.[5] Yet, theatre does not seem to be of particular interest to Philodemus. It is, however, quite central to the *De arte poetica* by Horace (65–8 BCE), a prominence which has long startled critics, as Horace himself never wrote drama. But it may well be the result of Horace's principal source, the third-century Peripatetic poet/ philosopher Neoptolemus of Parium, and its preferences.[6] The philosopher-poet Seneca (4 BCE–65 CE), one might think, would potentially be a rich source for philosophical reflection on theatre and drama, but there is an odd disconnect between Seneca's theatrical output (*if* the dramatic works transmitted under his name are in fact by him in the first place) and the lack of response to it in Seneca's preserved philosophical writings.[7] Looking at the bigger picture in the post-Aristotelian era, it does seem reasonably clear that Aristotle and his legacy in the form of the Peripatetic school of philosophy fundamentally reshaped the discourse within the philosophical interpretive community for centuries to come. The discussion moved away from moral and epistemological questions to a more formalistic type of analysis centred on issues like diction or plot construction – even if the moral dimension was never totally forgotten before rising again to great prominence with the emergence of Christian intellectuals who took aim at the contemporary pagan entertainment industry.

PLATO

Much of Plato's philosophical thinking is idiosyncratic by the standards of his time, and his take on the figurative and performative arts is no exception. In particular, his fierce anti-theatricalism stands out even more against the previously discussed backdrop of widespread acceptance of theatre in classical Greece (even it must be said at the outset that the very intensity of the philosopher's criticism is itself eloquent testimony to how much poetry in general, and theatre art in particular, actually mattered to him). The inherent drama and theatricality of Platonic dialogues, on full display in a work like the *Symposium*, has often been noted. This is clearly indicative of some personal affinity to things theatrical and, probably, an attempt by the philosopher to transcend, supersede and replace theatre, as a site of reflection on key matters of human existence, by another art form, the philosophical dialogue (itself a performative genre). And it is worth noting that ancient writers interested in Plato's biography regularly ascribe to him a strong affection for the mimes by the Sicilian Sophron, short comic prose pieces which were probably written not for theatres but for performance at drinking parties (*symposia*).[8] Making such a connection, whether ultimately true or not, seemed plausible to at least some in antiquity.

Plato's issues with theatre and performance are not of a narrowly aesthetic nature but are situated at the interface between epistemology and ethics, hence for Plato at the core of philosophy's task of reflecting on what constitutes a good and virtuous life. In the *Ion*, probably an earlier Platonic dialogue from the early fourth century BCE, a performer of epic poetry (*rhapsôdos*) is shown to be ignorant of any of the many subject matters covered by the Homeric poems, and to be 'artless' in the sense of not possessing a proper craft (*technê*, a term which in Greek, significantly, denotes both 'art' and 'craft'). Poets and performers of poetry like the rhapsode Ion, argues Plato, are not expert craftsmen of anything but produce by divine inspiration in the mental state of *enthousiasmos*, which means 'having the god in oneself' (*entheos*).[9] A poet is a mere vessel, an interpreter (*hermêneus*) of the divine, which renders the performer 'an interpreter of interpreters'.[10] From the perspective of a modern critic Plato's theory of *enthousiasmos* in the *Ion* may be reminiscent of the cult of the genius in Romanticism, hence complimentary in nature. But to an ancient Greek recipient the dialogue's conclusion that the rhapsode Ion is 'divine (*theios*) but not an expert (*technikos*)' rings distinctly ironic. What Plato insinuates here is that poets and performers are, at best, divinely mad. At worst, they are nothing but posers.[11]

In view of what Plato elsewhere has to say about the detrimental nature of the written word and the superiority of oral communication (*Phaedrus* 274b6–278b7), one might expect that for him the thoroughly performative nature of classical Greek theatre would go some way towards mitigating his criticism of it. But never is this possibility explored. On the contrary: in the final book 10 of his arguably most ambitious and far-reaching work, the *Republic*, Plato sets out to justify in detail the exclusion of mimetic poetry (which emphatically includes dramatic poetry) from the ideal state as previously advocated in books 2 and 3. The train of thought developed at the beginning of book 10 of the *Republic* (595a1–608b3) is in part epistemological and closely connected to Plato's theory of ideas, in part psychological and related to Plato's conception of the human soul. The latter line of argument posits that theatre appeals to the irrational part of the soul (*to anoêton*) at the expense of the rational one (*to logistikon*), in particular by making the spectators experience emotional extremes similar to those represented by dramatic characters onstage (esp. *Republic* 10, 605b9–d5). The epistemological argument, on the other hand, maintains that since our empirical world is itself ontologically removed from the world of ideas (which is accessible only to the mind), the mimetic artist who imitates the empirical world – Plato explicitly mentions painters and playwrights – is consequently one additional step further removed from the world of ideas:

> (Socrates) 'This, I believe, the god did knowingly, wanting to be truly the maker of a bed that existed truly, and not some bedmaker of some bed. That is why he made the bed one by true nature.'
> (Glaucon) 'So it seems.'
> (Socrates) 'Do you therefore want to call him the creator of this thing, or something along these lines?'
> (Glaucon) 'This is indeed justified', he said, 'since in its true nature he has created this thing and everything else.'
> (Socrates) 'How about the carpenter? Is he not the maker of the bed?'
> (Glaucon) 'Yes.'

(Socrates) 'And the painter – is he the maker and creator of such a thing as well?'
(Glaucon) 'Not at all.'
(Socrates) 'But what would you call him with respect to the bed?'
(Glaucon) 'To me at any rate', he said, 'he seems most appropriately be called the imitator of that which those others are makers of.'
(Socrates) 'So', I said, 'you are calling him the imitator of the third product from true nature?'
(Glaucon) 'Absolutely', he said.
(Socrates) 'So the maker of tragedies will be this as well, since he is an imitator, that is someone who is thrice removed from the king and the truth, and this applies to all other imitators as well.'
(Glaucon) 'It appears so.'

(Plato *Republic* 10, 597c11–e9)

As nothing but an imitator of the empirical world, which itself is nothing but a reflection of the world of ideas, the painter, the tragic playwright and figurative artists in general are in no position to provide insight and truth (something which for Plato remains the exclusive prerogative of the philosopher). In this context it is interesting to note that Plato never considers the hermeneutical status of actors and embodied performance, which presumably is an imitation (by performers) of an imitation (by playwrights), hence yet another step removed from the craft of the playwright and as a result four-times removed from the true world of ideas. But making this point would have been superfluous, as the decisive blow to theatre art has, of course, been dealt already: it is fundamentally flawed at its very inception, the creation of a script. A further important point here is the fact that when Plato talks about tragic playwrights, Homer is being subsumed under this label, as Plato explicitly considers him 'the leader of tragedy' and 'the first of tragedians' (*Republic* 10, 598d9 and 607a2, cf. 600e4f. and 605c10). This conflation, itself not surprising given the close and often observed affinity between Homer (especially the *Iliad*) and tragedy, is crucial for justifying Plato's most radical move, the banning from the ideal state of all poetry including Homer with the exception of hymns to the gods and songs of praise for good men (*Republic* 10, 607a2–5). But it is also a helpful reminder of the important fact that Plato's anti-theatricalism is embedded within a much larger cultural critique which, especially when extended to the uncontested cultural icon of Homer, goes to the core of Greek identity and cultural self-perception. And the prominent, indeed indispensable (if negative) role which tragedy assumes in Plato's argument only confirms its enormous and pervasive cultural presence. Plato himself is keenly aware of this, and in the closural remarks to this section of the *Republic* (10, 607b1ff.) adopts a mode of rhetoric which appears to be more conciliatory. After all, Plato concedes, poetry (especially that of Homer) has an enchanting spell (*kêlêsis*) that has been deeply engrained since childhood. Since this spell of poetry is potentially dangerous, philosophical argument can and needs to be used as a counter-spell against it. In this context, Plato also points out that the preceding reflections are only part of a larger and long-standing polemical argument between poetry and philosophy about their respective roles and merits, and it is conceded that, should poetry find astute defenders who could convincingly argue that poetry might actually be useful to the well-governed city, its (re)admission into the community is a distinct possibility.

ARISTOTLE

The interpretive community of philosophers had, for all we can tell, limited appeal, visibility and reach in antiquity. This applies to many important areas of people's lives. Religion is one of them, theatre is another: Plato did not re-configure the ways in which Greeks navigated their complex religious system, and he certainly did not manage to stop them from flocking *en masse* to theatres in antiquity. Yet, the philosophical interpretive community was to become a major force in Western cultural discourse beginning with the Renaissance, far exceeding the limited influence it had exercised during antiquity. In large part this is the result of the meteoric rise to fame of one specific work, Aristotle's *Poetics*. This treatise, however, is a somewhat unlikely super-star. It is, like all non-fragmentary works by Aristotle (384–322 BCE) that have reached us, a so-called 'esoteric' work, i.e. intended for internal circulation within the academic community of Aristotle's philosophical school (the Lyceum); it had, for all we can tell, no discernible impact in antiquity; and a major part of it, Aristotle's discussion of comedy in the lost second book of the *Poetics*, has not survived the perils and vagaries of the medieval textual transmission.

It is also important to realize that the *Poetics* is only one of several other lost works, recoverable for us only in limited ways, in which Aristotle tackled issues related to drama, and that as a text designed for internal circulation it seems to use at critical junctures concepts in shorthand format that presumably received more detailed discussion somewhere in those lost works (the infamous term *katharsis* being a notorious example). The fullest and most prominent treatise on poetry, including drama, is likely to have been Aristotle's dialogue (in three books) *On Poets* which was an 'exoteric' work, i.e. written for public dissemination outside the Lyceum.[12] The *Homeric Problems* (in at least six books) must also have been important in this context, not least because the *Poetics* regularly compares and contrasts epic and drama (esp. in chapter 26). Moreover, we know that Aristotle engaged in important data collection by assembling the official lists of victors in the dramatic competitions at the Great

Dionysia in Athens. This taxonomical research by Aristotle, although lost to us as well, was to become foundational for scholars working on drama from the Hellenistic period onwards (see further Hanink in this volume on 'theatrical scholarship'). Among the preserved Aristotelian works the *Politics*, the *Nicomachean Ethics* and especially the *Rhetoric* cover some of the ground that the *Poetics* is also concerned with, even if the perspectives and priorities differ in each work. The *Poetics* cannot be dated with precision and, given its nature as an inner-circle treatise, may well be diachronically cumulative and combine thinking from various stages of Aristotle's career. That said, there is a tendency in scholarship to view the *Poetics* in the form we have it as a later work from the second Athenian period (335–323/2 BCE) in the philosopher's life which presupposes and synthesizes earlier thinking.[13]

Aristotle was a student of Plato's and spent twenty or so years from his late teens onwards in Athens at Plato's philosophical school, the Academy. It therefore comes as no surprise that the *Poetics*, and presumably all of Aristotle's writing on theatre, is a critical response to Plato. The general stance adopted by Aristotle is decidedly pro-theatrical, hence anti-Platonic (even if the *Poetics*, at least in the form we have it, contains no overt polemics against Plato).[14] For Aristotle, there is no question that theatre is ethically, intellectually and socially legitimate. It is also, Aristotle maintains (*Poetics* chapter 4), ultimately an in-built anthropological necessity, hence natural and inevitable. This is because the activity of mimesis ('representation') is shared by the members of humankind (as opposed to all other beings) from their childhood days onwards, providing knowledge, skills and not least pleasure. Mimesis for Aristotle is not the fraudulent distortion disabling human capacity for rational thought that it had been for Plato but, on the contrary, an enabler fundamental for human learning, growth and indeed well-being. Theatre as *the* mimetic art form is therefore an eminently constructive and socially beneficial form of natural human activity.

The preserved *Poetics* follows a clear structure. After setting out the means, objects and modes of mimesis (chapters 1–3) as well as the natural causes of poetry (chapter 4), Aristotle proceeds to make intriguing remarks about the historical development of tragedy and comedy and Homer's role in it (chapter 4–5). The centrepiece of the preserved *Poetics* is Aristotle's discussion of tragedy (chapters 6–22), followed by a discussion of epic (chapters 23–26) which culminates in an evaluative comparison of epic and tragedy, with the latter emerging as the superior art form. The end of chapter 26 has a distinctly closural feel and is quite certain to mark the end of book 1. We know from other ancient sources that the *Poetics* consisted of two books. Since at the start of chapter 6 (i.e. the beginning of the big tragedy section), Aristotle promises to discuss epic and comedy at a later point, and because epic does receive considerable attention in chapters 23–26, the main subject of the lost book 2 of the *Poetics* must have been comedy (a genre which Plato had referred to only occasionally).[15]

Throughout, the mode of argumentation pursued in the *Poetics* is an interesting hybrid of the historically descriptive and the normatively prescriptive. This is a direct function of Aristotle's mode of philosophical thinking in general which is teleological. Such an explanatory model assumes that on the basis of a variety of causes (*aitiai*) the constituents of the natural as well as the social world develop towards a specific goal (*telos*). As a result, any description and analysis of teleological development, notably in the social sphere, by default has to combine the historical ('how did tragedy develop?') with the normative ('what is the goal of tragedy?'). This approach is well illustrated by two of the most central chapters of the *Poetics*, chapters 6 and 14. In the former Aristotle begins his discussion of tragedy by introducing the following definition of the art form:

> Tragedy is the representation (*mimesis*) of a serious and complete action of magnitude, in its parts written in embellished language distinct in each of its forms, of action and not by report, bringing about through pity (*eleos*) and fear (*phobos*) the cleansing (*katharsis*) from such emotions.

Aristotle's definition combines formal and material features with functional and reception-oriented ones. Its most famous aspect, and notorious challenge, is Aristotle's use of *katharsis* in it. The problem is much aggravated by the fact that the term is being used as a shorthand here and not laid out elsewhere in Aristotle's other preserved writings (with the exception of a passage in *Politics* book 8 (1341b38ff.) which, however, deals not with *katharsis* in poetry but in music).[16] Interpretations of tragic *katharsis* have ranged widely over the centuries: as a means of moral improvement for the spectator; as an agent of moderation, closely tied to the notion of the mean which is fundamental to Aristotle's ethical thinking; or as a medical process of purgation which reduces excess and restores healthy harmony. In this maze of interpretations and receptions, it is easy to lose sight of a few important points that hold true regardless of which precise view of tragic *katharsis* is being adopted. One is that tragic *katharsis* is without doubt something positive and beneficial, which flies in the face of Plato's case against tragedy. Secondly, it is worth noting Aristotle's orientation towards the audience, be it as a spectator of tragedy performed in the theatre or as a reading recipient. Tragedy, via its ultimate goal which is to create *katharsis*, is conceptualized in such a way that its audience and the communicative relationship with it become integral and indispensable. This is a fundamental insight, and it has been crucial to much work in more contemporary Theatre and Performance Studies over the past decades which in general has been characterized by forcefully moving *away* from Aristotelian modes of theatre analysis and their emphasis on plot ('the soul, as it were, of tragedy', in Aristotle's memorable formulation at *Poetics* 6, 1450a38) and character.[17]

Space constraints prohibit further detailed discussion of a text as rich and thought-provoking as Aristotle's *Poetics* (which has lost none of its appeal and importance in the current age of post-dramatic and immersive theatre forms). Suffice it to outline, in the briefest of manners, the following major points. First, it is worth pointing out that the discussion of tragedy in the *Poetics* has interesting 'blind spots': the chorus, surely a major aspect of the art form, hardly receives any attention, while in Aristotle's secularized formalism tragedy's metaphysical dimension, in particular its representation of divinity which had been so offensive in the eyes of Plato, is passed over entirely. Also, while French Neo-Classicism, enlisting the authority of the *Poetics* for its own aesthetic programme, idolized the notion of the 'three unities' (of action place, time and action), no such rigidity is in fact found in Aristotle, despite the fact that the 'wholeness' (*to holon*) of the plot is regularly emphasized. Throughout, it is important to bear in mind that Aristotle is not a theatre practitioner (although he did write poetry, of which one small lyric poem is preserved[18]), and the *Poetics* shows fairly little interest in the performative dimension of drama. But, contrary to what is sometimes insinuated, Aristotle is not anti-performative either: the visual dimension (*opsis*) is being acknowledged – but of the six parts of tragedy outlined in chapter 6 of the *Poetics* (1450a38–b20) *opsis* is 'the most artless and the least central' (*atechnotaton de kai hêkista oikeion*) and therefore at the bottom of his priority list, after plot (*muthos*), character (*êthos*), design (*dianoia*), diction (*lexis*) and music (*melopoiia*). This backgrounding of the performative dimension in Aristotle has to be seen as an integral part of a major interpretive shift away from occasion towards structure, from poetry seen as embedded in the context of an event or occasion towards poetry as a self-contained and detachable unit of analysis.[19] The *Poetics*, therefore, influentially marks the beginning of conceptualizing theatre as script and plays as texts, which was to remain the predominant mode of analysis until the emergence in the 1930s of theatre semiotics. As a result, reading rather than watching becomes the (self-)sufficient mode of consumption: 'Moreover, tragedy achieves what is proper to this art form also without movement, like epic. For through reading it is evident of what kind each tragedy is' (*Poetics* 26, 1462a11–13). These hermeneutical shifts have big sociological implications: while in performance tragedy is easily accessible to the large and socially stratified audiences of Aristotle's time, as a script it is by default only available for consumption by the select few who have the literacy level as well as the time required for reading. Aristotle's conceptualization of tragedy therefore safeguards this cultural commodity for the elite at a time when it had become most mobile, not only geographically but also sociologically.

LITERARY ARTISTS AND LUCIAN'S 'ON THE DANCE'

From early on, the appeal of theatre as an important cultural reference point to literary artists more generally was high. Tragedy stands out here, because it offered a particularly appealing range of 'crystallization points' for the interpretive community of literary artists: of all theatre arts, it connected most closely with the shared world of Greek myth and its boundless imaginative possibilities (only pantomime, tragedy's successor as a mass art form in late antiquity, is in a similar position); it had the highest cultural standing and visibility of all theatre arts, thereby appealing to the elite, who were most invested in literary activity; it showcased highly articulate heroes and, perhaps even more importantly, heroines with complex personal histories and psychologies; and it displayed a degree of overt self-reflexivity on the human condition (articulated by the choral voice in particular) which lent itself to trans-generic appropriation. What emerges is the manifold use, by a wide range of literary artists, of what may be called the 'tragic scheme': extreme situations and conflicts involving the highest stakes and morally complex choices; sacrilege and other transgressions of taboos, especially those surrounding kinship-relations (parricide, incest, infanticide, matricide); death and sacrifice (including self-sacrifice); suffering and revenge, with little if any prospect of lasting closure or redemption; and the problem of the limits of human autonomy and self-determination in a world order ruled by fate and unpredictable divinities.

Herodotus already shows keen awareness for this kind of tragic scheme,[20] and a number of his key narratives are shaped by it. Thus Gyges' ascent to the Lydian throne (Herodotus 1.8–13) involves breaking the taboo of a stranger seeing the king's wife naked and the offended queen's cruel revenge by forcing Gyges to choose between his own death and committing the crime of killing king Candaules (thereby assuming the reign himself). Not only are the parallels to tragic predicaments evident, but we know that the Gyges story was, in fact, the stuff of tragedy: a papyrus fragment published in 1949[21] contains part of a tragic speech delivered by the Lydian queen in what must have been a full 'Gyges tragedy' for the stage. The similarities with Herodotus are staggering, although it continues to be uncertain and controversial whether this tragedy preceded Herodotus and shaped his story or whether conversely it is modelled on the Herodotean narrative.[22] Either way, however, the main point, at least from the interpretive perspective, remains unaffected: Herodotus deploys a tragic pattern here. Other instances of tragic colouring, motifs and story patterns in the Herodotean narrative have been noted (involving, for instance, the figures of Croesus, Polycrates, Periander, Lycophron and Xerxes).[23] Their existence demonstrates ongoing interpretive engagement with tragedy by the historiographer, in whose hands tragedy becomes a vehicle for expressing emotionally and reflecting cognitively on fundamentals of the human condition as they manifest themselves in world history and its principal agents. Similar patterns of characterization and narrative strategies can be discerned in other historiographers (e.g. Thucydides) and historiographical writings (e.g. Plutarch's biographies or the opening of Tacitus' *Dialogue on Orators*), even if the formerly wide-spread assumption that a specific type of post-Thucydidean 'tragic historiography' existed probably overstates the case.[24] Beyond historiography, tragic colouring informed a wide range of genres, most notably epic (the portrayal of Medea and Dido in Apollonius and Virgil respectively are cases in point) and Ovid (especially in the *Metamorphoses*).[25]

A particularly valuable literary artefact, however, does not concern tragedy but its effective successor as a widely performed mass medium, pantomime. Lucian's treatise *On the Dance* (*Peri orchêseôs*), probably one of his earlier writings dating to the 160s CE at a time when pantomime and mime were becoming the predominant modes of theatrical entertainment in the Greek East, is a uniquely interesting (and still too little-known) document of ancient theatre history.[26] Framed as a philosophical dialogue between the Cynic philosophers Crato (who opposes pantomime) and the philosopher Lycinus (who vigorously defends it), the treatise is *prima facie* positioned as a conversation within the interpretive community of philosophers. The history of that discussion is in fact invoked more than once. There is, for instance, the story of the conversion of Demetrius the Cynic from a critic of pantomime (much along the lines of Crato) to an ardent admirer of the art (63), and within a similar narrative of conversion pantomimes are called 'manual sages' (*cheirisophoi*) (69). It is pantomime, argues Lycinus, which makes people morally and intellectually better, even more so than philosophy. In fact, pantomime *is* philosophy, because in characteristically integrative fashion it is capable of embodying the philosophical principles of Plato, Aristotle and Pythagoras (70), and because it combines the 'useful' (*chrêsimon*) and the 'pleasant' (*terpnon*) in a unique way (71, cf. Horace *Ars Poetica* 333f.).

Beyond such arguments, however, Lucian shows a discursive range which far exceeds anything we have from the philosophical community. In particular, the strong emphasis on the pantomime as *performer*, whose art requires him to meet steep physical and intellectual challenges (74f., 81), is (for us) unheard of in an ancient theoretical discussion of the theatre. The same applies to Lucian's keen and nuanced interest in *audiences*, including their competence level, their social composition and the therapeutic effect which pantomime has on them (76, 79, 81, 83f., cf. Libanius 64.112). This is in part due to the fact that Lucian's treatise is 'anti anti-theatrical': since polemicists against the theatre (across the ages) tend to zoom in heavily on performative aspects of their target and the allegedly detrimental effects on its audiences,[27] this tendency is reflected in Lucian's rejoinder. But in part it is also the result of the simple fact that Lucian's spokesperson Lycinus makes the case for pantomime, a theatre art which unlike any other in antiquity relied (almost) exclusively on non-verbal sign systems, especially the dance and gestures of the silent solo dancer (who was wearing a mask with no opening for the mouth), in conjunction with the imaginative collaboration of its audiences.

Lucian's gem of a treatise, which has its closest analogue not in Graeco-Roman material but in some of Zeami's writings on Noh theatre, contains extraordinarily interesting remarks about the 'protean' nature of the pantomime (19), resulting in frequent mask changes (66f.);[28] the universal repertoire of pantomime which covers the whole range of Greek traditional tale, from creation myths to the brilliant dynasts known from tragedy (37); pantomime's transparency (*saphêneia*: 62) and universal appeal to all social strata[29] and to non- or half-Hellenized spectators alike (64, 81); the dangers of over-acting and over-identification of the pantomime dancer with his role (83f.); the competition of pantomime actors with each other (84); and the various competence levels of pantomime's broadly stratified audiences (76, 83f.).[30] The specific criticism launched at pantomime of being an effeminate art (2) which appeals to 'women and madmen' (5) is countered by extensive sections on the history of dance (8–25) and the omnipresence of myth, from which pantomime draws its subject matter, in the Greek cultural sphere (36–61). Since pantomime's mode of presentation (dance) as well as its object (myth) are deeply rooted and positively connoted, the art form itself is vindicated. More than that, by the end of the dialogue pantomime has emerged as more than rehabilitated art form: it is a superior form of human expression and self-reflection, combining the physical, the emotional and the cognitive dimension in a uniquely holistic fashion.

THE CHRISTIAN INTERPRETIVE COMMUNITY

It was not until around 200 CE that Christianity achieved the social respectability and prominence to engage with pagan high culture on a literary level, although sub-literary, orally delivered sermons on this topic surely had existed for a while. Once Christian intellectuals started around this time to reflect in writing on a distinctly Christian stance towards the theatre, the addressees of their treatises, Christians (often new to the faith) who were seeking guidance on the crucial question of how to reconcile their Christian way of living with the pagan world they were operating in on a daily basis, constituted a large and ever growing interpretive community similar in social stratification to actual theatre audiences. Theatre, as Ruth Webb has pointed out, then functions as the perfect rival against which emerging Christianity is able to define itself.[31] For if theatre is portrayed as a demonic 'anti-Church' created by morally depraved stage performers (including women who would work as mime actresses) and catering to the hedonistic delights of the senses (especially sight), 'thinking against theatre' as practised by Christian intellectuals emerges as a perfect means to formulate, and canvass for, the new, Christian 'counter-identity' in ways that were accessible to anybody. More specifically, the issues (or 'crystallization points') around which the Christian interpretive community forms are two inter-connected ones: first, the representation of the divine, both on stage and as part of the religious rituals which had always been embedding the theatrical event in antiquity (see also chapter 1 in this volume on 'institutional frameworks'); and secondly, the moral effect of theatrical representation on the spectator, especially the on-stage depiction of violence, sexuality and the female body. These issues are for the most part not new, but pick up and further develop arguments that had for a long time been made in the philosophical community, especially by Xenophanes and Plato (see above). It is also true that regularly anti-theatrical Christian critics only exacerbate views held widely by their pagan contemporaries, as openly expressed by the low social, civic and legal status of stage performers.[32] But for Christians, the problems surrounding theatrical entertainment present themselves with a different kind of eschatological urgency not found in the pagan philosophers (not even Plato, who comes closest) or in pagan legislation. For Christians, the ultimate point of reference here is redemption and the possibility of an eternal life with God. It is, however, important to add that this eschatological perspective also means that Christian opposition to theatrical entertainment is, strictly speaking, not an absolute denial of pleasure but a mere *deferral* – to the blissful afterlife and its rewards that await the faithful.

On Spectacles by Tertullian (c. 160 until after 212 CE) is not only the first preserved self-positioning of a Christian writer relative to pagan entertainment culture but also one of the most aggressive.[33] This is explained in part by the zeal of the convert, since Tertullian, who had clearly received an excellent and thorough pagan education, had only recently become Christian before writing this treatise in Carthage in 196 or 197 CE. More than that, however, for Tertullian and his fellow Christians, persecution and gruesome publicly enacted forms of capital punishment were constant and very real dangers, and under these circumstances what in Tertullian (*On Spectacles* 30) may seem sadistic pleasure of watching former tormentors receive punishment on the day of the Last Judgement can more sympathetically be considered an understandable human reflex of 'getting back'. Theatre is but one of the areas of pagan entertainment spectacles for Tertullian, and only in select instances the focus of his attention (esp. *On Spectacles* 10, 17 and 22). Like the circus, the hippodrome and the gladiatorial combats in the amphitheatre (notoriously popular in Tertullian's hometown Carthage), the stage is the site of 'idolatry' (*idolatria*) and perverse, indeed diabolic worship, while true spectatorial pleasure is re-directed and deferred to Christian conversion and the advent of the 'New Jerusalem' (*On Spectacles* 29f.). A few centuries later, John Chrysostom (c. 349–407 CE) and

Jacob of Sarugh (born in 451 CE) will take a similarly aggressive and intransigent anti-theatrical stance in some of their sermons, co-incidentally providing us with precious and often uniquely attested glimpses into the performance culture of late antiquity.[34]

What effect did ringleaders like these actually have on the large and amorphous interpretive communities they were catering to? The theatre forms of late antiquity – mostly mime, pantomime and tragic or comic excerpts performed by solo artists (*tragôidoi* and *kômôidoi*) – certainly continued to be very popular in the Christian empire, and it stands to reason that the sheer aggressiveness of the anti-theatricalism voiced here all but masks the fact that many Christians did indeed frequent and enjoy the theatre. Also, there were other, significantly more nuanced responses to the allure of the stage, the recovering theatre addict Augustine (354–430 CE) being a particularly prominent one.[35] Most surprisingly, perhaps, the latest specimen of Christian discourse on theatre is a defence of the lowly mime by Choricius of Gaza.[36] This remarkable speech, held within the first quarter of the sixth century and entitled 'Speech on behalf of those who represent life in the theatre of Dionysus', shows a nuanced openness and receptivity to theatrical activity as a constructive and potentially beneficial cultural force which is reminiscent of Aristotle, and is a final high note in the polyphony that is the ancient debate on the value of theatre.[37]

CHAPTER SEVEN

Communities of Production

Pied Pipers and How to Pay Them; or, the Variegated Finance of Ancient Theatre

JANE LIGHTFOOT

This chapter attempts to trace the process by which theatre came to be constituted as commodity in classical antiquity, how its personnel developed into a profession, and how the whole business was funded. The process seems to have happened remarkably quickly, calling forth complex coping mechanisms (such as actors' guilds and associations) for the professionals involved in it, and equally complex and adaptable funding strategies. Any historical account is only as good as the sources on which it is based, and for each period reviewed here the evidence, its biases and limitations, must be taken into account. Literary evidence may tend to anecdote, scandal or salacity; inscriptions are liable to the changes of fashion, with different types of document showing up at different periods (Hellenistic victor-lists make way for inscriptions on statue-bases in the imperial period;[1] contractual documents for stage artists disappear); and sometimes there is a disconcerting lack of fit between different sorts of evidence, as when epigraphy fails to marry up with the archaeological evidence of theatre buildings.[2] But our sources range widely, and epigraphy is a resource from which many more important discoveries may confidently be expected. Let us begin with settings. What sort of festivals does drama belong in?

CLASSICAL ATHENS

Drama's original home was the Athenian City Dionysia; that was the setting for Thespis' inaugural victory in a tragic contest in 534. It was the climax of a festival cycle, increasingly packed with drama, that had already begun in the winter months with the Rural Dionysia[3] and continued with the Lenaea and the Anthesteria, the latter of which included a comic *agôn* by the mid- to late-fourth century if not before.[4] There was room for a lot of drama here. In the City Dionysia, three tragedians each produced three tragedies and a satyr play, and, though comedy was a later introduction (in 486?), five comic poets one play each. In the Lenaea, into which comedy was introduced c. 440 and tragedy about a decade later, there were again five comedies, but only two tragedians competing with two plays each, and no satyr play.

Drama, as well as the choral song known as dithyramb that was at home in the Dionysia, was funded by a combination of state and private finance, the latter known as *chorêgia*. This was a liturgy, an expense compulsorily undertaken by the wealthiest members of the community. It was a very familiar form of taxation, and liturgies funding festivals or parts of them (including major components of the Panathenaia) were one of its principal forms; Dionysia-related liturgies formed an especially large proportion of the liturgies in any given year.[5] It is so familiar in classical Athens that one is inclined to credit it with an intrinsically democratic character, but in fact it is unclear whether its origins are with Cleisthenes – records apparently begin in 502/1[6] – or whether it already existed earlier in the sixth century under the tyrants (ps.-Arist. *Oec.* 1347A). In the institution's classical form, once the Eponymous Archon had 'granted a chorus' to the poets for the forthcoming Dionysia (which he did at the beginning of his year of office, eight months before the festival itself), he would allocate them *chorêgoi*.[7] This was probably by lot. The *chorêgoi* would then provide finances for training the choruses in question. It was not an artistic but a financial role: these funds had to maintain the chorus during the rehearsal period, as well as pay for costumes (including masks), other props and scenery, musicians and the eventual victory banquet. The Attic orators attest huge levels of expenditure: Lysias 21.1–4 gives figures of 3,000 and 5,000 drachmas (this latter including the monumental tripod erected by the victor) for tragic *chorêgiai*, as well as 1,600 drachmas for a comic chorus; costs might exceed the equipping of a trireme (Dem. *Meid.* 80) and dwarfed those of, say, a Panathenaic chorus (300 drachmas according to Lysias).[8] No wonder that those chosen were 'from all the Athenians the very richest' (*Ath. Pol.* 56.3). They had to be Athenian citizens, although metics could hold the office in the less prestigious Lenaea.

It was possible to object to taking up the *chorêgia*, and the *antidosis* procedure, whereby a man who claimed that another was richer than himself could insist on an exchange of estates if the latter did not agree, worked against foul play. But it was not possible to wriggle out of a duty. Nor, it seems, was there much desire to. On the contrary, so far from dragging their feet, moneyed elites regarded *chorêgia* as a great occasion for self-display. It was no tangible reward for which they were competing – the prize for a tragic *chorêgos* was merely an ivy crown – but prestige, which in could be converted into other sorts of benefit, for example political influence (so that it is no accident that notable public figures such as Themistocles and Pericles are known to have acted as *chorêgoi*, the latter for no less a play than Aeschylus' *Persae*). Strikingly, whereas *chorêgia* was often shared in the Rural Dionysia, as well as in the ruinously expensive trierarchy, we hear of only one *synchorêgia* in the Dionysia, and in a year of financial stress at that.[9]

As well as rich individuals, the state had a big input.[10] It paid the poets: at least, we hear about *misthos* for comic poets in Ar. *Frogs* 367f. (as well as for dithyramb[11]), so *a fortiori* there was presumably tragic poets' pay as well. It also paid for actors. Although much is unclear at this date, prizes for actors were instituted, in the Dionysia for tragedy from 449 (*IG* ii.^{2} 2325), though not for comedy until the last decades of the fourth century, and in the Lenaea perhaps c. 442. With the emergence of stars, it became necessary to contract actors in advance, sometimes for enormous sums;[12] we shall return to the subject of hiring (*misthôsis*) below. Other state expenses included the pipers (originally hired by the poets, but the charge assumed by the state at some point before the middle of the fourth century), maintenance of the theatre and employment of the stage hands (doubtless the responsibility of the Archon in charge of the festival), possibly the actors' costumes, and certainly the considerable expenses of the procession and sacrifices.[13]

None of this came cheap, and it seems that the cult of Dionysus was lacking in one of the major sources of state funding for cults and festivals – real estate and leasable property.[14] But it is highly plausible, given what we know of the leasing of theatres outside Athens, and given, too, that the stone theatre on the south slope of the Acropolis was not even completed until a remarkably late date (the 330s), that the Athenian state contracted out the construction of a theatre – a temporary one, in wood – for each new Dionysia festival.[15] The lessees (*theatrônai* or *theatropôlai*) saw to the construction of the wooden seating for spectators (the *theatron*, literally the viewing-place) in return for the rights to the takings on the door. This could, in turn, explain what is otherwise an anomalous detail, the entry charge, which we may take for granted, but which is unusual in an ancient context. After the completion of the permanent theatre, the system lost its rationale, but persisted, with the money retained by the state, a source of income well attested in Attic demes in the fourth century and elsewhere in the Hellenistic period.[16]

In Athens itself, entrance charges were all the more remarkable in that they came to be offset by yet another anomalous expense from the opposite direction, the payment of theatre-goers for attending the theatre. (Anomalous, because although the state paid its citizens for participating in its institutions – the assembly, the council, the courts – it did not otherwise pay them for cultural activities or 'luxuries'.) The payment is usually inferred to have been two obols, although other sources which mention a drachma might be referring to the price of three days' entertainment.[17] It was not means-tested, and all theatre-goers were eligible, but the date of its introduction is unclear, and hence how long the expense of theatre-going was uncompensated by a state benefit (with possible implications for bias in the plays themselves towards a certain type of audience[18]). Some sources trace the inception of payments to Pericles, but it is unclear how systematic any Periclean payments were, and an alternative view places it as late as the middle of the fourth century.[19]

Athens is our best-known case, and one whose changes we can to some extent follow through time. Our last choregic inscription referring to the City Dionysia dates from 319. The next record, an inscription of 307/6, gives the role of the *chorêgos* to the *dêmos* and refers to an individual *agônothetês*. However the transition occurred, and whatever its motives,[20] the replacement of the *chorêgos* by a single elected official in control of state funds by no means had an anti-sumptuary effect. For the *agônothetês*, no less than the *chorêgos*, continued to be obliged (or had the opportunity) to dip into his own pockets, in one case to the tune of the enormous sum of 63,000 drachmas.[21] One question is the extent to which this funding model – a complex mixture of public and private, which developed in one very particular environment – is typical of the ancient world, either ipso facto, because that is how the ancient economy worked, or because of direct cultural influence from the mother-city of drama.

BEYOND CLASSICAL ATHENS: FESTIVALS AND PROFESSIONALS

As we move outwards from Athens, we need to consider the increasingly diverse environments in which drama is found.[22] The aim is not merely to show how drama becomes a must-have item in any self-respecting civic festival, but also to suggest the implications for organization and finance and for the participation and remuneration of the artists involved. The old forms first developed in classical Athens remained resilient and adaptable. Festivals patterned on the Dionysia were the natural home of drama, with competitions in tragedy, comedy and choral song accompanied by a piper. But scenic events also figure as one component of 'musical' festivals alongside 'thymelic' elements (musical competitions that took place in the orchestra where the altar, or *thymelê*, was located). A good example is the Mouseia of Thespiae, whose evolution we can trace from the third century BCE to the third century CE.[23] Whether or not drama was there from the start, its core events were in place by the third century, and first-century CE inscriptions show a finely-differentiated system with comedy and tragedy old and new, actors' prizes for each, and (new) satyr play, though without actor's prize.[24] Drama is still there three centuries later, but shrunk to contests for tragic and comic actors. Imperial festivals such as the Lysimachea in Aphrodisias[25] and the festival set up by C. Julius Demosthenes at Oenoanda remain true to this traditional pattern, the latter an astonishing three-week affair, perhaps reflecting the tastes of the Hellenophile emperor Hadrian.[26] Prize lists are preserved from both festivals, and it is interesting to see tragedy valued more highly than comedy, although comedy elsewhere seems the more popular genre in purely quantitative terms, as in Hellenistic Iasos (below).

Other festivals were spectacular occasions where music and drama were programmed beside athletics and, in the most ambitious, equestrian contests as well. In Naples, the Sebasta, founded by Augustus, although modelled on the Olympic games, had a major musical/dramatic element, perhaps an addition to the original programme.[27] There are many cases where drama was a later addition (for instance the Panathenaia, which had drama from the second century BCE to the first century CE, and even the Pythian Games in the imperial period[28]). Conversely, athletics may be added to an originally musical festival, such as the Delphic Soteria after its reorganization in the 240s (below). At Thebes, formerly separate musical and athletic festivals, the Agrionia and Iolaeia/Herakleia, seem to coalesce into a joint festival in the second century CE, the Dionysia Herakleia Kommodeia; what has become of the original tragedy and comedy is unclear, but a pantomime artist – on whom more below – proudly boasts that he has won the first competition in his speciality.[29]

We should also note the increasingly diverse forms of theatrical presentations. Quite apart from the osmosis of drama into new contexts, such as gala performances in the retinues of kings,[30] a broad distinction might be drawn between two types of presentation, the competitive *agôn* and the non-competitive display or *epideixis*. On the one hand, the *agôn* remained the traditional setting for drama, but with increasingly elaborate prizes – monetary or honorific – for victorious poets (where the drama was not a revival) and actors. On the other, the *epideixis* was a special performance, outside the formal framework of a festival, often put on for reasons of (avowed) piety, or simply because a performer was passing through.[31] This type of performance is particularly well attested in honorific inscriptions, especially from Delphi, and in the archons' records in Delos.[32] At the former, for instance, the tragic actor Nikon of Megalopolis offered the god a whole day's performance in 165 BCE and was commemorated for his pains.[33] The Delian records of those who have 'put on a display' or 'competed' for the god (the verbs are *epideixasthai* and *agônisasthai*, the latter irrespective of the fact that the performances are non-competitive[34]) are particularly striking, because after the lists of comic and tragic artists and high-status musicians who have offered their services are numerous lower-status performers including several conjurers (one of them female), along with a dancer, puppeteers, and a *rhômaistes* (whatever 'romanizing' is).[35] These lower-status performers – the mimes and conjurers, jugglers, tumblers and acrobats – also turn up in later inscriptions which seem to indicate that they have been hired in by festival-organizers to complement the more prestigious entertainments on offer.[36] They do not compete (although, as we shall see, competitive events *did* eventually accommodate some of them). The state of affairs in the Dionysia of second-century BCE Iasos seems somewhat betwixt-and-between competition and display.[37] Individual benefactors pay for (*epididonai*) specific performances, with named artists hired for a particular day or number of days. Some seem to have been hired again and again by popular demand: for instance, a *komôidos* for five and even six days, a *tragôidos* for four.[38] These do not look like competitive events, but when hire and expenses could so dramatically out-distance prize money (below), perhaps the agonistic element was less significant.

This, then, was the ever-evolving institutional setting for theatre professionals. They had come a long way from the earliest days, when Thespis won his first victory at the Athenian Dionysia in 534 BCE. He acted in his own plays, which seems to have remained the norm for the period down to Sophocles, whose non-participation is noted as an innovation (*Vit. Soph.* lines 21f. Radt). The next stage was for the playwright to choose his own actors, which may imply the importance of kinship-networks already in early theatre;[39] then for the protagonists to be allocated to the poets by the state and distributed by lot. The final stage, reached at the latest by the mid-fourth century, was that the tragic protagonists were distributed across the plays of each of the three poets, rather than being wedded for that year to the compositions of a single individual.[40]

Attention centres on these stars of the stage. Specialists of an always-emotive art form, the best could move their audiences to tears.[41] Their delivery and charisma might have been an asset in other fields as well, such as diplomacy.[42] Inevitably, they commanded huge fees, and this remained true throughout antiquity, from late classical Athens into the Roman Empire, with awed anecdotes circulating about the biggest names centuries after their death. Of course, it is doubtful how much any of this really tells us. Exceptional cases form no useful basis for generalization, and it is here that epigraphy is invaluable in providing a counter-weight to the sensationalist and usually contextless anecdotes about the likes of Neoptolemus, Polus and Aristodemus, instead shedding light on the more day-to-day business of acting and how the theatre professionals earned a living.

For professionals they now were. For one thing, they were now called upon to be technically proficient beyond the capabilities of any amateur. Musical developments required artistic virtuosity, from both the actors and the pipers who accompanied their increasingly lyrical roles;[43] papyri document the development of this taste, which reached the point where Lucian in the second century complains about a *tragôidos* who chants his iambic lines (*periaidôn ta iambeia*) as well as lapsing into monodies at the drop of a hat (*Salt.* 27).[44] Aspects of their art, such as their platform boots or *kothornoi*,[45] were becoming stylized to the point of mannerism. At the same time, some of those trained within the theatrical profession were capable of moving around comfortably within it. Inscriptions sometimes give intriguing instances of multi-tasking.[46] One memorable instance is the actor who boasted of his victories in sturdy roles (Heracles and the like) in revived dramas at various festivals, but who was also a victorious pugilist at the Ptolemaia in Alexandria.[47] Some of the contestants at the Amphictyonic Soteria in Delphi reappear in records from Delos and Athens, and yield instances of *didaskaloi* (producers? managers?[48]) reappearing as chorus-members, tragic actors and pipers reappearing in comedy, and even a piper reappearing as costumier.[49]

Deriving their livelihood from the theatre, these artists were obliged to be on the move, to travel the rounds of a festival circuit – which as a result had to be carefully coordinated. Decrees establish festivals and lay out the requirements in terms of personnel and finance; artists' guilds lay out their terms for participation; honours are granted to individual performers. Inscriptions do not always tell us as much as we would like to know. The general convention is to name simply the *tragôidos* or *kômôidos*, the protagonist (in the case of 'old', revived, drama, *hypokritês* for new works), and leave the fellow-members of his troupe implicit; in Iasos, it is the chief artists who are designated to take part in the Dionysia, and they are to bring their *hypêresiai* (crews, support staff) with them (I. Iasos 152.17, 37). But there are exceptions, notably the inscriptions from the Amphictyonic Soteria at Delphi (some time before 246/5),[50] which, by listing *everyone* involved, reveal the full configuration of a dramatic troupe. There are three actors in both tragedy and comedy (showing continued adhesion to the three-actor rule) accompanied by a *didaskalos* and piper; there are three each of these troupes in tragedy and comedy, or once, for comedy, four. There are also comic choruses of seven or eight members (a much smaller number than the classical twenty-four, unless supplemented by locals – an entirely hypothetical possibility). They apparently divide their services between the troupes (suggesting a generic rather than particularized choral identity). There is no trace of a tragic chorus, and while the fate of the classical chorus is too vast a subject to tackle here, it is notable that in the inscription for the Sarapieia of Tanagra (second century BCE) choruses have dwindled so far that the payment to the clothier (*himatiomisthês*) dwarfs that for the choruses and their pipers.[51] The small fry – the tragic and comic *synagônistai* – are to be found in the inscriptions if we look for them. One particularly nice example comes from Dura Europos on the Euphrates, apparently from the headquarters of a troupe of artists serving the Roman garrison in the middle of the third century CE – a tragic actor, Romanos, and his assistant (*hypotragôidos*) Theodora, right on the outposts of the empire on the eve of the Persian conquest.[52]

Epigraphy also throws light on the low-status performers who appear on the festival fringes.[53] We are still learning how these performers related to the more mainstream or normative art forms in the festivals in which they participated, and also how their forms and status changed over time. The enormous number of terms for various kinds of mime artist in ancient inscriptions, papyri, and lexica, suggests fascinating diversity. The Delian *rhômaistês* we have already met; the *neaniskologos* apparently acted the part of young men; the *archaiologoi* perhaps specialized in 'ancient' subject-matter (myth?); the *Homeristês* must have acted out scenes from Homer (a particularly intriguing case of the hybridization of genre).[54]

Above we encountered a distinction between artists who competed in contests and those who performed on the sidelines. In some cases the vocabulary indicates that the latter (*hoi kata kairon theatrizontes*, 'the occasional givers of shows', as opposed to *hoi agônisamenoi*, 'the competitors') are pantomimes.[55] A clear distinction should be drawn between the pantomime (Figure 7.1) and the mime.

The latter category was amorphous to the point of bewilderment, but the pantomime was a distinctive art, a sort of ancient ballet performed by a male soloist, accompanied by chorus and instrumentalists.[56] The subject-matter was drawn from mythology (unlike the quotidian subject-matter of the mime) and was not comedic. It was not so much an indication of the low status of the artists as of the passions they stirred up that pantomimes were repeatedly exiled from Rome (but repeatedly returned). But it is an indication of the increasing status of their art that they seem to have penetrated the festival circuit, from their appearance in the inaugural *ludi Augustales* in Rome, in the year 14 CE,[57] to their admission to contests in the Neapolitan Sebasta in the 160s, and in Asia Minor by the reign of Commodus (180–92 CE), now explicitly in the most prestigious, 'sacred', games.[58] Their acceptance may reflect the influence of Roman tastes in festivals sponsored by priests of the imperial cult.[59] Mimes, the less prestigious artists, were slower to be admitted to competitions, though admitted they eventually were – certainly, by the late second or early third century, to games with money prizes and eventually, conceivably (though as yet this is unverified), to crowned games as well.[60]

FIGURE 7.1: Late antique ivory plaque (late fifth century CE) depicting a pantomime dancer. Staatliche Museen zu Berlin, Antikensammlung (inventory no. TC 2497). Photo: Ingrid Geske.

ARTISTS' GUILDS

What all this means is that, from the classical period, an international complex of festivals did not cease to ramify until late antiquity. The financial systems that supported it, while sharing certain themes, were vertiginously complex, and the logistics of negotiating the circuit in a world often torn by conflicts, local and international, led to the development of regional associations to assist the huge personnel who made their livings in and from this complex environment which, to some extent, they attempted to coordinate. Stage artists were not the only competitive professionals to band together. Athletes did the same, but in their case our evidence only begins in the first century BCE.[61]

In the case of stage artists, an inscription from Chalcis, Euboea, preserving a decree issued by four cities of the island who were attempting to secure artists for their festivals, is the first pointer to the existence of a guild.[62] No guild is explicitly mentioned, but a gathering of the artists (*technitai*) is implied to which the festival organizers in Chalcis make application. The first positive evidence comes from two almost synchronous inscriptions, one honouring the '*koinon* of artists who travel in common to the Isthmus and Nemea', the other responding to an embassy from the *technitai* in Athens.[63] Soon afterwards comes evidence for guilds in Egypt (dedicated to Dionysus and the Sibling Gods, i.e. the ruling Ptolemies) and an Ionian-Hellespontine Guild, centred at Teos.[64] Also at Teos is attested a guild of *synagônistai*, variously interpreted as a guild for non-leading actors, and as a looser and large association of affiliates.[65] By the early empire, first attested under Claudius, a universal guild of artists has emerged, although the titulature of some of the old organizations continues to resonate.[66]

Our evidence concerning these associations includes decrees from cities and leagues, from the guilds themselves, and correspondence with Hellenistic kings and Roman officials and emperors. The material is organizational, contractual and honorific, and illustrates both the practicalities of their business and the light in which they wished to present themselves (observe for instance the neologism in *OGIS* 51.11, where *techniteuma* is modelled on *politeuma*, as if the guild wished to constitute itself as a city). They were involved at various levels in the organization of festivals, responding to requests from organizers in order to ensure the events were fully manned, or sharing jointly in the organization, and occasionally even organizing them themselves.[67] Above all, what they did for their membership – which, because they offered an all-in package for the festival management, extended not only to artistic personnel, but also to artisans, the mask-makers and costumiers and presumably makers of other stage properties[68] – was to establish clarity about the terms on which they were engaged. For nothing less than the livelihoods of their members might be at issue.

Of course, for the stars securing contracts had never been a problem. As early as the late classical period, the biggest names were being approached by the state, with the actor under obligation to appear on pain of punitive fines.[69] An inscription from the end of the fourth century shows how stars were able to dictate their own terms: Polus is praised for his good will and virtue by the Samians, for an arrangement which was evidently most advantageous to himself.[70] On the other hand, for the much smaller fry, and for a lesser festival (apparently the Rural Dionysia), the leaders of the troupe (but did the leaders always equate with the protagonists?) hired the men they needed for the smaller roles (Dem. 18.262, whose interest is in making the process sound as mean and degrading for the third actor as possible). The organizations of the Hellenistic period will have taken the arbitrariness out of the process. In the Chalcis inscription (above) the festival organizers send delegates to the artists to conclude contracts in a process called *ergolabia*, 'the undertaking of work',[71] and the artists evidently then distribute the work amongst themselves. It is true that guilds are not expressly mentioned here, but the process is presumably a model for what happened when a city or league approached the artists' associations; they explained their requirements, and the *technitai* allotted the performers.[72] The associations thus entered into binding agreements with the organizers of festivals, and could be penalized, or penalize their own members, for no-shows: this was obviously important in contractual situations where artists were paid in advance.

Nor is this all. The associations secured privileges for their members, both negative and positive.[73] The former included *asylia*, inviolability from attack, an important consideration in the often war-torn territories that *technitai* were obliged to cross (*SIG*³ 399) and *ateleia*, exemption from various tax burdens and liturgies (Diod. Sic. 4.5.4); already Demosthenes could assume the entitlement of stage artists to exemption from military service (*Meid.* 15, cf. 58f.). The latter included the honours accorded to civic benefactors, such as (in Delphi) special rights at the oracle, privileged seating and rights of prior access to justice (*SIG*³ 460). The entitlement to these and other privileges, such as honorific dress, will have been underscored by the guilds' religiosity, striking even by the standards of the ancient world, where the general embeddedness of religion in civil and political life saw priests at the head of many ancient clubs and societies. The devotion to Dionysus embedded in their titulature will not only have emphasized their piety, but was calculated to pitch an appeal to those rulers, like the Ptolemies in Egypt, the Attalids in Pergamum, Mark Anthony, and numerous Roman emperors, who promoted a connection with the culture-bringing deity.[74]

It is to the most philhellenic of Roman emperors that we owe a dossier of letters, discovered in Alexandria Troas and dated to 133–4,[75] which illuminates both the day-to-day business with which the guilds were concerned and the familiar way they communicate with the emperor.[76] True, this focus on minutiae is characteristic of imperial administration in general, but it is also eloquent about Hadrian's particular cultural tastes. In these documents, Hadrian addresses himself to the 'travelling thymelic union of artists associated with Dionysus [and] victorious in sacred and crowned contests', grappling with various organizational problems that had been brought to his attention during the celebration of the *Sebasteia Italika* games in Naples a little earlier that year (August/September 134). The first letter tackles various malpractices: the failure to hold festivals that had been advertised; the malappropriation of festival funds for other purposes, such as building; foot-dragging by agonothetes in the payment of prize money, which is henceforward to be counted out in the presence of the Roman magistrate and deposited in sealed containers beside the crowns (Figures 7.2 and 7.3). Moreover, prize money is to be handed over on the day it is due, and no attempt is to be made to substitute wheat or wine for cash. The second letter devotes itself to the niceties of a timetable, so that all the festivals could follow in sequence. And the third guarantees the artists' right to a banquet – again with the implication that agonothetes were trying to scrimp and save. Soon we shall turn to prizes and festival funding, which certainly did not exercise the *technitai* in the reign of Hadrian alone.

FIGURE 7.2: Four crowns and two money bags for the contest between Pan and Eros (mosaic from Room 35 in the Villa Romana del Casale, Piazza Armerina). Photo: R.J.A. Wilson.

FIGURE 7.3: Two crowns and two money bags for the musical and theatrical competitions shown in the mosaic below (mosaic from Room 34 in the Villa Romana del Casale, Piazza Armerina). Photo: R.J.A. Wilson.

Although they are relatively well documented, much remains unclear about ancient artists' guilds – above all the size of their membership and the proportion of stage artists that actually belonged to them. It is an easy assumption that any *technitês* was ipso facto a *technitês Dionysou*, a guildsman; but in only a disconcertingly small number of cases (in fact about 16 per cent) do we have proof of membership of an association.[77] It may be, then, that precisely those inscriptions that mention 'contractors' (*ergolaboi*) are the ones where guilds are *not* in question; representatives of the actors' troupes, and authorized to act on their behalf, they conclude contracts directly with the organizers of the festival (as in Euboea), the job that is otherwise undertaken by the guilds, and hence point to a different procedure.[78] We do know of contracts between states and individual artists;[79] when the theatre-loving Iasians in the second century hired favourite artists for performance after performance (above), did they do so through a guild or not? The extent to which they dominated the festivals in which they participated is also moot. Some evidence suggests that more than one association of artists was present at certain festivals in the Hellenistic period,[80] in which case was it possible for unaffiliated artists to perform there as well?[81] The analogy with trades unions is an obvious one, but limited, and it is possible that the closed shop is not the correct model. It does seem inherently plausible that one might sometimes act within and sometimes without a guild.

In any case, it is reasonable to hope for the discovery of more documents concerning the *technitai*; further insights are assured.

FINANCING GREEK AND GRAECO-ROMAN FESTIVALS

We turn next to the funding of festivals – to the sources of funds, and to their distribution in the form of hiring fees, prizes, and so on, to the artists who took part in them. Our evidence comes partly from literary texts, which contain both 'hard' historical data (such as ps.-Aristotle's *Constitution of Athens*) and anecdote, and partly inscriptions. We are fortunate that accounts survive in particular detail for Athens and for the Apollonia and Dionysia in Delos, and in some cases by agonothetes for the games for which they were responsible; numerous decrees also regulate the running of festivals. The picture that emerges is one of huge diversity – adaptations of existing models, *ad hoc* responses to new situations, an evolving culture of euergetism (private benefaction) – but with combinations of state and private finance a running theme. Sources of state finance – in the Chalcis inscription (above), it is the cities that dispatch ambassadors and pay the artists and artisans, and in the Troad a confederation of cities leagued together to fund the Panathenaia of Athena Ilias, a particularly splendid occasion big enough to warrant the minting of a special festival coinage[82] – included leases on state land and properties, and taxes. Tax revenue would ipso facto be increased by the concourse during a festival, which might thus, to some extent, become self-funding. Given the setting of drama in a religious festival, sacred funds are naturally available; they too come from leases, on sacred property, also from tithes and other sources, such as the sale of the hides of sacrificed animals. But in practice, even those agonothetes with state funds at their disposal might find themselves meeting additional out-of-pocket expenses, and indeed take special care to publicize the extent of their personal generosity, over and above what their office required of them.[83] The agonothete who has left us such a detailed set of accounts of the Sarapieia of Tanagra (although there is no mention here of a city or its funds) notes carefully that he paid for the feasting of the participants, judges, choruses, and victors, and for incense.[84]

To follow the evolution of classical *chorêgia* is to watch a method devised for one particular context as it is translated into very different environments. Its abandonment in Hellenistic Athens, perhaps under the influence of Aristotle-influenced theory that frowned upon, and desired to rationalize, burdensome expenditure, was only temporary.[85] At least one factor in its later incarnation was the archaizing look of the thing, suggesting that it had become bound up with the institution of theatre as a whole, and that what was important was the sense of cultural heritage that it carried with it. But two testimonies from the later first century show how much things had changed: from the first we learn that the expatriate prince Philopappos of Commagene, regal in his expenditure, served as universal *chorêgos* in the Dionysia; from the second, that all *chorêgoi* and choruses withdrew and declared the *demos* the winner. Was it that no one was prepared to compete at all, or that the spirit of collegiality triumphed over the *philotimia* that fired the old competitions?[86]

Forms of *chorêgia* are attested elsewhere outside Athens, but one of the most interesting comes from the corpus of inscriptions from early second-century Iasos.[87] True, it comes from a period when the city is under exceptional stress (earthquake, change of masters, civil strife), so the evidence may be ungeneralizable; on the other hand, for that very reason it may be all too typical of the vicissitudes of life in Hellenistic antiquity. In the earliest inscriptions, an agonothete and *chorêgoi* pay their share towards the Dionysia, but both they and other citizens pledge further, voluntary, contributions, or *epidoseis*. We should imagine public-spirited individuals responding to calls from the assembly, or festival organizers, with pledges from which it was then morally very difficult to back down, but which of course conferred prestige in proportion to their munificence. As we have seen, they bought in popular performers, actors and instrumentalists; a few contributed to renovation work (I. Iasos 179f., 182f.). Then, over the years 185–180, the system seems to have been regularized so as to make it less unpredictable and to remove the burden from the officials in charge by standardizing donations, which are expressly pledged in advance of the next year's Dionysia. The sums recorded are by no means colossal – the total of 1,200 drachmas, which had to buy in lyre-players, pipers, harpists-plus-chorus, comic and tragic actors, would barely have bought one boys' chorus in classical Athens. But this – plus the generosity of the *technitai* in contributing some of their services free of charge[88] – made it possible for the Iasians not to sacrifice the spectacles they loved.

The *epidosis* was a familiar model of private finance in antiquity; on two occasions it is used to finance, not spectacles, but the construction of theatres themselves.[89] Another is the interest-free loan. A third, popular throughout the Hellenistic and imperial periods, is for benefactors to set up endowment funds, which the state would curate, usually through a board of trustees or commissioners, by loaning them out at interest until the funds grew sufficient for a specific purpose, say for a building project or to fund an ongoing festival. One example is from Hellenistic Corcyra, in which a magistrate and his wife make a donation to the city in order to establish a biennial Dionysia festival for which artists are to be hired (there is mention of *technitai*, but not specifically of guilds); the moneys are to be made over to magistrates, who are to be severely fined for not adhering to the provisions of the council decree concerning the administration of the funds.[90] Another, from the reign of Hadrian, is the donation of C. Julius Demosthenes, former procurator of Sicily, to fund a penteteric musical festival, including scenic and thymelic events, in his native city of Oenoanda in Lycia.[91] The inscription is remarkable for the minute precision with which the benefactor details how the donation is to be invested and the money grown until it can be ploughed back into prizes, judges' fees, distributions and handouts. It is explicitly provided (l. 31) that the agonothete manages the fund and renders an account of it, but adds nothing from his own pocket. How utopian a wish is that?

The Oenoanda inscription is also of interest, as we have seen, for its enumeration of prizes and the entrenched values attached to particular events; and it is time now to turn to the question of awards and payments which had grown ever more complicated with the increasing complexity of festivals themselves. Already in classical Athens, the fact that artists were not going to compete for a purely honorific award (as athletes did at the pan-Hellenic games) was already acknowledged by the existence of actors' prizes, advance contracts, and doubtless other 'honours' such as bankable gold crowns; the business of theatre was on the way to professionalization in a way that that of an athlete was not (or at any rate, not yet). And if we look forward a century to the Chalcis decree, we begin to find a roster of ways a competitor could make money.[92] Players received *misthoi* (hire, for up-front sums specified in the decree) as well as living expenses (*sitêresia*) in addition to eventual prizes (which the inscription does not specify); at Corcyra (*IG* IX.1² (4) 798.87) and elsewhere it is a similar state of affairs, and pipers at the Delian Apollonia receive a package of fees, grants, and sweeteners (*misthos*, *sitêresia*, *chorêgêmata* – whatever they are – and *xenia* or 'guest-gifts') which dwarf the eventual prize.[93]

An additional complication arises when drama begins to appear in crowned, or 'stephanitic', events, where the reward was supposed to be purely honorific (this is the case, for instance, in the Delphic Soteria and then, as 'honours inflation' gets underway, in a host of imperial festivals). Here one often finds honourable fudges – the fig leaf of stephanitic status, but in fact a host of lucrative incentives for competitors. One ruse was to offer gold crowns of a specified monetary value; the Delphians adopted this method, but for some reason got a bad conscience and put an end to the practice in the middle of the first century BCE.[94] Or the organizers of crowned festivals could lean on the cities of victors to provide the meaningful prizes; if they themselves offered valuable wreaths of precious metal, it was in the firm expectation that they would be returned to the temple treasury to be recycled the next year.[95] Sometimes these *real* prizes were sizeable indeed, so that there might be considerable foot-dragging on the part of the home-cities before they signed up to the festival in question. By the imperial period some victors were entitled to pensions, and the point at which this entitlement begins is a bone of contention in Hadrian's first letter to the *technitai*; it was also important to be very precise about the tax exemptions victory in sacred games implied.[96] In time the fig leaf simply came to be discarded. The regulations for the Sebasta at Naples distinguish prizes (*epathla*) from *opsônia* (another term for maintenance grant, here paid for a thirty-day period before the festival) and *timai* (crowns, symbolic honours) – thereby coming clean about the fact that games aspiring to stephanitic status were actually offering filthy lucre.[97]

In sum, glittering prizes *were* to be had, in many cases quite literally. But to keep it in proportion, it is only fair to point out that inscribed prize-lists often show the rewards for stage artists outdistanced by those of other virtuosi. A well-known case are the *chorauloi* (pipers who accompanied a chorus) at the Apollonia in Delos, where the annual payments of 3,470 drachmas for two artists were so enormous that there had to be a special fund to deal with them.[98] Singing to the lyre (citharody) was a lucrative business as well, neck-and-neck with, or surpassing, the lead role in tragedy; such hierarchies reflect entrenched notions of cultural value that can be traced back well into the Hellenistic period.[99] And in imperial Aphrodisias actors and instrumentalists alike were put to shame by the athletes, who could win three times as much as the best-paid stage artist.[100]

THE ROMAN WEST

If we look across to the Roman world, we find both analogies and dissimilarities with Greek practice. In Rome, *ludi scaenici* – games with a theatrical element – were first performed in 390, but the starting point for formal drama was 240, when Livius Andronicus produced Latin adaptations of a Greek tragedy and comedy at the *Ludi Romani*.[101] These and other games (the *Ludi Plebei*, *Apollinares* and *Megalenses*) saw the first performances of Plautus and Terence and of Ennius' tragedy *Thyestes* (at the *Ludi Apollinares*), while more drama was to be had in settings like triumphs and funeral games (including two of Plautus' plays at the funeral games of L. Aemilius Paullus in 160 BCE). The festivals were organized by a state official – generally the curule or plebeian aedile, from Augustus' time the praetor, outside Rome the aediles or duumvirs. He managed a budget called the *lucar*, literally the revenue from a sacred grove or *lucus*, but, like many a Greek agonothete, was expected to supplement it from his own pocket. A good illustration comes from the Lex Coloniae Genetivae, the foundation document of a Caesarian colony in Baetica, which expressly lays down what the duumvirs and aediles can expect from the state and what they had to spend from their own pockets.[102] Given the enormous pressure to spend, there were sometimes imperial interventions to cap outlay[103] – though the Spanish *Lex* in fact stipulates the minimum spend rather than the maximum one.

The epigraphy of the Roman theatre presents a different pattern from that of the Greek.[104] A good number of inscriptions pertain to the *ludi* (ILS 5051–5316), to the construction (especially in the second and early third centuries, and especially in Spain and North Africa) and maintenance of theatres, to the establishment of festivals (often upon entry into some office, magistracy or priesthood), and to their financing (as in the Greek world, often from the interest on an invested sum of money); and there are copious honorific inscriptions and epitaphs for mimes and other performers and for administrators and imperial officials who sponsored theatre. But certain areas remain much less well documented than in Greece and the Greek East, especially matters of procedure and the day-to-day business of the theatre, the terms on which artists were engaged, the salaries and prizes they received. For the period of Plautus and Terence, it is assumed that the official in charge of the festival dealt directly with actor-managers – men like Ambivius Turpio[105] and Publilius Pellio,[106] who became celebrities as Plautus and Terence themselves became classics – and that the latter engaged the rest of their troupe, or *grex*. Given that they were known as *domini* and portrayed (whether or not in jest) in a position of dominance over their players,[107] the latter may well have been slaves, though this must be balanced against evidence for freeborn Romans on the stage, which drew increasing opprobrium as the Republic wore on. Later evidence suggests that actors received, like other workmen, state pay on a daily basis, the *diurnum*; an anecdote in Sen. *Ep.* 80.7f. concerns very low-status players, but even the vast stipend of the celebrity Roscius (with a leap from five denarii a day to 1,000) is described as *merces diurna* (Macrob. 3.14.13). This could, however, be supplemented in other ways. As well as prizes of palm branches (presumably of no monetary value, ever at risk from corruptible judges[108]), there were gifts and gratuities, *corollaria* (derived by Varro from floral tributes thrown to actors on stage) that in Caligula's case helped to empty the state coffers.[109] Crowns of precious metal were introduced into the Roman *ludi*, presumably on the analogy of Greek practice (Pliny dates their introduction to around the turn of the second century BCE[110]), but it is unclear how they worked (were they convertible into cash? Or decorative and to be returned to the festival organizers?). Were there also cash prizes? Unfortunately, the whole question of competitions in Roman *ludi* is still obscure. Plautus refers to competitions for actors and 'artists' (*artifices*, a word of broad and uncertain scope), and on one occasion to victory for an entire *play*, not just for an individual artist.[111] Of course, all the usual prizes were available for contests at *Greek* games. But as we shall see, the artists who performed competitively *par excellence* were, in the imperial period, pantomimes.

Another point of comparison and contrast with Greek practice is that of artists' guilds and associations. One might expect Greek influence from the fact that many of those involved in the earliest days of Roman theatre came from the south of Italy, where Greek culture had deep roots, though in practice what we see of Italian societies is very different from the Greek *synodoi* with their very pluralist membership. Instead, we hear of *collegia* or *societates* of minute specificity but sometimes perplexing shape, such as Greek singers (who included an usher: *CIL* I² 2519), Roman pipers, harp-players, and *scabellarii* (players of a sort of clapper-board worked by the foot, used to keep time for pantomimes and others).¹¹² We know that their membership overlapped, and we know that they cooperated – a necessity, when Roman festivals included so many different kinds of entertainment – for example when the collegium which provided the instrumentalists for religious worship helped out the stage companies (*CIL* VI. 2193 = 4416). But most of these Roman guilds are too badly documented for us to be able to follow their workings in detail. Several inscriptions refer to men, clearly involved in the performing arts, who are described as *adlecti* or 'chosen' associates of some sort of professional body; but what might that body have been?¹¹³ The partial exception to this obscurity are the 'Parasites of Apollo', for whom most of our evidence – two literary references and twelve inscriptions – comes from the second century CE, all from Rome or its environs, and all involving (where specified at all) mimes or pantomimes.¹¹⁴ Genres which had for centuries existed on the fringes of the performing arts (the association may have taken its name from the performers who honoured Apollo outside the main festivals on Delos) have now acquired a status and dignity which recalls that of the Greek *technitai*, and it is possible, though not certain, that some of them even served as priests in the universal guild of artists in the Hadrianic period.

The inscriptions that shed light on the activities of the Greek associations for the most part do not survive in the West, but the same conditions obtained. Stage performers were required to travel from festival to festival (albeit under more settled conditions than in the Hellenistic kingdoms), and the empire-wide nature of the enterprise is revealed by inscriptions of the guild in Nîmes, two of whose members (both from the Greek East) are on record as having performed in *agônes* on Roman soil, while a Neapolitan *synodos*, in turn, apparently went to perform in Nîmes.¹¹⁵ Hadrian's letters show how calendars had to be rationalized to ensure a smooth succession of festivals (although not all the local organizers were willing to accept changes imposed from above, not even by an emperor), and festival organizers obliged to deliver what they promised. But the emperor could also contribute to scenic festivals more directly by supplying the artists himself, thereby flaunting his own largesse and perhaps also unburdening provincial worthies in the process. There is evidence for travelling pantomimes in the second half of the second and early third centuries, in some cases specifically at the behest of the emperor.¹¹⁶ We know, too, that the imperial household – like other aristocratic households, but on a grander scale – maintained its own company of stage artists, the *summum choragium*, with their own department of accounts and bureaucracy.¹¹⁷ All its known members are pantomimes, the very players attested on tour outside Rome, and an inscription from Latium may reveal something of their business arrangements when it refers to *mancipes* (normally, 'contractors') of the emperors' troupes (note the continued use the terms *domini* and *greges*, familiar from the republican period) and to a *locator* (normally, someone who hires out a property) of the *corpus scaenicorum Latinorum*. The interpretation, however, is still unsettled: is the *locator* the troupe's representative and the *mancipes* the third parties who do the hiring, or is the *locator* an agent providing the troupes with personnel, and the *mancipes* his business partners?[118]

LATER ANTIQUITY

For later antiquity, the nature of our sources changes yet again.[119] Epigraphy is petering out, so we are more dependent on literary evidence, including Christian diatribes, and on legal sources which show, not what it was like for the participants and professionals, but what efforts the state made to regulate it.[120] This distribution of evidence coincides with, and perhaps fosters, an impression of greater centralization in the control of festival finances in the hands of the imperial government.[121] For theatre at this stage may have been increasingly a matter of mimes and pantomimes[122] and theatrical spectacles, but it was something that the central government cared to maintain, despite the onslaughts of Christians, and despite occasional attempts at partial restriction (no theatre on Sundays!) because it was so popular. Even Christian emperors speak of games as a right which people are not to be denied.[123]

It is an interesting moment when, at the very end of our period, Theoderic writes to the former city prefect Symmachus with permission to recoup the costs of the restoration of the Theatre of Pompey in Rome from his own private chamberlain, accompanying his letter with a long lecture on the history of drama. It appears that in the old capital of the empire the theatre was so bound up with Rome's urban heritage that the Ostrogothic king wished to contribute to the preservation of its memorials even if the glory went to his official.[124] But most of our sources present matters scenic, not as a matter of pious antiquarianism, but of very real and live concern. The higher magistrates were (as ever) supposed to finance the games, with somewhat different systems in the eastern and western halves of the empire.[125] In the east, we hear only of games paid for by praetors, while at different times in the west there were games funded by quaestors, praetors, and consuls, specifications for whom, laid down by Justinian,[126] give a fair idea of what was involved. While most of the seven shows officially prescribed were not a matter of theatre at all, but of horse-racing, wild animal shows, and general pageantry, the fifth was to exhibit *pornai* (show-girls, presumably), clowns, *tragôidoi*,[127] choruses (still) on the *thymelê*, and 'all sorts of diversions for eye and ear'. Whatever one may feel about the level at which these entertainments were pitched, they called for expenditure that was no less stupefying than at any other period of classical antiquity, and their staging is a story of imperial attempts both to coerce fluctuating numbers of office-holders into taking up their duties and to rein in the biggest spenders; the drive to competitive expenditure was still felt by magistrates, even when it was no longer a question of the need to curry favour with an electorate.[128] And however much the stage artists remained, as they had been under the late Republic, *infames*, sumptuary legislation targeting mime artists suggests the wealth which those at the top of their profession could afford to flaunt.[129]

EPILOGUE

The enormous timescale of this chapter both encourages 'big' questions and discourages precise answers. One common theme is the constant negotiation of the relationship between public and private finance (and indeed the questionable nature of the distinction in many environments in classical antiquity), another the ebb and flow of conservatism (the preservation of traditional funding models because associated with a venerable institution) and innovative responses to changing political, economic, and social conditions. One is struck by an apparent contrast between artistically exciting and intellectually challenging citizen-funded drama at the beginning of the period and state-funded fodder for the masses at the end, and even if this is re-pointed by noting the undoubted presence of sub-literary mimes in the early days and private reading and study of high-brow drama as antiquity came to an end, it is still the case that Aeschylus, on the one hand, and *pornai*, on the other, were what the moneyed elites were funding. The contrast invites reflection.

CHAPTER EIGHT

Genres

Drama and its Many Unhappy Returns

DONALD SELLS

Given the comparatively limited and often fragmentary evidence for antiquity's diverse dramatic literature, any study of genre and repertoire that hopes to be balanced, thorough and engaging recognizes that literary culture comprises numerous moving parts constantly developing in changing cultural and historical conditions. There is no ideal starting point for this work, but the next best thing may be an axiom of early genre theory that genres are functions, and not categories, of literature. As Alasdair Fowler noted, genre is less like a pigeonhole, more like a pigeon. The kind of animal matters less than its organic and evolving quality.[1] Given the cultural emphasis of this series, Gian Biagio Conte's definition of genre as an idea mediating between the literary work and various cultural discourses, and social functions, within which that literature operates, best captures culture's significance to ancient theatrical genre and its development in Greek and Roman society.[2]

This chapter examines five major theatrical genres of Graeco-Roman antiquity – tragedy, comedy, satyr play, mime and pantomime – along intra- and inter-generic vertices. We can perhaps best understand the organic social and cultural development of the repertoires of these forms if we consider how they come to be and evolve in proximity to each other. My focus is less on formal features – although these are occasionally considered – than on the cultural subtexts they express. The hero or protagonist who is critical to drama in most cultural and historical contexts is the subject of the first section, on the heroic paradigms of tragedy and comedy, specifically the evolution of tragedy's elite hero as well as comedy's formulation of its own brand of heroism in reaction to its loftier rival. In classical Athens, tragedy often (but not always) reconsiders heroic achievements, achievements upon which the social status of its epic heroes rests, in light of the democratic values of its fifth-century performance context. One excellent, controlled frame for isolating the heroic persona from different perspectives in the three canonical Athenian tragedians is the *nostos* ('homecoming') plot made famous by Homer's *Odyssey*. Tragedy's scrutiny of the heroic past furthermore underscores the provocative departure of comedy's heroic paradigm, which is typically predicated on the success and wish-fulfillment, i.e., looking forward rather than backward, of the comic project.

The second section on 'Female Agents' builds upon these canonical texts to explore the rise of the female in fifth-century Old Comedy and her status as a fixture of Greek and later Roman theatre. Of particular interest is the popular adultery novella that eventually made its way into theatre culture, I suggest, through one of Conte's 'places of expectation', the fertile generic margins between mainstream genres that give rise to new forms.[3] Sometime during the Hellenistic period, the popular adultery tale began its evolution into the wildly popular adultery plot that, along with other skits of the mime's vast repertoire, dominated the ancient stage for seven centuries. In the last section of this chapter, I treat the gods as an index of genre in both Greece and Rome, with particular emphasis on two important developments: first, later New Comedy's adoption of tragedy's divine prologue as a part of its change of tone under Menander; secondly, pantomime's extreme remediation of mythology from the various verbal and visual codes of dramatic performance to the primary visual mode of dance.

Before diving into genre's form and content, the most explicit determinant of classification in Graeco-Roman performance culture should be acknowledged, i.e., context. The 'classical' theatrical genres, tragedy and comedy (and, for Greeks, satyr play) were performed in designated public spaces as part of civic, and often ritually sanctioned, events. In Greece, these performances were part of the festivals of Dionysus, while Romans enjoyed drama, mime, and pantomime during its celebration of regular and occasional games, *ludi*.[4] Greek and Roman spectators were thus never in doubt as to which genre they were watching, and not just because of the specific institutional context of most performance: tragic acting was grand and attractive; comedy, originally ugly and obscene, eventually became lighthearted and fun; satyr play featured satyrs. As one critic states, while 'contextual determination' is a given for these plays, confirming, qualifying, or even challenging that reconstructed performance text is the task of readers and interpreters.[5] This task is the focus of the present chapter.

HEROIC CODES

In tragedy, the epic-heroic biography that forms the basis of the protagonist's elevated social and political status is often the background of his plight in the uniquely democratic present. The *nostos*, or 'day of homecoming', is a relatively stable plot-type predicated upon the dynamic tension between epic past and tragic present.[6] Given tragedy's preferred setting before the house, and between public and private spheres, the *nostos* provides an excellent dramaturgical vehicle for highlighting tragedy's concern with events of the past in the context of present problems. Moreover, the *nostos* provides an excellent measure of the parameters of the tragic repertoire. It derives from the *Nostoi*, a lost epic poem on the homecomings of various Greek heroes in the aftermath of the sack of Troy, the greatest achievement of Graeco-Roman antiquity.[7] The sole extant version of an epic *nostos* is the account of Odysseus' ten years of wandering during his return home to Ithaca in Homer's *Odyssey*, which generates suspense by alluding to the experiences of other Trojan war heroes, particularly Agamemnon. The commander of the Greek army quickly and safely returned home only to be slaughtered at the dinner table by his wife's lover, Aegisthus (*Od.* 11.422). A central conceit of the *nostos* is thus the imminent danger awaiting the vulnerable hero in his own home and the critical importance of his kin, particularly his wife, to his survival.

Extant tragic *nostoi* describe homecomings of all kinds, and not simply those relating to the Trojan War. However, the most famous *nostos* of the tragic stage is doubtless Aeschylus' *Agamemnon*, the first installment of his *Oresteia* (458 BCE). Aeschylus spends the first two thirds of the play building a sense of apprehension and uncertainty by drawing out the king's return to Argos after Troy's fall.[8] Entrances by the chorus of Argive elders, queen Clytemnestra and the king's herald repeatedly disrupt audience expectation of Agamemnon's inevitable fate. Choral stasima and characters' statements imbue his achievement with deeper, ill-omened significance by emphasizing the enormous costs in human life of the Atreids' punishment of Paris and Troy at the order of Zeus (59–67): Agamemnon's sacrifice of his own daughter, Iphigenia (205–15); the losses of the Argives (436–55); and the suffering of Trojan innocents (111–39). These horrors reveal the force of the retributive justice about to crush Agamemnon at his moment of greatest glory.

Tragedy's relatively sparing use of physical properties acquires greater significance in Agamemnon's arrival, staged grandly through the king's entrance on a chariot. The famous purple textiles queen Clytemnestra lays over the entrance to the palace for the barefoot king to tread represent the kind of ill-gotten wealth whose possession corrupts and whose destruction attracts the gods' interest for the wrong reasons. The dark purple hue of the woven walkway may have produced the striking visual effect of a stream of blood flowing from the palace's open door,[9] an allusion to the house's past violence and anticipation of Agamemnon's approaching death. Entrapping him in the bath with a robe, Clytemnestra stabs him three times, ostensibly for his earlier sacrifice of their daughter, Iphigenia, for the sake of the expedition. The 'man-counseling heart' (11) with which Clytemnestra carefully planned and carried out the assassination of her husband and seizure of power in Argos exhibits the kind of gender inversion that Greek tragedy sometimes thematized. Although far from a good or decent man, we think of Agamemnon as a tragic hero because his death is the outcome of what many would describe as an impossible choice imposed upon him: to sacrifice his daughter for the expedition and ensure the justice of Zeus, or refuse and become the target of its wrath.

Edith Hall[10] identified a common element of female transgression in tragedy as a temporarily or permanently husbandless woman whose lack of supervision leads to her disastrous attempt at self-assertion. On the scale of tragic femininity, sitting at the end opposite to the evil Clytemnestra is Deianira of Sophocles' *Trachiniae* (date unknown), the gut-wrenching treatment of the death of the pan-Hellenic hero Heracles. Sophocles' contribution to the *nostos* pattern was his recasting of epic's jealous, man-killing Deianira into a vulnerable, sympathetic primary focalizer of events beyond her control. While the imminent arrival of Aeschylus' Agamemnon is assessed from various perspectives, Sophocles 'transfocalizes' the heroic *nostos* by reducing multiple perspectives to the individual, personal reaction of a Greek housewife.[11] Sophocles places his own stamp on the neglected, forgotten Deianira by defining her marital unhappiness as the perpetuation of the uncertainty and emotional turmoil of the newly married Greek maiden who typically departed the sheltered life of her father's house for the bed of an unknown man twice her age (141–54). Since this is tragedy, the loneliness of Deianira's life is extreme. Although rescued from her first suitor, the monstrous river god Achelous, by her current husband, life with the latter has its own problems:

> Finally, Zeus of the contest arranged all well,
> if it really is well. Since our marriage, I feed
> one fear after the next, constantly worrying
> about him. Each night dissolves one difficulty
> and brings on another. We have children, which
> he sees only once at sowing and once at reaping,
> as a farmer visiting a distant field. Such is the
> life of this man, always sending him to and from
> home and in service to another.
>
> (26–35)

The geographical and emotional detachment of Heracles is representative of the larger-than-life, uncompromising and fiercely independent Sophoclean hero, which here reinforces the gulf between the lonely housewife and the monster-slaying son of Zeus. This is not a civilized man of the polis: Heracles acquired his wife as a prize in a primitive contest with Achelous where the 'crashing of hands and bows', 'mix of bull-horns', 'grapplings' and 'deadly head-butts' (516–21) permit no distinction between hero and monster.[12] It is not too difficult to imagine that a man who won his wife in combat might not sufficiently appreciate the value of marital and domestic tranquility, and the demands of maintaining it.

Deianira's emotional limbo and failed incorporation into her husband's house as a bride destroys their family when Heracles finally returns. In a marked departure from Clytemnestra's meeting with the enslaved Trojan princess Cassandra in *Agamemnon* (1035–71), Deianira's encounter with the enslaved princess Iole and gradual recognition of the maiden's threat to her position eventually prompts her own destructive attempt to protect her domestic role. As a former innocent prize of war and object of Heracles' bestial libido herself, Deianira sympathizes with Iole (296–313), but not without realizing the girl's potential to replace her. She therefore attempts to retain her husband's affections quietly and naïvely with a false love-charm given to her by his enemy, the dying centaur Nessos. Mortally wounded with one of Heracles' poison-tipped arrows, he gave her a measure of his blood as a guarantee of her husband's *erôs*. After sending the approaching Heracles a blood-smeared robe by messenger as a gift – as in *Agamemnon*, the robe is an instrument of death – Deianira realizes too late that the blood was tainted with the corrosive poison of the arrow. Upon learning of the poison's horrifying effect on her agonizing husband, Deianira silently leaves to hang herself, never actually receiving the husband whose absence caused so much distress. The tragedy climaxes with a grotesque *nostos* in which the incapacitated and emasculated Heracles arrives on a stretcher, screaming in agony and for his wife's immediate death. His callous disregard of the feelings of his son Hyllus, who attempts to defend his mother, is the final image of this complicated hero's inhumanity.

Agamemnon and Heracles come to such violent ends, in part, because their choices, as heroes, privilege their public obligations to the extreme detriment of their households, where a man's public and financial standing was thought to be most vulnerable. The final *nostos* inverts core features of the template. Despite his previous military victory, the 'down-and-out' hero of Euripides' fragmentary *Telephus* (438 BCE) reluctantly returns in disguise to his now hostile homeland with the intention of staying hidden. *Telephus* expanded a marginal episode of the Trojan War from the cyclic *Cypria*, the aftermath of a battle between Telephus – king of barbarian Mysia but Greek son of Heracles and the Tegean princess Auge – and the Achaeans, who mistakenly attacked his city, Teuthrania, thinking it was Troy.[13] While repulsing the Greek army, Telephus was wounded in the thigh by Achilles' spear. After an oracle stated that the festering wound could only be healed by the one who dealt it, Telephus travelled to Argos to infiltrate the Achaean Assembly in disguise as a beggar in hopes of getting close enough to appeal to Achilles' humanity.

While he was not the first to dramatize this episode, Euripides exploited the full cultural, social and theatrical potential of this novel *nostos*. Upon arrival in Argos, a wounded and desperate Telephus describes himself as a 'king of barbarians, though Greek' in the surviving portion of the prologue (fr. 696). The hero's transformation to a ragged beggar to conceal his identity was apparently noteworthy for its detail in prop-averse tragedy, for it inspired Aristophanes' famous parody of this scene thirteen years later in his *Acharnians* of 425 BCE.[14] That parody implies that Telephus' social and political status expanded the ethical range of the hero in tragedy. His Odyssean deception of his enemies by such means was unconventional, even provocative, as was his quintessentially Euripidean lameness.

Textual and visual evidence indicates that Telephus was eventually exposed when he spoke passionately in defence of himself and the Mysians in the hostile assembly. This kicked off an explosive dramatic sequence culminating in the hero's flight to an altar for refuge while holding the baby Orestes hostage,[15] behaviour that in tragedy at least is more typical of women and old men, not valiant kings of heroic lineage in the prime of life.[16] Ultimately, the Achaeans were persuaded of the fairness of his case and their shared kinship, which was affirmed by his election as guide of the renewed expedition to Troy (fr. 727c). Telephus' famous defense of his people may allude to contemporary social tensions in Athens between the banausic lower classes increasingly empowered in the democracy and the traditional elites who sought to control them (see Roselli, forthcoming). The hero's exceptional rhetorical acumen, in fact, may have evoked the increasing influence of working-class demagogues in the popular assemblies. While comedy implies that Telephus' foreign associations, self-abasement, loquaciousness and unconventional heroism were untypical of tragedy, it seems that Euripides' character exploited the full social and ethical potential of the genre.

Telephus is among a handful of Greek tragedies that passed through the culturally Greek regions of fourth-century Southern Italy and Sicily before being adapted into Latin by Republican tragedians in Rome.[17] Unfortunately, Roman Republican tragedy's disappointing remains provide very little sense of its heroic agents, let alone its treatment of the *nostos*, apart from scattered anecdotes.[18] Agamemnon's *nostos* in Accius' *Clytemnestra* (along with Naevius' *Trojan Horse*) in celebration of the general Pompeius Magnus' completion of his stone theatre in 55 BCE emphasized Pompeius' own recent victory in the east after a six-year war.[19] In this play, the thematic and geographical relevance of Agamemnon's return from the east was highlighted by an over-the-top triumph of 6,000 mules and 3,000 ornamental bowls. While the frequency of such dramatic experiments in aristocratic self-promotion is unknown, the politically-charged Roman theatre, where spectators reacted to the presence of spectating public figures and political allusions in the performance itself, surely affected Roman tragedy's take on the original spirit of Greek models.[20] The extant titles – *Achilles, Aegistos, Ajax the Whipbearer* (Livius Andronicus); *Aesiona, Danae, Hector Departing, Iphiginia, Lucurgus* (Naevius); *Trojan Horse* (both) – suggest the Republican tragedians were working within the traditions of Aeschylus, Sophocles and Euripides.[21]

Arguably Rome's most distinctive contribution to theatrical culture was its development of the unique *praetexta* subgenre, named for the purple-bordered toga worn by the Roman magistrate or general.[22] These historical dramas memorialized significant events in Rome's history with dramatizations analogous to that of the pan-Hellenic aetiologies of fifth-century tragedy, in an effort to cultivate the people's sense of their origins and national pride. This might partly explain ancient scholars' frequent alignment of the *praetexta* with Greek tragedy, despite the form's narrower commemorative aim. The single extant *praetexta* of ancient Rome, the *Octavia* attributed to Seneca, was produced sometime during the Imperial period. While the genre's meagre remains in the Republican period – ten known titles, fewer than fifty total lines – reveal only the most general affinities, they suggest the glorification of a central figure and his exploits. Accius' *Brutus* celebrated Marcus Junius Brutus' role in expelling the Tarquins and establishing the Republic, while legendary narratives of Rome's very beginnings, for example the birth of Romulus and Remus, preserved even older traditions.

Comedy

Telephus shows that not every tragedy ends with suffering and misfortune. Some tragedies ended with the survival of the focal character(s) – albeit often in new and unfavourable circumstances – and even their rescue and triumph. The Greek tragedians' particular interest in the human response to such suffering and misfortune illuminates the heroic paradigm of the other, primary dramatic genre, at least in fifth-century Athens.[23] Comic heroes often exploit the knowledge gained from their own suffering, with fantastic results. In Euripides' *Suppliant Women* (late 420s BCE) the aged and helpless father Iphis witnesses his own daughter Evadne's self-immolation on the pyre of her dead husband. The bereaved father laments that mortals cannot be young and old twice: if only this were possible, they might correct earlier mistakes in their first life (1080–6). This variation of the impossible wish is in some ways fundamental to comic heroism,[24] where aged Athenian citizens worn down by frustration and grief seize the initiative to change their circumstances at moments of political or cultural crisis.[25]

Comedy's vast repertoire is partly a product of the hero's fantastic 'comic project' in the gritty, contentious world of everyday Athens. Nothing is impossible. Heroes form their own societies by magically acquiring private peace treaties, end wars by flying to Olympus on monstrous dung beetles, or organize worldwide sex-strikes; others reform Athens' dysfunctional political situation by resurrecting great leaders of the past, founding utopian cities, or reviving the powers of decrepit divinities. Other plays grapple with seemingly intractable cultural or social ills and end in chaotic fashion, without reaching any perceivable solution (e.g., *Wasps*, 422 BCE). But in each and every extant case, the comic hero enjoys some degree of *success*, in some form. His presumption and insistence that he really *is* heroic, even when his often shameless conduct would be unethical and even criminal in the real world, is to some degree shared by all protagonists.[26] The aggressive, primal egotism of the hero is in some ways symbolized by the phallus – the leather penis stitched to the male costume – which male heroes can grasp as a threat to enemies or an expression of intentions toward a sexually available female.

Comic heroism also extends to the poet himself, particularly when the protagonist becomes his mouthpiece. When Dicaeopolis impersonates Euripides' Telephus in *Acharnians* to elicit pity and sympathy from the hostile Acharnian chorus, the persona of the aged farmer recedes and Aristophanes himself emerges to construct and circulate his own heroic biography. In this instance, Aristophanes compares his political crusade against the demagogue Cleon, who attempted to indict him for statements in his comedy, to Telephus' demand for justice in the Achaean Assembly. Comedy itself is made a heroic labour through the formal mechanism of the comic *parabasis*, where the chorus steps aside from its fictional role to speak in the voice of the poet claiming to educate the audience and protect its interests.[27]

Between the end of Aristophanes' career and the next extant complete Greek comedy, Menander's *Dyscolus* (316), appears a new hero, the young lover, whose comic agency originates in his heart, not his phallus. Unlike his ugly, shameless and egotistical predecessor, the physically and ethically beautiful young man of New Comedy works *within* the existing structures of the *polis*, instead of going beyond or outside them.[28] His aim is overcoming all obstacles to his goal, usually (but not always) marriage to his love interest, an Athenian girl whose citizenship may or may not be known. The plot of *Dyscolus* ('The Bad-Tempered Man') follows the wealthy Sostratus' multiple failed approaches to the maiden's father, the bitter old misanthrope of the title, for permission to marry his daughter.[29] The maiden of *Aspis* is betrothed to an unscrupulous older uncle who invokes his right to marriage when her guardian, her brother, is thought to have died. The friends and extended relations of the absent youth work together to trick the villain to dissolve the engagement. An elaborate attempt to conceal a maiden's pregnancy in *Samia* creates even more obstacles to overcome before she and her child's father can be married. In other words, marriage is the goal of the comic project in the late fourth century because it is the *sine qua non* of its conception of utopia, an idealized Athens populated by citizens born of other virtuous and compassionate citizens joined in lawful marriage. Where the Aristophanic hero's greatest asset was his imagination and audacity, the most important resource of the hero in Menander, as well as later Roman comedy, is typically the trusted agents of his kin, i.e., family, friends, and especially his slave.

FEMALE AGENTS

Though not a focal point of the previous discussion, the agency afforded Clytemnestra and Deianira in Greek tragedy is considerable. Women in tragedy and comedy wield significant power despite their marginal status in real life.[30] While tragedy and comedy's fixation on the disastrous potential of unsupervised women reflects male anxiety, the comic poets at least recognized the dramatic potential of women bent on evil or good to offer new content and expand their repertoire.[31] Comedy's development of the female-citizen type can illustrate its competitive 'marketplace' of innovation, where poets sought the next new thing by drawing on a common pool of options and refashioning as necessary. The rapid evolution of themes and ideas in this competitive frame throws the comparatively gradual and much less perceptible changes of other fifth-century genres, tragedy and satyr play, into sharp relief.

While attempts to identify the origin of a topos with any certainty are difficult (and often misguided), Aristophanes' *Knights* (424) is not a bad place to start for the comic 'wife'. By 'wife' I mean a heavily stylized female with whom comedy's poet-hero seeks a permanent, sexual relationship for some greater benefit, as opposed to a marriageable woman according to the stricter norms of Athenian society.[32] In *Knights*, the poet imagines the rapid ascent of his young career through his imagined courtship and seduction of the demanding *Kômôidodidaskalia* ('comic production'), whose interest his comic predecessors could never sustain (517–19).[33] One such predecessor, Cratinus, responded by expanding this courtship conceit into something grander in his *Pytinê* ('Wine Flask') the following year, making himself both the hero and spouse of *Kômôidia* ('Comedy'), with whom he had become estranged thanks to his drinking. The plot followed their marital struggles and inevitable reconciliation that proved, once again, Cratinus' sole right to the genre in a way Aristophanes could only pretend.

As personified abstractions, *Kômôidodidaskalia* and *Comedy* represent a transition from comedy's earliest females, Olympian goddesses in older mythological burlesque, to the fictional citizen-wives of Aristophanes' groundbreaking 'women plays' of 411.[34] The comic wife opened up the theme of Athenian women and their own domestic world to representation that had been hitherto forbidden for most of the fifth century.[35] Readers will be most familiar with the wives of *Lysistrata*, whose sex-strike ends the Peloponnesian War by asserting the polis' complete dependence on their essential contributions to its domestic sphere. However, Aristophanes' portrayal of female agency in his second play of that same year, *Thesmophoriazusae* ('Women at the Thesmophoria Festival'), may offer greater insights into the evolution of this key part of the comic repertoire. At an all-female religious festival, Athens' wives conspire to destroy the tragedian Euripides for his putatively misogynistic portrayals of them. To avert his own destruction, Euripides convinces his brash and buffoonish 'Inlaw' to infiltrate the festival as a woman and deliver a speech to dissuade his enemies. When his turn to denounce Euripides arrives, the tactless Inlaw instead defends his kinsman by rehashing some favorite misogynistic vignettes of popular tradition as types of women that Euripides *did not include* in his tragedy, beginning with his own marriage:

> I'd been married only
> three days, and my husband was sleeping beside me.
> But I had a boyfriend who'd deflowered me when I
> was seven and was still hot for me. He came
> scratching at my door and I knew right away who
> it was. I start to steal downstairs, and my husband
> asks, 'Where are you going downstairs?' 'Where?
> My stomach is churning, husband, so I'm going to
> the shitter.' 'Go on then.' And he starts grinding
> up juniper berries, dillweed, and sage, while I pour
> water into the door socket and go out to meet my
> lover. Then I bend over, holding onto the laurel tree
> by Apollo's Pillar, and get my grinding . . .
>
> (478–89)

The corrupted wife's shameless liaison inverts the gender roles of her marriage by reducing her husband to the kitchen while she copulates in public. Neither, Inlaw continues, does Euripides reveal how wives sleep with slaves and stable-boys (491f.), nor how they chew garlic, to mask the scent of lovers who have ravished them, when their husbands return from work in the morning. Nor does he mention the wife who, upon being surprised by her husband's arrival home, spreads out her 'weavings' in the sun's light to impress her husband while her lover makes a quick escape unseen. The speech climaxes with the corruption of the household's biological integrity, the worst evil:

> And I know another wife who pretended to be in
> labour for ten days, until she could buy a baby, while

her husband was running all over town buying medicine
to quicken birth. An old woman brought it in a pot,
the baby I mean, its mouth stuffed with a honeycomb
so it wouldn't cry. Then the old woman gave the signal
and the wife yells, 'Out you go, husband, out you go;
this time I think I'm giving birth!' Yes, the baby had
kicked the pot's belly! He ran out joyous, she unplugged
the child's mouth, and it raised a shout. Then the dirty
old lady who'd brought the baby runs out to the husband
smiling and says, 'You've got a lion, sir, a lion, the very
image of yourself, sir, with everything a perfect match,
its little weenie too, curled over like an acorn!'

(502–16)

The rapid, abbreviated form of this comic bricolage suggests that the audience's familiarity with its content could be assumed. Inlaw's claim that 'Euripides has not shown' such things seemingly invites the audience to identify it with another repertoire. While hardly any trace of such narratives is found in the extant fragments of earlier comedy,[36] the evil, self-indulgent and/or adulterous wife dates from Hesiod's didactic epic as well as iambic poetry of the Archaic period. Semonides of Amorgos' poem of over a hundred lines on the animal origins of different kinds of women is an early example of the kind of misogynistic attitudes permeating Greek literature.[37]

At some point, the popular adultery narrative of such colourful variety in the speech of Inlaw became a centrepiece of one of the most popular dramatic genres of Graeco-Roman antiquity, the mime.[38] The origins of Greek mime are debated and the date at which it achieved some formal stability is unknown. While some sources claim that the mimes of the Syracusan poet Sophron were popular in fifth-century Athens, the genre's influence on other literary forms first becomes apparent in the Hellenistic period.[39] In Rome, a separate tradition of popular improvised street performance preceded mime's inclusion at the *Floralia* (or *Ludi Florales*), a festival created in the late third/early second century BCE. I bypass the complications of distinct Greek and Roman traditions by focusing primarily on the 'adultery plot' that remained both popular and relatively stable in its repertoire for seven centuries.[40] The *nostos* quality of its plot-scheme is striking. Typically, a suave adulterer (*cultus adulter*) seeks and gains access to a newly married woman (*callida nupta*), while her naïve husband (*stupidus*) is away. Wives also sleep with slaves and attempt to poison their husbands, while enraged husbands pursue elusive adulterers around the house. The well-attested seduction plot turns on the husband's sudden return just as the lovers get down to business, which forces the intruder into hiding, usually in a chest that becomes the locus of comic business.[41] Skits concluded with the discovery of the adulterer and an eruption of slapstick violence (or chaos) until the husband is sufficiently humiliated and the seducer able to escape. Horace provides a sense of the chaos in one of his *Sermones* (published c. 35 BCE), thought to borrow from an adultery scenario:

> The door shatters, the dog barks, the house everywhere explodes with crashing, as the wife deathly pale leaps from bed, the complicit maid laments her fate, she fears for her legs, the woman for her dowry, I for myself, as I am forced to flee barefoot with my tunic undone, lest my finances, ass, or in any case my reputation pay the price.
>
> (1.2.128–34)

In its corporality, slapstick, and 'busyness', mime exhibits clear affinities with Greek and Roman comedy.[42] A script partially preserved on the verso of a papyrus (*P. Oxy.* 413) and dated to a century or two after Horace (c. first/second century CE) entitled 'The Adulteress' shows a mistress' savage reaction to being rebuffed by one of her slaves, who loves another slave. The obscenity ('fuck': 108), frenetic stage action of repeated entrances and exits, and the mistress' plot to poison her husband (161–2) echo the misogynistic tropes of earlier Greek poetry. In performance, at least, Old Comedy anticipated many other mime tropes including the nighttime rendezvous, hoodwinked husband, adulterer's infiltration of the house, the mistress' sex with slaves, etc.[43]

This is not to suggest that mime was confined to the adultery plot. Mime in fact possessed the widest repertoire of any dramatic genre of antiquity, and in scope ranged from short pieces of one or two scenes (*paignia*) to longer narratives with a plot (*hypotheseis*).[44] Although it frequently treated real life, it also burlesqued myth by setting the gods in the everyday world in the style of fifth- and fourth-century comedy.[45] It also parodied classical works. On the recto of *P. Oxy.* 413, a party of Greeks consisting of a heroine named Charition, her brother, a ship captain and a buffoon attempt to escape a barbarian horde and their king on an unknown foreign coast off the Indian Ocean. The action broadly resembles that of a romantic adventure plot from the Greek novel, possibly even Euripides' *Iphigenia Among the Taurians*, but with farting.[46]

The adultery mime merits particular attention for what it reveals about the comic treatment of a significant cultural anxiety and its consistent popularity for centuries. Its appeal was probably less its eroticism, which appeared often enough in comedy, than its *mimesis* of adultery and the performance of a wife's corruption. For it is one thing to allude to something, and a completely different thing to perform it. Mimic performance apparently specialized in portraying things which comedy, for example, only alluded to.[47] For comparison, consider the comedy that most closely resembles the adultery mime, the *Amphitruo* of Plautus, Rome's prolific comic poet of the late third and early second century. A randy Jupiter transforms himself into Alcumena's husband, Amphitruo, who is away at war, and seduces his young wife. Mercury has similarly transformed himself into Amphitruo's slave, Sosia, to act as Zeus' lookout before the house, where the action is confined. Slapstick, comic violence, misrecognitions and disorientation follow, although neither Jupiter's seduction of the married Alcumena nor the inner space of Amphitruo's house are ever revealed to the spectators. This particular case of adultery was uncontroversial because of its mythological currency and happy ending, the birth of Heracles, greatest culture hero of antiquity. The final *deus ex machina* ('god from the machine'), i.e. the sudden introduction of a god with the theatrical crane to effect a solution to the onstage conflict, confirms as much: Jupiter somewhat amusingly tells the newly arrived Amphitruo to forgive his wife's affair because she could not help it. The emergence and widespread popularity of the mime, by contrast, seems to exemplify not just genre's mediation of literary culture and social context, but the successful expansion of its repertoire by appropriating territory either unclaimed by or inaccessible to other, more mainstream forms.

ACTS OF GODS

The dramatic resolution imposed by Zeus the Adulterer is a good segue to the final aspect of dramatic repertoire in this chapter, divine agents. At the first mention of gods in Graeco-Roman theatre, most undergraduates, for example, immediately think of the *deus ex machina*. But such neat epiphanies are merely the most explicit intrusion of the divine in the (largely) human plots of drama. Gods are pervasive in drama by virtue of the form's origins in the cult of Dionysus, a vegetation god associated with wine, revelry and the freeing of boundaries generally.[48] But Dionysus' role in early tragedy is hazy, as are most of the Dionysiac aspects of its repertoire. And ancient sources in fact claim that the decline of the Dionysiac precipitated the introduction into the festivals of satyr play and its chorus of Dionysus' boon companions, the goat-human man-child satyrs, who maintain the god's regular connection to the theatre. While he appears infrequently in the extant evidence for satyr play – a central conceit of the genre is the satyrs' separation from their master – Dionysus is frequently present *in the spirit* of symposiastic practice as a benign force.[49] For example, in the sole extant satyr play, Euripides' *Cyclops*, the god is embodied in the wine of Maron, which inebriates the cannibalistic Polyphemus and liberates Odysseus, his men and the satyrs. The god seems to be evoked generally by the constant horseplay and search for sex, drink, music and other leisure activities characterizing the satyrs' behaviour. Their frequent involvement in aetiologies, such as the foundations of critical, pan-Hellenic institutions, e.g., an athletic festival (Aeschylus' *Theôroi*), the acquisition of fire (*Prometheus the Fire-Bearer*), the invention of the lyre (Sophocles' *Trackers*), stresses the god's status as a culture hero.[50]

Unlike the Dionysiac in satyr play, the gods of fifth-century tragedy oversee the mortal world with a harsher, darker form of justice without empathy or regret, and with only occasional benevolence.[51] Although he does not appear, *Agamemnon*'s Zeus, for example, enforces moral law with little thought for the circumstances of his human agents. In fact, tragedy's Zeus almost never appears in person.[52] The Furies, Apollo and Athena in the same poet's *Eumenides*, by contrast, appear in person to debate Orestes' fate, and the *Prometheus Bound* has more divine than mortal characters. Sophocles' gods seem especially cruel for their disinterest in human suffering, as the Apollo of *Oedipus Tyrannus*, whose communication through oracles at the beginning of the play is only slightly less unsettling than his silence at the end. Zeus simply looks on as Heracles, his son, perishes in excruciating pain in *Trachiniae*.

The gods' influence is more explicit in Euripides, and communicated typically from the margins, perhaps most idiosyncratically in divine prologues. Whether their intentions are good or evil, his gods calibrate audience expectations by sharing with the spectators their privileged knowledge, which is concealed from those onstage.[53] *Hippolytus'* Aphrodite outlines the revenge she plans against Hippolytus, son of the Athenian king Theseus, so that the audience recognizes the reason for his stepmother's overpowering lust for him. Although the goddess' cool admission of the suffering in store for the unsuspecting mortals has proven to be more memorable, the more uplifting plans of benevolent figures like the Apollo of *Alcestis* (438) and (especially) the Hermes in *Ion* (late 410s) have arguably exerted a more distinctive, farther-reaching effect on Greek and Roman drama. In the latter prologue, Hermes' remarks set the stage for the audience: the Delphic location, Apollo's rape of Creusa, Ion's birth, Creusa's marriage to Xouthus and, most importantly, Apollo's plan for a happy ending. The audience can therefore enjoy the events without despairing for the hero.

Sometime in the second half of the fourth century, comedy began incorporating this prologue, among other features, in its departure from certain comic conventions and cultivation of greater affinities with tragedy and its divine universe. Divine prologues, attested in at least seven Menandrian comedies, separate the divine and mortal worlds that earlier comedy took great pleasure in collapsing. At a basic level, this connection of the everyday events of the plot to divine providence aggrandizes the ordinary world of its fictional characters, and aligns audience sympathy with some against others. Certain ethical and comic effects like dramatic irony allow audiences to enjoy characters' distress with the assurance of a happy ending.[54] Menander's preference for benevolent divine personifications – 'Chance' (*Aspis*), 'Ignorance' (*Peirikeiromenê*), 'Refutation' (play unknown, fr. 507) – may attempt to distance his world from the cruel associations of the Olympians in tragedy, or even the ridiculous figures of early fourth century BCE comic burlesque.[55] The later Roman comic poets Plautus and Terence generally observe a similar separation, which underscores the uniqueness of *Amphitruo*.[56]

Since the gods of Roman Republican tragedy and *praetexta* are unknown, only those of the extant imperial tragedy of the stoic philosopher Seneca remain. The stoic belief that the gods do not perniciously act against human will has sometimes been taken as an explanation for their omission as significant agents in Seneca's plays. They usually do not appear in the flesh, but Seneca's gods are repeatedly linked to crime and punishment.[57] At one extreme is the *Thyestes* with its horrible centrepiece of the protagonist's feast on his own children, which reduces the gods to mere spectators who eventually abandon the cosmic structure to collapse in the 'star ode' (789–884). Perhaps more representative is the shadowy Venus who may or may not be influencing the events of Seneca's *Phaedra*, which responds partly to Euripides' *Hippolytus*.[58] By removing the prologue and understating Hippolytus' relationship with Diana, Seneca diminishes the divine to the extent that its existence is open to question. Phaedra herself understands her passion (124–8) as Venus' retaliation against the descendants of Helios: the Sun, Phaedra's grandfather, exposed Venus' affair with Mars in the archetypal adulterer story found as early as Homer (*Od.* 8.266–320).[59] The goddess' motive elegantly fits within the larger thematic nexus of adultery imposed on the Hippolytus myth by Seneca. Phaedra's passion strikes during her husband's absence in Hades, where he abets Peirithous' shameful attempt to abduct Persephone. In the Euripidean model, Theseus was abroad (piously observing *theôria*). This is the same Peirithous whose father, Ixion, attempted to seduce Hera and was confined to the Underworld on a burning wheel. These connections make divine involvement difficult to articulate, but this may be precisely the effect Seneca sought.

The mythological narratives of the Graeco-Roman tragic repertoire eventually won even greater popularity in the altogether different genre of pantomime.[60] Its earliest appearance in the extant literature may be found at the end of Xenophon's *Symposium*, where the dinner guests of the wealthy Athenian Callias were treated to a short performance of the 'marriage' of Dionysus and Ariadne sometime in 422 BCE:

> Then Ariadne appeared, dressed as a bride, and sat down on a chair. Although Dionysus had not yet appeared, a Bacchic rhythm struck up on the flute. And [the guests] admired the dancing master. And Ariadne immediately upon hearing the music made known to all that she listened with pleasure. She

turned to the sound, and did not rise, but was remaining calm with difficulty. When Dionysus saw her, he danced over and sat her on his lap in an affectionate way, and then embracing her, gave her a kiss. She acted modestly, but still embraced him passionately. As they watched, the guests clapped and cheered. And as Dionysus rose, he stood up Ariadne with him, and then they acted kissing and caressing each other. Beholding the beauty of Dionysus and the bloom of Ariadne, who weren't burlesquing the myth but kissing honestly, the guests watched all aflutter. For they heard Dionysus asking her if she loved him, and she swore – not only to Dionysus but to all present – that she did, as any boy and girl had ever loved one another. And they did not seem like they were playing roles, but actually doing what they had long desired . . .

(3–6)

While the genre of this performance is not stated explicitly, the evidence on the whole inclines to pantomime ('one who imitates all things'), albeit with some exceptional features.[61] Dionysus' 'marriage' to the scorned Ariadne, Phaedra's elder sister, is one of the divine amours described by the second-century CE writer Lucian (*Salt.* 59–60) as a standard subject of the dance-performance. Pantomime reached its most developed form during the Augustan period, when several sources date the innovations of the tragic and comic dancers Pylades of Cilicia and the Alexandrian Bathyllos, respectively. Yet performances similar to that enjoyed by Callias' guests are attested in Greece hundreds of years earlier than Pylades and Bathyllos.[62]

The scale of pantomime was anywhere from that of a theatrical production, i.e., three or more actors with musicians, to a single actor dancing in a private residence. Though often supported by an *aulos*-player (flutist), percussionist and singer(s), the pantomime's body was the focal point and primary medium of the performance. In his dialogue *On the Dance*, Lucian claims that the repertoire of a competent pantomime included theogonic, dynastic, aetiological, heroic and even historical myth. Yet he frustratingly offers only the barest hints as to how dancers conveyed such mythological narrative through 'postures' (*schêmata*; ibid. 36) and nuances of movement that enabled audiences to 'hear' (62) and discern seamless shifts between personas, actions and scenes. One ancient anecdote claims that in Nero's reign, the cynic philosopher Demetrius complained during a pantomime that the excellence of the performance was due to the skill of the musicians and singer, not the dancer. After silencing the music, the dancer quieted his critic with an impressive performance of the affair of Ares and Aphrodite that proved pantomime's excellence lay primarily in the dancing. The story nicely illustrates pantomime's striking reduction of tragedy's numerous parts and codes – multiple actors, chorus and musicians performing in the same space – to a concentrated focus on a single dancer (albeit supported by musicians) performing a multiplicity of roles in a paratactic narrative without pause:⁶³ the nameless pantomime of the anecdote danced the illicit love-making of the gods; the 'tattling' of the sole witness, Helios; Hephaestus' trap; the enjoyment of Olympian witnesses; Aphrodite's shame; and Ares' helplessness. Myth is remediated from speech, action, and choral dance to a silent dancer whose body becomes a 'mouth' (*Anth. Lat.* 100.9f).⁶⁴

Pantomime's dance may have required a greater imaginative contribution from audiences, who needed to fill conceptual gaps when, for example, the pantomime was imitating the dance of a pair,⁶⁵ and recognize the visual vocabulary of emotion and character. But if performers exploited the extant choreographic repertoires of the countless public forms of cultic and secular dance, this interpretative matrix may have been easier to acquire than we might think.⁶⁶ Some anecdotes imply that pantomimes expressed a kind of universal language, one capable of bridging cultures, as an explanation of the genre's great popularity.⁶⁷ Dancers' representation of gender, particularly male mimicry of femininity through fluid, effeminate movements of the neck and upper body, convinced critics of the corrosive effects of such androgynous gestures on dancer and spectator.

The above anecdote of Lucian about the philosopher Demetrius hints at a certain defensive attitude of practitioners and partisans of the pantomime, who may have felt obliged to defend that aspect of the performance against more established arts like music. Lucian's explicit comparison of pantomime performance to that of the tragic actor elaborates the pantomime aesthetic, and its premium on fluidity, virtuosity and immediacy in comparison to the repellent, frightful and ill-proportioned tragic actor. The latter's elevated stature, oversized mask with gaping mouth and body padding enhance the unpleasantness of his lamentations (27). Aside from tragedy's alleged physical ugliness, the speaker imputes a static, artificial quality to its aesthetic compared to the dancer, whose attractive (29) yet non-committal face expressed a greater range of emotion and better complemented the performance's aggregate parts of body and song. This showcase of pantomime's attractions against the genre with which it shared its mythological content suggests that, at least during Lucian's time, the two genres competed for the same audience.

CONCLUSION

The texts and historical developments of repertoire in this chapter illustrate the function of genre as mediating concept between culture and society and theatrical performance of antiquity. The unique approach to the cultural world through each genre's distinctive repertoire is strikingly illustrated by its variation of the adultery scenario that features throughout the discussion, beginning with the *nostos* subplot. Sophocles' shift of perspective from Aeschylus' conniving adulteress, Clytemnestra, to the lonely housewife, and his remotivation of a sympathetic heroine, creatively (and cruelly) elaborates this cultural anxiety. His *Trachiniae* is thus testimony to the breadth of the tragic repertoire of the *nostos*, which could pivot on the horrible mistake of even the most loyal, well-intentioned wife. It seems that Euripides' *Telephus* shifts the focus of the *nostos* towards class and status and away from female danger by investing it with different social and ethnic subtexts. The particular threat faced by Mysian Telephus, his fellow Greeks, may reveal tensions among ethnic groups and classes in contemporary Athens.

The clearest example of a genre's evolution by the incorporation of content typically imagined as 'non-art' is Greek comedy's reaction to tragedy, particularly its interest in the suffering of its heroes and portrayal of women. In comedy, the suffering of the comic hero is commonly not the end of the road, but a spur to action, the point of departure for a project that secures future glory and a higher-quality second life. The rebirth and quasi-divine agency of the aging comic hero performs what a tragic hero beaten down by the world but resurrected for a second shot at life could look like. The same wish-fulfillment, but in a far more subdued, culturally normative form is enjoyed by the youthful hero of later Greek and Roman New Comedy, whose story inevitably reaches the happy outcome described in a divine prologue. The unique opportunism of the comic genre can be seen in its treatment of gender, which comic poets realized they could present as popular entertainment. As the zenith of comedy's respectable female character, the maiden or wife of New Comedy is the end of a process that began in Old Comedy's gradual expansion into real women's domestic world. This critical exploration of the comic repertoire, exemplified by Aristophanes' women plays of 411, was almost certainly driven by comic poets' interest in offering themes and content beyond the reach of other forms.

In similar fashion, the emergence of mime and pantomime, which did not become fully developed theatrical forms until the Roman period, may have been occasioned by the stagnation of tragedy and comedy. Mime developed into the most popular form of drama in part by its expansive mimesis of topics seemingly off-limits to the major genres, most probably adulterous seduction. In presenting an unfiltered look at marital infidelity as an independent narrative, literary and sub-literary mime seems to have exceeded in popularity other forms of stage drama. Extant sources show that the partisans of the wildly popular pantomime argued for the genre's legitimacy by presenting it as a superior alternative to other theatrical conduits of myth, particularly tragedy, for whose active performance culture in later antiquity there is slim evidence. Dancers conceived their isolation and elevation of one dimension of the major dramatic forms, dance, as an improvement over older, fading genres.

If the extant genres of Graeco-Roman theatre surveyed here share certain traits, among them are surely the requisite flexibility and responsiveness to develop their repertoires gradually in reaction to developments in other, rival forms. Opportunistic development and expansion into the margins between literary worlds, where new cultural topoi were waiting to be discovered, allowed these genres to sustain a long-term appeal that would lead to cultural relevance, and survival of the long journey from antiquity to our present day.[68]

CHAPTER NINE

Technologies of Performance

Machines, Props, Dramaturgy

PETER V. MÖLLENDORFF
(translated from German by Martin Revermann)

The history of ancient theatre cannot be described as a linear development. This is because its contexts (spatial, political, cultural) are too heterogeneous respectively, and the preserved pieces of documentation too discontinuous. The resulting impression is one of a series of disparate closed systems which as a whole share only quite general characteristics with each other. This general observation also applies to technologies of performance more specifically. In our time, technological development is almost by default considered to be a history of progress. As far as ancient theatre technology is concerned, however, such an assumption is not warranted by the relatively sparse evidence since, somewhat paradoxically, most is known about the use of performance technology in the earliest phase of institutionalized theatre in the fifth century BCE, less about Hellenistic theatre, and very little indeed about performance technology in the theatre of the Roman Republic, the imperial period and late antiquity, despite the fact that Greek and Roman theatre buildings show significant architectural similarities.[1]

This negative finding as far as Roman theatre is concerned is hard to explain. Apparently we have fallen victim to adverse chance. For by the first century BCE already Roman theatre had a penchant for the monumental and spectacular, as was noted critically by contemporaries. According to Horace, the content of the plays got lost among the spectators' loud conversation,[2] while Cicero remarks that the sumptuous use of props alone led to an atmosphere characterized less by 'serenity' (*hilaritas*) and 'entertainment' (*delectatio*) than by the 'admiration of the riff-raff' (*popularis admiratio*).[3] Livy even goes so far as to call the theatrical extravaganza of his time 'insanity' (*insania*).[4] In view of all of this it seems likely that, by the imperial period at the latest, Roman theatre had elaborate machinery which could be used for staging ever-changing spectacular surprises. To make those possible, most of the machinery needed would be hidden underneath the raised stage. Seneca (*Epist. mor.* 88.22) mentions 'machine workers' (*machinatores*) and their impressive technologies,[5] which were a good fit for the analogous phenomenon, the paratheatrical amphitheatre.[6] Whether in the *Ars Poetica* (191f.) Horace speaks of the *deus ex machina*, which would imply the use of a stage crane at his time, is not entirely clear from the context but possible. Mime and certainly pantomime (the two main forms of theatre in the Roman imperial period) presumably worked well dramaturgically without any machinery. But since only once in preserved Roman theatre scripts is the use of a mechanical device attested (in Seneca's *Medea*, on which see below), there is bound to be a focus in this chapter on Greek theatre of the classical period. For even Roman comedies, which contain a sufficient number of metatheatrical passages, tell us nothing on this matter (unlike Greek Old Comedy). This prompts the suspicion (certainty is out of the question here) that in this genre at least stage machines were not being used a great deal, and that when they were being used they did not leave a footprint in the scripts we have.

Cicero, however, does mention a theatre curtain (*aulaeum*) – a device unknown to the Greek theatre – which was dropped at the beginning of a play and raised at its end.[7] The right moment was indicated by the beat of wooden clappers (*scabella*). In the relevant passage Cicero maintains that lifting the curtain was designed to hide a dramatically inept ending which, for him, is typical of the mime. A similar verdict, this time about the use by tragic playwrights of the crane with a *deus ex machina* on it, is made by the fourth-century Greek comic playwright Antiphanes in his play *Poiêsis* (fr. 189.12–15 Kassel-Austin): 'Then, when they [i.e. tragic poets] have nothing more to say / and have totally run of steam in their plays, / they lift the crane like their finger, / and for the audience this is satisfactory.'

In general, the point has to be made that, with the exception of a limited number of passages in secondary texts, it is the ancient dramatic texts themselves which are our only source for questions to do with performance and the use of technology. For the latter in particular no information is provided by theatre-related vase paintings while archaeological remains of theatre machines reveal, at best, something about their position within a particular theatre building but little about their precise appearance and nothing about their actual use in concrete instances. In the preserved dramatic scripts, on the other hand, the use of stage technology is sometimes pointed out quite explicitly but in the vast majority of cases only implied. And since there is no paratext in the form of stage directions (which ancient playwrights do not seem to have written in the first place), the dramatic texts only permit interpretations and suggest certain modes of *mise-en-scène* while usually allowing for some hermeneutic leeway. Even if one were to take the (highly questionable) view that every significant action is reflected in the dramatic script,[8] this would only lead to a very limited impression of the stage action. More important and profitable than reconstructing precise performance details is analysing the specific dramaturgical and semiotic relevance associated with the use of theatre machines.

The Theatre of Dionysus in Athens in which most of the preserved classical plays appear to have been performed at one point[9] certainly had two specific machines, the *ekkyklêma* (also sometimes called *exôstra*)[10] and the crane.[11] It must remain open whether in addition there also were other, smaller machines and subterranean pathways, as is insinuated by the sophist Pollux of Naucratis (second century CE) who, however, may have conflated information about various theatres and from different time periods.[12] There can be no doubt that in the Athenian theatre there were machines capable of generating a variety of sounds (like thunder), because such were, for instance, needed for the appearance of the chorus of clouds in Aristophanes' comedy of the same title (see *Clouds* 291–4).[13] The ancient *Life of Aeschylus* assumes the frequent use of scenic technology of this dramatist (the first we have a significant amount of evidence for) in the 450s BCE at the latest.[14] Aeschylus' *Oresteia* (458 BCE) clearly presupposes the availability of a stage house (*skênê*), and on the assumption that not one and the same set of background painting (*skênographia*) was used to signify both Agamemnon's palace and the acropolis of Athens there also had to be the possibility of changing scenography.

CRANE AND *EKKYKLÊMA*

The crane, attested in a scene of Aristophanes,[15] resembled that of a modern ship.[16] It was anchored in a stone platform behind the middle of the *skênê* building,[17] and when not in use its arm (which could be swung to the sides and lifted up or down) was probably lying flat on the roof of the stage house (Figure 9.1).[18] Its function was to simulate flight, hence its predominant use in tragedy for sudden and spectacular entries, of divinities in particular. The ending of Euripides' *Electra* can serve as a good example. In this play (1221ff.) Orestes and Electra stand on stage in front of their mother's corpse and decide to cover her with a piece of cloth, intending to use this ritual action also to put

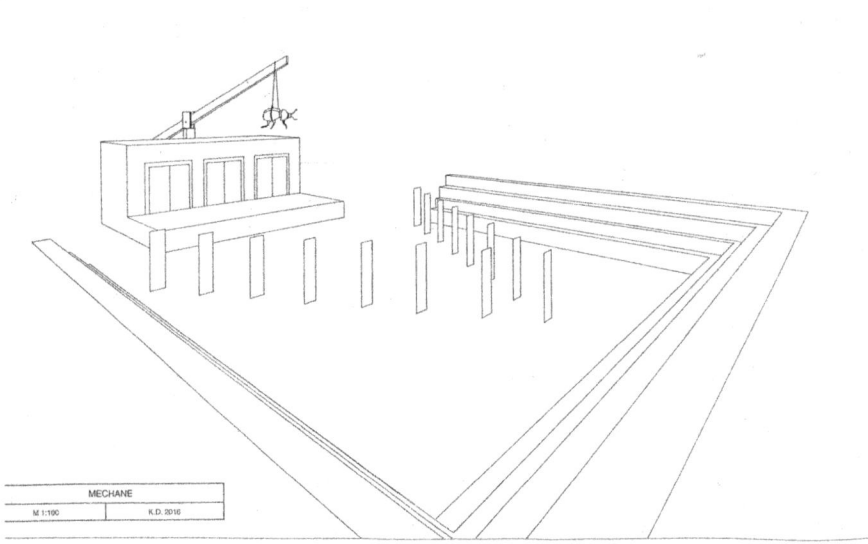

FIGURE 9.1: Schematic rendering of the stage with crane (loosely modelled on a scene in Aristophanes' *Peace*). The rectangles hint at a possible blocking of the chorus in the orchestra. It becomes strikingly clear how much audience perception was informed by the chorus and its movements. Drawing by Katrin Dolle.

a symbolic end to the concatenation of horrors which has been haunting the House of Atreus for several generations (1231f.). For acoustical reasons alone it seems obvious that while speaking these words the actors were turning their backs to the stage house and were looking downwards (since they were dealing with the body of Clytemnestra below them). The chorus, standing below the stage in the orchestra, looks up to them and suddenly spots the Dioscuri (Castor and Pollux) approach from the direction of the palace roof (1233–7).

The pointer to the gods' movements is not only semantic but also rhythmical in that there is a change from the lyric metres of Electra and Orestes to anapaestic dimeters delivered by the chorus. The reference to the top of the roof (*Electra* 1233) is decisive for assuming that the crane is being used here. The speed of its movement is measured, as is made clear by the repetition of the verb 'they are walking' (*bainousin*) (*Electra* 1233 and 1237). Since there is no physical contact, it seems correct to infer that the two deities were picked up behind the stage house, hidden from the spectators, moved towards the roof and then put down on it.[19] This movement may have started well before *Electra* 1233. If so, the audience saw the gods approach before they were being noticed by the members of the chorus (who were focused on Clytemnestra's body anyway). They were therefore able to savour the chorus' anxiety as well. The subsequent action was taking place on three planes simultaneously. At the end of the scene Orestes and Electra leave the stage via the two side entrances while Castor and Pollux evidently fly off on the crane again, because they explicitly mention (at *Electra* 1349) that they intend to travel via air to the Sea of Sicily. Depending on how much realism is to be assumed, swinging the crane back behind the stage house, i.e. towards the south-west where the Sea of Sicily is located relative to the theatre, would be appropriate for the play's fiction. The chorus alone remains, leaving pessimistic blessings for Electra and Orestes before departing from the orchestra. The action which had previously seemed to have come to an end has now literally exploded in all directions.

Only *prima facie* therefore does the use of the crane constitute a strong coda for the dramatic action. At a second glance the closure which the plot has arrived at turns out to be deceptive and opens up the action by identifying new dramatic necessities and activities. In Euripides' *Electra*, Agamemnon's children are given clear instructions by Castor and Pollux (1284–91): Electra is to accompany Pylades to his homeland of Phocis as his wife, whereas Orestes is to go to Athens to be purged from the murder he has committed. Not only are the siblings separated for good, only hours after they had found each other, but the close friends, Orestes and Pylades, have to leave each other as well. Contrary to their earlier assumption that the suffering had come to an end (*Electra* 1231f.) the evil continues: an end is now even further out of sight. If tragedy needs a clear closure by its nature, this would be an instance of an 'open ending'. This is not without precedent in previous Greek literature. Both *Iliad* and *Odyssey* finish with an open ending: after Hector's death the battle for Troy will go on, and Odysseus will have to leave his new-found Ithaca again to be purged, similar to Orestes, from an act of violence (in his case that of Polyphemus) by sacrificing to Poseidon. In a comparable fashion, Pindar always presents the extraordinary achievements of the athletes he celebrates as a continuum of previous exploits by mythical heroes and the expectation of further great deeds in the future.[20] Open narrative technique, therefore, may be a persistent concern of archaic and classical culture, and is being evoked in this instance by the deployment of a stage machine.

The *ekkyklêma* (Figure 9.2), explicitly mentioned in Aristophanes twice,[21] was a platform which could be wheeled out from the *skênê* onto the stage. On it the results of (usually lethal) action within the building were demonstrated and (re)integrated into the action. Depending on their dramatic functions, the *ekkyklêma* tends to be used in climactic moments, yet at points within the plot where conflicts might still be resolved or actions of integration and reconciliation are still possible. The crane, on the other hand, would normally be used in the closural sequence. Accordingly, the deployment of the *ekkyklêma* requires dramaturgical preparation. It turns out that around the appearance of the *ekkyklêma* a specific scene type starts to evolve which can be spotted across a

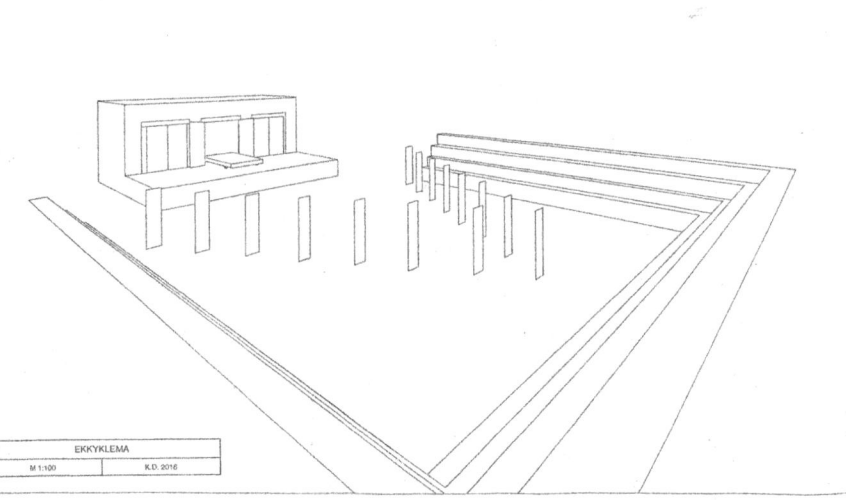

FIGURE 9.2: Schematic rendering of the stage with *ekkyklêma*. The rectangles hint at a possible blocking of the chorus in the orchestra. Here too the prominent role of the chorus in shaping audience perception is evident. For spectators in the lower tiers a good view of the *ekkyklêma* was not guaranteed when the chorus was moving in the orchestra. Drawing by Katrin Dolle.

significant span of time and in various tragic playwrights.[22] From the very start the chorus functions as spectator and therefore as a focal point for the audience. The chorus has learned, often by way of an eye-witness narrative, that some catastrophe has occurred within the stage house. Now the chorus is considering a possible intervention or invokes the suffering caused by the catastrophe. The premonition of the chorus is confirmed by a character who emerges from the *skênê*. The chorus demands that the door of the *skênê* be opened and the calamity be revealed: the door opens, the *ekkyklêma* with its tableau is being wheeled out, and the chorus, together with everyone else present on stage, reacts in horror and pain. Now the presentation of the *ekkyklêma*-based tableau segues into speech action. A rapport with the figures on the *ekkyklêma* is being established, and the tableau is being integrated into the scene on the main stage.

The *Heracles* by Euripides may function as an illustration of this scene type. The scene in question extends over c. 550 verses in the preserved playscript. The chorus has a premonition of the bloodbath caused by the mad Heracles in his own palace and verbalizes its anxieties (875–909). They are confirmed by a servant who emerges from the palace (910–1015), and the chorus starts lamenting (1016–27). Now the palace door opens, as is pointed out immediately (1028–38), and the *ekkyklêma* is brought out showing Heracles, a sight confirmed by the chorus (1028–38). They are joined by Heracles' father Amphitruo, later by Theseus as well. They establish contact with Heracles and lead him from the horror of his deed back into their community (1039–1163ff.). The eventual withdrawal of the *ekkyklêma* back into the stage house is being thematized only superficially at the very end of the play (1422), together with the request to bring the dead children (who must still be lying on the platform of the *ekkyklêma*) back into the palace.[23]

The tragic *ekkyklêma* therefore does not show anything new but summarizes, so to speak, an interior event and presents it in the form of a result. In so doing, this technology offers information that is complementary to the preceding report but also creates, by its picturesque nature and positioning on stage, a new permanence of the action, a kind of duration and memorability of impression which is usually not possible to generate in theatre with its relentless progression of presentation and reception. Put succinctly, the *ekkyklêma* functions as an inverted ekphrasis of sorts by providing the picture for the text. As a result, the picture has to be more than a mere documentation of past actions. On the contrary, it obeys different, pictorial rules of presentation (in the same way that in ekphrasis the verbal description has to superimpose a narrative character on the picture described). This is particularly evident in Euripides' *Heracles*, because in this play what is shown to the on-stage characters and the spectators is not the natural result of the action but purposefully arranged. For as the servant reports (971–1000), Heracles had killed the members of his family at various spots within the palace, but now they are all lying around the hero who is tied to a column. The event which was expansive in time and space has been concentrated, compressed and reduced to one single contracted chronotope. It would be interesting to know whether the arrangement of the dead bodies on the platform followed some discernible rule, for instance symmetry (like a funeral) or an intentional and forced asymmetry (like a battle scene) – such an insight would yield a lot for interpretation. At any rate, in this kind of arrangement there seems to be visible the hand of a director who in a metapoetic gesture shows something that we as spectators have to confront. There is a sense of stylization, of wanting to make an important point concisely, which can be found, in the medium of texts, as gnomic expression, a frequent feature of archaic and early classical Greek literature. This is because in gnomic expressions too an argument and train of thought ends up being expressed in a short, memorable statement. Perhaps what holds these *prima facie* different phenomena together is based on a unified cultural preoccupation, namely the need and wish to make the hidden visible (for all, i.e. publicly) and to turn what is complex and difficult into an object of reflection.

By way of contrast, it may be worthwhile at this point to look briefly at the analogous scene in the *Hercules furens* by the Roman playwright Seneca. In

Seneca's play the protagonist falls asleep after having committed the murders on stage (1044). Amphitruo has his weapons taken away from him (1054). The chorus laments the immense suffering, not least the death of the children whose path to Hades is being invoked (1122–35). Does the repeated exhortation to the children's bodies to 'go' (1130, 1131, 1135 and 1137) point to a movement, for instance into the palace which would now denote Hades – a movement which then could only have been performed by means of the *ekkyklêma*? This would hardly seem plausible, and even if this were the case, the intentional and deictic action found in the Euripidean version would be missing.

Provided that the preceding considerations are accurate, other plays too can be tested for this scene type which, if encountered, would in turn make the use of the *ekkyklêma* in this scene more than likely. Thus there is a long-standing and controversial debate on whether or not in Aeschylus' *Oresteia* the body of Agamemnon was shown on the rolling platform.[24] But the scene in question (*Agamemnon* 1072–1673) corresponds quite exactly to the type just discussed so that everything points to the murdered ruler being presented on the *ekkyklêma* at *Agamemnon* 1372–1406 (Figure 9.3).[25] In the two subsequent tragedies of the trilogy (*Libation Bearers* and *Eumenides*), however, this scene type is only rudimentarily present. The presentation of the dead Clytemnestra and Aegisthus (*Libation Bearers*) as well as that of Orestes sleeping in the Temple of Apollo at Delphi (*Eumenides*) therefore in all likelihood did not involve the

FIGURE 9.3: Clytemnestra on the *ekkyklêma*. Scene from Aeschylus' *Agamemnon* in the *mise-en-scène* by Peter Stein (Berliner Schaubühne 1981). Photo: Ruth Walz.

ekkyklêma. Note that the repeated use of this device within a connected trilogy would in fact diminish its impact anyway.[26]

In the parodies of tragedy that can be found in comedy, on the other hand, the modes of deployment typical of stage technology and the scene types associated with them are characteristically inverted. Thus Aristophanes in his *Peace* uses the crane right at the beginning of the play, thereby letting his protagonist fly not from heaven to earth like a god but the other way round, because the gods no longer save humankind (from war, in this case). On the contrary: in the hopeless situation of the long armed conflict humans have to take the power of making decisions away from the gods. As in tragedy's *deus ex machina* scenes human beings are deprived of the power to act decisively, so are the gods in comedy. The very choice of the animal which is suspended from the crane, the dung beetle, is also a parody of tragedy: Euripides' *Bellerophontes*, which showcased the flight of the protagonist on his winged horse Pegasus.

At the same time, comedy does not ignore the real-life existence of the crane as an auxiliary device. The flight of Trygaeus in *Peace* appears to stop time and again, as is shown by the insertion of spoken verse (in iambic trimeters) into the rhythmical representation of the flight movement by the the anapaestic dimeter.[27] Moreover, the crane appears to be lifting Trygaeus far too high initially, as is shown by him fearfully addressing the crane's operator (*mêchanopoios*) (*Peace* 173) before eventually being dropped off on the roof. The return to earth, however, does not involve the crane but is done by foot, a fact which is explicitly thematized (*Peace* 725): while the joke of the flight itself and its crude mechanics is used up, it still retains secondary force by having a character (the god Hermes) point out that the crane is not really needed to get up to the roof of the stage house. This kind of conclusion is less a parody of tragedy than a comic exploitation of the crane's full potential in a situation where tragedy with its self-contained fictionality would be forced to operate in a more reductionist manner.

In comedy, the use of the *ekkyklêma* too is part and parcel of parodying tragedy. The texture of such comic scenes, if analysed with the preceding considerations in mind, becomes transparent indeed, as can be demonstrated by looking at the entry of Euripides in Aristophanes' *Acharnians* (performed in 425 BCE). The play's comic protagonist, the Athenian Dicaeopolis, is fed up with the pro-war politics of his home city and decides to strike a private peace with the enemy, Sparta. When being attacked for this by a chorus of militaristic charcoal burners from the deme of Acharnai, Dicaeopolis is prepared to provide an account and a justification for this actions. To do this he would like to put on a tragic costume which he plans to borrow from none other than Euripides. In response to Dicaeopolis' repeated calling Euripides eventually rolls out of his house on the *ekkyklêma* while emphasizing that he has no time to 'come down' from the machine (*Acharnians* 408). Also on the *ekkyklêma* are all of his tragic props, which he passes to Dicaeopolis upon request. When his teasing becomes too much of a nuisance, Euripides orders his servants to pull back the *ekkyklêma*, at which point Dicaeopolis turns back to the chorus (*Acharnians* 395–479).

This scene is without doubt intended to be a caricature of tragic poetics, as is shown by the fact that the tragic playwright is being shown on the *ekkyklêma*. The standard dramaturgy and mode of operation of the *ekkyklêma* is consequently inverted in full. Thus the rolling out of the *ekkyklêma* is already unusual qua being almost entirely unprepared: Euripides enters at the very moment he is announcing his entry, mentioning the device explicitly (something which would be unthinkable in tragedy). An eye-witness narrative from within which would prepare for what will imminently become visible is missing almost completely in view of the fact that the preceding comments of the servant only deal with Euripides' poetic methods. The pushing back of the *ekkyklêma* is highlighted very strongly, something for which in tragedy only Sophocles' *Ajax* is comparable (and even this instance appears to be untypical of the genre). Also, in tragic scenes where the use of the *ekkyklêma* is likely the chorus tends to be heavily involved, whereas it is very much in the background during the Euripides scene in *Acharnians*. So while in tragedy the presentation of the *ekkyklêma* is embedded within a largely standardized sequence of scenes, comedy provides its viewers with a clearly demarcated and uniquely designed single scene. The intention is *not* to focus emotions and information, nor to provide complementary information. In a similar vein, the spectator is given hardly any opportunity to dwell on what is being presented. The interaction between stage and moving platform kicks off instantly and is significantly more intense than in tragedy because of the fact that objects are being passed down from the *ekkyklêma*. It is also striking how comedy relishes playing up the paradox of an interior world turned 'inside out', which in tragedy is almost completely played down. This is achieved not least by a quantitatively busy, hence funny arrangement of domestic objects on the *ekkyklêma*. Last but not least, the comic *ekkyklêma* scene of *Acharnians* is being used by Aristophanes for discussing tragic poetics (this applies to an even greater extent to its companion scene in the *Women at the Thesmophoria* (95ff.), performed in 411 BCE). This presumably shows that the previously mentioned metapoetic dimension of this technology (that is, the sense that the author-director is, as it were, co-present on stage when the *ekkyklêma* is being used) was keenly perceived as such in antiquity already, which is why comedy was able to capitalize on it by gross and aggressive distortion.

That Euripides is often chosen by Aristophanes for comically theatricalizing his tragic dramaturgy is not necessarily motivated by Aristophanes' general penchant for this particular tragic colleague of his rather than the result of the fact that Euripides, who was more a poet of innovation than tradition anyway, experimented with this stage technology, which in turn caught the attention of the alert comic playwright. Indeed, subtle uses of theatre technology were not alien to tragedy either, and Euripides in particular seems to have deployed stage machines regularly and in often unexpected ways (including instances where there were comic undertones, as in the previously mentioned scene from the *Bellerophontes*). For while the theatrical impact of the crane much depends on the character's sudden and unexpected appearance, the rolling out of the *ekkyklêma* is, on the contrary, usually prepared quite elaborately by the effectively standardized scene type described above which primes and prepares on-stage characters and spectators alike for what they are about to witness. In this way the *ekkyklêma* generates, in Aristotelian lingo, not horror (*phobos*) but pity (*eleos*) by gradual accumulation of lamentable elements.[28] These eventually materialize before our eyes in a deictic gesture (e.g. the command to open the palace doors), thereby complementing the spectators' mental image which has been generated by the preceding verbal information and turning into crystallization points of their emotions. Yet Euripides succeeds in combining these different dramaturgical effects when in his *Medea* he prepares the appearance of the *ekkyklêma* with Medea's dead children in a way typical of this device while then bringing the protagonist on stage with the crane, riding the serpent chariot of her father the Sun (*Helios*). Emotionally, we have been primed for sympathy and pain because of the innocent young victims, and Jason's predictable lamentation for his children could have been received as an incipient attempt at coping with this kind and magnitude of suffering. But Medea's triumphant entry, which turns her into a kind of inverted *dea ex machina* who does not solve but perpetuate the tragic dilemma, provokes nothing less than an emotional shock. The spectators are not being presented with the anticipated visual complement to what they know already but with a sudden and unexpected turn to the horrific.

Contrast the *Medea* by Seneca: here Boyle has assumed the use of the *ekkyklêma* for Medea's scene in her 'witch's kitchen' (Seneca *Medea* 740–848), because this was without doubt the representation of an interior scene.[29] It was shown above that in Greek drama the use of the *ekkyklêma* could not be reduced to such a narrowly technical function. At first glance, in the Senecan *Medea* scene there seems to be a scenic preparation roughly of the kind as is known from Greek dramatic texts, since the scene is preceded by an elaborate eye-witness narrative by the nurse about the events in the interior of the house (*Medea* 670–739). But then the nurse mentions steps (738f.): 'There – she made a sound with her crazed step and starts to sing' (*Sonuit ecce vesano gradu / canitque*). This reduces, in my view, the probability that the *ekkyklêma* is being used here. Also the fact that immediately after (740ff.) Medea is shown performing sacrifices rather supports the notion that Medea comes out of the stage house by foot and engages in her ritual actions at altars on the raised stage (*pulpitum*). Otherwise at the end of the scene (after line 848) Medea would have to be pulled back into the house on the *ekkyklêma*.[30]

It seems therefore that the use of such a machine, though possible, is not really endorsed by the text. If the *ekkyklêma* was deployed in this scene at all, its use was not dramaturgical but entirely technical. A slightly different case is the crane which is certainly used for the ending of the *Medea* (1022–5), because Medea, standing on the house, leaves on the serpent chariot. Her cynical remark 'This is how I usually escape' (1022: *sic fugere soleo*) can possibly be seen as a metatextual reference to Euripides.[31] All of this said, there is none of the subtle play with the dramaturgy of these stage technologies that is found in preceding Greek theatre. It may perhaps be justified to extrapolate from this that in Roman theatre stage machines were used as spectacular auxiliary devices which were denied dramaturgical value proper, and that this may precisely be the reason why, on the whole, the preserved playtexts provide hardly any indications of their use.

Returning again to Greek drama, a further example for a highly sophisticated and far from 'topical' use of these machines in the theatre of the Greeks is the (certain) deployment of the crane during Socrates' entry in Aristophanes' *Clouds* (218–38). The farmer Strepsiades has already been talking to the servant of Socrates when the philosopher appears on a rack functioning as a basket which is suspended with rope and hooks from the crane (*Clouds* 218, 226). The crane is not explicitly mentioned but unmistakably implied (*Clouds* 218, 225 and 237). Socrates uses it as a purely technical device in order to be closer to the 'things above' (*ta meteôra*) and to be able to conduct his observations of the sky. A genuinely and properly tragic element is then introduced by having Socrates address the peasant Strepsiades as 'creature of the day' (223: *ôphêmere*) and utter 'I airwalk and think around the sun' (225: *aerobatô kai periphronô ton hêlion*), which Strepsiades instantly translates into 'from your mat you think higher than the gods' (226: *apo tarrou tous theous hyperphroneis*). The ambiguous terminology of *periphronein* ('to think around', in the sense of thinking carefully) and *hyperphronein* ('to think beyond', in the sense of looking down on others) implies that Socrates believes to be far superior to ordinary human beings and even gods. If the peasant is nothing but an ephemeral being, then Socrates ought to be counted among the immortals, and his approach to the sky can be seen as a contemptuous act of hubris. Socrates is, quite literally, being 'put up' for the tragic fall, and his demise in the play's final moments will be all the greater: he is about to be burnt inside his house, while that ephemeral creature Strepsiades is now sitting on the roof, making fun of him by quoting Socrates' own 'I airwalk and think around the sun' (*Clouds* 1503). The use of the crane therefore can indeed not be considered paratragic.[32] Yet it marks the Socrates plot as a tragic one by invoking tragic associations connected with the use of the crane. And this in turn fits excellently within the tragico-comic design of *Clouds* as a whole.

A lot therefore supports the notion that the deployment of the crane could have been preceded by a corresponding use of the *ekkyklêma*. For Strepsiades, who is sold on the idea of taking rhetoric lessons with Socrates, will not let Socrates' disciples get rid of him (*Clouds* 132–80), similar to Dicaeopolis in the *Acharnians* who did not get chased away by Euripides' servant. Instead, he again knocks hard at the door (*Clouds* 181–3). On this occasion the spectators even get a prep talk of sorts about the scientific activities of Socrates which captivate the peasant so much that he now wants to see the master himself more than ever. The door opens, and Strepsiades is confronted with a sight that terrifies him at first: nothing but pale students,[33] engaged in a wide range of disciplines (astronomy and geometry, for instance). Since the master disciple says that they should not be exposed to the fresh air for too long (*Clouds* 195–9), it is natural to assume that with Socrates' appearance on the crane (*Clouds* 218) and the departure of the master disciple into the house (*Clouds* 221) the remaining disciplines too disappear into the stage house. Evidently a number of diverse instruments were visible with them, definitely a map of Greece (*Clouds* 206–17) which Strepsiades discusses with his master student. The *ekkyklêma* may therefore have been used for the disciples' entry.[34] But it must be emphasized that the sequence of events bears more similarity with the tragic scene type than with a parodic inversion (as is usually found in comedy). Here, too, *Clouds* turns out to be a tragico-comic text, with much comic effect deriving from the juxtaposition, even interweaving, of the *ekkyklêma* scene and the crane scene: the house of Socrates – his 'Thinkery' (*phrontistêrion*) – is marked as heavily 'tragic' by this intense and compressed use of stage technology which is, in this density and compression, not attested in preserved tragedy and may therefore at the same time convey a comic overtone.[35]

SCENOGRAPHY

While quite a bit can be said about the various modalities with which stage machines were deployed, other technologies and their dramaturgical functions often permit only less precise analysis. The ones to be discussed here (if briefly) are scenery, props and masks. Aristotle (*Poetics* 1449a18) attributes the invention of scenery (*skênographia*) to Sophocles. More vaguely, the same is maintained of Aeschylus (*Life of Aeschylus* 14), whose productions are associated with the painter Agatharchus of Samos (Vitruvius *De architectura* 7, Preface 11); these should be reproductions of Aeschylus' plays in the last quarter of the fifth century as Agatharchus is to be connected to Alcibiades.[36] Since the construction of the *skênê*-building took place by the time of Aeschylus' *Oresteia* in 458 BCE (where, as mentioned previously, the availability of a stage house is presupposed) and because Sophocles, according to an important inscription called 'The Parian Marble' (*Marmor Parium*), celebrated his first victory in 469/8 BCE, the introduction of scenography can tentatively be dated to the late 460s BCE. Vitruvius further claims that for each of the three dramatic genres (tragedy, comedy and satyr play) there was a distinct scenery.[37] His description, however, of the comic scenery (private houses with balconies and windows) matches at best New Comedy but not Old Comedy. Scenery that could be pushed and/or turned, which Pollux mentions, did not exist prior to the late Hellenistic period at the earliest,[38] and it is still unclear where exactly such kind of scenery would have stood in front of a stone façade like that of the Lycurgan Theatre of Dionysus in Athens and its successors, let alone the very lavishly ornamental 'stage fronts' (*scaenae frontes*) of Roman stone theatres which rose to enormous height.[39] When plays were performed on wooden stages, scenic images would probably be suspended in between door openings.

Much therefore remains controversial: what precisely was shown, in what kind of perspective, even what precisely is meant by the term 'scenography'? Small has plausibly argued that scenography consisted only of oblique views of buildings.[40] From a dramaturgical point of view scenery, however, is not always a background of action which is weakly indicated semantically, but can be integrated into the action very prominently. Thus, in Aeschylus' *Agamemnon* the palace of the sons of Atreus is sometimes addressed directly, even treated as a distinct character in the prologue by the watchman (*Agamemnon* 1–39, esp. 18 and 37f.). And in the subsequent *Libation Bearers* the action, at least in the first part of the play, primarily revolves around the tomb of Agamemnon, the social symbol of the demise of the House of Atreus.

PROPS AND MASKS

Props are being used very differently in tragedy and comedy. Broadly speaking, tragedy operates intensively with few props whereas comedy deploys a plethora of props while devoting more cursory attention to them.[41] Methodologically, props which are not more than they seem to be need to be distinguished from props with additional symbolic value.[42] This symbolic value can exist on its own or be generated from scratch by the surrounding action. Using Electra's urn as an example (Sophocles *Electra* 1113–1229), Revermann points out that a prop can function as an 'emotional focalizer' of several dramatic characters.[43] Pollux (4.117) provides a list of typical tragic props.

The protagonist's sword in Sophocles' *Ajax* (esp. 657–65 and 815–22) illustrates well the dynamic complexity of tragic props. At least during Ajax's 'deception speech' the sword has been extensively presented to the audience.[44] Ajax received this sword in exchange for his own from his enemy, Hector. This fact makes it, first of all, a weapon designed to kill an opponent, whereas by virtue of the exchange it also acquires the connotation of friendship (*Ajax* 665 and 817f.). It has, however, not brought good fortune to its bearer. During the competition for the weapons of Achilles, Ajax was beaten by Odysseus, because he conquered Troy *without* a sword and solely by cleverness, an accomplishment which was denied to Ajax despite all his martial prowess. The sword therefore also symbolizes Ajax's defeat and, more than that, the fact that the power of the intellect has rendered obsolete the sword and the brute force it stands for. Thus it represents a kind of heroism which is in decline. In sum, the sword symbolizes a competition of values that overwhelms the straightforward Ajax. This in turn makes it the obvious instrument for his suicide being itself motivated by his inability to deal with conflicting values. At the other end of the spectrum there are striking examples in comedy for the ridiculous overflow of props, especially in *ekkyklêma* scenes where in a very small space one finds the accessories of a female bedroom (Aristophanes *Women at the Thesmophoria*), the chaos of the habitat of 'thinking men' (Aristophanes *Clouds*) or, precisely, the plethora of props in the study of a tragic playwright (Aristophanes *Acharnians*).

Very similar considerations, finally, apply to masks which could be worn in all dramatic genres, even if perhaps not in all periods.[45] That the masks connect theatre to the cult of the god Dionysus has been both emphatically postulated and rejected with equal vigour. But the question is of little relevance for the issue of their performative functionality.[46] From the perspective of performance, acting with a mask means, on the one hand, having to compensate for the loss of some expressive potentials, which remain hidden, by the use of text, voice, gesture, movement and body language. On the other hand, the mask predetermines the range of expressive possibilities from the very start if it happens to be the mask of a type or stock character, as is regularly the case in tragedy and New Comedy.[47] Especially with the masks of Old Comedy which grotesquely exaggerate some facial features (nose, mouth, chin) for comic effect these predeterminations are something the actor to a certain degree has to act against, so to speak. One advantage of the mask is the better visibility in theatres where spectators could be seated 50–60 metres away from the stage action. At the same time, the mask made high demands on the actor's vocal and enunciatory precision.

In addition, Old Comedy also worked with portrait masks when known personalities of public life were brought on stage, like Socrates in *Clouds*,[48] or perhaps Aeschylus and Euripides in *Frogs*. Here the mask is the iconic equivalent to individualized ridicule (*onomasti kômôidein*). In the *Knights* Aristophanes capitalizes on audience expectation to generate an additional joke by pretending that out of fear of the demagogue Cleon none of the mask makers dared turn the mask of the Paphlagonian into a portrait mask of Cleon.[49]

Like props, masks too could acquire symbolic meaning in the course of a play, even in comedy. Clouds make up the chorus in Aristophanes' play of the same name, and Socrates starts to reflect on the various shapes which can be adopted by them, offering everyone metaphorical mirrors of oneself.[50] But Strepsiades, and with him the audience, sees them as 'wooly creatures', with apparently exorbitant noses (*Clouds* 344). Köhnken, invoking a Greek phrase which describes deception, has interpreted this as a reference to Strepsiades' deceitful intentions.[51] The noses, initially nothing but a grotesque facial feature, now acquire meaning when confronted with Strepsiades. They become symbols which point ahead to the progression of the play and its ending.

PANTOMIME

Starting in the late Roman Republic, the new art form of pantomime rose during the imperial period and late antiquity to a superior status, increasingly surpassing in importance and cultural presence the traditional genres of ancient theatrical art.[52] In its standard form, pantomime featured a single, usually male performer who, supported by a speaker, singer and/or chorus and instrumentalists, would present mythical narratives by means of gesture and dance. Contrary to the traditional forms of theatre where, at least from our modern perspective, language was the prime communicative channel, pantomime prioritized the body and its meaning-generating capacities while language, in the last resort, had the status of scenery, hence of a second-order performance medium. Pantomime could be put on wherever a stage could be put up, including private homes. This suggests that the significance of additional technologies should not be over-estimated, also bearing in mind that the extant sources are particularly thin: not a single pantomime libretto has been securely identified.[53]

While we know that pantomime, when staged in theatres, could involve scenery, the use of technologies like the *ekkyklêma* or the crane would seem intrinsically unlikely, not least because the contrast between rapid movement and sudden, statuesque 'freezing' was considered a hallmark of pantomimic art.[54] Thus, via body control, the pantomime achieves precisely what in traditional theatre was achieved by, for instance, the *ekkyklêma* (hence the term 'technology of the body' has justifiably been used).[55] Deploying a machine as an auxiliary, so to speak, would almost have detracted from the pantomime's art. The use of machines is therefore to be considered less typical of pantomime, also considering that not all devices will have been available at the various sites where pantomime could and would be performed. That said, mention must be made of the loud water-organ that was used in (large) theatres according to the poem *Aetna* (which is wrongly attributed to Virgil and must pre-date the eruption of Mount Aetna in 79 CE).[56] This does not, of course, preclude the use of 'special effects'. Thus Apuleius (*Met.* 10.30–34) has a pantomime troupe put on 'The Judgement of Paris' at the theatre of Corinth, which involves water games, live animals, scent dispensers and, as a dramatic climax, sinking an artificial mountain into the ground. But in this passage, too, it is evident that the spectator devotes significantly more attention to the pure achievement of the pantomime and the bodies of the dancers. The 'special effects' only serve to enhance the overall appeal and highlight the largesse of the event's organizers, but are not an indispensable part of the art of pantomime. There are also legitimate doubts as to how realistic Apuleius' description is as a whole, and what in his description is owed less to the reality of pantomime than to the author's intention to place at the end of his novel a final meta-fictional *mise-en-abyme* of the metamorphosis story.[57] Costumes too were more sparingly used. After all, it was the dancer's body which was to achieve the presentation in and of itself. Only the dancer's cloak is mentioned as a medium of representation to be used in manifold ways.[58] Similarly, the pantomime dancers were wearing masks (which had closed mouths; see Figure 7.1), and other props could be used, surely with similar implications as have been set out above.

CHAPTER TEN

Knowledge Transmission

Ancient Archives and Repertoires

JOHANNA HANINK

In the earliest surviving Greek comedy, Aristophanes' *Acharnians* (Athens, 425 BCE), the comic hero Dicaeopolis calls on the tragedian Euripides at the playwright's home. Dicaeopolis wants to borrow a tragic costume (and a tragic conceit) from Euripides: he asks for the 'tatters' or 'rags' (*rhakion*) of an 'old drama'.[1] Euripides offers to loan him a variety of choices from his work's most famous beggars and poor men (Oineus, Philoctetes and Bellerophon) before Dicaeopolis finally settles on the rags worn by the title-character of the now-lost tragedy *Telephus*.[2] This scene offers an orientation to the subject material of this chapter, which surveys how knowledge about the theatre was generated, preserved and transmitted in Graeco-Roman antiquity. *Rhakion*, the word for 'rag', refers to the raggedy costumes themselves (the material remains of performance) and to the 'tatters' of the papyrus rolls that would have preserved Euripides' scripts (the material vehicle of textual transmission).[3] But the scene also dramatizes a more abstract mode of theatrical survival, as Euripides' play *Telephus* is set to be extensively parodied and so embedded and, after a manner, transmitted, in Aristophanes' comedy (one of our best sources for the lost play). Finally, the ancient scholarly tradition around this scene as documented by *scholia*, or notes in the margins of medieval manuscripts, reveals that, in postclassical antiquity, Aristophanic comedy's recherché cultural references already presented an interpretative challenge. These marginal notes, made by scholars for whom classical Athens was also very 'ancient' indeed, are today some of our best evidence for Greek performance records, realities and practices.[4]

Aristophanes' scene gives us a framework for thinking about the variety of paths of transmission, but the organization of this chapter will also be guided by Diana Taylor's influential distinction between 'archive' and 'repertoire' as vessels of cultural and performance memory. According to Taylor's schema, 'archival' memory exists as documents, maps, literary texts, archaeological remains, bones, videos, films, CDs, all those items supposedly resistant to change'.[5] The repertoire, on the other hand, is more evanescent; it resides in embodied practice and knowledge: muscle memory, gestures, poses, facial expressions, etc. The difficulty presented by the ancient theatre is, of course, that our archive of evidence is, in Taylor's terms, only 'archive': we have *only* scripts, ruins, art, etc. to go on in attempting to reconstruct ancient theatrical practices. Nevertheless, our archival sources do provide glimpses at the modes of knowledge and memory transmission that took place via and thanks to a vibrant 'repertoire'.

GREECE

Archive

The Euripides scene in the *Acharnians* spotlights the role that playwrights themselves played as keepers and transmitters of knowledge about their productions. In the scene Euripides, who in antiquity was famous for his large private library,[6] keeps a personal archive of both scripts (*rhakion* as papyrus tatters[7]) and theatrical costumes (*rhakion* as shabby garments).[8] We might imagine that Euripides' son (or nephew) Euripides 'the Younger', a tragic playwright himself, inherited the collection: in Greek antiquity, dramaturgy was very much a family business (see again below). We know little of what became of dramatic sets, though scattered sources refer to the existence of treatises on scene-painting and set design.[9] (Other treatises *On the Chorus* are said to have been composed by working tragedians, including Sophocles.[10]) In much later antiquity, the marionetteer Potheinus supposedly paid to purchase the *skênê*, or stage building, used by Euripides and his contemporaries.[11] Though its historical truth is suspect, this story attests at least to the possibility of long-term preservation (perhaps even by the state) of theatrical paraphernalia.

Victorious playwrights and *chorêgoi*, or financial sponsors ('producers') of plays, made lavish dedications in honour of their victories which were also celebrated with parties – such as the one thrown by the tragic playwright Agathon in Plato's *Symposium*.[12] Dedications tended to consist in monuments with inscriptions giving notice of the victory,[13] but could also include the masks worn by actors in the prize-winning productions (the masks seem to have most usually been dedicated in the sanctuary of Dionysus around the theatre, the

Dionysion).[14] In a speech delivered after the fall of the Thirty Tyrants (in 402 BCE), the defendant of Lysias 21 claims that as a comic *chorêgos* he spent a total sixteen minae on the production itself and the post-victory dedication of the theatrical 'equipment' and/or 'attire' (*skeuê*, equivalent to Latin *apparatus*).[15] Such dedications would have contributed to the museum-like quality of the Theatre of Dionysus and its surrounding precinct, a quality only enhanced in later years by the addition of statues of illustrious playwrights and inscribed records of past competitions (see below and Figure 10.1).

The third quarter of the fourth century BCE in Athens saw both consolidation and curation of knowledge about theatre history. Under the stewardship of Lycurgus, overseer of the state treasury, the Athenians worked to advertise their city's status as birthplace of the Greek theatre.[16] Lycurgus himself is credited with moving a decree to erect statues of the three great tragedians (Aeschylus, Sophocles and Euripides) outside the entrance to the theatre and to deposit official copies of their texts in a state archive.[17] The tragedians' statues may well have been meant as finishing touches on the magnificent new and enlarged stone Theatre of Dionysus.[18] (During the fifth and at least the first half of the fourth century, the seating at the theatre had consisted in much more ephemeral 'bleacher' type benches built and dismantled each season by contractors; see also Wiles in this volume.[19]) The project of building a stone theatre was begun under Lycurgus' predecessor Eubulus and not completely finished until after Lycurgus' death, but ancient sources credit its completion to Lycurgus and so suggest that the theatre was viewed as part of his broader package of cultural initiatives.

At the end of the fourth century (around 306?), a monumental inscription recording the name of victors (playwrights, *chorêgoi*, and actors from between 450–447 onwards) at the Great Dionysia was inscribed and displayed, likely near the Erechtheion temple on the Acropolis.[20] In the early third century, more complete dramatic records, which included the names of second- and third-place (i.e., not just victorious) competitors, were also put up outside the Theatre of Dionysus.[21] These large-scale inscriptions, compiled from state archives and possibly records assembled by Aristotle,[22] stood as testimonies to the historical significance of Athens' long and illustrious theatrical tradition. Thus in the course of the lifetime of ancient Greece's most celebrated comic playwright, Menander (c. 340–290 BCE), much of Athens' great theatrical history came to be enshrined in monuments (architectural, epigraphic and sculptural) concentrated around the theatre.

As the popularity of Athenian theatre spread throughout the Greek world in the fifth and fourth centuries BCE, so too did the manufacture of vases with painted scenes depicting dramatic productions.[23] During the later fifth century BCE, Athenian artists first depicted choral performances (theatrical and otherwise), then from about the 430s moved on to add to their repertories

FIGURE 10.1: An actor looks on as a woman dedicates a tragic mask to the gods. Wallpainting from Herculaneum. Museo Archeologico Nazionale, Naples, Italy. Scala/Art Resource, NY.

representations of scenes with dramatic actors.[24] In the early fourth century, Southern Italian vase-painters also began painting tableaux from tragedies by (at least) Aeschylus, Sophocles and Euripides,[25] and we currently know of nearly 600 vase-paintings that seem to have been inspired by comic drama.[26] These vases are an important testament to the westward diffusion of Athenian theatre into Italy (see also Hadley in this volume).[27] Drama's spread is more easily traced within Attica by means of theatre buildings and local inscriptions,[28] and in the Greek East through notices of theatrical productions put on by Alexander the Great in the third quarter of the fourth century.[29] From the fourth century

BCE onwards, terracotta figurines depicting theatrical masks and (especially) masked comic actors also materially attest to the development of a kitsch souvenir (or 'downmarket merchandise'[30]) market around the persistent popularity of dramatic productions.[31]

Repertoire

Our archive of evidence for the Greek theatre affords glimpses of how theatrical knowledge was transmitted from person to person, as embodied knowledge and practice. The Greek, and even just the Athenian, theatre industry required an enormous amount of manpower – during the classical period, the Great Dionysia alone saw the debut of as many as seventeen new plays a year – and most knowledge and expertise of theatre production would have been transmitted personally, and even within families: playwriting in particular was passed down through generations, with strict divisions between 'tragic' and 'comic' families[32]. The Ancient Greek verb used of putting on plays, *didaskô*, is the same verb that has the blanket meaning of 'to teach'; likewise the title of a chorus director was *chorodidaskalos*, or 'teacher of the chorus' – a role that, in at least the fifth century, the playwrights themselves assumed.[33] We know little about the ancient rehearsal process, though the scraps that shed light on it attest to its intensity and the high stakes involved.[34] Antiphon's speech *On the Choreute* (between 422 and 411 BCE) is a defense speech for a *chorêgos* charged with murder: one of his young male chorus members had died from taking a 'performance enhancing drug' intended to improve his singing voice.[35] As part of his defence, the *chorêgos* opens a window onto the everyday realities of training a chorus (Antiphon 6.11–13):

> I served as a *chorêgos* as best and fairly as I was able. First I outfitted an exceptionally well-suited training room in my house (*didaskaleion*, the 'teaching place'), in which I also trained a chorus for the Dionysia. Then I put together a chorus as best as I could . . . When the boys first arrived, I didn't have time to attend to them myself . . . [The *chorêgos* names three men whom he appointed to look after the boys.] . . . There was still yet a fourth man, Philippos, who was charged with spending money on whatever purchases the poet/director (*didaskalos* = 'teacher') or anyone else instructed him, so that the boys might be trained up superbly well for the chorus.

Training a chorus was thus a rigorous, costly and intimate process – too intimate, it seems, on some occasions. Aristotle mentions a law which stipulated that, in the case of choruses for the boys' dithyramb (non-theatrical choral productions), the *chorêgos* had to be a minimum of forty years old, to prevent improper relationships with the young choreutes.[36]

We know less about how actors would have learned their lines, though an ancient 'cue script' (a script containing just one actor's lines) for Admetus' part in Euripides' *Alcestis* survives from later antiquity (first century BCE–first century CE).[37] We have slightly more evidence for debates about actors' methods, the kind of embodied knowledge that would have been transmitted from actor to actor. A passage in Aristotle's *Poetics* (c. 330 BCE) documents an ancient controversy about to what extent gestures and poses should be used by tragic actors: the older fifth-century BCE actor Mynniskos supposedly called his younger colleague Kallippides an 'ape' because of his excessive histrionics. The anecdote seems most urgently to reflect (reactions to) a later fifth-century movement towards greater 'realism' in acting, especially in actors' portrayals of different cross-sections of the population, including women, foreigners and slaves.[38] While Kallippides stood for a new style that allegedly pandered to more vulgar audiences, Mynniskos conservatively defended a more restrained method of acting, as befitted the decorum of tragedy and its grandiose characters.

By the fourth century BCE, some actors had achieved true international celebrity.[39] They travelled the Greek world performing at theatre festivals, and some accompanied Alexander the Great as part of his retinue.[40] Actors were even used on diplomatic missions, particularly between Athens and Macedon in the 340s and 330s BCE.[41] Thus, thanks to the combination of their crowd-drawing power and itinerary, they surely had a large hand in the spread of the Athenian theatre and transmission of knowledge about it. Some of the surviving plays also seem to bear traces of lines changed or introduced by actors ('histrionic interpolations'[42]), who also levied their status to shape the formats of dramatic festivals. In 386 BCE, it was likely a group of tragic actors who first arranged for a new category of 'revivals' of previously-produced tragedies at the Great Dionysia (a similar revival category was introduced for comedy in 339).[43] By the first decades of the third century, actors and other theatre professionals had also formed guilds, institutionalized networks and clusters of theatrical knowledge. These groups were called the 'Artists of Dionysus', in homage to the god of theatre (see Lightfoot in this volume).[44]

The actors' introduction of an 'old drama' performance category to the Great Dionysia in 386 is just one example of antiquity's lively culture of theatrical reperformance. Formal reperformance, or full-scale revivals of entire plays, seems to have occurred from an early date in the Attic demes (the regions of Attica outside the city of Athens).[45] Audiences unable to attend the great theatre festivals celebrated in the city, the Great Dionysia and the Lenaea, would still have had opportunities to see the plays performed in their local theatres (in this volume Wiles discusses the case of the deme theatre at Thorikos).[46] But reperformance also occurred more 'informally'. Like the case of Euripides' *Telephus* in Aristophanes' *Acharnians*, comedies often included scenes of 'paratragedy', or parody of tragic scenes, characters, dialogue and song (see Sells in this volume).[47] Beginning in the 340s, tragedy was also sometimes quoted for the wisdom and authority of its dignified verses during high profile Athenian trials;[48] as early as 422 BCE, however, the comic hero of Aristophanes' *Wasps*, Philocleon, explained that one of the perks of jury service was the possibility of forcing famous actor-defendants to perform.[49] Revermann has calculated that celebrations of the Great Dionysia could have required as many as 165 choreutes each year for the theatrical productions alone,[50] and surely these chorus members, too, kept memories of their former performances alive through the oral tradition (we can easily imagine that ex-choreutes merrily sang at symposia with former chorus-mates, and even bored younger generations with stories about their participation in theatre festivals past). Theatre in the Greek world was a mainstay of cultural and social life, and in Athens in particular its ubiquity was both a symptom and cause of its deep intertwining with the city's sense of its own identity, particularly as Greece's self-proclaimed cultural capital.

BETWEEN GREECE AND ROME I: THEATRICAL SCHOLARSHIP

One mode of preservation of knowledge about the Greek theatre that sets it apart from its Roman (or at least Latin-language) counterpart is a rich and relatively well-preserved tradition of ancient scholarship (see also Revermann in this volume on 'interpretive communities'). From the fourth century BCE onwards, scholars dedicated themselves to the recovery and preservation of knowledge about theatrical texts, practice and even particular productions.[51] This kind of work, and the people who undertook it, constituted a critical link in the transmission of Greek theatrical knowledge to Rome. Scholars also worked at a juncture between archive and repertoire: their research relied upon information contained in archives (primarily scripts and other works of scholarship), yet some scholars were active dramatic poets. Throughout the Hellenistic Period living performance traditions continued: new tragic and comic plays were still composed and performed,[52] and the poorly documented performance genre of comic mime also flourished (mime consisted in scenes performed by one or two unmasked performers).[53] It is also difficult to imagine that any of the theatre scholars had no personal experience of contemporary productions.

Scholarship on the theatre effectively began in Athens during the Lycurgan Era, when the city archived scripts by Aeschylus, Sophocles and Euripides, and Aristotle began pursuing research into historic victors at the city's theatre festivals (three lost works testify to his work in this area: *Victories at the Dionysia, On Tragedies* and *Didascaliae*[54]). At roughly the same time that Aristotle was busy with his archival work, he was also delivering lectures on his observations about tragic poetry and production. A form of those lectures has been preserved as his celebrated treatise *Poetics*, which also includes reflections on the contrast between tragedy and comedy. Aristotle's students carried the torch and in the later fourth to third centuries BCE a number of figures associated with the Peripatetic School in Athens produced treatises on various aspects of the theatre, especially tragedy. Surviving titles include Aristoxenus' *On Choruses, On Tragic Dance* and *On the Tragic Poets*; Heraclides of Pontus' *On Euripides and Sophocles* and *On the Three Tragedians*; an *On Aeschylus* by both Theophrastus and Chamaeleon; and Duris of Samos' *On Tragedy* and *On Euripides and Sophocles*.[55]

In the early third century BCE, this kind of work only intensified in the context of the great Library at Alexandria.[56] Within the library, and under the patronage of Ptolemy II Philadelphus (who reigned from 283 to 246 BCE), a number of scholar-poets worked to chronicle and catalogue the entire inheritance of Greek literature. Alexander Aetolus and Lycophron, both tragic poets themselves, supposedly 'corrected' the collection's tragic and comic texts.[57] During the reign of Ptolemy III Euergetes (246–241 BCE), the Library is said to have used duplicitous means to acquire the Athenian ('Lycurgan') copies of plays by the three great tragedians. Galen, the famed physician (late second century CE), reports that an edict was issued requiring all ships weighing anchor at Alexandria to forfeit any books on board for copying. The Athenians were encouraged to bring their tragic texts for this purpose, and were paid an enormous deposit for them.[58] But the library kept the exemplars, and was content to let the Athenians have the money.

The colorful anecdote may well be a fiction, but even if so it is a telling one. Here a tale of textual transmission – of some of the most valuable holdings in the Athenian theatrical 'archive' – effectively allegorizes the transmission of the Greek world's centre of theatrical knowledge and learning (and so to important aspects of its repertoire), from Athens to Alexandria. In the next generation or so, Aristophanes of Byzantium (head librarian at Alexandria from about 200 BCE) devoted substantial attention to drama. He is often credited with the first scholarly edition of Athenian tragedies (though no good evidence assures this), and is named as author of a number of 'hypotheses', or summaries of plays, which often contain notices about the original productions.[59] Aristophanes' interests seem to have extended beyond matters of poetry to ones of production, as he is also said to have written a work *On Theatrical Masks*.[60]

Other major centres of learning developed as well. The Library of Attalid Pergamum, in Asia Minor, had a collection of both books and scholars working in its employ to rival that of Alexandria,[61] and a number of observations made by its scholar and librarian Crates of Mallus (second century BCE) are preserved in the scholia to Euripides (Crates also authored a treatise *On Comedy*[62]). Crates was a critical living link in the chain of transmission of Greek literary and philosophical knowledge; during a visit to Rome, he fell into an open sewer and passed his days convalescing in bed and giving lectures.⁶³ A century later, the immensely prolific Alexandrian scholar Didymus (credited with some 3,500 works, many of them compilations of earlier scholarship) may also have served as an important conduit of Alexandrian learning.⁶⁴ Didymus lived during the first century BCE, the same century that also gives us our first evidence of Roman theatrical scholarship. Some of that scholarship was written in Latin and dedicated to native Roman dramatic history (see below), but other works were written in Greek, and here (as is often the case) it becomes difficult to pigeon hole scholarship as either distinctly 'Greek' or 'Roman'. One of the most important theatre scholars of the period was of North African origins: Iuba II of Mauritania, who had been brought to Rome in 46 BCE after the defeat of his father, Iuba I, composed a *Theatrikê Historia* (*Theatrical History*) in Greek.⁶⁵ This work went on to influence subsequent generations of theatre scholars including Julius Pollux, a Greek from Egypt who composed an *Onomasticon* (*Terminology*) while serving as the emperor Commodus' appointed 'Chair of Rhetoric' in Athens during the late second century CE. The *Onomasticon*, which still survives, includes a substantial section on technical words associated with the Greek theatre.⁶⁶ Thus from the first century BCE, scholars from every corner of the Roman Empire were positioned at the intersection of archive and repertoire, but also at a cultural crossroads between Greece and Rome.

ROME

Tacitus' *Dialogue On Orators* (*Dialogus de Oratoribus*, c. 102 CE) begins with a rich vignette about the aftermath of a performance event. Curiatius Maternus has given a reading of his historical tragedy on Cato,⁶⁷ which apparently offended the ruling powers. The day after the reading, Tacitus, in the company of two high-profile public intellectuals, Marcus Aper and Julius Secundus, goes to visit Maternus, whom they find at home holding the offending tragedy (a book, *liber*) in his hands. Maternus, who had also composed a *Medea*, informs his callers that he has imminent plans to give a reading of his new *Thyestes*. But Aper cannot share his enthusiasm and asks Maternus whether composing plays is really the best use of his time: to Aper's mind Maternus can hardly do justice to his forum obligations as it is, let alone with the extra *negotium* of 'adding our own stories and Roman names to Greek dramas' (*Graeculorum fabulis*).⁶⁸

Being a tragedian in imperial Rome could be a risky business, as the cases of Maternus and Seneca (the dramatist, philosopher and statesman sentenced to suicide under Nero in 65 CE) serve to highlight. But even the earliest sources for Roman theatre showcase the scepticism with which theatrical productions were often regarded. Many days of the Roman calendar were given over to games and spectacle, yet the theatre was often disdained for its associations with loose morality, and feared for its power to incite mobs. Whereas in classical Athens we see near obsession with commemoration and documentation, particularly of theatrical victories, the early Roman material bears signs of a commitment to ephemerality: when the performance ended, the spectators disbanded, the stage was dismantled, and business as usual resumed in the forum. Thus in general, the preservation and transmission of theatrical knowledge is weaker, and a couple of points from the dramatic frame of Tacitus' dialogue help to showcase why. Roman dramas (including Maternus' *Medea* and *Thyestes*) were often based on Greek myths and/or adapted from Greek plays, and by the Imperial Era (and likely earlier) many were designed to be read or recited, rather than performed with full theatrical casts (Julius Caesar and Augustus are known to have composed such plays).[69]

More importantly, though, the Roman and Greek theatre industries operated against entirely different sets of social contexts and expectations. The evidence for classical Athens' theatrical life is so rich largely because the state itself celebrated it as a dignified and even quintessentially Athenian institution.[70] *Chorêgoi* were selected from among the wealthiest citizens and pressed into service by the state; some tragic playwrights were remembered as civic role models, and acting was a career open to respectable Athenians. This was not the case in Rome itself, where playwrights could belong to the world of the elite, but actors were technically *infames* ('disreputable' and without full citizen rights or permission to serve in the army),[71] and the first permanent theatre structure was built only in 55 BCE. Roman comments about actors and the theatre are thus often couched in works, such as Tacitus' *Dialogus*, whose primary subject is oratory – a more 'socially acceptable' form of performance. The sources that we do have make clear that the theatrical life of early Rome was busy, vibrant and complex, but the general elite stance of wariness made for fewer sure routes of material endurance and transmission, even in antiquity.

Archive

Roman theatre, like the great poet (and dramatist) Ennius, had three hearts: Greek, Roman and native Italian (in this case both Oscan and Etruscan).[72] Both the 'Atellan farce', an Oscan (native Italian) form of comedic performance built largely around stock characters, and mime (performed at the *Ludi Florales* in 239 BCE) existed in parallel with early Roman tragedy and comedy, but as far as we can tell these traditions remained sub-literary – and so entrusted to the 'repertoire' – until the first century BCE.[73] On the other hand, the Greek theatre's movement westward from Athens, into Sicily and Southern Italy (Magna Graecia) continued north and heavily influenced productions at Rome. We know of about ninety titles of plays by the four great Roman Republican tragedians (Naevius, Ennius, Pacuvius and Accius), whose combined careers spanned from about 240 to 85 BCE. Of these, seven point to tragedies that, like Maternus' piece on Cato, took their plots from 'our own stories and Roman names' – the so-called *fabulae praetextae* first composed by Naevius.[74] The remaining majority of the titles represent plays largely translated and adapted from Greek originals (*fabulae cothurnatae*);[75] Roman comedy was also similarly divided along Greek-inspired versus 'native Roman' lines (*fabulae palliatae* versus *fabulae togatae*). Many modern scholars have emphasized the curiousness of the origins of Roman literary culture in a mass project of literary translation: in this case, the geographical movement of part of Greece's theatrical archive gave birth to a new, even if 'hybrid', theatrical culture and set of performance traditions (see also Hadley in this volume).[76]

During the Republic plays were first staged as part of official 'festival games' (*ludi*; called *ludi scaenici* when they featured theatrical performances); the first 'formal' drama was performed at the *Ludi Romani* of 240 BCE (see also Lightfoot in this volume). Theatrical performances at Greek festivals usually took place in the framework of competitions, and the material remains of victories – in the form of inscribed records and dedications – marked a significant mode of transmission of knowledge about the theatre and its participant-competitors. Less evidence clusters around the context of Roman theatrical performances at *ludi scaenici*, though magistrate lists would have helped to date productions (on Roman theatrical inscriptions see Lightfoot in this volume). There is also evidence that poets and actors had permission to make dedications (*dona ponere*) in the Temple of Minerva on the Aventine hill.[77] Ovid refers to the *palma* awarded to victors at the festivals (e.g. at *Fasti* 5.189), but the *didascaliae* (notices about first productions) that have been transmitted with five of Terence's comedies do not provide any information about Terence's competitors, if indeed there was an agonistic frame to the festivals' performances.[78]

As in Greece, masks were artifacts in the theatrical archive. Ancient sources do not accord on the date of masks' introduction into Roman performances (the Latin word *persona*, 'mask', hence *dramatis personae* 'cast of characters', is, like *histrio*, 'actor', of Etruscan origin).[79] The surviving mask typologies come from relatively late sources. In the first century CE, the rhetorician Quintilian identifies the 'countenance' (*vultus*) as the most expressive part of the body, and observes that theatre practitioners (*artifices*, the Latin equivalent of Greek *technitai*) design their masks accordingly: 'in tragedy Aerope is sad; Medea fierce; Ajax frantic; Hercules ferocious.'[80] In his *Onomasticon* (see also above) Julius Pollux refers to forty-four different masks of Greek New Comedy, each used by a different stock character type, and these may well apply to Roman comic characters as well. Pollux's work again illustrates the difficulty of discerning between strictly 'Greek' and 'Roman' traditions, particularly from the later Imperial Era.

Visual representations also aided in the transmission of knowledge about Roman costumes, masks and props: ancient theatre-themed frescoes and mosaics survive (in Rome, Pompeii and elsewhere),[81] as do much later illustrations of Terence's comedies in the γ-family of medieval manuscripts, though these images are most likely derived from the plays themselves, rather than from direct knowledge of stage practice.[82] In literature of the first century BCE, remarks on the sumptuousness of stage apparatus are commonplace. Cicero, for example, laments in a letter to Marcus Marius the extravagant stagecraft of the performances put on at the inauguration of the Theatre of Pompey (see also below): 'Really what pleasure is there in 600 mules in *Clytemnestra* or 3,000 wine bowls in *The Trojan Horse*, or the various arms and armour of infantry and cavalry in whatever battle? All this earned the people's admiration, but would have brought *you* no real pleasure.'[83] A recent archaeological (re-)find has even allowed scholars to attempt to reactivate knowledge about Roman masks and the skills required for their production. In 2009, a set of fifteen plaster masks and moulds was rediscovered in Pompeii (they had first been unearthed in 1749), and on the basis of these, attempts have been made to reproduce masks as Roman craftsmen once made them.[84] This cache marks a rare instance of the material survival of Roman dramatic apparatus, and it is still the case that much of the 'evidence' for Roman theatrical masks, costumes and set design must be deduced from dialogue in the scripts.

From at least the first century BCE, the history of the Roman theatre was an object of historical and philological inquiry. At that time scores of plays were circulating under the name of Plautus, and according to Aulus Gellius it was Varro who narrowed down the 'authentic' *corpus* to just twenty-one (plays known as the *fabulae Varronianae*).[85] Later in the century, Horace composed (in verse) the great surviving Augustan-era treatise on dramatic poetry and performance, the *Ars Poetica*. As a child, Horace may well have heard news about the construction of Rome's first permanent theatre structure, the Theatre of Pompey, in 55 BCE.[86] Before that date, Roman performance spaces had no real material permanence (contrast the museum-like qualities of the sanctuary of Dionysus discussed above, and see also Wiles in this volume). Temporary seating was installed for festivals, often in the forum, then dismantled, all on an *ad hoc* basis. The persistence of this practice is generally attributed to the elites' general wariness towards the theatre, but it is also the case that plays were regularly performed before the temple of the god honoured by the particular *ludi*, whereas in Athens performances were restricted to the sanctuary of Dionysus, and the construction of permanent structures to host productions in all of these spaces would have been impractical.[87] Roman temporary structures did, however, achieve impressive proportions: the three-storey theatre built by the aedile M. Scaurus in 58 BCE supposedly had a capacity of 80,000, as opposed to the 44,000 accommodated by the Theatre of Pompey.[88] Information about Roman theatre design from a theoretical standpoint is preserved in Book 5 of Vitruvius' *De Architectura* (dedicated to the emperor Augustus), where Vitruvius notes, for example, that at Rome most of a play's action takes place on the stage itself (and not in the orchestra), the implication being that Roman stages were deeper than Greek ones.[89]

Repertoire

Evidence about the theatre industry's personnel allows us to imagine a robust repertoire for the transmission of embodied performance knowledge and memory. Roman playwrights had a lesser hand in bringing their scripts to life than did their early fifth-century Athenian counterparts, and once a magistrate charged with organizing *ludi scaenici* had purchased a play the practicalities of its production were left largely in the hands of a professional 'impresario' (Manuwald's term; Latin refers to this person only as *actor*, from the verb *agere*, 'to lead').[90] An impresario was also the head of the play's acting troupe (Latin *grex*, a 'company' or 'group' of people; also the word used for 'flocks' and other groups of animals). A Roman *choragus*, on the other hand, had a much different hand in the *ludi scaenici* than did the Greek *choregos*-producer. Internal evidence from Roman comedies indicates that this *choragus* was contractually responsible for providing costumes and props (collectively the *choragium*); in the days before permanent theatres he may also have filled a position of something like head 'roadie', overseeing the construction of the stage and seating.[91] His role was thus more strictly devoted to the material requirements of the theatre than to the supervision and organization of performers, which in Rome was the purchase of the so-called impresarios.

Organized acting troupes were contracted for celebrations of *ludi*, but later actors were also kept in the private employ of emperors and other aristocrats (Alexander the Great provided an early example of royal theatrical patronage).[92] As in Greece, some of these actors, such as Roscius, known primarily for comedy, and the great tragic actor Antiphon, achieved enormous celebrity.[93] The role played by seasoned actors as mentors to the next generation is attested by Cicero's comments on Panurgus, an actor-slave who was pupil of the great comic actor Roscius.[94] Much of our evidence for Roman acting methods and practices is scattered in rhetorical treatises, and Roscius himself supposedly wrote a work comparing oratory and acting, *eloquentia* and *histrionia*.[95] Despite the elite's customary disdain for actors, aspiring orators did need to acquire similar skill sets; like actors they were instructed in complex sets of gestures,[96] and underwent vocal training. In Cicero's *De Oratore* (composed in 55 BCE, though set in 91) the speaker Catulus highlights the exceptional expressiveness of certain actors: he remarks that he has seen the 'eyes of the actor appear to flash from behind the mask'.⁹⁷ Some modern scholars have attempted to recover aspects of Roman actors' methods on the basis of ancient theatre iconography and clues in dramatic dialogue.⁹⁸

In Rome, the organization of the guild (*collegium*) of dramatic poets and actors alike (*scribae* and *histriones*) seems to have owed much to the Greek precedent of the Artists of Dionysus;⁹⁹ from the first century BCE there is also evidence of a group called the *Parasiti Apollinis* ('Parasites of Apollo') that constituted a kind of guild for performers of mimes.¹⁰⁰ Playwrights, many of whom were elite Romans, had their own association, the 'Guild of Poets' (*Collegium Poetarum*).¹⁰¹ But knowledge of the theatrical tradition was in Rome, as in Greece, also transmitted via numerous restagings of old plays by celebrated playwrights of the past, both at public *ludi* and in the case of performances before 'private' audiences (at the imperial court, for example).¹⁰² And although a smaller percentage of the total population played a direct role in the theatrical life of Rome than of Athens, audiences still constituted vehicles of memory and knowledge transmission. Aspects of theatrical productions (songs, for example) filtered, in some cases in traceable ways, into the everyday popular culture of the Roman *plebs*.¹⁰³

BETWEEN GREECE AND ROME II: A GLANCE AT LATER ANTIQUITY

Native Italian traditions helped to shape Roman theatrical life, but the theatre of Rome and its empire was on many counts 'Hellenized'. The influence did however go both ways, and by the first century CE Greece's own dramatic industry had acquired a Roman flavour. Athens, which had once lavishly celebrated its imperial might at the festival of the Great Dionysia, now belonged to the Roman province of Achaea, and Roman poets entered the competitions with their own Greek-language plays. The emperor Nero (who reigned from 54 to 68 CE), an ardent fan of the theatre and enthusiastic actor, funded a new stage front for the Theatre of Dionysus.¹⁰⁴ In the late first or early second century CE, Dio Chrysostom bewailed how the iconic theatre had come to be used for gladiatorial competitions.¹⁰⁵ Details of full-scale performances of comedies and tragedies are difficult to trace for the later Imperial Era, which, particularly in the Graeco-Roman East, saw a boom in theatre construction and in mosaic-based representation of theatrical scenes.¹⁰⁶ Now, however, the genres of (comic) mime and (tragic) pantomime reigned on the stage.¹⁰⁷ Pantomime, often associated with the Greeks of Southern Italy was thought to have originated in the reign of Augustus. Evidence for competitions, however, clearly emerges only from the later second century CE, when visual evidence preserving depictions of 'closed-mouth' pantomime masks also multiplies.¹⁰⁸

Pantomime featured a solo masked dancer, a musician and a chorus that sang the libretto (*fabula saltica*, 'danced story'). Its repertoire consisted in part of a variety of genre-specific dance and mimetic techniques;[109] pantomime performances were also a major conduit for the transmission of public knowledge of 'classic' tragic scenes, though here, too, the influence appears bidirectional, as aspects of Senecan tragedy show evidence of pantomime's influence.[110] Although no actual pantomime libretto has survived (the 'Barcelona Alcestis' papyrus is the best candidate currently known[111]), it is nonetheless clear that many pantomime libretti were adapted directly from tragedies,[112] and in a handful of inscriptions from Delphi and the Graeco-Roman East pantomime is even designated as 'rhythmic' tragedy or 'tragic dancing'.[113] One of our best archival sources for performance in this period is Lucian's dialogue *On Dance* (see also Revermann in this volume), in which Lycinus attempts (successfully) to win over the Stoic Crato to the virtues of pantomime; the dialogue also features our most detailed account of a pantomime's performance.[114] Dio Chrysostom also lamented the loss of song from tragic performances (see below), but even without full-scale productions, theatrical knowledge continued to be transmitted in both material and embodied form. Modes of performance and the expression of that knowledge (as through pantomime) had, however, shifted and evolved.

CONCLUSION

This chapter has focused on the theatre's 'knowledge transmission' within antiquity itself, rather than strictly upon the textual and material preservation of ancient theatrical culture to the present day. The archive/repertoire distinction provided a schema for reconstructing the evidence, though on many points those fields have proven difficult to disentangle, not least because our ancient evidence for the 'repertory' is entirely dependent on the surviving 'archive'. Yet despite the difficulty of drawing clear lines between the evidence of the archive and the evidence of the repertoire, this division is a useful guide for the ancient material in part because a similar distinction was already suggested in Graeco-Roman antiquity. Dio Chrysostom bemoaned that in his day (c. 100 CE) tragic performances were not what they used to be. He explains that, while all of the original parts of comedies are still performed, in the case of tragedy 'only the strong bits, it would seem, remain' (he means the tragic iambic lines, or lines of metrical dialogue). But, he continues, the lyric (that is, sung) parts have 'melted away'. The bone versus flesh analogy that Dio goes on to develop maps well onto Taylor's own categories: 'It is', Dio reflects, 'just like how the firm parts of old people's bodies resist the passage of time – the bones and the muscles – but the other parts shrivel.'[115] This chapter has necessarily privileged the 'strong parts' – the bones – of the ancient theatre, but has also done its best to look for traces of the flesh that once gave those bones life.

NOTES

Introduction: Cultural History and the Theatres of Antiquity

1. Suffice it to point to the work of August Böckh on the financing structure of the Athenian dramatic festivals in his *Die Staatshaushaltung der Athener* (1817), Albert Müller *Lehrbuch der griechischen Bühnenaltertümer* (1886), the range of issues covered especially in the first of the three volumes of the commentary on Euripides' *Heracles* (first published in 1889) by Ulrich von Wilamowitz-Moellendorff, or the discussion of Roman theatre in Ludwig Friedländer's *Sittengeschichte Roms* (1862–71).
2. A telling landmark is Walter Burkert's highly influential 1966 article on 'Greek tragedy and sacrificial ritual'.
3. Marshall 2006 and Manuwald 2011: 68–80.
4. On these two genre labels, and the quite opaque third notion of a 'Middle Comedy' in between these two, see Konstan 2014 and Sidwell 2014.
5. Griffith in Revermann and Wilson 2008: 73–87.
6. Webb 2008: 95–138 (Greek mime) and Panayotakis 2010: 1–32 (Roman mime). Important earlier studies are Wiemken 1972 and Maxwell 1993.
7. Pantomime has more recently started to receive the attention it commands in several excellent contributions: Garelli 2007, Lada-Richards 2007, Hall and Wyles 2008 and Webb 2008: 58–94.
8. Welch 2007: 146f., Coleman 2006: 62–8 and 82–96.
9. Reynolds and Wilson 2013 is the key reference work for the transmission of ancient literature.
10. Depending on whether the *Rhesus* is considered Euripidean or not (the latter view is now prevalent, see Liapis 2012: lxx–lxxv).
11. Csapo 2010: 1–82, Taplin 2007 and Csapo in Revermann 2014: 95–127.
12. Csapo and Slater 1995: 1–88, Wilson 2000, Millis in Csapo, Goette, Green and Wilson 2014: 425–45.
13. Manuwald 2011: 225–34 and 244–57, Fontaine in Revermann 2014: 404–22.

14. Boyle 2006. Two volumes of a much-needed new edition of all fragmentary Roman tragedy have been published so far: Schauer 2012 and Manuwald 2012.
15. Panayotakis 2010.
16. Webb 2008: 97–115, Wiemken 1972.
17. *P. Oxy.* 5187–9, published by Parsons in vol. 79 of *The Oxyrhynchus Papyri* 2014: 13–41.
18. Hall in Hall and Wyles 2008: 258–82. On pp. 378–419 this important volume also contains an excellent selection of source texts (in the original language and in translation).
19. The standard date given for the first Great Dionysia festival, and therefore tragic performances, is 534 BCE under the tyrant Pisistratus, although this is not uncontroversial (Parker 1996: 92f., Rhodes 2003: 106f.). See also Chapter 1 in this volume on institutional frameworks.
20. For Athens see Csapo and Slater 1995; for Sicily, Bosher 2012 and Bosher in Revermann 2014: 79–94.
21. Kowalzig in Revermann and Wilson 2008: 128–57.
22. Greek theatres were multi-functional spaces which would regularly host assemblies and could be used for show trials or public executions (cf. Plutarch *Timoleon* 34.4f.).
23. Harris 1989, Johnson and Parker 2009. In his discussion of the evidence Harris ends up assuming literacy rates of no more than 10–15 per cent among the adult population throughout Graeco-Roman antiquity.
24. Schauer 2012: 21–65 (fragments and testimonia), Manuwald 2011: 15–40, Fantham 2013: 16–19 and Feeney 2016: 92–151 (general discussions).
25. Sear 2006: 57–67, Manuwald 2011: 55–68.
26. Burckhardt 1872: 1998. The oldest and perhaps most vivid expression of Greek competitiveness is Hesiod's description of good 'strife' (*eris*) and its beneficial social effects at *Works and Days* 17–26.
27. Revermann 2006a: 5–7 and 19–23. Osborne 1993 outlines the annual calendar of competitive Athenian festivals.
28. Wilson 2000.
29. Biles in Revermann 2014: 43–59.
30. Lucian *On Dancing* 2 (cf. 32 and 83f.).
31. Webb 2008: 31, Barnes 2010: 319f.
32. Plautus *Amphitruo* 69–78 and *Poenulus* 36–9, Terence *Hecyra* 29–48.
33. A good example is a serious incident under Tiberius where the theatre became the platform of the masses for articulating, 'with more licence than usual against the emperor', their dissatisfaction with the high price of corn (Tacitus *Annals* 6.13). Soldiers on stand-by: Tacitus *Annals* 13.24.
34. Csapo and Slater 1995: 315f. and 321f., Csapo 2010: 190f.
35. Panayotakis 2010, esp. 33–57.
36. See the papers by Moloney and Le Guen in Csapo, Green, Goette and Wilson 2014: 231–74.
37. *Monumentum Ancyranum* 20.1, 21.1, app. 3 and 4.
38. Csapo 2010: 182f.

39. Csapo 2010: 140–204. 'Trimalchio's Feast', which constitutes the bulk of the fragments that we have from Petronius' novel, gives some impression at least of the musical entertainment at the parties of the elite (or of those aspiring and pretending to be part of it).
40. The Colosseum, the largest and best-known of them, would hold at least 50,000 spectators, but even the amphitheatre in Pompeii, by all measures a fairly insignificant town in its day, held about 22,000 spectators (on both see Welsh 2007). Pompeii is an illuminating example in general: since the second century BCE, Pompeii had a stone theatre which was rebuilt in the Augustan period when it seated c. 3,500. It also had, since c. 75 BCE, a smaller roofed theatre (or *odeum*) seating c. 1,500 (Sear 2006: 130–2). In other words, both permanent theatres in Pompeii pre-date the first permanent theatre in Rome (!).
41. Sear 2006: 396f. with further literature.
42. Papastamati-von Moock in Csapo, Goette, Green and Wilson 2014: 15–76.
43. Bosher 2012 and Taplin 1999.
44. Braund, Hall and Wyles (forthcoming), Braund and Hall in Csapo, Goette, Green and Wilson 2014: 371–90.
45. Revermann 1999–2000: 457f. A dramatic papyrus (probably from a tragedy) was found at Ai Khanoum, so there were not only spectators but also readers of drama at this remote outpost.
46. Goldberg 1998: 13–6.
47. Sear 2006: 57–67. Sear's magisterial architectural study, consisting of a catalogue and detailed overview chapters, is the fullest and most authoritative discussion of Roman theatre buildings in general.
48. The best collection of audience-related sources, in English translation and with commentary, for Greek and Roman theatre can be found in Csapo and Slater 1995: 286–330. More specialized discussions of theatre audiences are Roselli 2011 (on Greece in the fifth and fourth century), Revermann 2006b (on audience competence in classical Greece), Ruffell in Revermann and Wilson 2008: 37–58 (on audience and emotion in Greece) and Manuwald 2011: 98–108 (on Republican Rome).
49. The closest we get to non-fictional eye-witness accounts are some poems by Calpurnius Siculus, Statius and above all Martial in his book *On Spectacles*, a collection of epigrams to celebrate the opening of the Colosseum in Rome in 80 CE (see Coleman 2006 and Welsh 2007: 142–7). But the events here are all para-theatrical (gladiatorial combat etc.).
50. Barish (1981), an important and fascinating work.
51. On Greek comedy, Biles and Marshall in Revermann 2014: 43–59 and 131–46; on Roman comedy, Slater 2000.
52. Roselli in Revermann 2014: 242–6 summarizes and in part re-frames this much-contested issue. Roman theatre culture did allow female spectatorship, even if women were usually seated separately (Sear 2006: 2).
53. The preserved evidence for such an arrangement, however, only dates from Roman times: three inscribed statue bases dedicated by three of the ten Athenian tribes respectively (see Csapo and Slater 1995: 289f.). Note that these ten tribes (*phylai*)

were competing against each other in the dithyrambic competition which was part of the Great Dionysia festival.
54. Epicharmus fr. 237 (Kassel-Austin). Plato (*Laws* 659b5–8) mentions, perhaps polemically, that in Sicily and Southern Italy it is the audiences, and not any judges, who determine the winner in the dramatic competitions.
55. Hegelochus: Scholion on Euripides *Orestes* 279; the incident is ridiculed at Aristophanes *Frogs* 303f., Sannyrio fr. 8, Strattis frr. 1 and 60; Eros: Cicero *Pro Roscio* 30 (cf. Cicero *Stoic Paradoxes* 3.26).
56. Aristotle *Poetics* 17,1455a28; 18,1456a18f.; 24,1459b31, cf. Demosthenes 19.337.
57. Plautus *Amphitruo* 67; serious riots (at a pantomime performance): Tacitus *Annals* 1.77, and see Slater 1994.

Chapter One: Institutional Frameworks: Enabling the Theatrical Event

1. The exact meaning of the expression 'thrower of stones', which also seems to involve a pun, in the Pythia's oracular response is somewhat nebulous ('insignificant soldier', 'someone involved (actively or passively) in stoning', perhaps as part of a scapegoating ritual?). But its abusive gist is clear: the Pythia mocks Cleisthenes as a political lightweight.
2. As Hornblower 2013 (on Herodotus 5.67.5) puts it: '"Tragic" means what is says. [. . .] if Herodotus had meant dithyrambs, he had the vocabulary to say so'. On this passage, and on hero cult more generally, see also Parker 2011: 118.
3. Parker 2011: 171–223, Osborne 1993 (on theatre within the Athenian festival calendar), Beard, North and Price 1998 *passim* (on Rome).
4. Parker 2011: 103–23.
5. Slater 2007: 21.
6. Goffman 1974, see also Lemert and Branaman 1997.
7. Good remarks on this in Eco 1984 (comic frames, which initially appear to destabilize, only re-affirm *authorized* transgression).
8. Ancient theatres have therefore rightly been called 'engines of honour' (Wilson 2007: 5).
9. Gildenhard 2010: 165 juxtaposes classical Athens and mid-Republican Rome along these and similar lines in a chart.
10. Csapo 2010: 168–204.
11. Currie 2005, esp. chapters 7 to 9.
12. *Vita Aeschyli* 11f. in Radt 1985: 34f. On the practice of establishing hero cults for poets (e.g. Sophocles or Archilochus) see Clay 2004.
13. Jordan 2007 on a curse tablet from Gela mentioning *chorêgoi*. Note that Aeschylus spent time in Gela in the 470s and returned there in the 450s for the few final years of his life. Epicharmus (fr. 237 Kassel-Austin) uses the proverbial expression 'it lies in the lap of five judges', see Revermann 2006a: 21 n. 37.
14. On Hellenistic, especially Macedonian, theatrical frameworks see the contributions by Moloney and Le Guen in Csapo, Goette, Green and Wilson 2014; on a particularly well-attested festival, the Dionysia at Iasos, see Crowther in Wilson 2007 (the whole volume is fundamental for the study of festivals on the basis of the epigraphic record); recently published letters by the emperor Hadrian to theatrical guilds (the

Artists of Dionysus) provide fascinating evidence for the international theatre circuit at the time of the High Empire, see Petzl and Schwertheim 2006 and Slater 2008; on late antiquity see Webb 2008: 24–43 (a very important book on the performance culture of late antiquity in general).

15. The standard reference works for the Athenian dramatic festivals on which my (necessarily compressed) account of them is based are Pickard-Cambridge 1988: 25–125 and Csapo and Slater 1995: 103–85 (where the sources are provided in English translation, with incisive introductions and short but very valuable individual commentaries). Both works need to be consulted for a more detailed and nuanced presentation than can be offered here of the often complex literary, epigraphic and papyrological evidence.
16. Parker 1996: 92f. and Rhodes 2003: 106f.
17. Csapo 2013, esp. 50–64 (on the phallic choruses in the procession) and 64–80 (on generic interactions).
18. On these announcements and their ideological significance see Wilson 2009.
19. On the issues concerning the voting procedure see Csapo and Slater 1995: 157–60 and Marshall and van Willigenburg 2004.
20. Csapo and Slater 1995: 107 and 135.
21. No tragic tetralogy is preserved (although in a number of cases the titles of the four individual plays are known). The best case in our evidence is the Aeschylean trilogy *Agamemnon*, *Libation Bearers* and *Eumenides*, which was followed by the (lost) satyr play *Proteus*. For all we know, this type of a thematically connected trilogy (or even tetralogy, where the satyr play has some thematic link with the preceding tragedies) is the exception and not the rule, see Revermann 2008: 240 n. 11.
22. These aspects receive detailed discussion in Wilson 2000: 51–70.
23. These passages are the above-mentioned fr. 17 by Cratinus and Aristophanes fr. 590.27–9 Kassel-Austin.
24. Scholium on Aristophanes *Wasps* 1109 and Plato Symposium 194b3f., respectively. On the *proagôn* see Csapo and Slater 1995: 109f., Wilson 2000: 96f. and Revermann 2006a: 169f.
25. *Life of Euripides* 11 (in Kannicht 2004: 48).
26. Plato's *Symposium* is fictitiously set after Agathon's victory in the tragic competition of 416 BCE (whether at the Lenaea or the Great Dionysia is not entirely clear). On the social capital gained by the wealthy *chorêgoi* and their ways of spending it see Wilson 2000 (esp. 236–44 on their attempts to make visible victory in the dramatic competition where, by contrast with victory in dithyrambic competition which was rewarded with a tripod, there was no prize of material durability to display).
27. On performance time see Revermann 2006a: 333–7.
28. More recent contributions to this debate are Rhodes 2003 and Wilson 2009.
29. This point is explicitly made by the commentator preserved in *P. Oxy.* 2737 (see Csapo and Slater 1995: 135 no. 71).
30. See also Goette 2014 who provides, among other things, a catalogue of twenty-five deme theatres.
31. Csapo and Slater 1995: 127f.
32. Csapo and Slater 1995: 125 no. 49G and 129 no. 52A.

33. Manuwald 2011: 22–6, Feeney 2016: 104f. and 201–3. On Livy 7.2 see Oakley 1998: 40–72. The possibility of influence from Carthage, Rome's big early rival, must also seriously be entertained. It is worth mentioning in this context that by the time of Tertullian in the late second century CE, Carthage was (still?) a hotspot for entertainment culture.
34. Improvised Latin drama based on Greek myth? Shows performed in Oscan? Latin historical drama? Greek drama performed in Greek by Greek troupes? Any combination of the above? See Feeney 2016: 105–10, which is part of his larger discussion (92–151) of festivals as catalysts for the development of a Roman vernacular literature.
35. Cicero *Brutus* 91, Cicero *Tusc.* 1.3, Cicero *Cato* 50 (= T4–T6 in Schauer 2012: 21f.). On the much-discussed significance of this event see Gildenhard 2010: 156–60 and Feeney 2016: 92–151.
36. The nomenclature (*scribere, componere*) used in some later sources (T20, T21 and T25 in Schauer 2012: 26f.) seems to preclude translation in the strict sense.
37. See Csapo and Slater 1995: 207–20, Manuwald 2011: 41–54.
38. Goldberg 1998. Four of the comedies of Terence were staged at this festival in subsequent years (*Andria* in 166, the first *Hecyra* in 165, *Heautimôroumenos* in 163 and *Eunuchus* in 161).
39. Panayotakis 2010: 6f. and Sells, this volume.
40. Enumerated, with documentation, by Manuwald 2011: 47f.
41. Manuwald 2011: 51 provides examples from the Republican era.
42. Panayotakis 2010: 15f.
43. Cicero *Phil.* 1.36, *Att.* 16.2.3 and 16.5.1.
44. Slater 1994.
45. Manuwald 2011: 52–4.

Chapter Two: Social Function? Making the Case for a Functionless Theatre

1. Homeric Hymn to Hermes 433–62.
2. On Damon see Wallace 1991, Wallace 2004 and 2005.
3. Plato *Republic* 398d–399d.
4. Empedocles A 86 *Diels-Kranz*.
5. Gorgias B 11.10–4 *Diels-Kranz*.
6. Hippocrates *Regimen* 2.61.
7. See Wiles 1999: 43, Mitchell-Boyask 2007: 85–114 and Hartigan 2009.
8. Plato *Republic* 445c and 544dff.
9. Plato *Republic* 398d–399d.
10. Plato *Republic* 386a–399d.
11. Plato *Republic* 603e–607b.
12. Aristotle *Politics* 1339a11–1342b35.
13. Aristotle *Poetics* 1449b25ff.
14. Especially Halliwell 1998.
15. Cicero *De re publica* 1.52, *De officiis* 2.57f. (cf. Tacitus *Annals* 13.25), *De oratore* 29 and *Pro Murena* 40.
16. Aristophanes *Frogs* 1417–75.

17. *Contest between Homer and Hesiod* 322.
18. Aristotle *On Interpretation* 16a4–9.
19. See Asmis 1992 and Janko 2000 for useful, if older, overviews.
20. Horace *On Poetry* 333f.
21. Proclus *Commentary on Plato's Republic* 49.13–51.25.
22. Augustine *Confessions* 3.2.
23. Augustine *City of God* 1–2.
24. Readers interested in following social-functionalist readings of ancient literary practice can do no better than to start with the work of Tom Habinek, especially Habinek 1998 and Habinek 2005.
25. A point made most exhaustively by Goldhill and Osborne 1999.
26. Wilson 2000: 101f. only shows that Aristophanes uses a conventional synecdoche according to which the judicial body is said to the equal to *demos*.
27. Plutarch *Cimon* 8.7–9.
28. Terence *Hecyra* 1–57 and *Phormio* 30–4 with Manuwald 2011: 100f.
29. Sude O 806, Zenodotus 5.40. 'Nothing to do with Dionysus' is traditionally associated with the introduction of satyr play, see Seaford 1976: 209–21 and Shaw 2014: 79f. Csapo and Miller 2007 argue for the close affiliation between ritual and drama but it is more convincing as an inquiry into drama's origin than its generic reference.
30. See Rosenbloom 1993.
31. See Hubbard 1991.
32. The best (and judiciously agnostic) account of the evidence and available interpretations of drama's origins in Greece is to be found in Lesky 1965. See also Storey 2010 for a good recent discussion. I limit my remarks to the specific event of drama's institutionalization at the City Dionysia and make no claims about its earlier forms or its relationship with cognate musical practices.
33. See Osborne 1993, with further references.
34. Thucydides 3.104.
35. Herodotus 5.67.5 (with the useful comments in Hornblower 2013: 204f.).
36. See, in particular, Calame 2001 and Kowalzig 2007.
37. See Pickard-Cambridge (et al.) 1988: 77.
38. Wilson 2000: 314 n. 18 with references.
39. Rancière 2009: 23.
40. Rancière 2009: 24f. In a memorable phrase, Rancière remarks that while there is always power, there is rarely politics: the latter occurs when the former's normal operations are disrupted.
41. I do not want simply to adopt Rancière's diagnosis of art. His account of the political role of what he calls the 'aesthetic regime' in art fails to fit with the situation of ancient drama in at least one respect: if the modern work of art derives its political charge from its autonomy because it creates a singular space for interaction, the ancient drama arguably does the opposite in that tragedy and comedy display the *excluded*, and their autonomy is based on a gesture of exclusion (see also immediately below).
42. Adorno 1997 and Adorno 2007.

Chapter Three: Sexuality and Gender: Off-stage and Centre-stage

1. For the mask, see Wiles 2007 and 2008; for komastic costume, see Sifakis 1971, Rothwell 2007, Lissarrague and Frontisi-Ducroux 1990. On origins more generally, see Csapo and Miller 2007.
2. In non-dramatic performance outside Athens there is more evidence for female performance, not least Archaic Sparta, see Calame 2001.
3. For comedy, see MacDowell 1994 and Marshall 1997.
4. On *chorêgoi*, see Wilson 2000 and Lightfoot (this volume); for selection of actors, see Csapo and Slater 1995: 228–30, Pickard-Cambridge 1988: 93–5; for poets Pickard-Cambridge 1988: 84. For gender and law, Just 1989.
5. Zweig 1992.
6. For the grotesque body, see Foley 2000 and Ruffell 2015.
7. See, for example, Duckworth 1952: 39f. and Manuwald 2011.
8. For the mask, see Bieber 1961 (esp. 154–60), for the process of adaptation, see especially Handley 1968, Fraenkel [1922] 2007, Bain 1979 and Anderson 1993: 3–29.
9. On Roman mime, see Panayotakis 2010: 1–32 (esp. 18f.), and on female participants, Panayotakis 2006. For the status of Roman actors, especially female actors, see Duncan 2006.
10. See Webb 2002 and 2008: 44–57.
11. So Henderson 1991: 140f. and Csapo and Slater 1995: 291.
12. Alexis *Gynaikokratia* fr. 41.
13. Henderson 1991 and, at greater length, Roselli 2011; Goldhill (1994) is sceptical. See also Pickard-Cambridge 1988: 264f., Csapo and Slater 1995: 290–2.
14. *Life of Aeschylus* 9; Pollux 4.110.
15. *IG* ii.² 5063 A, 5093–164. See Sear 2006: 3 and 389.
16. Goldhill 1994; Henderson 1991 already distinguished between actual and notional audiences.
17. Ruffell 2011: 264–86.
18. Manuwald 2011: 98–108, with bibliography.
19. On audience composition, see Duckworth 1952: 80–2, Goldberg 1998: 14f. and Fontaine 2010: 183–7.
20. Nevett 2010: 48–50.
21. Dover 1974: 98 and 207–12, Schaps 1977, Sommerstein 1980, Henderson 1987b: 106f.
22. Courtesan plays are associated with Pherecrates, who began working in the early 430s: see Henderson 2000. Another working character, the bread-seller Myrtia, insists on naming herself and her citizen parentage 1396–8.
23. See Lewis 1955 and Henderson 1987a: xxxvi–xli.
24. On citizenship and legitimacy at Athens, see Ogden 1996 and, in New Comedy, Lape 2004. Traill 2008 discusses women in Menander generally.
25. See Treggiari 1991: 13–35, who cites (34) the Lex Cincia of around 204 regulating gifts between husband and wife: wives *in manu* would not own property.
26. For the interest in female agency, see also Sells in this volume.
27. For the *Oresteia*'s aetiology of misogyny, see Zeitlin 1978.

28. Gould 1980 is the classic statement.
29. For character types, see Ruffell 2014 with bibliography.
30. Perhaps spotted by ancient scholars, who labelled it 'rather satyric' (*satyrikôteron*, Hyp. b).
31. For Old Comedy, Ruffell 2013; for satyrs' lack of sexual satisfaction, Seaford 1984: 39 and Griffith 2002: 214–7.
32. Taplin 1977a: 306–16.
33. Sourvinou-Inwood 1989.
34. For *Lysistrata* on the modern stage, see Hardwick 2013.
35. Others include Erotium in *Menaechmi* (*The Brothers Menaechmus*) and Phronesium in *Truculentus*.
36. Thus Selenium in *Cistellaria* and Philematium in *Mostellaria*, and perhaps Philaenium in *Asinaria*.
37. For Menander, see Traill 2008; for gender and sexuality in Terence, see James 2013.
38. Segal 1987: 21–31 discusses such relationships. On *Plocium*, see Ruffell 2010 with bibliography.
39. See especially Miller 1999; for post-sympotic scenes, see Lissarrague and Frontisi-Ducroux 1990.
40. On the first *Hippolytus*, see Hutchinson 2004.
41. A label with even less history than 'homosexuality', but for non-binary approaches to gender across cultures, see, for example, Herdt 1996. For Athenian practice, see n. 39.
42. On Achilles in Greek tragedy, see Michelakis 2007.
43. See Dover 1978. Notwithstanding criticism of the Dover/Foucault model by Davidson 2001 and 2007, an ideology of power and penetration clearly underlies the invective of comedy and similar genres and cultural contexts.

Chapter Four: The Environment of Theatre: Experiencing Place in the Ancient World

1. See Wiles 2003 for bibliography on the phenomenology of place. Wiles 1997 focused on the structuring of space. On sensory archaeology, see Hamilakis 2013.
2. Greek months began with the first sighting of the new moon; the festival took place on days 10–14.
3. Roselli 2011: 63–86 summarizes current opinion. Goette 2007 assembles the archaeological data, along with an unhelpful reconstruction.
4. Papastamati-von Moock 2014: 21, on the basis of recent excavation suggests that the semi-circular conception nevertheless emerged in the fifth century, the age of Pericles. Moretti 2014 in the same volume cautions on the difficulty of extrapolating from stone structures to wooden structures.
5. Wiles 1997; 42f.
6. On this theatre see Mussche et al. 1975 and Mussche 1998.
7. Ober 2008: 206 and Paga 2010: 380. Paga surveys the phenomenon of deme theatres. So also does Goette 2014, who believes that neighbouring demes converged on this theatre.
8. Palyvou 2001 analyses the geometry.

9. Parker 2005: 71f. and Parker 2011: 112.
10. See Taplin 1999.
11. Csapo and Slater 1995: 127f.
12. See Csapo 2013.
13. See Csapo 2007.
14. Csapo and Slater 1995: 301–5.
15. Wallace 1997.
16. Plutarch *Moralia* 756b = Euripides fr.480 Kannicht.
17. Csapo and Slater 1995: 267f.
18. See most recently Papastamati-von Moock 2014.
19. Hanink 2014.
20. See Wiles 1997 36–8, and on the city, Roy 2007.
21. Polybius *Histories* IV.20. My translation.
22. This is the title given in the prologue l.54; the play is more normally known as 'The Little Carthaginian', or in Latin *Poenulus*.
23. *Amphitruo* 65–90.
24. Plays were also performed at the Plebeian games in the Circus Flaminius. On these festivals, see Manuwald 2011: 41–5.
25. Wiles 2003: 32–4 and 98–103; Marshall 2006: 36–44.
26. See Purcell 1989 for some of the problems involved in interpreting the Forum.
27. On the theatre, see especially Gleason 1994, Temelini 2006, Gagliardo and Packer 2006. Primary sources are gathered in www.theaterofpompey.com. Sear 2006 is a useful survey of Roman theatre buildings.
28. These are surveyed in Sear 2006. Manuwald 2011: 55–61 considers why temporary theatres persisted.
29. Favro 1998.
30. Hopkins 1983: 3–5.
31. On masks see Wiles 2007.
32. On seating see Rawson 1987, Edmondson 2002 and Wallace-Haddrill 2008: 167–9.

Chapter Five: Circulation: Theatre as Mobile Political, Economic and Cultural Capital

1. Greenblatt 2010: 84.
2. See the excellent discussion of this type of research, and a very good example of it, in Taplin 1999.
3. Taplin 1999: 54–7.
4. For a full collation of all the ancient evidence on Aeschylus' visits to Sicily, see Herrington 1967.
5. Bosher 2012a. For a summary of the debates concerning the entrance of Darius in *Persians*, and the 'rather feeble explanation' of the staging that is required in the absence of an underground tunnel, see Garvie 2009: l–liii.
6. Taplin 1999: 47, Scott 2010.
7. See especially Dougherty 2001.
8. Giovannini 2008 argues that the wealth Athens poured into artistic and cultural projects was both immense and completely independent of the tribute paid for

military protection by her allies. Drama, then, would have been seen as a truly 'Athenian', rather than a 'Delian' invention.

9. Giovannini 2008: 182–4, Hall 1989: 160–200 and *passim*; Vlassopoulos 2013: 61–4.
10. Bosher 2012a: 105f. was only the most recent scholar to suggest a first Syracusan performance, with Kiehl having proposed the idea in 1852, and Willamowitz in 1897.
11. Bosher 2012a: 108–11.
12. Green 2007 asserts that 'it is arguable that drama [of the later years of the fifth century] was already coming to be regarded as standing for Greek culture by people in colonial contexts, something it demonstrably did later.'
13. For the most succinct treatment of this vast topic, see Ferrari 1990. More detailed discussions can be found in Crotty 2009, the articles in Destrée and Hermann 2011, and Halliwell 2002: 37–147, inter alia.
14. Dearden 1999: 226.
15. Emlyn-Jones 1996: 68. Taplin 1999: 39 has also correctly understood the meaning of these lines.
16. See Taplin 1993: 5 on *Clouds* 518 ff. (not invalidated by Wilson 2007: 68f.).
17. Revermann 2006a: 70 and Harvey 2000: 114 ff.
18. Revermann 2006a: 254–60.
19. The sources for these anecdotes are given in Kovacs 1994: 24f. and 122–5. They receive excellent discussion, which I have followed, in Taplin 1999: 42f.
20. *Bibliotheca Historica* 15.74. For an excellent discussion of Dionysius' theatrical ambitions and accomplishments, see Duncan 2012. For the text of the treaty and a discussion of its circumstances, see Rhodes and Osborne 2003: 160–9.
21. Dearden 1990: 234.
22. For the debates on the connection of these passages to Epicharmus, see Olson 1998 *ad loc.* and Cassio 1985, who references the excellent discussion in Pickard-Cambridge 1962.
23. Taplin 1999: 35. See also Scodel 1999: 216f. These numbers, of course, do not account for comedians, among whom non-Athenian talent figures so prominently that, in the (as yet unpublished) words of Martin Revermann, we can say 'post-Aristophanic comedy, call it "Middle" and "New Comedy" or not, is "Attic" only in the sense that this dialect is accepted as the dialect of the genre'.
24. Csapo 2010: 86.
25. Taplin 1999: 35, with literature.
26. See Taplin 1999: 38 and Csapo 2000: 125f. Anne Washington's *Mr. Burns: A Post-electric Play*, itself concerned with the functions of touring repertoire troupes struggling to draw audiences, contains a brilliant instance of this same phenomenon in the form of song-and-dance routines amalgamating recent popular music. The performances in Toronto in 2015 featured more local and recent music in these routines than those which were (or could have been) part of the initial production in New York in 2012.
27. Csapo 2010: 89–94. For more detailed inscriptional evidence of the Attic theatres and festival circuits, see Goette 2014 and Millis 2014.
28. Taplin 2012: 238 with literature.

29. Ibid. and Taplin 1993: 4f., Goette 2014.
30. For the funding models of the Athenian festivals, see Wilson 2008 and Roselli 2011: 96–105.
31. Csapo 2010: 86.
32. See the ancient sources on the Tarentines' addiction to theatre cited at Taplin 1993: 14. We cannot, of course, rule out a degree of hyperbole in the stories told of the Tarentines' theatrical hedonism, but the exaggerated reputation itself is telling of the ancient perception of Taras' theatrical culture.
33. Carpenter 2014.
34. Taplin 2007: 2–46.
35. Taplin 2007: 27f. See also Osborne 2008: 412f.
36. See Taplin 1993: 36–41 and Csapo 2010: 54–9.
37. Csapo 2010: 57.
38. On Greek symposia in general, see Murray 1990. For the more demotic elements of the symposium, see Jones 2014.
39. Taplin 2007: 14.
40. For which, see Csapo 2007: 205–10.
41. Csapo 2010: 62, Dearden 2012: 284, Taplin 1993: 41–7.
42. Dearden 1990 and 2012.
43. Green 2007.
44. The nature of the relationship between Greek source materials and their Latin adaptations by Plautus and Terence is a matter of much fascinating and long-standing discussion. The standard work on the subject remains Fraenkel [1922] 2007. For a more digestible treatment, see Fontaine 2014, and for the particular case of the *Casina*, see O'Bryhim 1989.
45. Green 2007, Taplin 1993: 27.
46. Taplin 1993: 41. My summary of this vase and its meaning closely follows Taplin 1993: 40f.
47. Carpenter 2014. For more detailed discussions of the Pronomos Vase and its meaning(s), see Taplin and Wiles 2010.
48. Revermann 2010.
49. Green 2007. See, however the criticism of Csapo 2007 of assumptions concerning the relation between tragedy and Dionysiac mysteries on tragedy-related vases found in tombs.
50. Robinson 2014: 327.
51. Robinson 2014.
52. Carpenter 2014.
53. Robinson 2014: 323f.
54. Moloney 2014: 234–40, Revermann 2000: 454 and *passim*.
55. See the presentation of Euripides in Aristophanes' *Frogs*. For an evaluation of Aristophanes' presentation of Euripides in this play, see especially Hunter 2010: 10–52.
56. Revermann 2000.
57. Moloney 2014: 243f.
58. On Alexander's travelling performances and theatrical foundations, see Csapo 2010: 173–7, Le Guen 2014a, Revermann 2006: 456 ff. On Hellenistic culture in

the Far East, see Mairs 2014 and Rapin 1990. On the potential tragic texts at Ai Khanoum, see Rapin et al. 1987: 255–7.
59. Csapo 2010: 172–8, Moloney 2014: 244–8.
60. I use the word 'command' instead of 'private' in order to acknowledge the semi-public, or at least ambiguously private nature of an immense performance put on for an entire military camp or significant portion of a population.
61. Csapo 2010: 176.
62. Csapo 2010: 179–92.
63. Manuwald 2011: 32f.
64. Manuwald 2011: 188–90 gives an excellent discussion of the debated timeline for Andronicus' first production in Rome.
65. Manuwald 2011: 194.
66. Erasmo 2004: 18. The oft-repeated quote about Ennius' three hearts is found at Aulus Gellius, *NA* 17.17.1, listed as T73 in Manuwald 2012.
67. Manuwald 2011: 42–8, Duckworth 1952: 76–8.
68. On these communities of production, see Jane Lightfoot's chapter of the same name in this volume, as well as Lightfoot 2002 and Manuwald 2011: 41–119.
69. Manuwald 2011: 49–68.
70. Erasmo 2004: 83–91, Manuwald 2011: 62f.
71. Cassius Dio 43.49.3, cf. Erasmo 2004: 173 n. 14.
72. Sear 2006: 12.
73. Barnes 1996: 164, Mitchell 1987.
74. Barnes 2010: 317–22.
75. See Zenobi 2008 and Zimmerman 2008.
76. For various takes on this scene, see Bosher 2012: 101, Dover 1993: 320f. and Garvie 2009: 53–7.
77. See, e.g., 933, when Aeschylus loses his patience and chastises the buffoonish Dionysus for not understanding his description of the paintings on the prows of Greek ships.
78. Aristophanes *Frogs* 1112, Harris 1989: 87.
79. Halliwell 1998: 337–43, Revermann 2006a: 13.
80. On the contrast between poor rowers and the wealthy classes, see Dover 1972: 99, Ehrenberg 1962: 300f.
81. The nature of literacy in the ancient world is a large subject, treated extensively and carefully by Harris 1989. Silent reading was not common in the ancient world, but it certainly was possible, see Vatri 2012.
82. Fantham 2004: 84.
83. See the index and its cited passages in Wright 1931: 110.
84. In a rather touching moment that highlights Cicero's hopes for his younger brother at an earlier time, before his political career had come to naught, Cicero shows this very process in action, when the young Quintus Cicero spontaneously translates and remarks upon the power of the opening lines of Sophocles' *Oedipus at Colonus* while touring Attica with his brother and a retinue of companions in the wake of Sulla's seizure of power at Rome (*Fin.* 5.3).
85. Webb 2008: 197–216.
86. Webb 2008: 199.

87. Browning 2001: 875, Nervegna 2013: 254.
88. On Terence, in particular, the literature is very rich. See, e.g., Black 2001, Herrick 1950 and Cain 2013.
89. As quoted in Wilson 2007: 10. See Hadley 2015 for the role of Aristophanes in the Renaissance.
90. Hadley 2015: 152.
91. On this production see Flashar 2009: 25–32 and Macintosh 2009: 70–3.

Chapter Six: Interpretations: The Stage and its Interpretive Communities

1. Sear 2006: 48–50.
2. The evidence is discussed in detail by Manuwald 2011: 57–61.
3. Safety concerns, which would make a permanent site intrinsically preferable, seem to have been irrelevant – although temporary theatres could, and did, collapse (cf. Tacitus *Annals* 15.34 on one such incident involving a theatre, fortunately empty, at Naples in Nero's time).
4. Paulson 1992 and Walden 1894.
5. Janko 2011.
6. Neoptolemus of Parium, however, is little more than a name to us (Janko 2000: 152f.). On the *Ars Poetica* see Laird 2007, Reinhart 2013 and, most comprehensively, Brink 1963.
7. The search for the philosophical (esp. Stoicism) in Seneca's eight tragedies is a long-standing concern in Seneca research, see many of the chapters in Damschen and Heil 2014, for instance.
8. Hordern 2004, esp. 8f. and 26.
9. Plato *Ion* 533c9–535a10 is the key passage.
10. Plato *Ion* 535a9.
11. This position is not inconsistent with remarks given to Socrates in Plato's *Phaedrus* (245a1–7), a later dialogue quite safely datable to 370–350 BCE (Yunis 2011: 22–5, also on the problematic chronology of Plato's dialogues more generally). Here Socrates singles out poetry as an area of beneficial madness (*mania*), on par with the madness of prophets, ritual healers and, ultimately, the divine madness of *erôs* ('love'). But the fact that only the beneficially mad poet produces superior poetry says nothing about the moral or epistemological quality of that poetry.
12. The 2011 edition by Richard Janko of Philodemus' treatise *On Poems* (= Janko 2011), which in its fourth and fifth book polemicizes against Aristotle, has significantly enlarged the number of fragments that can plausibly be considered as originating from Aristotle's *On Poets*. Heath 2013, however, argues in detail that Janko's methods and conclusions have to be treated with caution.
13. Halliwell 1998: 324–30 on the date. Halliwell's monograph-length discussion of the *Poetics* as well as his book on mimesis (Halliwell 2002a) are fundamental. Hanink 2014a: 199–220 perceptively situates the *Poetics* within the theatre culture of fourth-century Athens. A particularly noteworthy article-length contribution with wide-ranging observations is Heath 2009. Shorter remarks on the place of the *Poetics* in early tragedy reception in Revermann 2016: 22–4. The extensive critical edition of the Greek text by Tarán and Gutas 2012 is the first one which fully

takes into account the extant Arabic translations, even if Kassel's edition of the text (Kassel 1965) as well as Halliwell's Loeb-edition (Halliwell 1995) remain important.

14. In the fifth century CE the neo-Platonic commentator Proclus, however, remarks that Plato's exclusion of tragedy and comedy from the ideal state 'gave Aristotle much incentive for criticism' (Proclus *On Plato's Republic* 1 p. 49 Kroll).
15. An ambitious and thought-provoking attempt at reconstructing the lost second book of the *Poetics* has been made by Janko 1984.
16. Halliwell 1998: 190–201 and 350–6 is a full and appropriately balanced discussion of *katharsis* in Aristotle's *Poetics* and the history of its interpretation. For possible new insights via Philodemus' *On Poems* see Janko 2011 (but note the cautioning remarks made by Heath 2013). Apart from music and tragedy, *katharsis* was probably also invoked by Aristotle for comedy, see Halliwell 1998: 274f. and Janko 1984: 136–51.
17. Lehmann 1999 on 'post-dramatic' theatre (the English translation is Lehmann 2006) has been ground-breaking. Lehmann 2013 pursues these issues for tragedy in the tradition he calls 'dramatic' theatre.
18. Ford 2011.
19. Ford 2002 situates this shift, and Aristotle's role, within the tradition of Greek critical and meta-poetic discourse.
20. Another interpretive community contemporary with Herodotus, that of comic poets, similarly shows keen awareness for tragic plot patterns. Aristophanes, our (by far) best preserved witness, is a good indicator of this, even if his penchant for tragedy may be exceptional by the standards of the genre. See Revermann 2006a: 101–4.
21. Fragment 664 in Kannicht-Snell 1981: 248–51.
22. Fr. 664 in Kannicht-Snell 1981: 248–51. Some of the long-standing and controversial discussion of this quite sensational fragment is presented in Kotlińska-Toma 2015: 178–85.
23. Saïd 2002, Griffin 2006.
24. Walbank 1960, Rutherford 2007.
25. See, for instance, Keith 2010.
26. Lada-Richards 2007, Garelli 2007 *passim*, Schlapbach 2008, Webb 2008: 58–71. On the (belated) second-century CE rise of pantomime in the Greek East, see Lada-Richards 2007: 23 and 63, Barnes 2010: 320.
27. Barish 1981, still the standard discussion of 'the anti-theatrical prejudice'.
28. The word 'pantomime' means, after all, 'the one who imitates everything' (i.e. by non-verbal representation, like the modern mime). In Lucian's words, the pantomime 'pulls together' everything that is done separately in other performance genres (68).
29. Libanius, writing his oration *Against Aristides on Behalf on the Pantomimes* about 200 years after Lucian in (probably) 361 CE, called pantomime 'some kind of instruction (*didachê*) for the masses in things of old' (64.112; cf. also Molloy 1996: 269 and Hall 2008: 6).
30. The praise of the sophistication with which audiences at Antioch relate to pantomime (76) is peculiar and is one indication that points to the 160s CE as the date of composition, when the Roman emperor Lucius Verus, a strong supporter of the pantomime (and the theatre arts more generally), spent several years in that city.

31. Webb 2008: 197–223 (esp. 201f.).
32. This is duly pointed out by Tertullian *On Spectacles* 22. Also, John Chrysostom in fact repeats criticism launched against pantomime by Aristides some 200 years earlier (Barnes 2010: 327).
33. Barnes 1985: 93–6, Turcan 1986, Barish 1981: 36–65 (esp. 44–51).
34. Theocharidis 1940, Hall and Wyles 2008: 412–9. On John Chrysostom see also Halliwell 2008: 495–512 (from a different yet related angle, his views on laughter).
35. Barish 1981: 52–65, Lim 2012.
36. Reich 1903: 204–30, Barnes 2010: 327–30 who voices and then retracts doubts about Choricius being a Christian, while accurately pointing out that even if Choricius were pagan, the fact that he sets out to defend the mime would remain remarkable.
37. I wish to thank Johanna Hanink and Donald Sells for very helpful comments on this chapter.

Chapter Seven: Communities of Production: Pied Pipers and How to Pay Them; or, the Variegated Finance of Ancient Theatre

1. Robert 1969: 680.
2. Slater 2007: 25.
3. Csapo 2004: 57–66, Wilson 2010.
4. Plut. *Mor.* 841F, cf. Philochorus, *FGrH* 328 F 57.
5. Davies 1967: 33f.
6. Pickard-Cambridge 1988: 103.
7. *Ath. Pol.* 56.3, adding that at some point the allocation of *chorêgoi* to comic poets passed from the Archon to the tribes, although the competition remained non-tribal.
8. Davies 1971: xxi–xxii, Wilson 2008: 112–14.
9. Wilson 2000: 265.
10. Wilson 2008: 91–111.
11. Isocr. *Antid.* 166 (an exceptionally high sum), cf. Pind. fr. 76 Maehler.
12. Strattis fr. 1, Wilson 2008: 106.
13. Wilson 2008: 98–100, 108f.
14. Wilson 2008: 110f., with some other possible sources of income.
15. Csapo 2007; cf. the Piraeus lease, Lalonde et al. 1991, L13 (324/3 BCE).
16. Csapo 2007: 95f., Migeotte 2010: 142.
17. Pickard-Cambridge 1988: 265–8.
18. Sommerstein 1997: 66f., 70f., Roselli 2011: 87–117.
19. Wilson 2008: 94f.
20. Csapo and Wilson 2010, Wilson and Csapo 2012, Hanink 2014a: 225-30. The role of the philosopher-statesman Demetrius of Phaleron, who headed the Athenian administration under Macedonian rule until democracy was restored in 307, is disputed. The first agonothetic inscription is *IG* ii.^{2} 3073.
21. *IG* ii.^{2} 834, Mikalson 1998: 57.
22. Ceccarelli 2010: 100f.
23. Manieri 2009: 313–40, 347–423.

24. Manieri 2009: 333–8.
25. Roueché 1993: 173f., no. 53.
26. *SEG* xxxviii. 1462 (English translation in Mitchell 1990: 183–7), cf. Wörrle 1988 (esp. 227–58), Jones 1990.
27. *IvO* 56, Geer 1935: 218–20.
28. Sifakis 1967: 61f. and 95.
29. *SEG* xix. 379 (c. 228 BCE) ll. 34f., I. Ephes. 2071.
30. Csapo 2004: 58f. and 2010: 86 (Macedon), Plut. *Crassus* 33.2–4 (Parthia).
31. *IG* XII.7 226 (Amorgos).
32. Sifakis 1967: 19f. and 148–52.
33. *SIG*^{3} 659.
34. Slater 2007: 34f.
35. Robert 1969: 680, Sifakis 1967: 19f., Milanezi 2004: 200f., cf. 196; see esp. *IG* XI.2 133.78–81.
36. Robert 1969, 662–4 (*I Priene* 113.63–6); id. 1969: 607–10 (*SEG* vii. 825, *IGRR* iv. 1270). The Oenoanda foundation (n. 26, ll. 23, 44f.) calls for *paramisthômata* ('rentals'), including mimes; cf. Wörrle 1988: 251–3.
37. Migeotte 1993, Crowther 2007.
38. Migeotte 1993: 270f.
39. Csapo 2004: 54, 68.
40. Pickard-Cambridge 1988: 93f.
41. Pickard-Cambridge 1988: 168, 176.
42. Pickard-Cambridge 1988: 279.
43. Sifakis 1967: 75–80.
44. Nervegna 2013: 80–8.
45. Pickard-Cambridge 1988: 204–8.
46. Le Guen 2001: ii. 125–30.
47. *SIG*^{3} 1080; Nachtergael 1977: 359–61.
48. Sifakis 1967: 80f., Slater 2010a: 254, Nervegna 2013: 82.
49. Sifakis 1967: 80f., Nachtergael 1977: 243 n. 165. For the Delphic Pythaides, Sifakis 1967: 93, Chaniotis 1990: 92f.
50. Sifakis 1967: 71–83, Nachtergael 1977: 309–13.
51. *ArchEph* 1956: 34–72 + *SEG* xix. 335, Slater 1993: 189–99 and 2010a: 279.
52. Stephanis 1998, no. 448; for *hypotragôidoi*, cf. also Luc. *Jup. Trag.* 1, Philostr. *Vit. Soph.* 1.18 (507). Women *tragôidoi* are also implied by the tonal register of P. Berol. inv. 6870; cf. Dioscorides 2 G.-P.
53. Robert 1930 and 1936 (foundational); excellent overview in Slater 2010b.
54. Roueché 1993: 18 and 22, Nagy 1996: 164–72.
55. *SEG* vii. 825, with Robert 1969: 607–10.
56. Hall and Wyles 2008, Slater 2010b.
57. Tac. *Ann.* 1.54, Slater 2010b: 536.
58. Lucian *Salt.* 32 (Sebasta, 162–5 CE), *FD* iii. 1, 551 and I. Eph. 2070f., cf. Slater 1995 and Bowersock 2008: 74f.
59. Robert 1969: 683f., Slater 1995: 281f., Hunt 2008: 181–3.
60. Roueché 1993: 23f., I. Tralles 110.
61. Pleket 1973 and 2004: 104f.

62. *IG* XII.9, 207 and p. 176, *IG* Suppl. p. 178, *SEG* xxxiv. 896 (294–287 BCE), Le Guen 2001, i. 41–56.
63. *SIG*³ 460 (soon before 279) = Le Guen 2001, i. 129–32, *IG* ii.² 1132 + *SIG*³ 399 (c. 279/8) = Le Guen 2001, i. 57–61. First literary reference Chamaeleon fr. 44 Wehrli.
64. *OGIS* 50f. = Le Guen 2001, i. 293–300, *SIG*³ 507 (c. 227) = Le Guen 2001, i. 199–202.
65. Michel, *Recueil* 1016B, Pickard-Cambridge 1988: 293, Poland 1934: 2487f., Le Guen 2001, i. 230, Aneziri 2003: 324–7.
66. Pickard-Cambridge 1988: 297–302, Aneziri 2009: 222f., *BGU* iv. 1074 (273/4 CE). Frisch 1986, no. 1.
67. Aneziri 2003: 267–89, Le Guen 2004a: 296f.
68. *OGIS* 51.66, a *skeuopoios*, *SIG*³ 424.85, *himatiomisthai* (Sifakis 1967: 81f., Nachtergael 1977: 313), Aneziri 2003: 208f.
69. Aeschin. *Fals. Leg.* 19 (and Σ ad loc.), Plut. *Alexander* 29.3.
70. *SEG* i. 362 (c. 306), Csapo 2004: 57 and 2010: 87.
71. *IG* XII.9 207.12–17.
72. On *nemêsis* ('allocation'), Aneziri 2003: 283 n. 71, 284–5; Slater 2010a: 263–8; I. Iasos 152.12.
73. Poland 1934: 2488.46–2492.20, Le Guen 2001: ii. 70f., Aneziri 2003: 243–54 and 2009: 229–32.
74. Le Guen 2004a: 286, Ceccarelli 2004: 135–8.
75. Edited by Petzl and Schwertheim 2006; see Jones 2007, Slater 2008 and Le Guen 2010b.
76. Millar 1977: 458–63.
77. Le Guen 2004b: 91.
78. Le Guen 2004b: 98f. and 103.
79. Sifakis 1967: 139.
80. Sifakis 1967: 140–6.
81. Le Guen 2004a: 297f. and 2004b, but cf. Jory 1970: 248, on the apparent restriction of (imperial) *hieroi agônes* to guildsmen.
82. Thonemann 2011: 118, an *agôn tôn tragôidôn* in I. Ilion 2.41.
83. Slater 2004: 158f.
84. *SEG* xix. 335, Migeotte 2010: 136f.; see also n. 21.
85. Wilson 2000: 270–6, Csapo and Wilson 2010.
86. Plut. *Mor.* 628A, *IG* ii.² 3114, Geagan 1967: 136–8, Wilson 2000: 276–8, Follet and Peppas Delmouzou 2001.
87. See n. 37 with main text.
88. I. Iasos 152.
89. Chaniotis 2012 (92 on Iasos) and Ellis Evans 2012.
90. *IG* IX.1 694 = IX.1² (4), 798 (before 229 BCE, or second century), Le Guen 2004b: 97–9.
91. See n. 26 with main text.
92. Slater 2007: 38–44 and 2010a.
93. Sifakis 1967: 31 and n. 1, Le Guen 2001: ii. 71, Slater 2007: 42f., Ceccarelli and Milanezi 2007: 207 n. 49, Wilson 2008: 108, Migeotte 2010: 129.
94. Slater 2007: 40f.

95. Slater and Summa 2006.
96. Spawforth 1989: 193, Slater 2007: 43f. and 2010a: 270f.
97. *IvO* 56, cf. *SEG* xxxvii. 356, second century CE; Slater 2007: 39f., Dunbabin 2010: 343–5; the first of Hadrian's letters (see n. 75) ordains that carefully-counted cash should be deposited beside the crowns.
98. Sifakis 1967: 38 (a skilled workman earned 2 drachmas a day, an unskilled one 2 or 3 obols), Migeotte 2010: 129; for the punitive costs of *choraulia*, see also Slater 2010a: 276–8 and 281.
99. Wörrle 1988: 234–6.
100. Roueché 1993: nos. 52. I, III.
101. Varro ap. Gell. 17.21.42.
102. *CIL* I^2 594 = II Suppl. 5439, §§lxx–lxxi; Crawford 1996, i. no. 25.
103. Leppin 1992: 84.
104. Blänsdorf 2004.
105. Prologue speaker of Terence's *Heauton Timoroumenos* and of the third performance of the *Hecyra*.
106. Plaut. *Bacch*. 215; the Didaskalia of the *Stichus* name him as leader of the troupe that produced it.
107. Plaut. *Cist*. 785.
108. Plaut. *Poen*. 36–9.
109. Leppin 1992: 85–7.
110. *NH* 21.6.
111. Plaut. *Amphitruo* 64–80 (awarded by the aediles), *Poen*. 36–9 (awarded by the *curatores ludorum*), *Trin*. 705f.
112. Jory 1970.
113. Jory 1970: 253, Leppin 1992: 184–6, *CIL* XIV. 2408 (Bovillae, 169 CE).
114. Jory 1970: 237–42, Leppin 1992: 93–5.
115. *IG* XIV. 2495 and 2499, Ghiron-Bistagne 1991.
116. Leppin 1992: 176–81, 196–8.
117. Boulvert 1970: 175f., Jory 1970: 244–7. For publicly-maintained troupes, cf. Leppin 1992: 90 and 237, Slater 2002: 315–20.
118. *CIL* XIV. 2299 (Ager Albanus, 161–212 CE), cf. Jory 1970: 247, Leppin 1992: 177f. and 279, Malavolta 2000, Blänsdorf 2004: 114. For other *locatores scaenicorum* see Csapo 2010: 201 n. 131.
119. Roueché 1993: 5.
120. Theocharidis 1940: 1–3 (literary sources), Blänsdorf 1990.
121. Roueché 1993: 7–11.
122. Theocharidis 1940: 20–48 and 67–119. *CIL* VI. 32328 contains Septimius Severus' decree for the celebration of the Secular Games of 204 CE, with detailed specifications for the performances of pantomimes, the individual artists and where they are to perform.
123. Roueché 1993: 6f.
124. Cass. *Var*. 4.51 (507 or 511 CE).
125. Jones 1964: 537–42.
126. Novellae 105.1.
127. Theocharidis 1940: 49–62.

128. Blänsdorf 1990: 263, Roueché 1993: 10.
129. Blänsdorf 1990: 268.

Chapter Eight: Genres: Drama and its Many Unhappy Returns

1. Fowler 1982: 38. Specific to genre in Greek tragedy is Donald Mastronarde's (1999–2000: 25; 2010: 47) helpful description of its social and cultural aspects as a slowly moving target.
2. As described by Charles Segal (1994: lx).
3. (1993).
4. Greece: Storey and Allan 2005: 14–24. Rome: Manuwald 2011: 41–9. See also Revermann, this volume, Chapter 1.
5. Silk 2013: 13.
6. For tragedy's *nostos* plot, see Taplin 1977a: 124–7; Hall 1997: 107–9.
7. For an overview of the poem, see West 2013: 244–50.
8. Taplin 1977: 297, 302–4.
9. Oliver Taplin has creatively compared this visual effect to the famous 'elevator scene' of Stanley Kubrick's *The Shining*.
10. Hall 1997: 107.
11. Deianira's thoughts are a heavily stylized, stereotyped version of a housewife's emotions, the accuracy of which is impossible to determine because no such perspectives survive. For transfocalization as a strategy of adaptation (typically between genres), see Genette 1997: 292f. and Sanders 2006: 48–62, 97–119.
12. Easterling 1982: *ad loc.*
13. *Cypria* Arg. 35–39 Bernabé with West 2013: 106f.
14. Note, however, that the hero in rags appears in the oldest extant tragedy, where the fallen Persian king Xerxes (see esp. 1017) returns to his court following the destruction of his navy in Aeschylus' *Persians* (472) (see Hanink, this volume).
15. Fifth- and fourth-century depictions of Telephus on Attic and Southern Italian vases showing him threatening the baby while propped on the altar attest to the impact of the scene. See Taplin 2007: 205–10.
16. Mastronarde 2010: 261.
17. Nervegna 2014a: 177. Other (Euripidean) tragic models both attested on Southern Italian vases and influential in Republican Roman tragedy include *Hecuba*, *Alexander*, *Medea*, *Melanippe*, and more.
18. For the different paradigms through which scholarship tends to view the Roman adaptation of Greek tragedy, 'Horatian' (cultured Greece captures savage Rome) *vs.* 'Ciceronian' (Rome aggressively appropriates Greek cultural goods), see Gildenhard 2010: 158f.
19. One famous, albeit biased, anecdote is Cicero's claim in the *Pro Sestio* (115–126; 56 BCE) that the famous actor Aesopus performed Accius' tragedy *Eurysaces*, the name of the son of Telamonian-Ajax, as an allegorical vehicle for Cicero's honourable suffering in exile from 58–56 BCE.
20. See Gildenhard 2010: 160–72.
21. For the fragments of Andronicus and Naevius, see Schauer 2012: 31–65, 73–123.
22. For Republican period *praetexta*, see Boyle 2008: xlii–lv; Manuwald 2011: 140–4.

23. For this aspect of tragedy, see especially the remarks of Scodel 2010: 12f.
24. See Collard (1975: 382–4) for commentary on the passage and parallels.
25. Faulkner (1995: 191) cites a body of fieldwork in anthropology that points to patterns of domestication and effeminization of men in old age, when increasingly involved in the care of the household and children, while older women progressively indulge their 'aggressive and egocentric impulses'.
26. Rosen (2014: 230–2) revises Whitman's (1964) famous definition of 'comic heroism' as a certain *ponêria* ('roguishness', 'rascality') driving the hero's project.
27. See in particular *Wasps* 1015–1059.
28. For changes in the physical appearance of the male protagonist in the visual record, see Green 2006.
29. See Goldberg's (1980: 72–91) dramaturgical study.
30. See Ruffell in this volume.
31. Comedy's emphasis on the political agency of ethically flawed women, whose sexuality is 'predominantly characterized by divergence from, and sometimes the flagrant transgression of, ideal *sôphrosunê*, "self-discipline"' (Halliwell 2002a: 125), produced critical advances in the genre's development.
32. First identified by Sommerstein 2005. See also Hall 2006 (= 2000): 170–83.
33. The passage's vocabulary of courtship and seduction has long been noted: Σ *Eq.* 517a; Henderson 1991a: 158, 160 (for additional citations); Biles 2002: 184f.
34. The domestic world of myth and the sexual escapades of gods and heroes are thought to have offered a path toward the depiction of mortal women (Bowie 2000), but when and how the leap from goddess to mortal was made is unknown.
35. Public mention of a free woman compromised the customary anonymity that guaranteed her chastity and fidelity. Thus identification (let alone satire) of a man's wife, daughter, or sister was tantamount to an attack on his house and honour. The *locus classicus* for the Athenian cultural enjoinment of female modesty is Pericles' encouragement to women to strive for anonymity in the Funeral Oration (Thuc. 2.45.2).
36. Though Davidson (2000) has identified one possible source of such scandalous episodes as the fifth-century poet Gnesippos (*floruit* 440s/430s) whose so-called 'adultery songs' lured women outside to their lovers, see the response of Hordern 2003. Cf. Eupolis, fr. 148; Cratinus, fr. 17; and Telecleides, fr. 36. Trenkner (1958) identified the adultery theme in contemporary Aesopic fable and the (now lost) 'Locrian Tale'.
37. An accessible translation is the colourful edition of Lloyd-Jones 1975.
38. Important studies of mime include Wiemken 1972 and Panayotakis 2010: 1–32 (whose focus is chiefly, but not exclusively, Roman mime).
39. For the few extant fragments of Sophron, see Hordern 2004. For mime influence on the Hellenistic poets Herodas and Theocritus, see Hunter 2002. The earliest explicit reference to mime may be the orator Demosthenes' condemnation (*Ol.* 2.19) of king Philip of Macedon's crass enjoyment of 'mime and shameful songs' (but see Sonnino 2014: 141 who argues that Aristotle preserves the earliest mention of literary mime). Early evidence for its public performance in Athens is a terracotta lamp (c. 225 BCE) depicting three performers of 'The Mother-in-Law' (Csapo and Slater 1995: 370).
40. Trenkner (1958: 6) identifies the adultery plot as the classic type of novella, and with connections to Aesopic fable.

41. That the chest was a traditional prop in such mimes is signaled by the Roman satirists Horace (2.7.58–61) and Juvenal (6.42–4).
42. Revermann 2006a *passim*. For the wife meeting her lover, sleeping with slaves, and plotting her husband's death as themes shared by Inlaw's speech and novella, see Trenkner 1958: 80–8.
43. Wives with slaves: Ar., *Th*. 491; fr. 592.29; fr. 715 ('you grind the mistress all night in sweet-smelling covers'); Eupolis fr. 192.100–2.
44. For these two types first defined by Plutarch, see Webb 2008: 95–138.
45. Tertullian (*Apol*. 15.1), for example, lists *Anubis the Adulterer, The Manly Moon, Diana Lashed, The Will of the Late Jove,* and *Three Starving Heracleses* as mime titles.
46. See Wiemken 1972: 48–80; Revermann 2006a: 320f.
47. While it is possible that Alcaeus' *Seduced Sisters* and Ameipsias' *Adulterers* portrayed seduction in some detail in late fifth-century comedy, their four meagre fragments tell us almost nothing,
48. The debate over the specifics of drama's development from the cult of Dionysus is a notoriously thorny problem and falls well outside the scope of this chapter. For an accessible discussion of this question, see Storey and Allan 2005: 24–34.
49. Griffith 2002: 202, 207. Dionysus may be the unnamed speaker complaining in Aeschylus fr. 78a.64–72, but this is uncertain.
50. Griffith 2002: 211–24.
51. For a useful, concise discussion of the different tendencies of the tragedians, see Rutherford 2012: 343f.
52. A possible exception is Aeschylus' *Psychostasia*.
53. Mastronarde 2010: 176.
54. Zagagi 1995: 142–4; Miles 2014: 83.
55. For the former explanation, see Miles 2014: 78.
56. While later Roman comedy adopts the free-standing prologue, it often introduces a generic prologue speaker, 'prologos', of analogous omniscience.
57. One exception is Juno's appearance at the beginning of Seneca's *Hercules Furens* 1–124.
58. Mayer 2002: 19–35.
59. Mayer 2002: 46f. reasonably considers this to be a flimsy pretext for Phaedra's bad behaviour, and perceives no divine scheme setting the agenda for the human agents. However, there are Senecan parallels for such inherited guilt (cf. *Pho*. 338, *Ag*. 233, *Thy*. 23–32), and it is quintessentially tragic. Venus' curse also has a precedent in Ovid (*Her*. 4.53ff.).
60. For a useful, concise overview of the genre, see Hall 2008: 1–40. In their appendix, Hall and Wyles 2008: 378–419 offer a collection of primary sources (with English translation).
61. Csapo and Slater 1995: 370; Hall and Wyles 2008: 378–80 (T1); Webb 2008: 60. Exceptional features include two dancers (as opposed to one), who are unmasked and also speaking.
62. Aside from Xenophon's proto-pantomime, the epigrammatist Dioscourides (*AP* 11.195 = T2 in Hall and Wyles 2008) laments his loss dancing the myth of the 'Temenidae' (perhaps from the Euripidean tragedy of the same name) in competition against an opponent performing the story of the 'Galli' in the middle of the third century BCE.
63. Webb 2008: 80.
64. See Lada-Richards 2007: 44–8; Webb 2008: 149.

65. Webb 2008: 84.
66. Lucian affirms the influence of earlier cultic dances on pantomime, specifically those of the cult of Cybele (8), and the mysteries and dramatic festivals (22, 26) of Dionysus.
67. Cf. Lucian's story (64) of the barbarian from Pontus. See Webb 2008: 59.
68. I would like to thank Martin Revermann and Ian Ruffell for their extremely helpful comments on an earlier draft of this chapter.

Chapter Nine: Technologies of Performance: Machines, Props, Dramaturgy

1. Both Greek and Roman theatres have a stage house (Greek: *skênê*, Latin: *scaena*) at the back with up to three doors; a slightly raised stage (Greek: *logeion*, Latin: *pulpitum* – although the attribution of the Greek term is not secure whereas the sheer existence of a raised stage in classical Greek drama certainly is, cf. Aristophanes *Wasps* 1342–1344 and Csapo/Slater 1995: 268); and an area in front of the stage (Greek: *orchêstra*, the dancing area of the chorus, Latin: *orchestra*; note that in Roman theatres senators could be seated here as well).
2. Horace *Epist*. 2.1.194–207.
3. Cicero *Ad fam*. 7.1.2.
4. Livy 7.2.13. In this chapter Livy dates the beginning of the Roman theatre business to 364 BCE and describes the evolution from pure dance to dramatic works (see Oakley 1998: 40–72, Feeney 2016: 99f.). In those early days, machines do not seem to be involved.
5. 'To them [i.e. the arts of the stage] you may add the machine workers who come up with stage machines which lift themselves up, silently rising platforms and other surprise effects where things which were connected drift apart, or things which were separated unite on their own, or things which were sticking up gradually collapse.'
6. Drama was also performed in amphitheatres of the imperial period, but then in the form of 'fatal charades' in which the characters (usually convicted criminals) were in fact killed according to their role, see Coleman 1990 (cf. Coleman 2006: lxv–lxxv). That the huge machinery of the amphitheatre was used on such occasions can hardly be doubted. Conversely, the staging of such charades will not have adhered to a dramatic text in the narrow sense of the term.
7. Cicero *Pro Caelio* 65, cf. also Manuwald 2011: 69f.
8. See the legitimate criticism of such a position, as for instance endorsed by Taplin 1971 and Taplin 1977a: 28–39, by Revermann 2006a: 46–65.
9. This also applies to the plays performed at the Lenaea festival, which until about the middle of the fifth century BCE were probably staged on the Athenian agora (cf. Pickard-Cambridge 1988: 37–9 and Csapo and Slater 1995: 123). That the first performance of comedies took place in Athens can be considered as fairly certain, while for tragedy there may be slight doubts. It is, however, important that there were frequent re-performances in the Attic deme theatres and outside of Attica (especially in Western Greece), not so frequently in the city of Athens before the fourth century (cf. Revermann 2006a: 66–95 and Lamari 2015). The existence of reperformances makes it possible that the basic technical equipment as described in this chapter was also available in deme theatres. Conversely, it is also possible that dramaturgy could be adapted to match local theatre resources which were less lavish than those found in the cultural capital, Athens.

10. Cf. Pollux 4.128.
11. Pollux 4.128 maintains that only in tragedy the crane was called *mêchanê* whereas in comedy it was called *kradê* (cf. also *P.Oxy.* 2742.3–19, probably a commentary on the *Seriphioi* by Cratinus; cf. Csapo and Slater 1995: 269).
12. Pollux 4.127–32. This source, however, is only reliable for the time after late Hellenism, a period for which we lack dramatic texts.
13. On the acoustics of the Athenian Theatre of Dionysus generally see Kampourakis 2008.
14. *Vita Aeschyli* 14.
15. Aristophanes *Peace* 79–178.
16. Cf. Lendle 1995.
17. The necessary supporting structure for the crane can now also be considered documented in the archaeological record for the classical phase of the Athenian Theatre of Dionysus, in the form of the much-discussed foundation T (cf. Papastamati-von Moock 2014: 63–72 and Papastamati-von Moock 2015: 69–71).
18. This function can be derived quite plausibly from Antiphanes fr. 189 Kassel-Austin (see also n. 5 above).
19. For a reconstruction of the scenic ensemble and the crane model used see Papastamati-von Moock 2014: 71. Her drawing, however, lacks a raised stage (which would have been wooden, hence leaving no archaeological trace). Also, her rendering of the height of the back portico which is slightly elevated relative to the stage house has to be questioned, since in this case the crane could not have been swung towards the back of the stage house. It remains unclear how the crane could have picked up actors without spoiling the surprise for the audience.
20. Cf., for instance, Currie 2005: 71–84.
21. Aristophanes *Acharnians* 407–479 and *Women at the Thesmophoria* 95–265.
22. On this whole topic see van Möllendorff 2015.
23. The push-back of the *ekkyklêma* can be passed over in silence or be heavily marked (as in Sophocles' *Ajax* 579–595).
24. See Taplin 1977a: 322–7 who decides against the use of the *ekkyklêma* and even argues (443) against its existence at so early a date.
25. Cf. van Möllendorff 2015: 53. Here too one may ask how this was staged. If Clytemnestra emphasizes that the platform of the *ekkyklêma* is identical with the site of murder, it would be not so much hyper-realistic but heavily symbolic to present the corpse in the bathtub. Such a stylizing presentation, which can also be witnessed in other plays – for instance Sophocles *Ajax* 347ff. (Ajax in the middle of the sheep and the ram murdered by him) and, as shown above, Euripides *Heracles* 1028ff. (Heracles asleep, leaning at a column with his murdered family around him) – would prominently highlight the vulnerability of the victim, the particular cowardice of the murderers and the metamorphosis of a place of relaxation into a site of cruel violence.
26. This also applies to the beginning of the *Eumenides* (cf. van Möllendorff 2015: 54f.). In particular, the *ekkyklêma* could in this case not present the result of an action the genesis of which had been described earlier. And would the Furies, who were not asleep according to the report of the priestess (*Eumenides* 54), have been put to sleep (*Eumenides* 67f.) by Apollo, before or perhaps while they were being rolled out on the *ekkyklêma*?

27. *Peace* 82–101: anapaestic dimeter; 102–153: iambic trimeter; 154–172: anapaestic dimeter; 173–179: iambic trimeter. On the whole scene see van Möllendorff 2002: 75–80. Mastronarde 1990: 285f. and Olson 1998: xliii–xlviii believe that the following scene (set in heaven) was staged in front of the *skênê*.
28. At *Poetics* 6.1449b24–28 Aristotle considers both these emotions as co-operating towards the overall impact of tragedy, while he also maintains that they do not have to manifest themselves simultaneously (cf. *Poetics* 11.1452a38–b3).
29. Boyle 2014: 312f.
30. Boyle 2014: 65 assumes an empty *ekkyklêma* being wheeled back while the characters walk or rush back into the palace. This seems to me to be an unnecessarily complicated way of staging.
31. See also Boyle 2014: 384 who points out that this is the only place in Seneca's plays where the use of the crane is certain.
32. But cf. the discussion by Revermann 2006a: 187–9 who insists on the 'comic point' of the philosopher's seriousness. This is certainly true, but I would like to focus on the specifically tragic dimension of this intellectual business doomed to fail at the end.
33. Against the background of the question pursued here it is not unimportant that Strepsiades (*Clouds* 186) compares their pallor with that of the Spartans who were defeated at Sphacteria and then brought to Athens as prisoners of war. In the year 423 (the year in which the first version of *Clouds* was performed) they had been detained for two years already and were therefore hardly in healthy condition (cf. Dover 1968: 120). If Socrates' house is compared to a PoW camp in this way, this can plausibly be seen as an equivalent to the horrific events that take place in the heroic palaces of tragedy.
34. Cf. already Dearden 1976: 65–7 and Sommerstein 1998: 170; for ancient commentators assuming the use of the *ekkyklêma* cf. Revermann 2006a: 186 n. 12 who himself opts for a staging with individual students bringing out one prop after the other. This is certainly not to be dismissed but perhaps underrates Strepsiades' astonishment when apparently being confronted with a number of students all at the same time (*Clouds* 184).
35. Newiger 1990 provides an overview of the use of both machines which is still valid and shows sound judgement, even if it may not be correct in all instances. (1) Crane: (a) Comedy: *Peace* 79–178, *Birds* 1196–1261, Aristophanes *fr.* 192 Kassel-Austin, *Clouds* 218–238. (b) Tragedy: Euripides *Medea* 1317ff., *Electra* 1233ff., *Heracles* 815ff, *Hippolytus* 1283ff., *Ion* 1549ff., *Helen* 1642ff., *Andromache* 1226ff. (in other words, only Euripidean plays). That the crane was used at Sophocles *Philoctetes* 1409–1417 cannot be proven from the text but perhaps might be indicated by the metre. (2) *ekkyklêma*: (a) Comedy: *Acharnians* 407–79, *Women at the Thesmophoria* 95–265 (for the passage of *Clouds* analysed in the main text above Newiger [1990: 42] is reluctant to assume the use of the *ekkyklêma*). (b) Tragedy: Sophocles *Ajax* 344–594, Euripides *Hippolytus* 808–1089, *Heracles* 875–1426. Of note is the observation that within tragedy Euripides not only uses these machines most often but also several times uses both of them within a single play. In the *Clouds* scene Aristophanes would therefore be taking his guidance from Euripides.
36. Cf. Plutarch *Alcibiades* 16.14, Demosthenes *Against Meidias* 147, Andocides *Against Alcibiades* 17.

37. Vitruvius *De architectura* 5.6.9.
38. Pollux 4.126.
39. Small 2013: 116f.
40. Small 2013.
41. See Revermann 2013: 79. Tordoff 2013: 100 and 103 offers a statistical analysis to support this distinction.
42. On this differentiation between the de- and connotation of props see Tordoff 2013: 94–6.
43. Revermann 2013: 85. Electra's monologue of despair about the assumed death of her brother is directed towards the urn which Orestes out of pity tries to take away from her until he can no longer contain himself and, against his earlier intention, discloses his true identity to his sister.
44. Whether the sword was also visible during Ajax's subsequent suicide speech continues to be controversial, as is the related question whether Ajax's suicide was visible on stage, see Finglass 2015b and Martinelli 2015. The question is not of vast importance to the problem discussed here, since the sword has been shown extensively to the spectators and, most of all, because its connection with Hector has been established at length by Ajax. Therefore, although it may later be invoked only verbally (even involving the use of demonstrative pronouns) without being visible any longer, the sword nonetheless has a semiotic presence on stage.
45. See the discussion in Manuwald 2011: 79f.
46. Extensive discussion in Csapo and Miller 2007, esp. the 'General Introduction' (1–38). Wiles 2007 and 2008 argues emphatically against an overly political and in favour of a cultic-religious reading of Greek drama.
47. Cf. Dugdale 2008: 114–24. Pollux devotes most of the theatrical section of his *Onomastikon* to naming and describing masks: masks of tragedy and satyr play (4.133–42) and masks of New Comedy (4.143–54). On the latter see also Ruffell 2014: 149–55.
48. The question of whether the character of Socrates was wearing a simple comic mask or a portrait mask, and the implication of either scenario, are discussed in Dover 1968: xxxiii.
49. Aristophanes *Knights* 230–233.
50. Aristophanes *Clouds* 348–350.
51. Köhnken 1980.
52. On pantomime see Lada-Richards 2007, Garelli 2007 and the contributions (including the excellent Introduction and appendix of sources) in Hall and Wyles 2008.
53. Cf. Hall's discussion of the fourth-century CE 'Barcelona Alcestis' papyrus as a libretto of Latin pantomime in Hall and Wyles 2008: 258–82. The text (124 hexameters) contains dialogues and monologues which may have been recited as background to the pantomime's dancing.
54. See, for instance, Plutarch *Sympotic Questions* 9.747c and Libanius *or.* 64.118.
55. Lada-Richards 2007: 38–55 (esp. 47).
56. *Aetna* 294–301, cf. Hall and Wyles 2008: 27.
57. On this topic see May 2008.
58. Cf. Fronto *On Orations* 5, p. 150 van den Hout, and Lada-Richards 2007: 40.

Chapter Ten: Knowledge Transmission: Ancient Archives and Repertoires

1. 'Old drama' (*palaion drama*) was the standard way of referring to a play that had premiered at a previous festival.
2. *Acharnians* 394–489.
3. Hall 2015: 1–2.
4. For a survey of *scholia* on dramatic texts see the relevant chapters in Dickey 2007.
5. Taylor 2003: 19.
6. Athenaeus 1.3a, cf. Knox 1985: 9; in Aristophanes' *Frogs* Euripides' use of books is mentioned at 943 and 1409.
7. Ancient plays have been transmitted with minimal stage directions, though Taplin argued that stage directions are implicit in the dialogue (for an overview of his theory see Taplin 1977b and 1978); for discussion and critique see Revermann 2006a: 46–65.
8. On costume in Greek tragedy see Wyles 2011; in comedy see Compton-Engle 2015. On stage props see Revermann 2013 and Tordoff 2013; on the evidence for 'technologies of performance' (such as stage machinery) see von Möllendorf in this volume.
9. Vitruvius 7.11; the authors named are Agatharchus, Anaxagoras and Democritus.
10. *Suda* σ 815.
11. Athenaeus 1.19e.
12. On the Greek institution of the *chorêgia* see Wilson 2000 and Lightfoot in this volume.
13. For an overview of choregic monuments see Townsend 2010.
14. Duncan 2015: 'Dramatic masks were portable, physical, and non-ephemeral items of theatre which, when part of a winning production, were publically dedicated in the Dionysion.' Cf. Aristophanes F 130 K-A on the dedications of masks in the Dionysion. For an overview of the use of masks in Greek tragedy see Wiles 2007.
15. Lysias 21.4; see Green 1982 on such dedications. For a highly speculative account of costs associated with the material reality of the Great Dionysia see Wilson 2008.
16. For a full-length study see Hanink 2014a; see also Lambert 2008 for evidence of the use of theatre as a political/diplomatic tool in this period.
17. [Plu.] *Lives of the Ten Orators* 841f; see the discussion and bibliography at Hanink 2014a: 60–89. The law is often seen as an attempt to curb the introduction of actors' interpolations into the tragic scripts. The question of how early musical notation was introduced into dramatic scripts is still debated: see esp. Fleming 1999 and, for a more cautious view, Prauscello 2006.
18. See esp. Papastamati von Moock 2014.
19. Csapo 2007.
20. On the date see Tracy 2015, esp. p. 559 on the inscription's date and location. For an edition of this inscription, *IG* II² 23218 (the 'Fasti') see Millis and Olson 2012 (scholars prior to Tracy had dated the inscribing of the Fasti to a year between 347 and 342 BCE).
21. On this set of inscriptions, the 'Didascaliae', see most recently Tracy 2015: 560–6 and Millis and Olson's 2012 edition.

22. Hanink 2014a: 191–220.
23. Hart 2010, Green and Handley 1995, Taplin 1997 and Csapo 2014 are accessible overviews of the iconographic evidence for the Greek theatre. For panoramas of the spread of Athenian theatre throughout Greece see esp. Taplin 1999 and Csapo 2010: 83–116.
24. See esp. Csapo 2010: 1–37.
25. See esp. Taplin 2007 and 1997 on the 'pictorial record' for tragedy generally.
26. On these vases see esp. Taplin 1993 and Csapo 2014. For 'theatre realistic' art in the Greek West see also Csapo 2010: 38–82.
27. On Greek theatre in the West see the volume edited by Bosher 2012.
28. On the evidence for the so-called 'rural' celebrations of Dionysia festivals see Goette 2014.
29. See recently Le Guen 2014a and Moloney 2014.
30. Csapo 2010: 75.
31. On theatre-related terracotta figurines as evidence for 'regional' theatre see Green 2014; more generally see *passim* in Hart 2010 and Green and Handley 1995.
32. Sutton 1987.
33. An anecdote about Euripides as *didaskalos* (director) at Plutarch *Mor.* 46b (*De audiendo*); about Aeschylus teaching dance steps at Athenaeus 21d–22a: see Marshall 2004.
34. On rehearsals of comedy see Revermann 2006a: 87–94; for a comparative approach with Elizabethan theatre see Ley 2013.
35. Antiphon 6.11–13; discussion at Wilson 2000: 116–20. The victim was a boy named Diodotus who was training with a chorus slated to perform at the festival of the Thargelia. The chorus was thus not a part of a theatrical production, but the practice of training dramatic and non-dramatic choruses was likely similar.
36. Aristotle *Constitution of the Athenians* 56.3.
37. *P.Oxy.* 4546. See Marshall 2004 and Revermann 2006a: 88–93; at p. 87 Revermann notes that ancient comedy preserves no 'rehearsal scene' along the lines of what we find in, e.g., Shakespeare's *A Midsummer Night's Dream*.
38. Csapo 2010: 117–39; see also Hunter 2002; for the evidence about ancient acting practice that is preserved in Aristotle's works see Sifakis 2002. On 'styles of performance' in Greek antiquity see also Valakas 2002 and Green 2002: 105–21, who makes helpful use of material artifacts depicting actors in performance.
39. Easterling 2002, Hall 2002 and Csapo 2010: 83–116.
40. Moloney 2014; Le Guen 2014a. Some actors were in such demand that fines were introduced for those who failed to fulfil commitments to perform (at least in Athens): Hanink 2014a: 70–2.
41. Hanink 2014a: 68–70.
42. See, most recently, Finglass 2015a.
43. *IG* II² 2318.1009–11 Millis-Olson. The significance of the reform is discussed by Hanink 2015.
44. On the *technitai Dionysiou* see also Lightfoot 2002. Le Guen 2001 collects the epigraphical sources.
45. On early reperformances see esp. Nervegna 2007, Lamari 2014, Nervegna 2014a, Vahtikari 2014 and the collected papers in Lamari 2015.

46. On deme theatres and theatrical performances see Goette 2014.
47. The topic of paratragedy is extremely rich; for a survey with bibliography see Hanink 2014b: 264–6.
48. Wilson 1996, Ford 1999 and Scodel 2007: 133–42.
49. Aristophanes *Wasps* 579–80: if Oeagrus (the tragic actor) is brought to court, the jurors might force him to perform a part of (Aeschylus'?) *Niobe*.
50. Calculations at Revermann 2006b: 108, in the context of an illuminating discussion of the competence of Athens' theatrical audiences to recognize e.g. parody of and intertextuality with previous plays.
51. On ancient scholarship in general see esp. Pfeiffer 1968 (the classic account) and now Montanari, Matthaios and Rengakos 2015 (2 vols.; the first is of more general use). Reynolds and Wilson 2013 is a time-tested handbook (in its fourth edition) to the transmission of ancient texts. For an overview of ancient scholarship on comedy see Dobrov 2010; on tragedy see Hanink forthcoming.
52. On comedy see Le Guen 2014b; on tragedy see Kotlinska-Toma 2015.
53. On Hellenistic mime (and its influence on Hellenistic poets and Roman performance) see Hunter 2002 and Panayotakis 2014 respectively; on mime plots and their impact see Sells in this volume.
54. Listed at Diogenes Laertius 5.26 (*opera* 135–7); see Reisch 1903, cols. 396–9.
55. On Peripatetic scholarship see Pfeiffer 1968: 87–95, on Peripatetic scholarship on tragedy see Wartelle 1971: 125–34.
56. For an excellent overview of the library and its legacy see Hall 2015.
57. Pfeiffer 1968: 95; see Richardson 1993 on links between Athens' Peripatos and the Library of Alexandria.
58. Galen *In Hippocratis epidemiarum* iii 17a.607.5–17 Wenkebach.
59. For Aristophanes of Byzantium's theatrical scholarship see esp. Kovacs 2005: 384–6. On his *hypotheseis* see Pfeiffer 1968: 192–6, Dickey 1999: 92–4, Mossman 2010 and Bing 2011.
60. Athenaeus 14.695a = Aristophanes of Byzantium F 373 Slater.
61. On scholarship in Pergamum see Nagy 1998.
62. Diogenes Laertius 4.23.
63. Suetonius *On Grammarians* 2.1.
64. On Didymus' theatrical scholarship see Zuntz 1965: 253–4, Pfeiffer 1968: 277f. and Wartelle 1971: 185–95.
65. The work is lost, but is celebrated by many theatre historians as the founding work of their field: Schoch 2012. On Iuba II see Roller 2006.
66. Csapo and Slater 1995: Appendix A consists in an introduction and English translation of the theatre-related entries.
67. *Dialogus* 2: *Curiatius Maternus Catonem recitaverit*. See Manuwald 2001 on Maternus in the *Dialogus*.
68. *Dialogus* 3.
69. Boyle 2006: 145; for passages attesting to 'nonperformed drama' see Csapo and Slater 1995: 37f. Aristotle even refers to *anagnôstikoi*, tragedians' whose work is better suited to reading: *Rhetoric* 1413b12f.
70. See e.g. Goldhill 1987 on the relationship between Athenian tragedy and Athens' empire.

71. Cf. Cornelius Nepos *Preface* 5 on the distinction between views of actors in the Greek and Roman worlds: in Rome, unlike Greece, being an actor brings *infamia*. Livy 7.2.12 attests to the prohibition of actors from military service, which was not in force for performers of Atellan farce; though see Jory 1970: 230–3 on the difficulties presented by the passage.
72. Ennius *TRF* Vol. II (= Manuwald 2012) test. 73. For an overview of theatre during the Roman Republic see esp. Manuwald 2011. On the Etruscan influence see esp. Wiseman 1988: 1–13.
73. On the Atellan farce see recently Manuwald 2011: 169–77 and Petrides 2014; on Roman mime (Latin *planipes*, meaning 'a barefoot actor') see Manuwald 2011: 178–83 and Panayotakis 2010: 1–32. On the importance of improvisation even in Roman comedy see Marshall 2006: 245–79.
74. Feldherr 1998: 172, citing Zehnaker 1983: 32 for the numbers.
75. For an overview see Boyle 2006: 27–55.
76. On translation in the early Republic and its immense significance for the development of Roman culture see Feeney 2016: 17–64.
77. Festus 446 Linds (the source is the first-century BCE Verrius); see the discussion in Jory 1970: 225–8.
78. The didascaliae are preserved by Donatus (Rome, fourth century CE); on his commentaries on Terence see Demetriou 2014. For an overview of theories about the origins of the information in the *didascaliae* (in Terence's own time, with Varro, or in the imaginations of Imperial-Era antiquarians) see Moore 2012: 8f.
79. On masks in Roman drama see esp. Marshall 2006: 126–58.
80. Quintilian 11.3.72–3. In the next section (74) Quintilian lists a series of comic stock characters. See Marshall 2006: 83–125 for an overview of actors' roles in Roman drama.
81. See Baker 2005 on a digital project on the relationship between Pompeiian frescos and stage practice.
82. Victor 2014: 701–6; see Wright 2006, Nervegna 2014b: 727–31 and Radden-Keefe 2015 on the illustrations. Dutsch 2007 attempts, on the basis of these miniatures, to recover information about ancient actors' gestures.
83. *Ad familiares* 7.1; cf. Horace *Epistles* 2.182–207 (*Ars Poetica*). In the *Poetics* (1450b17) Aristotle had also located *opsis* (often translated as 'spectacle') as the least important aspect of tragedy.
84. Hamilton 2011. See also Williams 2004 for a digital project that has created enlargements of New Comedy masks depicted by miniature terracotta figurines.
85. Athenaeus 3.3.3; 130 plays ascribed to Plautus were apparently circulated in Athenaeus' time (3.3.11–14). See esp. Gunderson 2015: 19–24. Livy's account (7.2) of the early stages of the Roman theatre owes much to Varro as well. On the passage see Feldherr 1998: 178–82; for an account of Varro, Livy, and the Christian author Tertullian on the origins of the Roman theatre see Waszink 1948.
86. See Gagliardo and Packer 2006 for a recent overview of the archeological evidence.
87. Goldberg 1998: 12.
88. Goldberg 1998: 13 citing Pliny *Natural History* 36.113–15. See also Livy 40.51.3 on a contract for theatre construction. On the early temporary theatres and their opulence see e.g. Beacham 1992: 56–85.

89. On Vitruvius and Roman theatres see esp. Sear 1990 and 2006: 24–36; Vitruvius' 'theoretical' prescriptions for theatre construction are notoriously at odds with the archaeological evidence of actual theatres.
90. Manuwald 2011: 80–90; see also Marshall 2006: 20–31 for the business side of Roman theatrical production.
91. Marshall 2006: 26–31; Manuwald 2011: 84 with note 143 for references to *choragi* made in comedies.
92. Csapo 2010: 168–204 provides an overview of theatre's 'privatization'.
93. See in particular Beacham 1992: 154–63 and Boyle 2006: 145 on specific Roman actors.
94. Cicero *Pro Roscio* 28–9.
95. Macrobius *Saturnalia* 3.14.12. For comments on acting from oratorical discussions see e.g. Quintilian 2.10.13 (comic actors add a touch of stage direction to common speech); 6.2.34 (on 'method acting': actors in tragedies depart the stage in tears); 11.3.11 (on the power of slow-paced delivery); Plutarch *Cicero* 5.3 (the actor Aesopus, playing Atreus, killed a stagehand with his sceptre). On how orators' delivery (should) differ from actors' see e.g. *Rhetorica ad Herennium* 3.15; Cicero *Orator* 25.86; Quintilian 11.3.57 and 181.
96. Cf. Quintilian 11.3.65–49 with Boyle 2006: 147–8 with n.18 on 261. For an attempt at reconstructing Roman actors' repertoires of gesture see Dutsch 2013.
97. *De Oratore* 2.191: *ex persona mihi ardere oculi hominis histrionis viderentur.*
98. See, respectively, Csapo 1993 and Marshall 1999.
99. On these *collegia* and their influence by Greek models see esp. Jory 1970.
100. Festus 436–8, discussed by Jory 1970: 237–42.
101. See e.g. Manuwald 2011: 90–7 on the social status of dramatic poets.
102. See Boyle 2006: 145 with n.7 on 260 and Jory 1970: 244–9 on actors kept in the imperial household.
103. Horsfall 2003 esp. 11–19 and 31–74.
104. On the transformations of the Theatre of Dionysus under the Romans see Welch 2007: 165–78.
105. *Oration* 31.121.
106. See Dunbabin 2014 and Csapo 2010: 140–67 on theatrical mosaics in the Graeco-Roman East.
107. In the *Encomium of Demosthenes* attributed to Lucian (thus mid-second century CE), it is observed that 'there is a dearth of new poetry for Dionysus, whether comedy or tragedy' (27).
108. On pantomime masks and their iconography see Jory 1996 and 2001; Huskinson 2008 examines pantomime imagery on sarcophagi.
109. See esp. Webb 2008: 72–93 on the pantomime dancer's embodied knowledge.
110. Zanobi 2014.
111. (Latin) text with (English) translation in Hall and Wyles 2008: 404–12 (with Hall's article on this papyrus in the same volume).
112. Easterling 1997: 220–1. See Jory 2008 on the pantomime libretti; Lucian *On Dance* 61 names myths danced in pantomime. On mime and pantomime in late antiquity (second to sixth centuries CE) see Webb 2008. On pantomime see also Garelli 2007 and the essays in Hall and Wyles 2008.

113. Robert 1930; cf. Athenaeus 1.20d.
114. *On Dance* 63; cf. Petrides 2013 for the light that the dialogue sheds on the pantomime mask.
115. *Oration* 19.5.

BIBLIOGRAPHY

Anderson, W.S. 1993. *Barbarian Play: Plautus' Roman Comedy*. Toronto: University of Toronto Press.
Adorno, T. 1997. *Aesthetic Theory*. Translated by R. Hullot-Kentor. New York: Continuum.
Adorno, T. 2007. *Philosophy of Modern Music*. Translated by A.G. Mitchell and W.V. Blomster. London: Continuum.
Aneziri, S. 2009. 'World Travellers: The Associations of Artists of Dionysus'. In *Wandering Poets in Ancient Greek Culture*, edited by R. Hunter and I. Rutherford, 217–36. Cambridge: Cambridge University Press.
Aneziri, S. 2013. *Die Vereine der dionysischen Techniten im Kontext der hellenistischen Gesellschaft: Untersuchungen zur Geschichte, Organisation und Wirkung der hellenistischen Technitenvereine*. Stuttgart: Franz Steiner.
Armstrong, R. 2006. *Cretan Women. Pasiphae, Ariadne, and Phaedra in Latin Poetry*. Oxford: Oxford University Press.
Asmis, E. 1992. 'Crates on Poetic Criticism'. *Phoenix* 46: 138–69.
Bain, D. 1979. '*PLAVTVS VORTIT BARBARE*. Plautus, *Bacchides* 526–61 and Menander, *Dis exapaton* 102–12'. In *Creative Imitation in Latin Literature*, edited by D.A. West and A.J. Woodman, 17–34. Cambridge: Cambridge University Press.
Baker, D. 2005. 'The Great Theatre at Pompeii and a Pompeian Fresco'. *Didaskalia* 6.2 (http://rae2007.cch.kcl.ac.uk/pompey/issues/vol6no2/baker.htm).
Barish, J. 1981. *The Antitheatrical Prejudice*. Berkeley, Los Angeles, London: University of California Press.
Barnes, T.D. 1985. *Tertullian: A Historical and Literary Study*. 2nd ed. Oxford: Oxford University Press.
Barnes, T.D. 2010. 'Christians and the Theatre'. In Gildenhard and Revermann 2010, 313–33.
Beacham, R.C. 1992. *The Roman Theatre and its Audience*. Cambridge: Cambridge University Press.
Beard, M., J. North and S. Price. 1998. *Religions of Rome*. 2 vols. Cambridge: Cambridge University Press.

Bernabé, A. 1996. *Poetae Epici Graeci. Testimonia et Fragmenta.* Pars I. Stuttgart/Leipzig: Teubner.

Bieber, M. 1961. *The History of the Greek and Roman Theater.* 2nd ed. Princeton: Princeton University Press.

Biles, Z.P. 2002. 'Intertextual Biography in the Rivalry of Cratinus and Aristophanes'. *Amercian Journal of Philology* 123: 169–204.

Bing, P. 2011. 'Anecdote, Hypothesis, and Image in the Hellenistic Reception of Euripides'. *Antike & Abendland* 56: 1–17.

Black, R. 2001. *Humanism and Education in Medieval and Renaissance Italy: Tradition and Innovation in Latin Schools from the Twelfth to the Fifteenth Century.* Oxford: Oxford University Press.

Blänsdorf, J. 1990. 'Der spätantike Staat und die Schauspiele im Codex Theodosianus'. In *Theater und Gesellschaft im Imperium Romanum/Théâtre et société dans l'empire romain*, edited by J. Blänsdorf, 261–74. Tübingen: Francke.

Blänsdorf, J. 2004. 'Das römische Theaterwesen der Kaiserzeit im Spiegel der Inschriften'. In *Theater, Theaterpraxis, Theaterkritik im kaiserzeitlichen Rom: Kolloquium anlässlich des 70. Geburtstages von Prof. Dr. Peter Lebrecht Schmidt 24./25. Juli 2003, Universität Konstanz*, edited by J. Fugmann et al., 103–31. Munich and Leipzig: K.G. Saur.

Bosher, K., ed. 2012. *Theater Outside Athens: Drama in Greek Sicily and South Italy.* Cambridge: Cambridge University Press.

Bosher, K., 2012a. 'Hieron's Aeschylus'. In Bosher 2012, 97–111.

Boulvert, G. 1970. *Esclaves et affranchis impériaux sous le Haut-Empire romain.* Naples: Jovene.

Bowersock, G.W. 2008. 'Aristides and the Pantomimes'. In *Aelius Aristides between Greece, Rome and the Gods*, edited by W.V. Harris and B. Holmes, 69–77. Leiden: Brill.

Bowie, A. 2000. 'Myth and Ritual in the Rivals of Aristophanes'. In Harvey and Wilkins 2000, 317–39.

Boyle, A.J. 2006. *An Introduction to Roman Tragedy.* London: Routledge.

Boyle, A.J. 2008. *Octavia. Attributed to Seneca.* Oxford: Oxford University Press.

Boyle, A.J. 2014. *Seneca: Medea.* Oxford: Oxford University Press.

Braund, D., E. Hall and R. Wyles, eds (forthcoming). *Ancient Theatre and Performance Culture around the Ancient Black Sea.* Cambridge: Cambridge University Press.

Brink, C.O. 1963. *Horace on Poetry.* Cambridge: Cambridge University Press.

Browning, R. 2001. 'Education in the Roman Empire'. In *The Cambridge Ancient History Volume XIV*, edited by A. Cameron, B. Ward-Perkins and M. Whitby, 855–83. Cambridge: Cambridge University Press.

Burckhardt, J. [1872] 1998. *The Greeks and Greek Civilization*, edited by O. Murray, translated by S. Stern. London: Harper Collins.

Burkert, W. 1966. 'Greek Tragedy and Sacrificial Ritual'. *GRBS* 7: 87–121.

Cain, A. 2013. 'Terence in Late Antiquity'. In *A Companion to Terence*, edited by A. Augoustakis, A. Traill and J. Thorburn, 380–96. Malden (MA) and Oxford: Wiley-Blackwell.

Calame, C. 2001. *Choruses of Young Women in Ancient Greece: their Morphology, Religious Role, and Social Function.* Translated by D. Collins and J. Orion. Lanham: Rowman & Littlefield.

Carpenter, T.H. 2014. 'A Case for Greek Tragedy in Italic Settlements in Fourth-Century B.C.E. Apulia'. In *The Italic People of Ancient Apulia. New Evidence from Pottery for Workshops, Markets, and Customs*, edited by T. Carpenter, K. Lynch and E. Robinson, 265–80. Cambridge: Cambridge University Press.

Cassio, A.C. 1985. 'Two Studies on Epicharmus and His Influence'. *Harvard Studies in Classical Philology* 89: 37–51.

Ceccarelli, P. 2004. '"Autour de Dionysos": remarques sur la dénomination des artistes dionysiaques'. In *Le statut de l'acteur dans l'Antiquité grecque et romaine*, edited by C. Hugoniot et al., 109–42. Tours: Presses universitaires François-Rabelais.

Ceccarelli, P. 2010. 'Changing Contexts: Tragedy in the Civic and Cultural Life of Hellenistic City-States'. In Gildenhard and Revermann 2010, 99–150.

Ceccarelli, P., and S. Milanezi. 2007. 'Dithyramb, Tragedy and Cyrene'. In Wilson 2007, 185–214.

Chaniotis, A. 1990. 'Zur Frage der Spezialisierung im griechischen Theater des Hellenismus und der Kaiserzeit'. *Ktema* 15 (1990) [1994]: 89–108.

Chaniotis, A. 2012. 'Public Subscriptions and Loans as Social Capital in the Hellenistic City: Reciprocity, Performance, Commemoration'. In *Epigraphical Approaches to the Post-Classical Polis: Fourth Century BC to Second Century AD*, edited by P. Martzavou and N. Papazarkadas, 89–106. Oxford: Oxford University Press.

Clay, D. 2004. *Archilochos Heros: The Cult of Poets in the Greek Polis*. Washington, DC: Center for Hellenic Studies.

Coleman, K. 1990. 'Fatal Charades: Roman Executions Staged as Mythical Enactments'. *Journal of Roman Studies* 80: 44–73.

Coleman, K. 2006. *M. Valerii Martialis Liber Spectaculorum*. Oxford: Oxford University Press.

Colesanti, G., and M. Giordano, eds. 2014. *Submerged Literature in Ancient Greek Culture: An Introduction*. Boston/Leiden: De Gruyter.

Collard, C. 1975. *Euripides. Supplices* (Vol. II, Commentary). Groningen: Bouma's Boekhuis.

Compton-Engle, G. 2015. *Costume in the Comedies of Aristophanes*. Cambridge: Cambridge University Press.

Conte, G.B. 1992. 'Empirical and Theoretical Approaches to Literary Genre'. In Galinsky 1992, 104–23.

Conte, G.B. 1994. *Genres and Readers. Lucretius, Love Elegy, Pliny's Encyclopedia*. Translated by G. Most. Baltimore: Johns Hopkins.

Crawford, M.H., ed. 1996. *Roman Statutes*. 2 vols. London: Institute of Classical Studies.

Crotty, K. 2009. *The Philosopher's Song: The Poets' Influence on Plato*. Lanham (MA): Lexington Books.

Crowther, C. 2007. 'The Dionysia at Iasos: its Artists, Patrons, and Audience'. In Wilson 2007, 294–334.

Csapo, E. 1993. 'A Case Study in the Use of Theatre Iconography as Evidence for Ancient Acting.' *Antike Kunst* 36: 41–58.

Csapo, E. 2000. From Aristophanes to Menander? Genre Transformation in Greek Comedy. In *Matrices of Genre: Authors, Canons, and Society*, edited by M. Depew and D. Obbink, 115–33. Cambridge (MA): Harvard University Press.

Csapo, E. 2004. 'Some Social and Economic Conditions behind the Rise of the Acting Profession in the Fifth and Fourth Centuries BC'. In *Le statut de l'acteur dans l'Antiquité grecque et romaine*, edited by C. Hugoniot et al., 53–76. Tours: Presses universitaires François-Rabelais.

Csapo, E. 2007. 'The Men Who Built the Theatres: Theatropoloi, Theatronai, Arkhitektones'. In Wilson 2007, 87–115.

Csapo, E. 2010. *Actors and Icons of the Ancient Theater*. Malden (MA) and Oxford: Wiley-Blackwell.

Csapo, E. 2013. 'Comedy and the Pompe: Dionysian Genre-Crossing'. In *Greek Comedy and the Discourse of Genres*, edited by E. Bakola, L. Prauscello and M. Telò, 40–80. Cambridge: Cambridge University Press.

Csapo, E. 2014. 'The Iconography of Comedy'. In Revermann 2014, 95–127.

Csapo, E., and W.J. Slater. 1995. *The Context of Ancient Drama*. Ann Arbor: University of Michigan Press.

Csapo, E., and M.C. Miller, eds. 2007. *The Origins of Theater in Ancient Greece and Beyond: From Ritual to Drama*. Cambridge: Cambridge University Press.

Csapo, E., and P. Wilson. 2010. 'Le passage de la chorégie à l'agonothésie à Athènes à la fin du IVe siècle'. In *L'argent dans les concours du monde grec: actes du colloque international, Saint-Denis et Paris, 5–6 décembre 2008*, edited by B. Le Guen, 83–105. Saint-Denis: Presses universitaires de Vincennes.

Csapo, E., H. Goette, J.R. Green and P. Wilson, eds. 2014. *Greek Theatre in the Fourth Century BC*. Berlin and New York: De Gruyter.

Currie, B. 2005. *Pindar and the Cult of Heroes*. Oxford: Oxford University Press.

Damschen, G., and A. Heil. 2014. *Brill's Companion to Seneca. Philosopher and Dramatist*. Leiden: Brill.

Davidson, J.N. 2000. '*Gnesippus Paigniagraphos*: The Comic Poets and the Erotic Mime'. In Harvey and Wilkins 2000, 41–64.

Davidson, J.N. 2001. 'Dover, Foucault and Greek Homosexuality: Penetration and the Truth of Sex'. *Past and Present* 170: 3–51.

Davidson, J.N. 2007. *The Greeks and Greek Love: A Radical Reappraisal of Homosexuality in Ancient Greece*. London: Weidenfeld & Nicolson.

Davies, J.K. 1967. 'Demosthenes on Liturgies: A Note'. *Journal of Hellenic Studies* 87: 33–40.

Davies, J.K. 1971. *Athenian Propertied Families, 600–300 BC*. Oxford: Oxford University Press.

Dearden, C.W. 1976. *The Stage of Aristophanes*. London: Athlone Press.

Dearden, C.W. 1990. 'Fourth-Century Tragedy in Sicily: Athenian or Sicilian?' In *Greek Colonists and Native Populations: Proceedings of the First Australian Congress of Classical Archaeology Held in Honour of Emeritus Professor A.D. Trendall*, edited by J.-P. Descoeudres, 139–57. Oxford: Oxford University Press.

Dearden, C.W. 1999. 'Plays for Export'. *Phoenix* 53: 139–57.

Dearden, C.W. 2012. 'Whose Line is it Anyway? West Greek Comedy in its Context'. In Bosher 2012, 272–88.

Demetriou, C. 2014. 'Aelius Donatus and his Commentary on Terence's Comedies'. In *The Oxford Handbook of Greek and Roman Comedy*, edited by M. Fontaine and A. Scafuro, 782–99. Oxford: Oxford University Press.

Destreé, P., and F.-G. Hermann, eds. 2011. *Plato and the Poets*. Leiden: Brill.

Dickey, E. 2007. *Ancient Greek Scholarship*. Oxford: Oxford University Press.

Dobrov, G.W. 2010. 'Comedy and her Critics'. In *Brill's Companion to the Study of Greek Comedy*, edited by Gregory Dobrov, 3–33. Leiden: Brill.

Dougherty, C. 2001. *The Raft of Odysseus: The Ethnographic Imagination of Homer's Odyssey*. Oxford: Oxford University Press.

Dover, K.J. 1968. *Aristophanes: Clouds*. Oxford: Oxford University Press.

Dover, K.J. 1972. *Aristophanic Comedy*. Berkeley and Los Angeles: University of California Press.

Dover, K.J. 1974. *Greek Popular Morality in the Time of Plato and Aristotle*. Oxford: Blackwell.

Dover, K.J. 1978. *Greek Homosexuality*. London: Duckworth.

Dover, K.J. 1993. *Aristophanes: Frogs. Edited with Introduction and Commentary*. Oxford: Oxford University Press.

Duckworth, G.E. 1952. *The Nature of Roman Comedy: A Study in Popular Entertainment*, Princeton: Princeton University Press.

Dugdale, E. 2008. *Greek Theatre in Context*. Cambridge: Cambridge University Press.

Dunbabin, K. 2010. 'The Prize Table: Crowns, Wreaths and Moneybags in Roman Art'. In *L'argent dans les concours du monde grec: actes du colloque international, Saint-Denis et Paris, 5–6 décembre 2008*, edited by B. Le Guen, 301–45. Saint-Denis: Presses universitaires de Vincennes.

Dunbabin, K.M.D. 2014. 'Mythology and Theater in Mosaics of the Greco-Roman East'. In *Using Images in Late Antiquity*, edited by S. Birk, T.M. Kristensen and B. Poulsen, 227–52. Oxford and Philadelphia: Oxbow Books.

Duncan, A. 2006. 'Infamous Performers: Comic Actors and Female Prostitutes in Rome'. In *Prostitutes and Courtesans in the Ancient World. Papers from the Conference 'Prostitution in the Ancient World' Madison, April 12–14, 2002*, edited by C.A. Faraone and L. McClure, 252–73. Madison (WI): University of Wisconsin Press.

Duncan, A. 2012. 'A Theseus Outside Athens: Dionysius I of Syracuse and Tragic Self-Presentation'. In Bosher 2012, 137–55.

Duncan, A. 2015. 'Boogeymen in the Playwright's Closet: *mormolukeia*, Generic Aesthetics, and Adolescent Outreach in Old Comedy'. Abstract of paper presented at the 146th annual meeting of the Society for Classical Studies, New Orleans, January 8–11, 2015.

Dutsch, D. 2007. 'Gestures in the Manuscripts of Terence and Late Revivals of Literary Drama.' *Gesture* 7: 39–71.

Dutsch, D. 2013. 'Towards a Roman Theory of Theatrical Gesture'. In *Performance in Greek and Roman Theatre*, edited by G.W. Harrison and V. Liapis, 409–31. Leiden: Brill.

Easterling, P.E. 1982. *Sophocles. Trachiniae*. Cambridge: Cambridge University Press.

Easterling, P.E. 1997. 'From Repertoire to Canon'. In *The Cambridge Companion to Greek Tragedy*, edited by P.E. Easterling, 211–27. Cambridge: Cambridge University Press.

Easterling, P.E. 2002. 'Actor as Icon'. In Easterling and Hall 2002, 329–41.

Easterling, P.E., and E. Hall, eds. 2002. *Greek and Roman Actors. Aspects of an Ancient Profession*. Cambridge: Cambridge University Press.

Eco, U. 1984. 'The Frames of Comic Freedom'. In Sebeok 1984, 1–9.

Edmondson, J. 2002. 'Public Spectacles and Roman Social Relations'. In *Ludi Romani: Espectáculos en Hispania Romana*, edited by T. Nogales Basarrate and A. Castellanos, 21–43. Madrid: Museo Nacional de Arte Romano.

Ehrenberg, V. 1951. *The People of Aristophanes: A Sociology of Old Attic Comedy*. 3rd ed. New York: Schocken Books.

Ellis-Evans, A. 2012. 'The Ideology of Public Subscriptions'. In *Epigraphical Approaches to the Post-Classical Polis: Fourth Century BC to Second Century AD*, edited by P. Martzavou and N. Papazarkadas, 107–22. Oxford: Oxford University Press.

Emlyn-Jones, C. 1996. *Plato: Laches*. London: Bristol Classical Press.

Erasmo, M. 2004. *Roman Tragedy: Theatre to Theatricality*. Austin: University of Texas Press.

Fantham, E. 2004. *The Roman World of Cicero's De Oratore*. Oxford: Oxford University Press.

Fantham, E. 2013. *Roman Literary Culture*. 2nd ed. Baltimore: Johns Hopkins.

Faulkner, T.M. 1995. *The Poetics of Old Age in Greek Epic, Lyric, and Tragedy.* Norman: University of Oklahoma Press.

Favro, D. 1999. *The Urban Image of Augustan Rome.* Cambridge: Cambridge University Press.

Feeney, D. 2016. *Beyond Greek: The Beginnings of Latin Literature.* Cambridge (MA): Harvard University Press.

Feldherr, A. 1998. *Spectacle and Society in Livy's History.* Berkeley and Los Angeles: University of California Press.

Ferrari, G. 1990. 'Plato and Poetry'. In *The Cambridge History of Literary Criticism Volume I: Classical Criticism*, edited by A. Kennedy, 92–148. Cambridge: Cambridge University Press.

Finglass, P.J. 2015a. 'Reperformances and the Transmission of Texts'. *Trends in Classics* 7: 259–76

Finglass, P.J. 2015b. 'Second Thoughts on the Sword'. In *Staging Ajax's Suicide*, edited by G. Most and L. Ozbek, 193–210. Pisa: Edizioni della Normale.

Flashar, H. 2009. *Inszenierung der Antike: das griechische Drama auf der Bühne.* 2nd ed. Munich: C.H. Beck.

Fleming, T. 1999. 'The Survival of Greek Dramatic Music from the Fifth Century to the Roman Period'. In *La colometria antica dei testi poetici greci*, edited by B. Gentili and F. Perusino, 17–29. Pisa: Istituti editoriali e poligrafici internazionali.

Foley, H.P. 2000. 'The Comic Body in Greek Art and Drama'. In *Not the Classical Ideal: Athens and the Construction of the Other in Greek Art*, edited by B. Cohen, 275–311. Leiden: Brill.

Follet, S., and D. Peppas Delmouzou. 2001. 'Les dédicaces chorégiques d'époque flavienne et antonine à Athènes'. In *The Greek East in the Roman Context: Proceedings of a Colloquium organised by the Finnish Institute at Athens, 21-2 May 1999*, edited by O. Salomies, 95–117. Helsinki: Bookstore Tiedekirja.

Fontaine, M. 2010. *Funny Words in Plautine Comedy.* New York and Oxford: Oxford University Press.

Fontaine, M. 2014. 'The Reception of Greek Comedy in Rome'. In Revermann 2014, 404–23.

Ford, A. 1999. 'Reading Homer from the Rostrum: Poems and Laws in Aeschines' *Against Timarchus*'. In *Performance Culture and Athenian Democracy*, edited by S. Goldhill and R. Osborne, 231–56. Cambridge: Cambridge University Press.

Ford, A. 2002. *The Origins of Criticism: Literary Culture and Poetic Theory in Classical Greece.* Princeton: Princeton University Press.

Ford, A. 2011. *Aristotle as Poet: The Song for Hermias and its Contexts.* Oxford: Oxford University Press.

Fowler, A. 1982. *Kinds of Literature. An Introduction to the Theory of Genres and Modes.* Cambridge (MA): Harvard University Press.

Fraenkel, E. [1922] 2007. *Plautine Elements in Plautus.* Translated by Tomas Drevikovsky and Frances Muecke. Oxford: Oxford University Press.

Frisch, P. 1986. *Zehn agonistische Papyri.* Opladen: Westdeutscher Verlag.

Gagliardo, M.C., and J.E. Packer. 2006. 'A New Look at Pompey's Theater: History, Documentation, and Recent Excavation'. *American Journal of Archaeology* 110: 93–122.

Galinsky, K., ed. 1992. *The Interpretation of Roman Poetry: Empiricism or Hermeneutics?* Frankfurt am Main: P. Lang.

Garelli, M.-H. 2007. *Danser le mythe. La pantomime et sa réception dans la culture antique*. Louvain: Peeters.

Garvie, A.F. 2009. *Aeschylus: Persae. With Introduction and Commentary*. Oxford: Oxford University Press.

Geagan, D.J. 1967. *The Athenian Constitution after Sulla*. Princeton: American School of Classical Studies at Athens.

Geer, R.M. 1935. 'The Greek Games at Naples'. *Transactions of the American Philological Association* 66: 208–21.

Genette, G. 1997. *Palimpsests. Literature in the Second Degree*. Lincoln: University of Nebraska Press.

Ghiron-Bistagne, G. 1991. 'Les artistes dionysiaques de Nîmes à l'époque imperiale'. In *Realia: Mélanges sur les Réalités du Théâtre antique* (= *Cahiers du GITA* 6 [1990/91]), 57–78. Montpellier: Université Paul Valéry-Montpellier.

Gildenhard, I. 2010. 'Buskins & SPQR: Roman Receptions of Greek Tragedy'. In Gildenhard and Revermann 2010, 153–85.

Gildenhard, I., and M. Revermann, eds. 2010. *Beyond the Fifth Century: Interactions with Greek Tragedy from the Fourth Century BCE to the Middle Ages*. Berlin and New York: De Gruyter.

Giovannini, A. 2008. 'The Parthenon, the Treasury of Athena, and the Tribute of the Allies'. In *The Athenian Empire*, edited by P. Low, 164–84. Edinburgh: Edinburgh University Press.

Gleason, K.L. 1994. '*Porticus Pompeiana*: A New Perspective on the First Public Park of Ancient Rome'. *Journal of Garden History* 14: 13–27.

Goette, H.R. 2007. '*Archaeological Appendix*'. In Wilson 2007, 116–21.

Goette, H.R. 2014. 'The Archaeology of the "Rural" Dionysia in Attica'. In Csapo et al. 2014, 77–105.

Goffman, E. 1974. *Frame Analysis: An Essay on the Organization of Experience*. Cambridge (MA): Harvard University Press.

Goldberg, S.M. 1980. *The Making of Menander's Comedy*. London: Athlone Press.

Goldberg, S.M. 1998. 'Plautus on the Palatine'. *Journal of Roman Studies* 88: 1–20.

Goldhill, S. 1987. 'Civic Ideology and the Great Dionysia'. *Journal of Hellenic Studies* 107: 58–76.

Goldhill, S. 1994. 'Representing Democracy: Women at the Great Dionysia'. In *Ritual, Finance, Politics: Athenian Democratic Accounts Presented to D.M. Lewis*, edited by R.G. Osborne and S. Hornblower, 347–69. Oxford: Clarendon Press.

Goldhill, S., and R. Osborne, eds. 1999. *Performance Culture and Athenian Democracy*. Cambridge: Cambridge University Press.

Gould, J. 1980. 'Law, Custom and Myth: Aspects of the Social Position of Women in Classical Athens'. *Journal of Hellenic Studies* 100: 38–59.

Green, J.R. 1982. 'Dedications of Masks'. *Revue archéologique* 2: 237–48.

Green, J.R. 2002. 'Towards a Reconstruction of Performance Style'. In *Greek and Roman Actors: Aspects of an Ancient Profession*, edited by P.E. Easterling and E. Hall, 93–126. Cambridge: Cambridge University Press.

Green, J.R. 2006. 'The Persistent Phallos: Regional Variability in the Performance Style of Comedy'. In Davidson et al. 2006, 141–62.

Green, J.R. 2007. 'Art and Theatre in the Ancient World'. In *The Cambridge Companion to Greek and Roman Theatre*, edited by M. McDonald and J.M. Walton, 163–83. Cambridge: Cambridge University Press.

Green, J.R. 2014. 'Regional Theatre in the Fourth Century: The Evidence of Comic Figurines of Boeotia, Corinth and Cyprus'. In Csapo et al. 2014, 333–69.

Green, J.R., and E. Handley 1995. *Images of the Greek Theatre*. London: British Museum Press.
Greenblatt, S. 2010. 'Theatrical Mobility'. In *Cultural Mobility: A Manifesto*, edited by S. Greenblatt et al., 75–95. Cambridge: Cambridge University Press.
Griffin, J. 1998. 'The Social Function of Greek Attic Tragedy'. *Classical Quarterly* 48: 39–61.
Griffin, J. 2006. 'Herodotus and Tragedy'. In *The Cambridge Companion to Herodotus*, edited by C. Dewald and J. Marincola, 46–59. Cambridge: Cambridge University Press.
Griffith, M. 2002. 'Slaves of Dionysos: Satyrs, Audience, and the Ends of the *Oresteia*'. *Classical Antiquity* 21: 195–258.
Gunderson, E. 2015. *Laughing Awry: Plautus and Tragicomedy*. Oxford: Oxford University Press.
Habinek, T. 1998. *The Politics of Latin Literature: Writing, Identity, and Empire in Ancient Rome*. Princeton (NJ): Princeton University Press.
Habinek, T. 2005. *The World of Roman Song: From Ritualized Speech to Social Order*. Baltimore: Johns Hopkins University Press.
Hadley, P. 2015. *Athens in Rome, Rome in Germany: Nicodemus Frischlin and the Rehabilitation of Aristophanes in the 16th Century*. Tübingen: Narr.
Hall, E. 1989. *Inventing the Barbarian: Self-Definition Through Tragedy*. Oxford: Oxford University Press.
Hall, E. 1997. 'The Sociology of Athenian Tragedy'. In Easterling 1997, 93–126.
Hall, E. 2002. 'The Singing Actors of Antiquity'. In Easterling and Hall 2002, 3–38.
Hall, E. 2006. *The Theatrical Cast of Athens*. Oxford: Oxford University Press.
Hall, E. 2008. 'Introduction: Pantomime, A Lost Chord of Ancient Culture'. In Hall and Wyles 2008, 1–40.
Hall, E. 2015. 'Adventures in Ancient Greek and Roman Libraries'. In *The Meaning of the Library: A Cultural History*, edited by A. Crawford, 1–30. Princeton: Princeton University Press.
Hall, E., and R. Wyles. 2008. *New Directions in Ancient Pantomime*. Oxford: Oxford University Press.
Halliwell, S. 1995. *Aristotle Poetics*. Cambridge (MA): Harvard University Press.
Halliwell, S. 1998. *Aristotle's Poetics*. 2nd ed., Chicago: University of Chicago Press.
Halliwell, S. 2002a. *The Aesthetics of Mimesis: Ancient Texts and Modern Problems*. Princeton (NJ): Princeton University Press.
Halliwell, S. 2002b. 'Aristophanic Sex: The Erotics of Shamelessness'. In Nussbaum and Sihvola 2002, 120–42.
Hamilakis, Y. 2013. *Archaeology and the Senses: Human Experience, Memory, and Affect*. Cambridge: Cambridge University Press.
Hamilton, S.L. 2011. 'Making Roman Theatrical Masks: An Aspect of Ancient Performance Culture'. *Acta Iassyensia Comparationis* 9: 114–23.
Handley, E.W. 1968. *Menander and Plautus: A Study in Comparison. An Inaugural Lecture Delivered at University College, London, 5 February 1968*. London: Lewis.
Hanink, J. 2014a. *Lycurgan Athens and the Making of Classical Tragedy*. Cambridge: Cambridge University Press.
Hanink, J. 2014b. 'Crossing Genres: Comedy, Tragedy, and Satyr Play'. In *The Oxford Handbook of Greek and Roman Comedy*, edited by M. Fontaine and A.C. Scafuro, 258–77. Oxford: Oxford University Press.

Hanink, J. 2015. 'Why 386? Lost Empire, Old Tragedy and Reperformance in the Era of the Corinthian War'. *Trends in Classics* 7: 277–96.

Hanink, J. (forthcoming). 'Scholars and Scholarship on Tragedy'. In *Greek Tragedy after the Fifth Century*, edited by V. Liapis and A. Petrides. Cambridge: Cambridge University Press.

Hardwick, L. 2013. 'Lysistratas on the Modern Stage'. In *Looking at Lysistrata*, edited by D. Stuttard, 80–9. London: Bloomsbury.

Harris, W. 1989. *Ancient Literacy*. Cambridge (MA): Harvard University Press.

Hart, M.L. 2010. *The Art of Ancient Greek Theater*. Los Angeles: J. Paul Getty Museum.

Hartigan, K. 2009. *Performance and Cure: Drama and Healing in Ancient Greece and Contemporary America*. London: Duckworth.

Harvey, D. 2000. 'Phrynichos and His Muses'. In Harvey and Wilkins 2000, 91–134.

Harvey, D., and J. Wilkins, eds. 2000. *The Rivals of Aristophanes: Studies in Athenian Old Comedy*. London: Duckworth and the Classical Press of Wales.

Heath, M. 2009. 'Should There Have Been a *Polis* in Aristotle's *Poetics*?' *Classical Quarterly* 59: 468–85.

Heath, M. 2013. 'Aristotle *On Poets*: A Critical Evaluation of Richard Janko's Edition of the Fragments'. *Studia Humaniora Tartuensia* 14: (A1).

Henderson, J. 1987a. *Aristophanes: Lysistrata*. Oxford: Clarendon Press.

Henderson, J. 1987b. 'Older Women in Attic Old Comedy'. *Transactions of the American Philological Association* 117: 105–29.

Henderson, J. 1991a. *The Maculate Muse: Obscene Language in Attic Comedy*. 2nd ed. New York: Oxford University Press.

Henderson, J. 1991b. 'Women and the Athenian Dramatic Festivals'. *Transactions of the American Philological Association* 121: 133–47.

Henderson, J. 2000. 'Pherekrates and the Women of Old Comedy'. In Harvey and Wilkins 2000, 135–50.

Herdt, G. 1996. *Third Sex/Third Gender. Beyond Sexual Dimorphism in Culture and History*. New York: Zone Books.

Herrick, M. 1950. *Comic Theory in the Sixteenth Century*. Urbana: University of Illinois Press.

Herrington, C.J. 1967. 'Aeschylus in Sicily'. *The Journal of Hellenic Studies* 87: 74–85.

Hopkins, K. 1983. *Death and Renewal*. Cambridge: Cambridge University Press.

Hordern, J. 2003. 'Gnesippus and the Rivals of Aristophanes'. *Classical Quarterly* 53: 608–13.

Hordern, J. 2004. *Sophron's Mimes. Text, Translation, and Commentary*. Oxford: Oxford University Press.

Hornblower, S. 2013. *Herodotus: Histories V*. Cambridge: Cambridge University Press.

Horsfall, N. 2003. *The Culture of the Roman Plebs*. London: Bristol Classical Press.

Hubbard, T.K. 1991. *The Mask of Comedy: Aristophanes and the Intertextual Parabasis*. Ithaca: Cornell University Press.

Hugoniot, C., F. Hurlet and S. Milanezi, eds. 2004. *Le statut de l'acteur dans l'Antiquité grecque et romaine*. Tours: Presses universitaires François-Rabelais.

Hunt, Y. 2008. 'Roman Pantomime Libretti and their Greek Themes: The Role of Augustus in the Romanization of the Greek Classics'. In Hall and Wyles 2008, 169–84.

Hunter, R.L. 2002. '"Acting down": The Ideology of Hellenistic Performance'. In Easterling and Hall 2002, 189–206.

Hunter, R.L. 2009. *Critical Moments in Classical Literature: Studies in the Ancient View of Literature and its Uses*. Oxford: Oxford University Press.

Hunter, R.L. 2012. *Plato and the Traditions of Ancient Literature: The Silent Stream*. Cambridge: Cambridge University Press.

Huskinson, J. 2008. 'Pantomime Performance and Scenes on Roman Figured Sarcophagi'. In Hall and Wyles 2002, 87–110.

Hutchinson, G.O. 2004. 'Euripides' Other *Hippolytus*'. *Zeitschrift für Papyrologie und Epigraphik* 149: 15–28.

ILS Inscriptiones Latinae Selectae, edited by H. Dessau. Berlin and New York 1892–1916: Weidmann.

IvO Inschriften von Olympia, edited by W. Dittenberger and K. Purgold. Berlin and New York 1896: Asher.

James, S.L. 2013. 'Gender and Sexuality in Terenc'. In *A Companion to Terence*, edited by A. Agoustakis and A. Traill, 175–94. Chichester: Wiley-Blackwell.

Janko, R. 1984. *Aristotle on Comedy: Towards a Reconstruction of Poetics II*. London: Duckworth.

Janko, R. 2000. *Philodemus: On Poems, Book 1*. Oxford: Oxford University Press.

Janko, R. 2011. *Philodemus: On Poems, Books 3–4, With the Fragments of Aristotle On Poets*. Oxford: Oxford University Press.

Johnson, W., and H. Parker, eds. 2009. *Ancient Literacies: The Culture of Reading in Greece and Rome*. Oxford: Oxford University Press.

Jones, A.H.M. 1964. *The Later Roman Empire, 284–602: A Social, Economic and Administrative Survey*. Oxford: Oxford University Press.

Jones, C.P. 1990. 'A New Lycian Dossier Establishing an Artistic Contest and Festival in the Reign of Hadrian'. *Journal of Roman Archaeology* 3: 484–8.

Jones, C.P. 2007. 'Three New Letters of the Emperor Hadrian'. *Zeitschrift für Papyrologie und Epigraphik* 161: 145–56.

Jones, G.S. 2014. 'Voice of the People: Popular Symposia and the Non-Elite Origins of the Attic *Skolia*'. *Transactions of the American Philological Association* 144: 229–62.

Jordan, D. 2007. 'An Opisthographic Lead Tablet from Sicily with a Financial Document and a Curse Concerning *choregoi* '. In Wilson 2007, 335–50.

Jory, E.J. 1970. 'Associations of Actors in Rome'. *Hermes* 98: 224–53.

Jory, E.J. 1996. 'The Drama of the Dance: Prolegomena to an Iconography of Imperial Pantomime'. In *Roman Theater and Society*, edited by W.J. Slater, 1–27. Ann Arbor: University of Michigan Press.

Jory, E.J. 2001. 'Some Cases of Mistaken Identity? Pantomime Masks and their Context'. *Bulletin of the Institue of Classical Studies* 45: 1–20.

Jory, E.J. 2008. 'The Pantomime Dancer and his Libretto'. In Hall and Wyles 2008, 157–68.

Just, R. 1989. *Women in Athenian Law and Life*. London: Routledge.

Kampourakis, G. 2008. 'Die Akustik des Theaters'. In *Das Dionysostheater von Athen. Architektonische Gestalt und Funktion*, edited by S. Gogos, 108–30. Vienna: Phoibos.

Kannicht, R. 2004. *Tragicorum Graecorum Fragmenta*, vol. 5: Euripides. Göttingen: Vandenhoeck & Ruprecht.

Kannicht, R., and B. Snell. 1981. *Tragicorum Graecorum Fragmenta*, vol. 2. Göttingen: Vandenhoeck & Ruprecht.

Kassel, R. 1965. *Aristotelis De Arte Poetica Liber*. Oxford: Oxford University Press.

Keith, A. 2010. 'Dionysiac Theme and Dramatic Allusion in Ovid's *Metamorphoses* 4'. In Gildenhard and Revermann 2010, 187–217.

Knox, B. 1964. *The Heroic Temper. Studies in Sophoclean Tragedy*. Berkeley: University of California Press.

Knox, B. 1985. 'Books and Readers in the Greek World. I: From the Beginnings to Alexandria'. In *The Cambridge History of Classical Literature. Vol. I: Greek Literature*, edited by P.E. Easterling and B.M.W. Knox, 1–16. Cambridge: Cambridge University Press.

Köhnken, A. 1980. 'Der Wolken-Chor des Aristophanes'. *Hermes* 108: 154–69.

Konstan, D. 2014. 'Defining the Genre'. In Revermann 2014, 27–42.

Kotlińska-Toma, A. 2015. *Hellenistic Tragedy: Texts, Translations and a Critical Survey*. London: Bloomsbury.

Kovacs, D. 1994. *Euripidea*. Leiden: Brill.

Kovacs, D. 2005. 'Text and Transmission'. In *A Companion to Greek Tragedy*, edited by J. Gregory, 379–93. Malden (MA) and Oxford: Blackwell.

Kowalzig, B. 2007. *Singing for the Gods: Performances of Myth and Ritual in Archaic and Classical Greece*. Oxford: Oxford University Press.

Lada-Richards, I. 2007. *Silent Eloquence: Lucian and Pantomime Dancing*. London: Duckworth.

Laird, A. 2007. 'The Ars Poetica'. In *The Cambridge Companion to Horace*, edited by Stephen Harrison, 132–43. Cambridge: Cambridge University Press.

Lalonde, G.V., M.K. Langdon and M.B. Walbank. 1991. *Inscriptions: Horoi, Poletai Records, and Leases of Public Lands. The Athenian Agora XIX*. Princeton: American School of Classical Studies at Athens.

Lamari, A. 2014. 'Early Reperformances of Drama in the Fifth Century'. *CHS Research Bulletin* 2.2 (http://nrs.harvard.edu/urn3:hlnc.essay:LamariA.Early_reperformances_of_drama_in_the_fifth_century.2014).

Lamari, A., ed. 2015. *Trends in Classics* 7 (special issue: *Reperformances of Drama in the Fifth and Fourth Centuries BC*).

Lambert, S. 2008. 'Polis and Theatre in Lykourgan Athens: The Honorific Decrees'. In Μικρός Ιερομνήμων: Μελέτες εις Μνήμη *Michael H. Jameson*, edited by A.P. Matthaiou and I. Polinskaya, 53–85. Athens: Greek Epigraphic Society.

Lape, S. 2004. *Reproducing Athens: Menander's Comedy, Democratic Culture, and the Hellenistic City*. Princeton: Princeton University Press.

Le Guen, B. 2001. *Les associations de technites dionysiaques à l'époque hellénistique*. 2 vols. Paris: Diffusion de Boccard.

Le Guen, B. 2004a. 'Remarques sur les associations de technites dionysiaques de l'époque hellénistique'. *Nikephoros* 17: 279–99.

Le Guen, B. 2004b. 'Le statut professionnel des acteurs grecs à l'époque hellénistique'. In Hugoniot et al. 2004: 77–106.

Le Guen, B. 2010a. *L'argent dans les concours du monde grec: actes du colloque international, Saint-Denis et Paris, 5-6 décembre 2008*. Saint-Denis: Presses universitaires de Vincennes.

Le Guen, B. 2010b. 'Hadrien, l'Empereur philhellène, et la vie agonistique de son temps: à propos d'un livre récent: *Hadrian und die dionysischen Künstler: drei in Alexandreia Troas neugefundene Briefe des Kaisers an die Künstler-Vereinigung*'. *Nikephoros* 23: 205–39.

Le Guen, B. 2014a. 'Theatre, Religion and Politics at Alexander's Travelling Royal Court'. In Csapo et al. 2014, 249–74.

Le Guen, B. 2014b. 'The Diffusion of Comedy from the Age of Alexander to the Beginning of the Roman Empire'. In *The Oxford Handbook of Greek and Roman Comedy*, edited by M. Fontaine and A.C. Scafuro, 359–77. Oxford: Oxford University Press.

Lehmann, H.-T. 1999. *Postdramatisches Theater*. Frankfurt: Verlag der Autoren.
Lehmann, H.-T. 2006. *Postdramatic Theatre*, translated by K. Jürs-Munby. London: Routledge.
Lehmann, H.-T. 2013. *Tragödie und dramatisches Theater*. Berlin: Alexander Verlag.
Lemert, C., and A. Branaman, eds. 1997. *The Goffman Reader*. Oxford: Blackwell.
Lendle, O. 1995. 'Überlegungen zum Bühnenkran'. In *Studien zur Bühnendichtung und zum Theaterbau der Antike*, edited by E. Pöhlmann, 165–72. Frankfurt: Peter Lang.
Leppin, H. 1992. *Histrionen: Untersuchungen zur sozialen Stellung von Bühnenkünstlern im Westen des Römischen Reiches zur Zeit der Republik und des Principats*. Bonn: Rudolf Habelt.
Lesky, A. 1965. *Greek Tragedy*. London and New York: Ernest Benn-Barnes and Noble.
Lewis, D.M. 1955. 'Note on Attic inscriptions, II 23, Who was Lysistrata?' *Annual of the British School Athens* 50: 1–12.
Ley, G. 2013. 'Rehearsing Aristophanes'. In *Performance in Greek and Roman Theatre*, edited by G.W.M. Harrison and V. Liapis, 291–308. Leiden: Brill.
Liapis, V. 2012. *A Commentary on the Rhesus Attributed to Euripides*. Oxford: Oxford University Press.
Lightfoot, J.L. 2002. 'Nothing to Do with the *technitai* of Dionysus?' In Easterling and Hall 2002, 209–24.
Lim, R. 2012. 'Augustine and Roman Public Spectacles'. In *A Companion to Augustine*, edited by M. Vessy, 138–50. Malden (MA) and Oxford: Wiley-Blackwell.
Lissarrague, F., and F. Frontisi-Ducroux. 1990. 'From Ambiguity to Ambivalence: A Dionysiac Excursion Through the "Anacreontic" Vases'. In *Before Sexuality*, edited by D.M. Halperin, F.I. Zeitlin and J.J. Winkler, 211–56. Princeton: Princeton University Press.
Lloyd-Jones, H. 1975. *Females of the Species. Semonides on Women*. London: Duckworth.
Lowe, N.J. 2007. *Comedy*. New Surveys in the Classics, v. 37. Cambridge: Cambridge University Press.
MacDowell, D.M. 1994. 'Actors in Old Comedy'. *Classical Quarterly* 44: 325–35.
Macintosh, F. 2009. *Sophocles: Oedipus Tyrannus* (Plays in Production). Cambridge: Cambridge University Press.
Mairs, R. 2014. *The Hellenistic Far East: Archaeology, Language, and Identity in Greek Central Asia*. Oakland: University of California Press.
Manieri, A. 2009. *Agoni Poetico-Musicali Nella Grecia Antica*. Pisa and Rome: Università di Urbino.
Manuwald, G. 2001. 'Der Dichter Curiatius Maternus in Tacitus' *Dialogus de oratribus*'. *Göttinger Forum für Altertumswissenschaft* 4: 1–20.
Manuwald, G. 2011. *Roman Republican Theatre*. Cambridge: Cambridge University Press.
Manuwald, G. 2012. *Tragicorum Romanorum Fragmenta vol. 2 (Ennius)*. Göttingen: Vandenhoeck & Rupprecht.
Marshall, C.W. 1997. 'Comic Technique and the Fourth Actor'. *Classical Quarterly* 47: 77–84.
Marshall, C.W. 1999. '*Quis Hic Loquitur*? Plautine delivery and the "double aside"'. *Syllecta Classica* 10: 105–29.
Marshall, C.W. 2004. '*Alcestis* and the Ancient Rehearsal Process (P. Oxy. 4546)'. *Arion* 11: 27–45.
Marshall, C.W. 2006. *The Stagecraft and Production of Roman Comedy*. Cambridge: Cambridge University Press.

Marshall, C.W., and S. van Willigenburg. 2004. 'Judging Athenian Dramatic Competitions'. *Journal of Hellenic Studies* 124: 90–107.

Martinelli, M.C. 2015. 'Aiace e la spada'. In *Staging Ajax's Sucide*, edited by G. Most and L. Ozbek, 211–22. Pisa: Edizioni della Normale.

Martzavou, P., and N. Papazarkadas, eds. 2012. *Epigraphical Approaches to the Post-Classical Polis: Fourth Century BC to Second Century AD*. Oxford: Oxford University Press.

Mastronarde, D.J. 1990. 'Actors on High: The Skene Roof, the Crane, and the Gods in Attic Drama'. *Classical Antiquity* 9: 247–94.

Mastronarde, D.J. 1999–2000. 'Euripidean Tragedy and Genre: The Terminology and its Problems'. *Illinois Classical Studies* 24–25: 23–39.

Mastronarde, D.J. 2010. *The Art of Euripides: Dramatic Technique and Social Context*. Cambridge: Cambridge University Press.

Maxwell, R. 1993. 'The Documentary Evidence for Ancient Mime'. PhD thesis. Toronto.

May, R. 2008. 'The Metamorphosis of Pantomime: Apuleius Judgment of Paris (Met. 10.30–34)'. In Hall and Wyles 2008, 338–62.

Mayer, R. 2002. *Seneca: Phaedra*. London: Duckworth.

Meyer, E.A. 2013. 'Inscriptions and the City in Democratic Athens'. In *The Greek Polis and the Invention of Democracy: A Politico-Cultural Transformation and its Interpretations*, edited by J.P. Arnason, K.A. Raaflaub and P. Wagner, 205–24. Chichester: Wiley-Blackwell.

Michelakis, P. 2007. *Achilles in Greek Tragedy*. Cambridge: Cambridge University Press.

Migeotte, L. 1993. 'De la liturgie à la contribution obligatoire: le financement des Dionysies et des travaux du théâtre au IIe siècle avant J.-C.'. *Chiron* 23: 269–94.

Migeotte, L. 2010. 'Le financement des concours dans les cités hellénistiques: essai de typologie'. In Le Guen 2010a, 127–43.

Mikalson, J.D. 1998. *Religion in Hellenistic Athens*. Berkeley: University of California Press.

Milanezi, S. 2004. 'À l'ombre des acteurs: les amuseurs à l'époque classique'. In Hugoniot et al. 2004, 183–209.

Miles, S. 2014. 'Staging and Constructing the Divine in Menander'. In Sommerstein 2014: 75–89.

Millar, F. 1977. *The Emperor in the Roman World (31 BC–AD 337)*. London: Duckworth.

Miller, M.C. 1999. 'Reexamining Transvestism in Archaic and Classical Athens: The Zewadski Stamnos'. *American Journal of Archaeology* 103: 223–53.

Millis, B.W., and S.D. Olson. 2012. *Inscriptional Records for the Dramatic Festivals in Athens*. Leiden: Brill.

Millis, B.W. 2014. 'Inscribed Public Records of the Dramatic Contests at Athens: IG II^2 2318–2323a and IG II^2 2325'. In Csapo et al. 2014, 425–45.

Mitchell, S. 1986. 'Imperial Building in the Eastern Roman Provinces'. *Harvard Studies in Classical Philology* 91: 333–65.

Mitchell, S. 1990. 'Festivals, Games and Civic Life in Roman Asia Minor'. *Journal of Roman Studies* 80: 183–93.

Mitchell-Boyask, R. 2007. 'The Athenian Asklepieion and the End of the Philoctetes'. *Transactions of the American Philological Association* 137: 85–114.

Möllendorff, P. v. 2002. *Aristophanes*. Darmstadt: Wissenschaftliche Buchgesellschaft.

Möllendorff, P. v. 2015. 'Tragende Rollen. Das Ekkyklema auf der tragischen Bühne'. In *Translatio humanitatis. Festschrift zum 60. Geburtstag von Peter Riemer*, edited by C. Kugelmeier, 31–55. St. Ingbert: Röhrig Universitätsverlag.

Molloy, M. 1996. *Libanius and the Dancers*. Hildesheim, Zurich and New York: Olms-Weidmann.

Moloney, E. 2014. '*Philippus in acie tutior quam in theatro fuit* . . . (Curtius 9.6.25): The Macedonian Kings and Greek Theatre'. In Csapo et al. 2014, 231–48.

Montanari, F., S. Matthaios and A. Rengakos, eds. 2015. *Brill's Companion to Ancient Scholarship*. 2 vols. Leiden: Brill.

Moore, T.J. 2012. *Music in Roman Comedy*. Cambridge: Cambridge University Press.

Moretti, J.-C. 2014. 'The Evolution of Theatre Architecture Outside Athens in the Fourth Century', in Csapo et al. 2014, 107–38.

Mossman, J. 2010. 'Reading the Euripidean *hypothesis*'. In *Condensing Texts, Condensed Texts*, edited by M. Horster and C. Reitz, 247–67. Stuttgart: Franz Steiner Verlag.

Murray, O., ed. 1990. *Sympotica: A Symposium on the Symposion*. Oxford: Oxford University Press.

Mussche, H.F. 1998. *Thorikos: A Mining Town in Ancient Attika*. Ghent: Ecole Archéologique Belge En Grèce.

Mussche, H.F., P. Spitaels and F. Goemaere-De Poerck. 1975. *Thorikos and the Laurion in Archaic and Classical Times: Papers and Contributions of the Colloquium Held in March, 1973, at the State University of Ghent*. Miscellanea Graeca. Vol. fasc. 1. Ghent: Belgian Archaeological Mission in Greece.

Nachtergael, G. 1977. *Les Galates en Grèce et les Sôtéria de Delphes: recherches d'histoire et d'épigraphie hellénistiques*. Brussels: Palais des académies.

Nagy, G. 1996. *Poetry as Performance: Homer and Beyond*. Cambridge: Cambridge University Press.

Nagy, G. 1998. 'The Library of Pergamon as a Classical Model'. In *Pergamon: Citadel of the Gods*, edited by H. Koester, 185–232. Harrisburg (PA): Trinity Press International.

Nervegna, S. 2007. 'Staging Scenes or Plays? Theatrical Revivals of "Old" Greek Drama in Antiquity'. *Zeitschrift für Papyrologie und Epigraphik* 162: 14–42.

Nervegna, S. 2013. *Menander in Antiquity: The Contexts of Reception*. Cambridge: Cambridge University Press.

Nervegna, S. 2014a. 'Performing Classics: The Tragic Canon in the Fourth Century and Beyond'. In Csapo et al. 2014, 157–87.

Nervegna, S. 2014b. 'Graphic Comedy: Menandrian Mosaics and Terentian Miniatures'. In *The Oxford Handbook of Greek and Roman Comedy*, edited by M. Fontaine and A.C. Scafuro, 717–34. Oxford: Oxford University Press.

Nevett, C. 2010. *Domestic Space in Classical Antiquity*. Cambridge: Cambridge University Press.

Newiger, H.-J. 1990. 'Ekkyklema und Mechané in der Inszenierung des griechischen Dramas'. *Würzburger Jahrbücher* 16: 33–42.

Nussbaum, M.C., and J. Sihvola, eds. 2002. *The Sleep of Reason. Erotic Experience and Sexual Ethics in Ancient Greece and Rome*. Chicago: University of Chicago Press.

Oakley, S. 1998. *A Commentary on Livy Books VII–VIII*. Oxford: Oxford University Press.

O'Bryhim, S. 1989. 'The Originality of Plautus' *Casina*'. *The American Journal of Philology* 110: 81–103.

Ogden, D. 1996. *Greek Bastardy in the Classical and Hellenistic Periods*. Oxford: Oxford University Press.
Olson, S.D. 1998. *Aristophanes: Peace*. Oxford: Oxford University Press.
Osborne, R. 1993. 'Competitive Festivals and the Polis: A Context for Dramatic Festivals in Athens'. In *Tragedy, Comedy, and the Polis: Papers from the Greek Drama Conference, Nottingham, 18–20 July*, edited by A. Sommerstein et al., 21–38. Bari: Levante.
Osborne, R. 2008. 'Putting Performance into Focus'. In Revermann and Wilson 2008, 395–418.
Paga, J. 2010. 'Deme Theatres in Attica and the Trittys System'. *Hesperia* 79: 351–84.
Palyvou, C. 2001. 'Notes on the Geometry of the Ancient Theatre of Thorikos'. *Archäologischer Anzeiger*: 45–58.
Panayotakis, C. 2006. 'Women in the Greco-Roman Mime of the Roman Republic and the Early Empire'. *Ordia Prima* 5: 121–38.
Panayotakis, C. 2010. *Decimus Laberius: The Fragments*. Cambridge: Cambridge University Press.
Panayotakis, C. 2014. 'Hellenistic Mime and its Reception in Rome'. In *The Oxford Handbook of Greek and Roman Comedy*, edited by M. Fontaine and A.C. Scafuro, 378–96. Oxford: Oxford University Press.
Papastamati-von Moock, C. 2014. 'The Theatre of Dionysus Eleuthereus in Athens: New Data and Observations on its "Lycurgan" Phase'. In Csapo et al. 2014: 15–76.
Papastamati-von Moock, C. 2015. 'The Wooden Theatre of Dionysos Eleuthereus in Athens: Old Issues, New Research'. In *The Architecture of the Ancient Greek Theatre*, edited by R. Frederiksen et al., 39–79. Aarhus: Aarhus University Press.
Parker, R. 1996. *Athenian Religion: A History*. Oxford: Oxford University Press.
Parker, R. 2005. *Polytheism and Society at Athens*. Oxford: Oxford University Press.
Parker, R. 2011. *On Greek Religion*. Ithaca: Cornell University Press.
Paulson, T. 1992. *Inszenierung des Schicksals: Tragödie und Komödie im Roman des Heliodor*. Trier: Wissenschaftlicher Verlag.
Pelling, C., ed. 1997. *Greek Tragedy and the Historian*. Oxford: Oxford University Press.
Petrides, A. 2013. 'Lucian's *On Dance* and the Poetics of the Pantomime Mask'. In *Performance in Greek and Roman Theatre*, edited by G.W.M. Harrison and V. Liapis, 433–50. Leiden: Brill.
Petrides, A. 2014. 'Plautus between Greek Comedy and Atellan Farces: Assessments and Reassessments'. In *The Oxford Handbook of Greek and Roman Comedy*, edited by M. Fontaine and A.C. Scafuro, 424–43. Oxford: Oxford University Press.
Petzl, G., and E. Schwertheim 2006. *Hadrian und die dionysischen Künstler: drei in Alexandria Troas neugefundene Briefe des Kaisers an die Künstler-Vereinigung*. Bonn: Rudolf Habelt.
Pfeiffer, R. 1968. *History of Classical Scholarship from the Beginnings to the End of the Hellenistic Age*. Oxford: Oxford University Press.
Pickard-Cambridge, A.W. 1988. *The Dramatic Festivals of Athens*. 2nd ed., revised with addenda by John Gould and D.M. Lewis. Oxford: Clarendon Press.
Pleket, H.W. 1973. 'Some Aspects of the History of the Athletic Guilds'. *Zeitschrift für Papyrologie und Epigraphik* 10: 197–227.
Pleket, H.W. 2014. 'Inscriptions as Evidence for Greek Sport'. In *A Companion to Sport and Spectacle in Greek and Roman Antiquity*, edited by P. Christesen and D.G. Kyle, 98–111. Chichester: Wiley-Blackwell.

Poland, F. 1934. 'Technitai'. In *Paulys Realenzyklopädie der classischen Altertumswissenschaft*, edited by G. Wissowa, vol. 5 A, cols. 2473–2558. Stuttgart: Alfred Druckmüller.

Prauscello, L. 2006. *Singing Alexandria: Music between Practice and Textual Transmission*. Leiden: Brill.

Purcell, N. 1989. 'Rediscovering the Roman Forum'. *Journal of Roman Archaeology* 2: 156–66.

Radden-Keefe, B. 2015. 'Illustrating the Manuscripts of Terence'. In *Terence between Late Antiquity and the Age of Printing: Illustration, Commentary and Performance*, edited by A.J. Turner and G. Torello-Hill, 36–66. Leiden: Brill.

Radt, S. 1985. *Tragicorum Graecorum Fragmenta vol. III: Aeschylus*. Göttingen: Vandenhoeck & Ruprecht.

Rancière, J. 2009. *Aesthetics and its Discontents*. Translated by S. Corcoran. Cambridge: Polity Press.

Rapin, C. 1990. 'Greeks in Afghanistan: Aï Khanum'. In *Greek Colonists and Native Populations: Proceedings of the First Australian Congress of Classical Archaeology Held in Honour of Emeritus Professor A.D. Trendall*, edited by J.-P. Descoeudres, 329–42. Oxford: Oxford University Press.

Rapin, C., P. Hadot and G. Cavallo. 1987. 'Les Textes Littéraires Grecs de la Trésorie de Aï Khanoum'. *Bulletin de Correspondance Hellénique* 111: 225–66.

Rawson, E. 1987. 'Discrimina ordinum: The Lex Julia Theatralis'. *Papers of the British School at Rome* 55: 83–114.

Reinhardt, T. 2013. 'The *Ars Poetica*'. In *Brill's Companion to Horace*, edited by. H.-Chr. Günther 499–526. Leiden: Brill.

Reisch, E. 1903. 'Didaskaliai'. In *Paulys Realenzyklopädie der classischen Altertumswissenschaft*, edited by G. Wissowa, vol. V 1, cols. 394–401. Stuttgart: Alfred Druckmüller.

Revermann, M. 2000. 'Euripides, Tragedy and Macedon: Some Conditions of Reception'. *Illinois Classical Studies* 24/25: 451–67.

Revermann, M. 2006a. *Comic Business: Theatricality, Dramatic Technique, and Performance Contexts of Aristophanic Comedy*. Oxford: Oxford University Press.

Revermann, M. 2006b. 'The Competence of Theatre Audiences in Fifth- and Fourth-Century Athens'. *Journal of Hellenic Studies* 126: 99–124.

Revermann, M. 2008. 'Aeschylus' *Eumenides*, Chronotopes, and the "Aetiological Mode"'. In Revermann and Wilson 2008, 237–61.

Revermann, M. 2010. 'Situating the Gaze of the Recipient(s): Theatre-Related Vase Paintings and their Contexts of Reception'. In Gildenhard and Revermann 2010, 69–97.

Revermann, M. 2013. 'Generalizing about Props: Greek Drama, Comparator Traditions, and the Analysis of Stage Objects'. In *Performance in Greek and Roman Theatre*, edited by G.W.M. Harrison and V. Liapis, 77–88. Leiden: Brill.

Revermann, M. 2016. 'The Reception of Greek Tragedy from 500 to 323 BC'. In *A Handbook to the Reception of Greek Drama*, edited by B. van Zyl Smit, 13–28. Malden (MA) and Oxford: Wiley-Blackwell.

Revermann, M., and P. Wilson, eds. 2008. *Performance, Iconography, Reception: Studies in Honour of Oliver Taplin*. Oxford: Oxford University Press.

Revermann, M., ed. 2014. *The Cambridge Companion to Greek Comedy*. Cambridge: Cambridge University Press.

Reynolds, L.D., and N.G. Wilson. 2013. *Scribes and Scholars: A Guide to the Transmission of Greek and Latin Literature*. 4th ed. Oxford: Oxford University Press.

Rhodes, P. 2003. 'Nothing to Do with Democracy: Athenian Drama and the Polis'. *Journal of Hellenic Studies* 123: 104–19.

Rhodes, P.J., and R. Osborne. 2003. *Greek Historical Inscriptions 404–323 BC*. Oxford: Oxford University Press.

Richardson, N.J. 1993. 'Aristotle and Hellenistic Scholarship'. In *La philologie grecque à l'époque hellénistique et romaine*, edited by F. Montanari, 7–38. Vandoeuvres-Geneva: Fondation Hardt.

Robert, L. 1930. 'Pantomimen im griechischen Orient'. *Hermes* 65: 106–22 = Robert 1969: 654–70.

Robert, L. 1936. '*ARCHAIOLOGOS*'. *Revue des Études Grecques* 49: 235–54 = Robert 1969: 671–90.

Robert, L. 1969. *Opera Minora Selecta*, vol. 1. Amsterdam: Hakkert.

Robinson, E.G.D. 2014. 'Greek Theatre in Non-Greek Apulia'. In Csapo et al. 2014, 319–32.

Roller, D.W. 2006. *The World of Juba II and Kleopatra Selene*. London: Routledge.

Roselli, D.K. 2011. *Theater of the People: Spectators and Society in Ancient Athens*. Austin: University of Texas Press.

Roselli, D.K. (forthcoming). 'Kings in Rags and Working-Class Heroes in Greek Tragedy'.

Rosen, R.M. 2014. 'The Comic Hero'. In Revermann 2014, 222–40.

Rosenbloom, D. 1993. 'Shouting "Fire" in a Crowded Theater: Phrynichos's Capture of Miletos and the Politics of Fear in Early Attic Tragedy'. *Philologus* 137: 159–196.

Rothwell, K.S. 2007. *Nature, Culture and the Origins of Greek Comedy: A Study of Animal Choruses*. Cambridge: Cambridge University Press.

Roueché, C. 1993. *Performers and Partisans at Aphrodisias in the Roman and Late Roman Periods: A Study Based on Inscriptions from the Current Excavations at Aphrodisias in Caria*. London: Society for the Promotion of Roman Studies.

Roy, J. 2007. 'The Urban Layout of Megalopolis in Its Civic and Confederate Context'. *British School at Athens Studies* 15: 289–95.

Ruffell, I.A. 2010. 'Translating Greece to Rome: Humour and the Re-Invention of Popular Culture'. In *Translation, Humour and Literature*, edited by D. C. Chiaro, 91–118. London and New York: Continuum.

Ruffell, I.A. 2011. *Politics and Anti-Realism in Athenian Old Comedy: The Art of the Impossible*. Oxford: Oxford University Press.

Ruffell, I.A. 2013. 'Humiliation? Voyeurism, Violence and Humor in Old Comedy'. *Helios* 40: 247–77.

Ruffell, I.A. 2014. 'Character Types'. In Revermann 2014, 147–67.

Ruffell, I.A. 2015. 'The Grotesque Comic Body, between the Real and Unreal'. In *Carnaval et comédie: Actes du colloque international organisé par l'équipe PLH-CRATA les 9–10 décembre 2009 à l'Université de Toulouse – Le Mirail*, edited by M. Bastin-Hammou, 37–73. ISTA, Besançon: Presses Universitaires de Franche-Comté.

Rutherford, R. 2007. 'History and Tragedy'. In *A Companion to Greek and Roman Historiography*, edited by J. Marincola, 504–14. Malden (MA) and Oxford: Blackwell.

Rutherford, R. 2012. *Greek Tragic Style. Form, Language, and Interpretation*. Cambridge: Cambridge University Press.

Said, S. 2002. 'Herodotus and Tragedy'. In *Brill's Companion to Herodotus*, edited by E. Bakker, I. de Jong and H. van Wees, 117–47. Leiden: Brill.

Sanders, J. 2006. *Adaptation and Appropriation*. London and New York: Routledge.
Schaps, D. 1977. 'The Woman Least Mentioned: Etiquette and Women's Names'. *Classical Quarterly* 272: 323–30.
Schauer, M. 2012. *Tragicorum Romanorum Fragmenta, vol. 1*. Göttingen: Vandenhoeck.
Schlapbach, K. 2008. 'Lucian's *On Dancing* and the Models for a Discourse on Pantomime'. In Hall and Wyles 2008, 314–37.
Schoch, R. 2012. 'Inventing the Origins of Theatre History: The Modern Uses of Juba II's *Theatriké Historia*'. *Journal of Dramatic Theory and Criticism* 27: 5–23.
Scodel, R. 2007. 'Lycurgus and the State Text of Tragedy'. In *Politics of Orality* [=*Mnemosyne* suppl. 280], edited by C. Cooper. Leiden: Brill.
Scodel, R. 2010. *An Introduction to Greek Tragedy*. Cambridge: Cambridge University Press.
Scott, M. 2010. *Delphi and Olympia: The Spatial Politics of Panhellenism in the Archaic and Classical Periods*. Cambridge: Cambridge University Press.
Seaford, R. 1976. 'On the Origins of Satyric Drama'. *Maia* 28: 209–21.
Sear, F.B. 1990. 'Vitruvius and Roman Theater Design'. *American Journal of Archaeology* 94: 249–58.
Sear, F.B. 2006. *Roman Theatres: An Architectural Study*. Oxford: Oxford University Press.
Sebeok, A., ed. 1984. *Carnival!* Berlin and New York: Mouton Publishers.
Segal, C. 1994. 'Forward. Literary History as Literary Theory'. In Conte 1994: vii–xv.
Segal, E. 1987. *Roman Laughter: The Comedy of Plautus*. 2nd ed. Oxford: Oxford University Press.
Shaw, C.A. 2014. *Satyric Play: The Evolution of Greek Comedy and Satyr Drama*. Oxford: Oxford University Press.
Sidwell, K. 2014. 'Fourth-Century Comedy before Menander'. In Revermann 2014, 60–78.
Sifakis, G.M. 1967. *Studies in the History of Hellenistic Drama*. London: Athlone.
Sifakis, G.M. 1971. *Parabasis and Animal Choruses. A Contribution to the History of Attic Comedy*. London: Athlone Press.
Sifakis, G.M. 2002. 'Looking for the Actor's Art in Aristotle'. In Easterling and Hall 2002, 148–64.
Slater, N. 2000. *Plautus in Performance. The Theater of the Mind*. 2nd ed. Amsterdam: Harwood Academic.
Slater, W.J. 1993. 'Three Problems in the History of Drama'. *Phoenix* 47: 189–212.
Slater, W.J. 1994. 'Pantomime Riots'. *Classical Antiquity* 13: 120–44.
Slater, W.J. 1995. 'The Pantomime Tiberius Julius Apolaustus'. *Greek, Roman and Byzantine Studies* 36: 263–92.
Slater, W.J. 2002. 'Mime Problems: Cicero Ad fam. 7.1 and Martial 9.38'. *Phoenix* 56: 315–29.
Slater, W.J. 2004. 'Where are the Actors?' In Hugoniot et al. 2004, 143–60.
Slater, W.J. 2007. 'Deconstructing Festivals'. In Wilson 2007, 21–47.
Slater, W.J. 2008. 'Hadrian's Letter to the Athletes and Dionysiac Artists Concerning Arrangements for the Circuit of Games'. *Journal of Roman Archaeology* 21: 610–20.
Slater, W.J. 2010a. 'Paying the Pipers'. In Le Guen 2010a: 249–81.
Slater, W.J. 2010b. 'Sorting out Pantomime (and Mime) from Top to Bottom'. *Journal of Roman Archaeology* 23: 533–41.

Slater, W.J., and D. Summa 2006. 'Crowns at Magnesia'. *Greek, Roman and Byzantine Studies* 46: 275–99.

Small, J.P. 2013, 'Skenographia in Brief'. In *Performance in Greek and Roman Theatre*, edited by G.W.M. Harrison and V. Liapis, 111–28. Leiden: Brill.

Sommerstein, A.H. 1980. 'The Naming of Women in Greek and Roman Comedy'. *Quaderni di storia* 11: 393–418. Reprinted in Sommerstein 2009: 43–69.

Sommerstein, A.H. 1997. 'The Theatre Audience, the *Demos*, and the *Suppliants* of Aeschylus'. In Pelling 1997, 63–79.

Sommerstein, A.H. 1998. *The Comedies of Aristophanes vol. 3: Clouds*. 2nd ed. Warminster: Aris & Philipps.

Sommerstein, A.H. 2005. 'A Lover of His Art: The Art-Form as Wife and Mistress in Greek Poetic Imagery'. In Stafford and Herrin 2005, 161–71.

Sommerstein, A.H. 2009. *Talking about Laughter, and Other Studies in Greek Comedy*. Oxford: Oxford University Press.

Sommerstein, A.H., ed. 2014. *Menander in Contexts*. New York and London: Routledge.

Sonnino, M. 2014. 'Comedy Outside the Canon: From Ritual Slapstick to Hellenistic Mime'. In *Submerged Literature in Ancient Greek Culture: An Introduction*, edited by G. Colesanti and M. Giordano, 128–50. Boston/Leiden: De Gruyter.

Sourvinou-Inwood, C. 1989. 'Assumptions and the Creation of Meaning: Reading Sophocles' *Antigone*'. *Journal of Hellenic Studies* 109: 134–48.

Spawforth, A.J. 1989. 'Agonistic Festivals in Roman Greece'. In *The Greek Renaissance in the Roman Empire*, edited by A.M. Cameron and S. Walker, 193–7. London: Institute of Classical Studies.

Stafford, E., and J. Herrin, eds. 2005. *Personification in the Ancient Greek World: From Antiquity to Byzantium*. Aldershot: Ashgate.

Stephanis, I.E. 1988. *Dionysiakoi technitai: symboles stēn prosōpographia tou theatrou kai tēs mousikēs tōn archaiōn Hellēnōn*. Heraklion: Crete University Press.

Storey, I., and A. Allan. 2005. *A Guide to Ancient Greek Drama*. Oxford: Blackwell.

Storey, I., and A. Allan. 2010. 'Origins and Fifth-Century Comedy'. In *Brill's Companion to the Study of Greek Comedy*, edited by G.W. Dobrov, 179–226. Leiden: Brill.

Sutton, D.E. 1987. 'The Theatrical Families of Athens'. *American Journal of Philology* 108: 9–26.

Taplin, O. 1971. 'Significant Actions in Sophocles' Philoctetes'. *Greek, Roman and Byzantine Studies* 12: 25–44.

Taplin, O. 1977a. *The Stagecraft of Aeschylus. The Dramatic Use of Exits and Entrances in Greek Tragedy*. Oxford: Oxford University Press.

Taplin, O. 1977b. 'Did Greek Dramatists Write Stage Instructions?' *Proceedings of the Cambridge Philological Society* n. s. 23: 121–32.

Taplin, O. 1978. *Greek Tragedy in Action*. Berkeley and Los Angeles: University of California Press.

Taplin, O. 1993. *Comic Angels and Other Approaches to Greek Drama through Vase-Painting*. Oxford: Oxford University Press.

Taplin, O. 1997. 'The Pictorial Record'. In *The Cambridge Companion to Greek Tragedy*, edited by P.E. Easterling, 69–90. Cambridge: Cambridge University Press.

Taplin, O. 1999. 'Spreading the Word Through Performance'. In *Performance Culture and Athenian Democracy*, edited by S. Goldhill and R. Osborne, 33–57. Cambridge: Cambridge University Press.

Taplin, O. 2007. *Pots and Plays: Interactions between Tragedy and Greek Vase Painting of the Fourth Century B.C.* Los Angeles: J. Paul Getty Museum.

Taplin, O., and R. Wiles, eds. 2010. *The Pronomos Vase and Its Context*. Oxford: Oxford University Press.

Tarán, L., and D. Gutas. 2012. *Aristotle Poetics: Editio Maior of the Greek Text with Introductions and Philological Commentaries*. Leiden: Brill.

Taylor, D. 2003. *The Archive and the Repertoire: Performing Cultural Memory in the Americas*. Durham: Duke University Press.

Temelini, M.A. 2006. 'Pompey's Politics and the Presentation of His Theatre Temple Complex, 61–52 BCE'. *Studia Humaniora Tartuensia* 7. http://www.ut.ee/klassik/sht/2006/temelini1.pdf

Theocharidis, G. 1940. *Beiträge zur Geschichte des Profantheaters im IV. und V. Jahrhundert, hauptsächlich auf Grund der Predigten des Johannes Chrysostomos, Patriarchen von Konstantinopel*. Thessaloniki: M. Triantaphyllou.

Tordoff, R. 2013. 'Actors' Properties in Ancient Greek Drama: An Overview'. In *Performance in Greek and Roman Theatre*, edited by G.W.M. Harrison and V. Liapis, 89–110. Leiden: Brill.

Townsend, R.F. 2010. 'Choregic Monuments'. In *The Oxford Encyclopedia of Ancient Greece and Rome, Vol. II.*, edited by M. Gagarin, 90b–92a. Oxford: Oxford University Press.

Tracy, S.V. 2015. 'The Dramatic Festival Inscriptions of Athens: The Inscribers and Phases of Inscribing'. *Hesperia* 84: 553–81.

Traill, A. 2008. *Women and the Comic Plot in Menander*. Cambridge: Cambridge University Press.

Treggiari, S. 1991. *Roman Marriage: Iusti Coniuges from the Time of Cicero to the Time of Ulpian*. Oxford: Oxford University Press.

Trendall, A.D. 1991. 'Farce and Tragedy in South Italian Vase-Painting'. In *Looking at Greek Vases*, edited by T. Rasmussen and N. Spivey, 151–82. Cambridge: Cambridge University Press.

Trenkner, S. 1958. *The Greek Novella in the Classical Period*. Cambridge: University Press.

Turcan, M. 1986. *Tertullien: Les Spectacles (De spectaculis)*. Paris: Les Éditions du Cerf.

Vahtikari, V. 2014. *Tragedy Performances Outside Athens in the Late Fifth and Fourth Century BC*. Helsinki: Foundation of the Finnish Institute at Athens.

Valakas, K. 2002. 'The Use of the Body by Actors in Tragedy and Satyr-Play'. In Easterling and Hall 2002, 69–92.

Vatri, A. 2012. 'The Physiology of Ancient Greek Reading'. *Classical Quarterly* 62: 633–47.

Victor, B. 2014. 'The Transmission of Terence'. In *The Oxford Handbook of Greek and Roman Comedy*, edited by M. Fontaine and A.C. Scafuro, 699–716. Oxford: Oxford University Press.

Walbank, F. 1960. 'History and Tragedy'. *Historia* 9: 216–34 (also in Walbank, F. 1985. *Selected Papers: Studies in Greek and Roman History and Historiography*, 224–41. Cambridge: Cambridge University Press).

Walden, W.H. 1894. 'Stage-Terms in Heliodorus' *Aethiopica*'. *Harvard Studies in Classical Philology* 5: 1–43.

Wallace, R.W. 1991. 'Damone de Oa ed i suoi successori: un' analisi delle fonti'. In *Harmonia Mundi*, edited by R.W. Wallace and B. MacLachlan, 30–53. Rome: Ateneo.

Wallace, R.W. 1997. 'Poet, Public and "Theatrocracy": Audience Performance in Classical Athens'. In *Poet, Public and Performance in Ancient Greece*, edited by L. Edmunds and R.W. Wallace, 97–111. Baltimore: Johns Hopkins University Press.

Wallace, R.W. 2004. 'Damon of Oa: A Music Theorist Ostracized? In *Music and the Muses: The Culture of Mousike in the Classical Athenian City*, edited by P. Wilson and P. Murray, 249–68. Oxford: Oxford University Press.

Wallace, R.W. 2005. 'Performing Damon's Harmoniai'. In *Ancient Greek Music in Performance*, edited by S. Hagel and C. Harrauer, 147–57. Vienna: Wiener Studien Beiheft 30.

Wallace, R.W. 2015. *Reconstructing Damon: Music, Wisdom Teaching, and Politics in Perikles' Athens*. Oxford: Oxford University Press.

Wallace-Hadrill, A. 2008. *Rome's Cultural Revolution*. Cambridge: Cambridge University Press.

Wartelle, A. 1971. *Histoire du texte d'Eschyle dans l'antiquité*. Paris: Les Belles Lettres.

Waszink, J.H. 1948. 'Varro, Livy and Tertullian on the History of Roman Dramatic Art'. *Vigiliae Christianae* 2: 224–2.

Webb, R. 2002. 'Female Entertainers in Late Antiquity'. In Easterling and Hall 2002, 282–303.

Webb, R. 2008. *Demons and Dancers: Performance in Late Antiquity*. Cambridge (MA): Harvard University Press.

Welch, K.A. 2007. *The Roman Amphitheatre: From its Origins to the Colosseum*. Cambridge: Cambridge University Press.

West, M.L. 2013. *The Epic Cycle. A Commentary on the Lost Epics*. Oxford: Oxford University Press.

Whitman, C. 1964. *The Comic Hero*. Cambridge (MA): Harvard University Press.

Wiemken, H. 1972. *Der griechische Mimus. Dokumente zur Geschichte des antiken Volkstheaters*. Bremen: Schünemann.

Wiles, D. 1999. *Tragedy in Athens: Performance Space and Theatrical Meaning*. Cambridge: Cambridge University Press.

Wiles, D. 2003. *A Short History of Western Performance Space*. Cambridge: Cambridge University Press.

Wiles, D. 2007. *Mask and Performance in Greek Tragedy: From Ancient Festival to Modern Experimentation*. Cambridge: Cambridge University Press.

Wiles, D. 2008. 'The Poetics of the Mask in Old Comedy'. In Revermann and Wilson 2008: 374–92.

Willi, A. 2012. 'Challenging Authority: Epicharmus between Epic and Rhetoric'. In Bosher 2012, 56–75.

Williams, R. 2004. 'Digital Resources for Practice-Based Research: The New Comedy Masks Project'. *Literary and Linguistic Computing* 19: 415–25.

Wilson, N. 2007. *Aristophanea: Studies on the Text of Aristophanes*. Oxford: Oxford University Press.

Wilson, P. 1996. 'Tragic Rhetoric: The Use of Tragedy and the Tragic in the Fourth Century'. In *Tragedy and the Tragic: Greek Theatre and Beyond*, edited by M. Silk, 310–31. Oxford: Oxford University Press.

Wilson, P. 2000. *The Athenian Institution of the Khoregia: The Chorus, the City and the Stage*. Cambridge: Cambridge University Press.

Wilson, P., ed. 2007. *The Greek Theatre and Festivals: Documentary Studies*. Oxford: Oxford University Press.

Wilson, P. 2008. 'Costing the Dionysia'. In Revermann and Wilson 2008, 88–127.

Wilson, P. 2009. 'Tragic Honours and Democracy: Neglected Evidence for the Politics of the Athenian Dionysia'. *Classical Quarterly* 59: 8–29.

Wilson, P. 2010a. 'How Did the Athenian Demes Fund their Theatre?' In Le Guen 2010a, 37–82.

Wilson, P. 2012, and E. Csapo. 'From *Chorêgia* to *Agônothesia*: Evidence for the Administration and Finance of the Athenian Theatre in the Late Fourth Century BC'. In *Greek Drama IV: Texts, Contexts, Performance*, edited by D. Rosenbloom and J. Davidson, 300–21. Oxford: Oxbow Books.

Winkler, J., and F. Zeitlin, eds. 1992. *Nothing to Do with Dionysus? Athenian Drama in its Social Context*. Princeton: Princeton University Press.

Wiseman, T.P. 1988. 'Satyrs in Rome? The Background to Horace's *Ars Poetica*'. *Journal of Roman Studies* 78: 1–13.

Wörrle, M. 1988. *Stadt und Fest im kaiserzeitlichen Kleinasien*. Munich: C.H. Beck.

Wright, D. 2006. *The Lost Late Antique Illustrated Terence*. Vatican City: Biblioteca apostolica Vaticana.

Wright, W.F. 1931. *Cicero and the Theater*. Northampton (MA): Smith College Classical Studies XI.

Wyles, R. 2011. *Costume in Greek Tragedy*. London: Bristol Classical Press.

Yunis, H. 2011. *Plato: Phaedrus*. Cambridge: Cambridge University Press.

Zagagi, N. 1995. *The Comedy of Menander. Convention, Variation, and Originality*. Bloomington: Indiana University Press.

Zanobi, A. 2014. *Seneca's Tragedies and the Aesthetics of Pantomime*. London: Bloomsbury.

Zehnacker, H. 1983. 'Tragedie pretexte et spectacle romain'. In *Théâtre et spectacles dans l' Antiquité: acte du colloque de Strasbourg, 5–7 novembre 1981*, edited by M. Zehnacker, 31–48. Leiden: Brill.

Zenobi, A. 2008. 'The Influence of Pantomime on Seneca's Tragedies'. In Hall and Wyles 2008, 227–57.

Zimmerman, B. 2008. 'Seneca and Pantomime'. In Hall and Wyles 2008, 218–26.

Zuntz, G. 1955. *The Political Plays of Euripides*. Manchester: Manchester University Press.

Zweig, B. 1992. 'The Mute Nude Female Characters in Aristophanes' Plays'. In *Pornography and Representation in Greece and Rome*, edited by A. Richlin, 73–89. Oxford: Oxford University Press.

INDEX

Accius (Roman tragic playwright) 32, 148, 149, 191
actors 9, 22, 26, 27, 32, 87, 121–41, 186, 193
    guilds 96, 130–4, 138f., 194
Adorno, Theodor 45
Aeschylus 5, 6, 22, 159f.
    Agamemnon 156
    Eumenides 50, 156
    Oresteia 28, 53f., 57, 145f., 165, 170f., 175, 176
    Persians 41, 64, 84f., 97f., 123
    Prometheus Bound 156
agôn (both formal element of comedy and name for 'competition' in general) 8f. *see also* competition
Ai Khanoum 12
Alcidamas 37f.
Alexander the Great 94f., 184, 193
amphitheatre 4
Antiphanes (comic playwright) 164
Antiphon 185
Apuleius 13, 178f.
Argos 17f.
Aristophanes 3, 54, 61, 87, 101, 160
    Acharnians 28, 55, 91, 148, 150, 171f., 177, 181f., 186
    Assembly Women 52, 58
    Birds 49
    Clouds 28, 165, 174f., 177f.
    Frogs 28, 37, 91, 97f.
    Knights 151, 177
    Lysistrata 48, 52, 55, 56, 58, 152
    Peace 49, 171
    Wasps 87, 150, 182
    Women at the Thesmphoria 42, 52, 60, 89–91, 152f., 172, 177
Aristophanes of Byzantium 188
Aristotle 37, 41, 111–14, 183, 187
    Poetics 14, 42, 112–14, 173, 175, 186, 188
'Artists of Dionysus' *see* actors' guilds
Asclepius 35, 41
'Atellan farce' 190
Athens 6, 7, 23–9, 88
    Theatre of Dionysus 12, 14, 50, 67, 72f., 77, 165, 176, 183, 194
audience 11–15, 32, 49f., 69, 80f., 84, 103, 116, 186, 194
Augustine 119
Augustus 8, 11, 81, 194
Aulus Gellius 192

books 8
Burckhardt, Jacob 8

Caesar 32, 80, 96
Cato 53, 189
chorêgia/chorêgos (sponsorship/sponsor of dramatic and dithyrambic performances) 9, 20, 24, 27, 43f., 122f., 134f., 182f., 185, 190, 193

Choricius of Gaza 119
chorus 3, 40f., 43f., 127f., 140, 195
Christianity 117–19, 140
Cicero 32, 37, 79, 98–100, 164, 192, 193f.
citharody 9
class 2
coins 2
Colosseum *see* Rome
comedy 3, 9, 13, 42, 149–53, 177f.
competition 8f., 10, 21, 126
costume 3, 55f., 193
   see also masks; props
crane 165–75, 178
Crates of Mallus 188f.
Cratinus (comic playwright) 3, 6, 91, 151
curtain 164

Damon 35
Delos 125f., 127, 134, 137
Delphi 17f., 43, 125, 127, 136
Demetrius (ancient critic) 4
Democritus 107
deus ex machina 155, 164
Didymus 189
Dio Chrysostom 194, 195
Dionysus 7, 17–19, 22, 24, 35, 37, 43, 51,
   67, 70f., 131, 155, 177, 182
Diphilus (comic playwright) 91
dithyramb 9, 28

ekkyklêma (mobile stage platform) 165–75,
   178
Eleusis 29
elite 8, 10f., 14, 30, 32, 105f.
Empedocles 35
Ennius (Roman poet) 190, 191
Epicharmus (comic playwright from Sicily)
   9, 14, 23, 87
Epidaurus 6, 12, 66
Eros (Roman actor) 14
Etruscans 8, 29
Eupolis (comic playwright) 3, 6, 91
Euripides 3, 5, 6, 26, 27, 54, 87, 94, 152f.,
   172f., 182
   Alcestis 55, 156, 186
   Andromache 57
   Andromeda 98
   Bacchae 59f., 97f.
   Bellerophontes 171, 173
   Cyclops 56, 155

   Electra 165–7
   Erechtheus 73, 106
   Heracles 168f.
   Hippolytus 56, 59, 156, 157
   Ion 156
   Iphigenia among the Taurians 154
   Medea 61f., 173
   Suppliant Women 149
   Telephus 89f., 147f., 150, 160, 181, 186

fabula palliata 56, 191
fabula praetexta 149, 157, 191
fabula togata 191
festivals 3, 8, 9f., 17–33, 42f., 72f., 95f.,
   121–41, 144, 153, 191, 192, 193
frames 19–21

gods 155–9
Goffman, Erving 19f.
Gorgias 35
Great Dionysia (dramatic festival in Athens)
   3, 5, 7, 9, 23–9, 42f., 67, 70, 122–4,
   183, 185, 186

Hadrian 125, 131f.
Hegelochus (Greek tragic actor) 14
Heliodorus 106
Heraclitus 107
hero 17f., 145–51
Herodas (comic writer) 4
Herodotus 17–19, 43, 115f.
Homer 108f., 128, 167
   Homeric Hymn to Hermes 35
   Odyssey 85, 144, 145, 157
homosexuality 61
Horace 154, 164
   Ars Poetica 38, 107, 192

Iasos 126, 135
Iuba II of Maretania 189
inscriptions 6, 9

Jacob of Sarugh 119
John Chrysostom 119
judges 24, 40
Julian (Roman emperor) 51
Justinian 140

Laberius (Roman mime playwright) 4, 7
Lenaea (dramatic festival in Athens) 9, 28f.

Libanius 116
literacy 8
Livius Andronicus (playwright) 8, 30f., 95, 98, 137
Livy 29, 164
Lucian 7, 9, 116f., 127, 158, 195
Ludi Romani ('Roman Games') 29f., 31, 137, 191
Lycophron 188
Lycurgus 73f., 106, 183
Lysias 51f., 56, 183

Marmor Parium 24, 175
Martial 5
masks 3, 4, 48f., 79, 176–8, 179, 182, 185, 188, 191, 192, 194
mêchanê see crane
Megalopolis 74
Menander 3, 6, 53, 156f., 183
   Aspis 150
   Dyscolus 50, 55, 150
   Men at Arbitration 58
   Samia 58, 150f.
mime 4, 7, 9, 18, 32, 128f., 140, 153–5, 160, 164, 190, 194
mosaics 192

Naevius (Roman poet) 148, 191
Nero 5, 96, 189, 194
New Comedy 3, 56, 91, 93, 144, 150f., 160, 176, 177

Oenoanda 136
Ovid 80f., 116, 191

Pacuvius (Roman tragic playwright) 191
pantomime 4f., 7, 11, 18, 79, 97, 116f., 128f., 138, 140, 144, 157–9, 160, 164, 178f., 194f.
papyri 7
'Parasites of Apollo *see* actors' guilds
paratheatrical events 1f., 5
parody 4, 149–51, 180
Pausanias 74
Pericles 52, 123
Philodemus 38, 107
Phrynichus (Greek tragic playwright) 26, 41
Pindar 167
Plato 13, 35–7, 41, 49f., 74, 86, 100, 104, 108–11, 112, 118

Plautus (Roman comic playwright) 3, 6, 14, 31, 53, 59, 75, 137f., 192
   Amphitruo 155, 157
   Casina 56, 59, 92
   Poenulus (*Little Carthaginian*) 50, 75f.
   The Bacchis Girls 58f.
Plutarch 39, 87, 97, 116
Pollux 176, 189, 191
Pompeii 12
privatization 21f.
proagôn 26f.
Proclus 39
props 177–9, 193

Quintilian 191

Rancière, Jacques 44
Rome 76, 105f.
   Colosseum 5, 106
   Palatine Hill 75
   Theatre of Balbus 8, 12
   Theatre of Marcellus 8, 11, 12
   Theatre of Pompey 8, 11, 12, 50, 76–80, 140, 148, 192, 193

satyr play 3f., 5, 144
scenography 175f.
scripts (of plays) 5f., 27, 32, 83, 182, 188, 192
Seneca 5, 6, 54, 108, 149, 164, 189, 195
   Hercules Furens 169f.
   Medea 164, 173f.
   Phaedra 56, 61f., 157
   Thyestes 157
Sicily 6, 7, 12, 23
skênê see stage house
Socrates 28, 36–7, 72
Sophocles 6, 27, 159f., 175, 182
   Ajax 172, 176f.
   Antigone 58, 70–2
   Electra 176
   Oedipus the King 101, 104, 156
   Trachiniae 57, 146f., 156, 160
Sophron (comic writer) 4, 153
South Italy 6, 29, 88, 91–4, 105, 194
Sparta 51
stage directions 165
stage house (*skênê*) 41, 167f., 175f.
Stein, Peter 170

Tacitus 32, 50, 116, 189f.
Taras (Taranto) 89
Taylor, Diana 182
Terence (Roman comic playwright) 6, 14, 100, 138, 157
   Adelphoe 32
   Eunuch 59
   Heauton Timoroumenos 59
   Hecyra 32, 59
Tertullian 13, 104, 118f.
theatre buildings 6, 63–81, 105f., 163f., 176, 177, 192
Theatre of Dionysus *see* Athens
Theatre of Pompey *see* Rome
Thebes 17–19
Theodosian Code 51

Thespis 126
Thorikos 29, 66–70
Thucydides 116
Thurioi 89
tragedy 3, 5, 9, 18, 115, 143–61

Varro 192
vase paintings (theatre-related) 7, 13, 24, 48, 89–91, 93, 164, 183–5
Virgil 116, 178
Vitruvius 74, 176, 193

Xenophanes 107, 118
Xenophon 157f.

Zeami 117